Dr Robert Morkot studied Ancient History at University College London and at the Humboldt University in Berlin, where he specialized in the Kingdom of Kush (present-day southern Egypt, Nubia and Sudan). From 1987 to 1991 he was G A Wainwright Fellow in Near Eastern Archaeology at the University of Oxford. From 1992 to 1998 he was course director for the ancient Nubia Summer School, held first at the Institute of Archaeology, London University and later at Birkbeck College, London. He lectures on various aspects of the ancient world, but particularly on the later periods of ancient Egyptian history and Egypt's relations with other ancient societies. Since 1984 he has been guest lecturer on many tours of Egypt and Libya. He serves on the committees of the Egypt Exploration Society and ASTENE (the Association for the Study of Travel in Egypt and the Near East).

Dr Morkot is author of *The Penguin Historical Atlas of Ancient Greece* (Penguin, 1996); *The Empires of Ancient Egypt* (BBC, 2001); *The Black Pharaohs: Egypt's Nubian Rulers* (Rubicon Press, 2000); *The Historical Dictionary of Ancient Egyptian Warfare* (Scarecrow Press, 2003); *The Egyptians: An Introduction* (Routledge, 2005); and was coauthor with Peter James, I J Thorpe, Nikos Kokkinos and John Frankish of *Centuries of Darkness* (Jonathan Cape, 1991; Rutger's University Press, 1993), a controversial reassessment of Old World chronology. He has written and reviewed for the archaeology magazine *Minerva*, and has contributed to a number of dictionaries and encyclopaedias. He currently lectures for the University of Exeter.

(preceding page) *The Great Sphinx of Giza rises above the massive blocks that form of the core of the temple standing in front of it. Behind is the pyramid of Khafre, its summit still retaining some of the original casing.*

EGYPT
LAND OF THE PHARAOHS

Robert Morkot

Photography by
*Kazuyoshi Nomachi and
Anthony Cassidy*

Published by Odyssey Books & Guides, an imprint of
Airphoto International Ltd, 903 Seaview Commercial Building,
21 Connaught Road West, Sheung Wan, Hong Kong
Tel: (852) 2856 3896; Fax: (852) 2565 8004; E-mail: sales@odysseypublications.com
www.odysseypublications.com

Distributed in the United States of America by
W.W. Norton & Company, Inc.,
500 Fifth Avenue, New York, NY 10110, USA
Tel: 800-233-4830; Fax: 800-458-6515
www.wwnorton.com

Distributed in the United Kingdom and Europe by
Cordee Books and Maps,
3a De Montfort Street, Leicester LE1 7HD, UK
Tel: 0116-254-3579; Fax: 0116-247-1176
www.cordee.co.uk

Library of Congress Catalogue Card Number has been requested.
ISBN: 962-217-701-8

Grateful acknowledgement is made to the following authors and publishers for permissions granted:
Grove Press for *Letters from Egypt: A Journey on the Nile 1849–1850*, by Florence Nightingale
© 1988; Penguin for 'Letter to Jules Cloquet from Cairo on January 15, 1850', from *Flaubert in Egypt*, by
Gustave Flaubert, translated and edited by Francis Steegmuller © 1996; Editions Olizane, Geneva, for map
of the Silk Road, 'Land and Sea Trade in the First Two Centuries AD', reproduced from *Silk Road: Monks,
Warriors & Merchants on the Silk Road* (page 156), by Luce Boulnois, Airphoto International Ltd © 2004.

Editor: Carey Vail
Design: Alex Ng Kin Man
Map Design: Mark Stroud

Front cover photography (Cassidy): The façade of the main temple at Abu Simbel
Back cover photography (Cassidy): The head of Ramesses II, entrance to the Temple of Luxor;
The pyramids of Giza

Photography by Kazuyoshi Nomachi, with additional photography by Anthony Cassidy (1, 6–7, 14–15
[repeated on back cover], 100, 108, 118, 126–127 [repeated on front flap], 140, 184–185, 189, 199, 206,
207, 209, 212, 221, 224, 226–227, 293, 301, 304, 311, 314, 323 [repeated on front cover], 412, 424
[repeated on back cover]); Lorenzo Martinengo (50: upper and lower, 58–59, 69, 86); Christopher
Coplans (361); courtesy of the Egyptian Government, Ministry of Culture (back flap, 420, 421).

Production by Twin Age Limited, Hong Kong
E-mail: twinage@netvigator.com
Manufactured in China

The Mosque of al-Rifa'i, Cairo

PREFACE

irst, my thanks to Magnus Bartlett for asking me to produce a new edition of *Egypt*, for his continuing interest in it over many years, and for his suggestions for improvements and things to include. The first version of *Egypt* (1989) was written by the late Lorenzo Martinengo and myself and, although radically revised over the succeeding editions, something still remains of that text. My thanks also go to the editors and designers who have worked on the various editions, coaxing text, smoothing rough edges and creating a visually attractive book; and also to those who were, unintentionally, instrumental in my becoming associated with this project in 1988: notably, Robert Anderson, who introduced me to Liselotte Man (Henderson-Begg), and thus to Francis and Anthony Bartlett.

Since my first visit to Egypt in 1977, I have benefited from the expertise of a range of travel specialists in private visits and lecture tours: most enjoyably with Bales Tours, Martin Randall Travel, Misr Travel and Eastmar Travel.

Memories of travel are as much of travelling companions and of incidents as of old stones, however interesting. Fortunately, my own travelling in Egypt has rarely been done alone, and intelligent and amusing company has leavened the potential tedium of long uncomfortable desert journeys, the chill of the Aluminium Hotel in winter and the unforeseen delays that frustrate even the most careful plans. Over many years I have enjoyed the hospitality of friends and colleagues both Egyptian and Egyptologists: from Okasha el-Daly I have learnt much about modern as well as ancient Egypt; with Sue Carney and friends I have explored the Delta and Middle Egypt, the deserts and oases, when it was slightly less easy than now. Particularly, I remember Ann Peters, with whom I shared too few visits, but all of them with their own extraordinary piquancy.

So this book is dedicated to all amusing travelling companions, both past and future.

A NOTE ON SPELLINGS

There is no single system in use for rendering ancient Egyptian and modern Arabic names. Earlier Egyptologists often used forms that were derived from Greek versions of Egyptian names (eg Amenophis). Here I have chosen the forms for Egyptian names that are closest to a direct 'transliteration' from the Egyptian hieroglyphic. So Amenhotep, rather than Amenophis; Senusret, not Sesostris; Menkaure not Mycerinus.

In rendering Arabic names I have been inconsistent in the use of the definite article: using al- for most personal names (eg caliphs, sultans and their mosques), but the more familiar el- in place names (eg Tell el-Amarna, Deir el-Bahari).

(right) *Remains of a carving, Temple of Luxor*
(preceding pages) *The Temple of Hatshepsut at Deir el-Bahari, Western Thebes, has been extensively restored by the Polish Institute over many years. The austerity of its architecture was originally set off by gardens and groves of trees.*

CONTENTS

(left) *Carved relief at the Temple of Luxor*

(following pages) *Camel-riding against the magnificent backdrop of the pyramids of Giza*

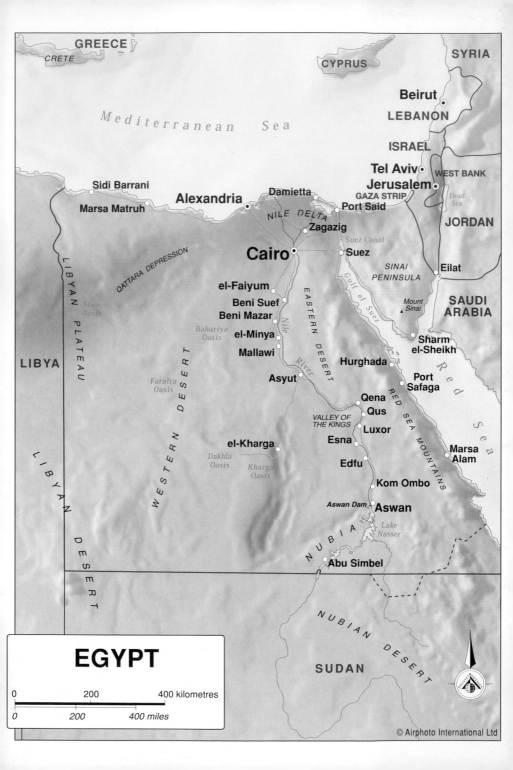

GREECE

CRETE

CYPRUS

SYRIA

Mediterranean Sea

Beirut
LEBANON

ISRAEL

Tel Aviv
Jerusalem
WEST BANK
GAZA STRIP
Dead Sea

JORDAN

Sidi Barrani

Marsa Matruh

Alexandria
Damietta
Port Said

NILE DELTA

Zagazig

Suez Canal

QATTARA DEPRESSION

Cairo
Suez

Eilat

SINAI
PENINSULA

LIBYAN PLATEAU

Siwa
Oasis

el-Faiyum
Beni Suef
Beni Mazar

Bahariya
Oasis

el-Minya

Mallawi

EASTERN

Nile

River

DESERT

Mount
Sinai

SAUDI
ARABIA

Sharm
el-Sheikh

LIBYA

Farafra
Oasis

Asyut

Hurghada

Port
Safaga

Red

Qena
Qus

VALLEY OF
THE KINGS

Luxor

RED

Sea

el-Kharga
Dakhla
Oasis

WESTERN

DESERT

Kharga
Oasis

Esna

Edfu

SEA

Marsa
Alam

Kom Ombo

MOUNTAINS

LIBYAN

Aswan Dam Aswan

Lake
Nasser

DESERT

NUBIA

Abu Simbel

NUBIAN DESERT

SUDAN

EGYPT

0   200   400 kilometres

0   200   400 miles

© Airphoto International Ltd

INTRODUCTION

EGYPT AND THE NILE

O f all ancient civilizations, Egypt is the one that seems to attract Western visitors the most. Egypt is part of our cultural past, appearing prominently in both the classical and biblical traditions and, certainly for the 18th, 19th and early 20th centuries, if not so much for us now, it also had the exotic associations of the Orient, the Islamic world and Africa.

The Greeks and Romans wrote extensively about Egypt: its history, its monuments, its customs and especially its religion. Through them the legends of Osiris and Isis were preserved. The Pyramids, sole survivors of the Seven Wonders of the World, could be seen by those Europeans who travelled to Egypt, and were a constant source of amazement and speculation. The conflict between Egypt and Rome—a turning point in European history—provided the background to one of the greatest romances of literature, the love of Antony and Kleopatra. Egypt also plays a prominent role in the biblical narratives, particularly the Old Testament. The stories of Joseph and Pharaoh and of Moses and the Exodus were the two major episodes, but other pharaohs were also named—Shishak, Tirhaka (Taharqo), Necho (Nekau II) and Hophra (Wahibre, or Apries). Even when Egypt is not central to the biblical narrative it remains a major background presence. For historical reasons, Egypt is far less prominent in the New Testament, but the 'Flight into Egypt' has been a popular subject for artists, although not acquiring truly Egyptian details for its setting until the 19th century. Egypt also played a major role in the development of early Christianity as the desert home of monasticism and numerous saints, notably St Anthony, St Paul of Thebes and St Catherine of Alexandria.

Even to the ancient world Egypt stood out as different. The Greeks and Romans were in awe of the monuments and of the country's antiquity—but we stand closer in time now to Kleopatra than Kleopatra did to the pyramid builders. In the Hellenistic and Roman periods, romantic novels and decorative arts used Egypt to provide a touch of the exotic, and its gods, especially Isis, acquired many devotees. Central to this image of Egypt was the Nile. Where did the river come from? And what caused the annual flood? These questions fascinated the Greeks and Romans. They are a significant element in Herodotos's description of Egypt, and were later said to

(following pages) *Paintings in the tomb of Sennefer, Western Thebes*

have motivated Alexander the Great of Macedon in his world travels. Indeed, at the time of his death (323 BC), Alexander was reputed to be arranging a further expedition into Aithiopia (modern Nubia, Sudan and Ethiopia) expressly to find the Nile's source. About 80 BC, at Palestrina (Praeneste), south of Rome, a huge mosaic depicting the festivals of the flooding Nile was placed in the temple of the goddess Fortuna, encapsulating the exotic and the religious aspects of Egypt, with temples and processions, crocodiles and hippopotami.

Even after Egypt was absorbed into the Roman Empire on Kleopatra's defeat and suicide in 30 BC, it remained in many ways distinct. It was a personal possession of the emperor, and members of Rome's governing elite had to have special permission to visit the country. It was important as a source of grain and of luxury commodities such as ivory, ebony and some of the animals used in the Roman Games. And many of these exotic luxuries, and Egypt's most important religious centres, lay far away from the Mediterranean, further up the Nile.

Before modern air-travel, most visitors to Egypt arrived either over the long desert road across northern Sinai from Gaza or by sea. Behind the sandy coastal ridges lies a series of large lakes and lagoons, in ancient times fringed with papyrus marsh: el-Manzala, el-Burullus, Idku and Maryut. Beyond lay the broad expanse of the Delta crossed by the seven branches of the river, with numerous towns rising on mounds from the flat plain. Although there were some coastal cities, such as Balamun, most of the ancient towns lay some way inland. Buto, Sau (Sais) and Djanet (Tanis), all standing on branches of the river, were each major ports playing a prominent role in Egyptian history at different periods. Naukratis was a Greek trading centre founded in the sixth century BC, and visited by Solon the Athenian lawgiver, Plato the philosopher and Herodotos, amongst many others. From 300 BC, Alexandria, on a coastal spit to the west of the Delta, grew to be the main port and entry to Egypt. From Alexandria it was two or three days sailing before the visitor arrived at the point where the river divides. Here, the medieval cities of Fustat and Qahira (Cairo) replaced the ancient ones of Iunu (Heliopolis) and Memphis. Sailing southwards into the Nile Valley, the limestone cliffs come in on both banks. Standing along the edge of the desert plateau, the pyramids dominate the western shore from Giza south to Dashur. For any visitor or invading army approaching from the north, these monuments would have impressed on the viewer the splendour of Egypt's past.

The great city of Memphis lay in the valley below the pyramids of Saqqara. At Memphis, tourists and pilgrims would have visited the desert temples and burial places of the sacred bulls and other animals, situated in the ancient necropolis. They would have viewed the ancient temples, sphinx-lined roadways and colossal statues within the vast city, still thriving in Ptolemaic and Roman times.

Sailing south the landscape opens out and through Middle Egypt the river runs close to the sheer limestone cliffs of the Eastern Desert, while on the west bank there are broad rich agricultural lands. Here the beauty of Egypt's landscape is revealed. Many of the ancient cities remained important and their temples became places of pilgrimage for devotees of the Egyptian cults. Khemenu (Ashmunein, Hermopolis), once one of the largest cities of Middle Egypt, was particularly revered as the cult centre of Thoth, the god of wisdom, identified with Hermes (hence Hermopolis). At Abydos, graffiti of Anubis, the jackal-headed god of embalming, wearing a Roman centurion's uniform, show his popularity with visitors to the temple of Osiris, god of the dead. The vast temple of the goddess Hathor at Dendera is one of the largest in Egypt, constructed by the Ptolemies and completed by the emperors Tiberius and Nero in the first century AD. No doubt the goddess's great Festival of Drunkenness was as popular as it had always been.

Politics and religious changes had their effects on other towns. By the first century AD the great city of Thebes was little more than a collection of villages dominated by the ruins of many of its magnificent temples. Once the burial place and a chief residence of the pharaohs at the height of Egypt's empire, Thebes had declined to a backwater. But it had many tourists, including the emperors Hadrian and Septimius Severus. They came to hear the colossal statues of Memnon (actually Amenhotep III) greet his mother at dawn. They visited the tombs in the Valley of the Kings, many of which lay open, and carved their names on them.

Beyond Thebes, the landscape begins to change, and the limestone cliffs are no longer so dominant. Just north of Silsila, sandstone replaces limestone and, passing through the narrow gorge of Silsila, the landscape changes, with more desert and narrower margins of cultivation. At Aswan the massive granite boulders and islands filled the river, creating rapids that obstructed the passage of those wishing to go further south. Much of the cataract disappeared beneath the two dams constructed in the late 19th and mid-20th centuries, but earlier travellers describe the exhilaration of being hauled up through rapids—or of sailing down them. At the head of the cataract, the southern border of ancient Egypt, was the small island of Philae, dedicated to Isis, and, by the Roman period, the focus of pilgrimages for her devotees. Beyond lay Nubia and the deserts.

(following pages) *Camel train near Kharga*

FLOATING UP THE NILE

W e shall have been on board a week tomorrow, and are now thoroughly settled in our house: all our gimlets up, our divans out, our Turkish slippers (mezd) provided, and everything on its own hook, as befits such close quarters. Now, if you ask how I like the dahabieh life, I must say I am no dahabieh bird, no divan incumbent. I do long to be wandering about the desert by myself, poking my own nose into all the villages and running hither and thither, and make acquaintances où bon me semble. I long to be riding on my ass across the plain, I rejoice when the wind is foul, and I can get ashore. They call me "wild ass of the wilderness, snuffing up the wind", because I am so fond of getting away. I dearly love our dahabieh as my home, but if it is to stay in it the whole day, as we are fain to do when the wind is fair, that is not in my way at all. However, I must tell what walks I have had. This morning I went ashore with one of the crew at sunrise; it was cold, as cold as an English morning in October, and there was even a touch of hoar frost. But when I got under the shelter of the palm trees it was warmer. We went inland to a village, the situation of which was marked to us by its fringe of palms. Whenever you see these, you are sure of finding houses. We met a woman leading out her flock to water at a pool left by the inundation of the Nile, her black goats and white sheep. A little further on, we came to a brick-field, mud bricks laid out to bake in the sun, and full of chopped straw to make them adhere. It made one think of Rebekah and the Hebrew's task, at every turn. Then we walked round the village. But no European can have the least idea of the misery of an African village; if he has not seen it, no description brings it home. I saw a door about three feet high, or a mud hut, and peeping in, saw in the darkness nothing but a white-horned sheep, and a white hen. But something else was moving, and presently crawled out four human beings, three women and a child; they made a miserable pretence of veiling their faces before my Efreet. The only reason why they had not their camel with them was because he could not get in; next door was a maize enclosure, which differed from the first only by being cleaner, and having no roof, I looked over and saw him. My Efreet is so careful of me that he won't let anybody come near me. If they do, he utters some dreadful form of words, which I don't understand, and they instantly fall back.

All the houses in the village were exactly like this, the mud walls very thick, nearly three feet. There appeared to me to be only one den inside, but I did not go in because I had promised not. Some little things were setting out to fetch water from the Nile, each with his amphora on the head, each with a rag which scarcely descended over the head, but shrouded the head (the Arab always covers his head). The dogs, who are like foxes, descended from the roofs at sight of me and my Efreet, but, awed by a similar charm, fell back.

The village, which seemed a considerable place, with a governor and a governor's house, possessed a Khan. I peeped in. Strings of camels lay round the walls—a few inner cells behind them, roofless and floorless, showed tokens of travellers. But I was afraid of a commotion: so veiled my face and passed on. A tray covered with the Turkish thimblefuls of coffee (which we also drink) was coming out—the only refinement the Arab possesses. In every village you see a coffee-house; generally a roofless cabin built of maize stalks, with mud benches round the inside, but always the thimblefuls of coffee, made, not like ours, but pounded, boiled for a moment, and poured off directly and drunk black. You cannot drink coffee in this climate with impunity; it is too heating. We walked round the village, the huts all tumbled together up and down, as animals build their nests, without regularity or plan. The pigeons seemed better lodged: they had round mud cones provided for them, taller than the houses, stuck full of pots at the top for them to build in, and sticks for them to perch on. There was not much curiosity about me, though they (the Arabs, not the pidgeons) could never have seen a European woman before; but they looked on me with the same interest which the dogs did—no more.

Florence Nightingale, Letters from Egypt: A Journey on the Nile 1849–1850,
Grove Press, 1988

Florence Nightingale (1820–1920), born in Florence, Italy, is regarded by many as the true founder of nursing as a profession. She took a team of nurses to Scutari (now Uskudar, Turkey) in 1854, into the Crimean War. By applying her scrupulous methods she reduced the hospital death rate from 42 per cent to 2 per cent. In 1856 she founded the Nightingale School & Home for Nurses in London, UK. She campaigned to improve health standards, hospital planning and organization, publishing 200 books, reports and pamphlets. Her awards included the Royal Red Cross, 1883 and the Order of Merit, 1907; she received the Freedom of City of London in 1908.

Now much of Nubia is covered by the waters of Lake Nubia (or Nasser), created by the High Dam. The Nubian desert was a source of gold, but from further south, in the northern parts of modern Sudan, came other valuable commodities: ivory, ebony, incense, animal skins, monkeys and slaves. In 593 BC Greek soldiers serving in the Egyptian army went far into Nubia, carving their names and places of origin on the colossi of the Temple of Ramesses II at Abu Simbel. Although they went beyond the Third Cataract of the Nile, and fought a battle there, they only reached the northern part of the kingdom of Meroe. Later, both Ptolemy II (reigned 285–246 BC) and the emperor Nero (reigned AD 54–68) sent fleets beyond Meroe (in Sudan) on peaceful missions, to further the trade in exotic produce and to find the source of the Nile. Travellers' tales about the regions around Meroe and further south entered the writings of Greeks and Romans, and were preserved in the encyclopedic works of Pliny, Diodoros and Strabo. The science fiction of its day, these tales described unfamiliar animals such as the rhinoceros, and people who had dogs' heads, or no heads at all: the myth of Africa was being created. But these writers served as the basis for Western knowledge of this region, and places such as Meroe were marked on maps long before the 'exploration' of Africa by Europeans began. These narratives also stimulated interest in the source of the Nile and ultimately led travellers like James Bruce to Ethiopia.

Throughout medieval and modern times, Egypt has been part of the Islamic world, and from AD 1517 specifically of the Ottoman Empire, distancing it from western Europe by religion as well as politics. Familiar to the West through the classical and biblical traditions and through preserved monuments, notably in Rome, yet not easily visited, Egypt became even more fascinating. The attraction of Egypt is clear in Western writing and painting from the Renaissance onwards, culminating in the military and scientific expeditions at the end of the 18th century, which opened the country to Europeans. Ancient, exotic, 'oriental', Egypt now inspired many artists and writers in works of figures as various as Jean-Léon Gérôme, David Roberts, Edward Lear, Gustave Flaubert, Gerard de Nerval and Amelia Edwards.

An important element in the West's fascination with Egypt lies in its religious and mystical tradition. Although academic Egyptology has been generally dismissive of this, it cannot be denied that since the Renaissance there has been a belief that esoteric wisdom was to be found in Egyptian texts.

This renewal of interest in Egypt naturally embraced the most celebrated of the Egyptian deities, Isis and Osiris, stimulated particularly by study of Plutarch's *On Isis and Osiris*. There were obvious parallels to be drawn between the god's death and

Granite colossus of king with chief queen before him, Karnak

resurrection and Christ's, and it was interpreted as an imperfect prefiguring of the Passion. Until recently, academic Egyptology tended to dismiss much that was written in western Europe between the Renaissance and early 19th century as nonsense: but attitudes are changing. We are now beginning to recognize that these writings are as serious in their intent as our own, and have validity. There were some important moves towards the modern discipline of Egyptology, including some serious studies of the pyramids of Giza and attempts at deciphering hieroglyphics. The most important steps in that direction were made by the brilliant Jesuit scholar Athanasius Kircher, who in the mid-17th century argued the connection of the language with Coptic. Although this was not developed further at the time, Kircher did stimulate interest in Coptic, which was almost a dead language, and it was Champollion's knowledge of Coptic that helped him in the decipherment of hieroglyphics.

Interest in Egypt continued throughout the later 17th and 18th centuries, and a few more Europeans began to travel south of Cairo. In France, enthusiasm for things Egyptian manifested itself in the Abbé Terrasson's *Sethos*, published in 1731. Purporting to be translated from Greek, the work of an Alexandrian of the second century AD, this influential work claimed to reveal the mysteries of Isis and Osiris. It was a fabrication but, nevertheless, it was used as a model for the rituals of the Freemasons in the 18th century. It also served as the source for Rameau's *The Birth of Osiris* (1751), which is probably the first 'Egyptian' opera. A later opera on the same theme, Johann Gottlieb Naumann's *Osiris*, was first performed at Dresden in 1781, only a few years before Mozart's *Magic Flute*, but a decade after James Bruce had 'discovered' the source of the Nile in Ethiopia. Bruce's travels were inspired by the classical sources, and on his return journey through northern Sudan he noted some ruins, and correctly identified them as the site ruins of ancient Meroe.

Mozart's *singspiel*, the *Magic Flute (Die Zauberflöte)* was first performed in Vienna in 1791. The work was a collaboration between Mozart and his friend and fellow Freemason, Emanuel Schikaneder. The plot was based on the Abbé Terrasson's novel *Sethos*, with additional elements from a collection of 'oriental' fairy tales by Christoph Martin Wieland, and considerable allusions to Masonic ritual and beliefs. The original stage sets and costumes for the production were a mixture of classical and oriental, rather than Egyptian, but following the publications of the Napoleonic expedition, spectacular and distinctively Egyptian images were introduced by Schinkel for the production in Berlin (1816) and Quaglio for that in Munich (1818).

It was only a few years after the *Magic Flute* that the French expedition (1798) arrived in Egypt. With military intent, it was also a scientific expedition in the 18th century manner, to examine every facet of Egypt, ancient and modern. The expedition is often thought of as the birth of academic Egyptology, and we obscure how much it owed not only to the classical and biblical sources, but also to the tradition of interest in Egypt that began with the Renaissance and continued with the esoteric traditions, as well as the influence of Freemasonry.

Whatever its inspirations, the French and British presence in Egypt resulted not only in the opening of Egypt to the western European powers, but a craze for all things Egyptian. The Egyptian style was perhaps most favoured in France, but pyramids, temples and sphinxes soon adorned gardens all over Europe.

The European consuls began to compete in acquiring collections of antiquities that now form the core of our museums. Henry Salt, aided by Giovanni Belzoni, formed three large collections, two now in London (British Museum), the third being sold to Paris (Louvre). Salt also acquired other significant pieces such as the sarcophagus of Sety I (London, John Soane Museum) and the sarcophagus lid of Ramesses III (Cambridge, Fitzwilliam Museum). Not to be outdone, Bernardino Drovetti made a splendid collection, which is now in the Museo Egizio in Turin; a second collection of Drovetti's went to the Louvre in Paris. The three collections formed by another Italian, Giuseppe di Nizzoli, who worked for the Austrians, are now central to the Kunsthistorisches Museum in Vienna, the Museo Archaeologico in Florence and the Museo Civico in Bologna. Giuseppe Passalacqua offered his large collection to the French Government in 1826, but it was rejected; however, Friederich Wilhelm of Prussia acquired it, and it now forms the foundation of Berlin's Egyptian Museum. In many years accompanying other travellers and scholars, Alessandro Ricci formed collections that are now divided between Dresden (Skulpturensammlung in the Albertinum) and Florence. Even the early Egyptologists such as Champollion (Louvre), Rosellini (Florence) and Lepsius (Berlin) continued to remove large numbers of antiquities: statues, stelae and smaller objects. Today, the activities of these men is regarded as little more than pillage—although that fails to appreciate the mentality of the times and the attitudes of all the parties concerned.

The 'opening' of Egypt also attracted a host of wealthy travellers, usually young men who were seeking something rather more adventurous and exotic than the 'Grand Tour' of Italy and western Europe. Most of them were well educated and able to employ artists to make a record of the sites they visited. In the period from

1815–1840 numerous books of travels appeared and knowledge of the monuments increased rapidly, and not only of those of the Egyptian Nile Valley. William Bankes of Kingston Lacy in Dorset travelled far into the Sudan, as did the Frenchman Frédéric Cailliaud. Cailliaud's publications were the first to present views of the pyramids of Meroe and the monuments of the oases of the Western Desert. Certainly some sort of adventure was an element, even if, as in Bankes's case, there was genuine interest.

The popularity of Egypt had its drawbacks: the Earl of Belmore travelled there with a large family group, causing the Comte de Forbin to complain that meeting an English nanny wheeling a baby took away any sense of adventure!

By the later 1820s many more travellers were arriving in Egypt. These included significant numbers of artists and architects who copied scenes from tombs and temples, and produced romantic views of the monuments. Many of these combine keen observation of the architecture and Egyptian style with a romantic and Orientalist sensibility, creating some of the most popular and enduring images of the period. The published versions of the work of these artists added not only to the developing discipline of Egyptology, but also stimulated the Egyptian taste in architecture and decoration. It was not just ancient Egypt that fascinated; the colours and 'exoticism' of medieval and modern Egypt had an equal allure, and Orientalism became another important feature of 19th-century art and literature. In painting, the ancient monuments might appear for their own sake; function as the backdrop to contemporary life; or be reconstructed in scenes from the biblical narratives (such as Joseph and Pharaoh, or the plagues of Egypt), the death of Kleopatra, or episodes from the new fiction set in ancient Egypt, or, as in the works of Lawrence Alma-Tadema, genre scenes.

Academic Egyptology grew out of this period of collecting antiquities and publication of the monuments. Champollion deciphered the hieroglyphic script and, following his early death in 1832, his successors made rapid advances in understanding the language. Egyptian texts were soon being read, and as knowledge of what the Egyptians themselves had written increased, the importance of the classical sources declined.

The changes in Egyptology are particularly notable in the career of Auguste Mariette, who was placed in charge of a newly created Antiquities Service in 1858. Mariette cleared many monuments of the sand and villages that covered them. He also started a national collection, now the Egyptian Museum in Cairo. Mariette's

Relief from the Temple of Hatshepsut, Luxor

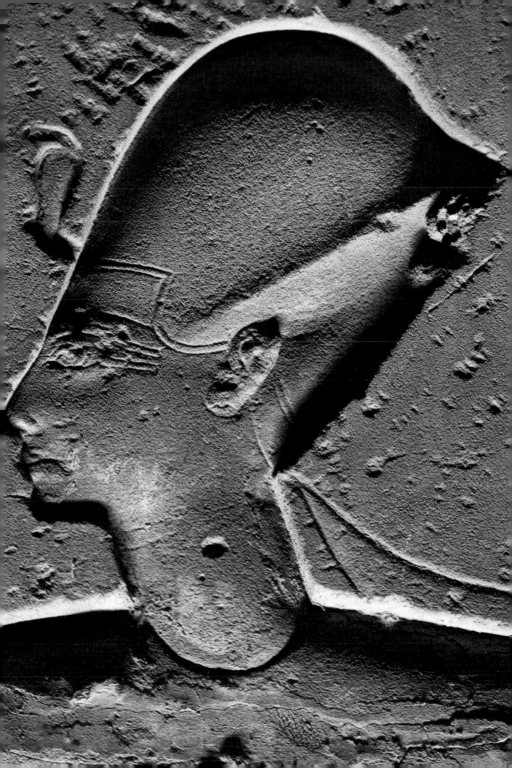

career also symbolizes another change in attitude toward Egypt. Mariette wrote the plot line for the most famous of Egyptian operas, Verdi's *Aïda*. The opera was first performed in Cairo on 24 December 1871, but not, as is often said, for the opening of the Suez Canal or Cairo Opera House (which opened with another Verdi work, *Rigoletto*), both of which took place in 1869. Mariette managed to create a classical romance with historical detail culled from the most recently discovered monuments. The conflict between Egyptians and 'Ethiopians' (Kushites or Nubians) reflects the narratives of historical inscriptions that had been found at Gebel Barkal in the northern Sudan, and the names of the 'Ethiopian' king, Amonasro, and Egyptian princess, Amneris, are those of historical characters (although we would read them differently nowadays). Although only 80 years separate Mariette's *Aïda* from Mozart's *Magic Flute*, they clearly show the dramatic change in European perceptions of ancient Egypt. *Aïda* has no themes of initiation into arcane knowledge, and attempts to be based in a 'factual' ancient Egypt, of the type being painted by contemporary 'archaeological' artists such as Alma-Tadema.

Popular interest in Egypt continued, still closely associated with the biblical narratives (which feature prominently in guidebooks of the period) and many more visitors were able to see the monuments when Thomas Cook began operating his first cruises on the Nile in 1869.

From 1850 on, academic Egyptology moved away from—positively rejected—the older esoteric European traditions about Egypt, in favour of increasingly more 'scientific' approaches, and history taken directly 'from the monuments'. Archaeology in Egypt, as opposed to simply clearing monuments and collecting objects, began with Flinders Petrie. An obsessive measurer, Petrie first went to Egypt in 1880 to measure the Great Pyramid. This was to test the theories of family friend Charles Piazzi Smyth, an influential writer who believed that the Pyramid's measurements encoded God's message to mankind. Petrie soon abandoned Smyth's interpretations, but did later dig sites with biblical associations as a way of encouraging wealthy sponsors. One of Petrie's own interests was early Egypt and he made pioneering excavations at Abydos and Naqada, laying the foundations for the study of Pre-Dynastic Egypt.

Collecting objects was as important for Petrie and his contemporaries as it had been for the preceding generation. The laws of the day allowed any excavator to bring away half of what they found, although the authorities selected the material that was to stay in Egypt. Petrie needed sponsors for his digs, and a way of encouraging them was to give them objects. Petrie's own interest in pottery and other small objects had the practical advantage that the more he kept of what he dug up, the more he had to give away. The collections formed by Petrie's sponsors, both private and academic, are central to many museums throughout the world from Britain, Europe and the United States, to South Africa, Australia and New Zealand.

Petrie and his successors broadened Egyptology from its base in texts and 'art' to a discipline with greater interest in urban sites, domestic life and its origins in the Pre-Dynastic periods. But, although important urban sites such as Amarna (ancient Akhetaten), Kahun and the very early settlements such as Nekhen (Hierakonpolis) were yielding enormous amounts of information on aspects of ancient Egypt previously unknown, rich patrons and the public always responded to the discovery of treasure. The American businessman Theodore Davis funded a series of excavations in the Valley of the Kings between 1903 and 1912, which resulted in important discoveries. He was followed in the valley by Lord Carnarvon and Howard Carter who, in 1922, made the biggest discovery of all: the tomb of Tutankhamun. This started another Egyptian craze, exploited by the popular press with the invention of the 'curse'.

The scale of Tutankhamun's burial overshadows other discoveries of its type. Even so, the royal tombs of Tanis, excavated by Pierre Montet in 1939, have never attracted as much popular attention as they merit. This is, no doubt, because they belong to the (apparently) unglamorous Libyan pharaohs, rather than one of the high points of Egyptian history. Egyptologists, in deciding what are 'high' points and periods of interest, have been significant in formulating public opinion and interests.

Public attention was again directed towards Egyptian archaeology during the late 1950s and 1960s, not by a major haul of gold, but by the construction of the High Dam at Aswan. This massive project, dominated by political issues associated with Egypt's new-found independence, was to result in a reservoir that flooded the whole of Nubia south of the First Cataract into northern Sudan. It necessitated the moving of the rock-cut temples of Ramesses at Abu Simbel and other temples to new locations, mostly on the shores of Lake Nubia (Lake Nasser). This was the most public feature of the archaeological work, but there was a huge survey of the entire region, with excavation of all the important sites, resulting in the rewriting of the history and archaeology of Nubia.

Throughout the 20th century Hollywood ensured that Egypt remained a significant part of popular culture. From the original silent version of Cecil B De Mille's biblical epic *The Ten Commandments* (1923), celluloid visions of Egypt have travelled via *The Mummy* (1932) and its numerous offspring; versions of the Kleopatra story with the lead played by icons of each generation; De Mille's 1956 remake with Charlton Heston as Moses and Yul Brynner as Ramesses II; and *Death on the Nile* to *Indiana Jones* and *The English Patient*. Archaeologists and Egyptologists in film have frequently been the victims of curses and attacks by mummies; they have been glamorized (*Indiana Jones*) too often; lampooned occasionally; and, on one occasion at least, sent to the other side of the galaxy (*Stargate*).

Although some Egyptologists still cultivate the 'Indiana Jones' image, the reality is generally less flamboyant. In recent years Egyptian archaeology has become more scientific and less intrusive than formerly. Whole regions, previously relatively ignored, are now being examined, minutely.

The German Archaeological Institute's excavations on Elephantine Island have continued for several decades, uncovering evidence of the early settlement, as well as many monuments of later periods. At Hierakonpolis (Nekhen) the work initiated by Michael Hoffman has shed considerable light on the political and cultural development of Upper Egypt in the Pre-Dynastic period.

The Delta has, at last, become the focus of many surveys and exploratory excavations, which will increase our understanding of its importance in ancient times. The many small towns and villages of the Ptolemaic and Roman periods in the Faiyum are now being examined for their archaeology, and not just the papyri sought by earlier diggers. Memphis, the key city of Egypt from the unification to the Ptolemaic Period, has been the subject of a major survey that is beginning to unravel the complex history of the movements of both the Nile and the main areas of the city.

Egyptology, both academic and popular, has tended to ignore the important monuments and sites that are not from the Pharaonic period. Indeed, some archaeologists destroyed the later (Roman and medieval) levels of sites to get at the dynastic material; others, presumably with a greater sense of guilt, waited for the local farmers to work their way down. Throughout Egyptology, there is now much greater interest in the Roman, Late Antique (Coptic) and early Islamic sites, and recognition of their importance. At the other end of the timescale, Egypt has provided some of the most important fossils of prehistoric mammals. Recently, in Bahariya Oasis, apart from the important discovery of the Valley of the Golden Mummies, one of the most significant deposits of dinosaur fossils has been rediscovered, yielding species previously unknown.

But soil cores, marl clays and pollen grains do not have quite the same allure as gold coffins and animal-headed gods. Inevitably, the increasingly scientific concerns of academic Egyptology have seen an ever-greater divide between 'academic' and 'popular' views of Egypt. The dramatic change in tourism in the past 20 years means that for Europeans, Egypt is easily accessible: a visit to Egypt is no longer a 'once in a lifetime', but something that can be accomplished relatively cheaply. It can also be done quite easily without using expensive tour operators and their guest Egyptologists. Many different groups with specialist interests—New Age, biblical, Afrocentrist, bird-watching—can easily organize their own tours to suit themselves. The many layers of Egypt's past and present are now available to more people than ever before, and despite all the attempts of academic Egyptology to reduce ancient Egypt to the study of potsherds, seeds and mud-bricks, the country still exerts its romantic lure. It is not surprising that many visitors seek a spiritual dimension that seems more achievable in Egypt's landscape and ruins than it does in Western cities. Academic Egyptology is beginning to respond to these 'alternative Egypts', both modern and those that are part of our Western inheritance. The future will no doubt see an increase in the breadth and depth of our knowledge about all periods of Egypt's past, but also a recognition that there is not just one Egypt, and its many layers will continue to allure us.

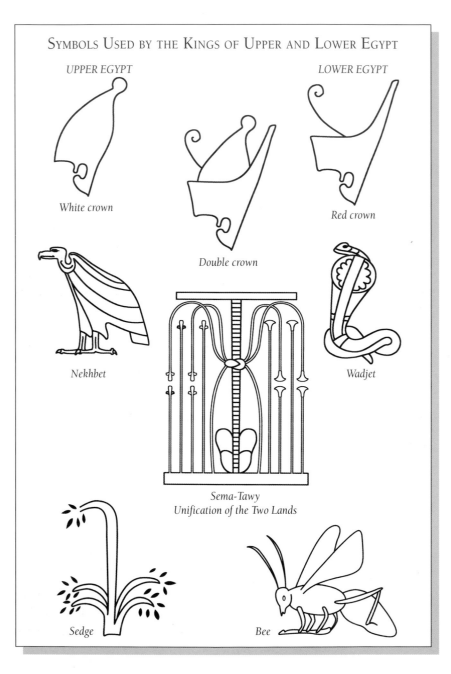

SYMBOLS USED BY THE KINGS OF UPPER AND LOWER EGYPT

UPPER EGYPT

LOWER EGYPT

White crown

Red crown

Double crown

Nekhbet

Wadjet

Sema-Tawy
Unification of the Two Lands

Sedge

Bee

EGYPTIAN HISTORY IN OUTLINE

A ncient Egyptian political history is little more than a king-list to which are added monuments and military activities of the rulers. It is the 'official view' that the Egyptian rulers wanted to tell posterity which forms the basis of our history. The main concern of these royal monuments was the relationship between the king and the gods, exemplified by the building of temples, the subjugation of chaotic forces and the maintenance of divine order. Occasionally documents and correspondence are discovered which shed more light upon events at the Egyptian court: the letters from Asiatic princes to Amenhotep III and Akhenaten, discovered at Amarna, detail events in an immediate way; the papyrus recording the trial of conspirators in a harem conspiracy against Ramesses III reveals something of the intrigues that went on in the palace. However, the historian most usually has to reconstruct turbulent aspects of Egyptian history from veiled references in the source materials, and this in turn has led to many alternative, and sometimes fanciful, interpretations.

Throughout Egyptian history the daily life of the majority of the people would have remained much the same. Records of strikes, and letters of complaint about the late supply of provisions, show that they were not always satisfied with their lot. These strikes were usually a reaction to the incompetence of bureaucrats and their failure to deliver foodstuffs or clothing. There is no evidence for large-scale popular uprisings against the central authority before the Ptolemaic period. Of course, that does not mean that there never was any.

PRE-DYNASTIC EGYPT

T he earliest important sites excavated in the Egyptian Nile Valley are in the Kom Ombo basin. Many cultures are known throughout the Mesolithic (c.10,000–5000 BC) and Neolithic (c.5000–3500 BC), particularly from the outer fringes of the Faiyum and Delta. Domestication of animals and cultivation of plants is thought to have been introduced from Western Asia at this time. There is no homogeneous culture in late Pre-Dynastic Egypt (c.3500–3100 BC) as is found in Mesopotamia, although there are similarities between the cultures known from many different sites. The artistic production, notably the pottery, already shows many characteristics of later Egyptian art. It is also clear from the religious symbols that many of the important cults were already established. The traditional interpretation of the development of Egyptian society proposes that during the later Pre-Dynastic Period a number of small districts, each with their own chiefs and gods, were eventually absorbed by conquest into two large kingdoms, Upper and Lower Egypt. The regions, with their deities, are seen as the origin of the nomes of the Dynastic Period. This system also serves as an explanation for the complexity of Egyptian religion with its many regional deities and different theologies. At the end of the Pre-Dynastic Period, a series of more powerful Upper Egyptian rulers, with their capital at Hierakonpolis, and later at Abydos, absorbed the Lower Egyptian state. With the defeat of the Lower Egyptian kings and the founding of Memphis, the united Egyptian state was born (c.3000–2950 BC). In recent years excavations at Hierakonpolis and Abydos, and surveys of rock drawings in the Eastern Desert of Upper Egypt, have produced a range of material that is causing Egyptologists to reassess both their traditional interpretation of the development of the united state, and the date at which it happened. Archaeology in the Delta region is also bringing to light new evidence from these very early periods, and showing that there were already strong trading contacts with western Asia. Evidence from the south shows that there was another trade network extending far into Nubia.

SITES

Few prehistoric or Pre-Dynastic sites remain to be seen easily.

MONUMENTS

Many museums have collections of pottery of the Naqada II or Gerzean Period with its characteristic red-on-white painting showing boats, often decorated with religious symbols. The large ceremonial slate palettes and mace heads of this period depict religious ceremonies and military events in the unification: the Battlefield Palette (London, British Museum and Oxford, Ashmolean Museum); the Bull Palette (Paris, Louvre); the Libya Palette (Cairo, Egyptian Museum). Ceremonial objects found at Hierakonpolis: Narmer Palette (Cairo, Egyptian Museum); Mace Head of King 'Scorpion' (Oxford, Ashmolean Museum).

EARLY DYNASTIC OR ARCHAIC EGYPT (Dynasties 1–2: c.3100–2686 BC)

The late Pre-Dynastic and early Archaic Period saw the creation of a centralized state with a god-king and powerful nobility. The benefits of the annual inundation were extended by a system of dykes and canals that exploited the agricultural potential of the land. Writing developed rapidly to facilitate the control of agricultural production by the officials. Architectural construction was sophisticated, surviving in the elaborate brick tombs and cenotaphs of the rulers at Saqqara and Abydos. Large blocks of hewn stone were used in construction, both limestone and granite. There was a high level of material culture within court circles. Stone vessels were produced in very elaborate forms, some imitating basketwork, others with remarkably thin walls in the shape of leaves. Schists and alabaster were favoured for larger vessels, amethyst for unguent vases. The earliest known statuary and relief work show rapid mastery of materials. The fine quality of the jewellery from the tomb of King Djer at Abydos (Cairo, Egyptian Museum) shows characteristics of later work, and is made of gold, lapis lazuli and turquoise, indicative of foreign contacts. Ivory carving was also of a high quality, being used for statuettes and furniture.

SITES

The remains of the massive brick monuments of the First and Second dynasties still exist at Saqqara and Abydos, but are mostly inaccessible at present.

MONUMENTS

Stele of King Djet from Abydos (Louvre); statues of King Khasekhemwy in schist (Cairo, Egyptian Museum) and limestone (Oxford, Ashmolean Museum) from Hierakonpolis.

OLD KINGDOM (Dynasties 3–6: c.2686–2181 BC)

During the Old Kingdom the state was headed by a god-king, many of whose chief officials were members of the royal family. They and the nobility were buried near him in large decorated tombs. The Step Pyramid complex at Saqqara, a revolutionary structure designed for Djoser by Imhotep, translates the architecture of wood, mud-brick and reeds into stone. But a new monumental style of stone architecture rapidly developed, epitomized by the pyramid complexes of the late Third Dynasty (Medum) and Fourth Dynasty (Dashur and Giza). Hard stones were brought enormous distances, granite from Aswan and diorite from the quarries of the Nubian Desert, to be used for statuary or as architectural elements. The geometrical austerity of the pyramid complexes was offset by the contrast of stones employed and the statuary and reliefs which decorated them. Private tombs had delicately painted (Medum) or carved relief (Saqqara and Giza) decorations, as well as much statuary. Funerary monuments and sculptures dominate our perception of the Old Kingdom, but the refinement of court taste can be seen in the objects from the burial of Queen Hetepheres, mother of Khufu (Cheops), discovered at Giza (Cairo, Egyptian Museum). The Fifth Dynasty witnessed the increased influence of the solar cult of Ra of Heliopolis, and the king was now regarded as the son of the sun god. The Fifth and Sixth dynasties saw the decline of royal and increase of noble power, evidenced by smaller and less well-constructed pyramids of kings (Abusir and Saqqara), and larger tombs for the nobility who intermarried with the royal houses. This situation came to a head in the Sixth Dynasty with the reign of Pepi II (94 years), one of the longest in history.

MAJOR SITES

Third Dynasty: Saqqara, Step Pyramid complex; Medum, pyramid of Huni and mastabas. **Fourth Dynasty**: Dashur pyramids; Giza pyramids, Sphinx and Temple of Khafre (Chephren). **Fifth Dynasty**: Saqqara, Unas pyramid and causeway, mastaba of Idut; Abusir, pyramids and sun temple at Abu Ghurob. **Sixth Dynasty**: Saqqara, pyramid of Teti, mastabas of Mereruka, Kagemni, Ptahhotep and Akhethotep, and Ti; Aswan, Tombs of the Nobles.

MONUMENTS

Statues of Djoser, Khafre (Chephren), Menkaure (Mycerinus), Rahotep and Nofret, the Sheikh el-Beled, Pepi I from Hierakonpolis (Cairo, Egyptian Museum); furniture of Queen Hetepheres (Cairo, Egyptian Museum); the Medum geese (Cairo, Egyptian Museum). Many museum collections have private statues of Old Kingdom date, and slabs of relief sculpture from mastabas.

FIRST INTERMEDIATE PERIOD (Dynasties 7–11: c.2181–2040 BC)

The centralized state broke down during the First Intermediate Period, perhaps as a result of the decline of Pharaonic prestige and increase of aristocratic power in the late Sixth Dynasty, but there is also the possibility of severe climatic changes. A series of low Niles may have affected agriculture, and there are some indications of times of drought and famine. The local rulers tried to provide for their people and some adopted royal style. The Seventh and Eighth dynasties comprise a large number of ephemeral rulers. There were regional dynasties at Herakleopolis (Ninth Dynasty) and Thebes (early 11th Dynasty), and individual notables such as Ankhtify of Moalla. These nomarchs (ie ruler of a nome) had private armies, and there were periods of conflict as rulers tried to protect their lands, and to keep out groups of people affected by the famine, whether coming from Asia, Libya or other parts of Egypt. Much of the art of the First Intermediate Period lacks the sophistication of the Old Kingdom, but can be more lively and innovative. The Memphite workshops continued to produce high quality material for the Herakleopolitan dynasts, but elsewhere a relative poverty can be noted until the latter part of the period.

SITES

Moalla, tomb of Ankhtify. Beni Hasan, the tombs of Khety and Baqet III both have a scene showing the siege of a town and military conflict.

MONUMENTS

Wooden soldiers from the tomb of Mesehti at Asyut (Cairo, Egyptian Museum).

MIDDLE KINGDOM (Dynasties 11–12: c.2040–1795 BC)

The princes of Thebes finally brought the whole of Upper Egypt under their control and Nebhepetre-Menthuhotep II subdued Lower Egypt and reunited the country. The artistic production of the **11th Dynasty** (c. 2040–1991 BC) is of a very high quality, and after the re-unification, Menthuhotep II brought sculptors from Memphis to oversee the rebuilding of his temple-tomb at Deir el-Bahari. The **12th Dynasty** (c.1991–1782 BC) was one of the most stable dynasties to rule in Egypt. The kings reasserted central authority and attempted to conciliate the nobility, but eventually were forced to curb their power by a reorganization of the state. This divided Egypt into two large administrative units, each with a vizier, rather than the old system of nomes. Co-regencies assured a strong succession. Expansion into Nubia brought control of the Nile as far as the Second Cataract into Egyptian hands. The Faiyum region was developed, and some kings built their pyramids at its entrance (Hawara and Illahun). The art of the early 12th Dynasty was modelled upon that of the late Old Kingdom, but it soon developed its own characteristics. There was much temple building throughout the country, although not on the monumental scale of the New Kingdom. The structures were small but elegant, and decorated in fine relief. The royal pyramids were of brick faced with limestone, and consequently are today less impressive than those of the Old Kingdom. In ancient times, however, the temple adjacent to the pyramid at Hawara was considered a greater wonder than the pyramids of Giza. At both Dashur and Illahun (Lahun), jewellery belonging to royal ladies was discovered, revealing a technical excellence and aesthetic refinement unequalled in Egyptian history.

MAJOR SITES

Eleventh Dynasty: Luxor, Temple of Nebhepetre-Menthuhotep at Deir el-Bahari. **12th Dynasty**: pyramids of Senusret I and Amenemhat I (Lisht), Senusret II (Illahun), Senusret III and Amenemhat III (Dashur); Hawara, pyramid and temple of Amenemhat III; Karnak, White Chapel of Senusret I and other architectural fragments reconstructed in the Open Air Museum; Beni Hasan, tombs; Aswan, tombs of the nomarchs and Heqaib sanctuary on Elephantine.

MONUMENTS

Eleventh Dynasty: statue of Nebhepetre-Menthuhotep from Deir el-Bahari (Cairo, Egyptian Museum); sarcophagi of wives of Nebhepetre-Menthuhotep from Deir el-Bahari (Cairo); wooden models from tomb of Meket-re at Thebes (Cairo); chapel of Menthuhotep III from Dendera (Cairo); statues of Menthuhotep III (Luxor Museum). **12th Dynasty**: statues of Senusret I from Lisht, and from Karnak temple (Luxor Museum); statues of Amenemhat III from Tanis (Cairo); of Senusret III from Deir el-Bahari (British Museum); jewellery of princesses from Dashur (Cairo) and Illahun (New York, Metropolitan Museum of Art).

SECOND INTERMEDIATE PERIOD (Dynasties 13–17: c.1782–1550 BC)

The **13th Dynasty** (c.1782–1650 BC) began strongly, and in artistic terms followed the Middle Kingdom traditions, but the country again broke down into regions and there were about 50 kings in a period of little more than a century. There were settlers from western Asia, notably in the eastern Delta, and some of their rulers assumed Pharaonic style. They are generally known as the Hyksos (from Egyptian: rulers of foreign lands). The territory gained by the 12th-dynasty pharaohs in Nubia was seized by the kings of Kerma (in northern Sudan). Again Thebes became the centre of a local dynasty (the **17th**) which claimed to be the legitimate power. These princes challenged the Hyksos rule in the north, but at least one of them (Seqenenre) was killed in battle. Kamose re-established Egyptian garrisons in Nubia before turning north and attacking the Hyksos capital, Avaris.

MONUMENTS

Some architectural elements can be found in the Open Air Museum at Karnak. *Ka*-statue of King Hor (Cairo, Egyptian Museum). Head of Amenemhat V from Elephantine (Vienna). Statues of King Sobekhotep IV (Paris, Louvre; London, British Museum). Stele of Kamose from Karnak (Luxor Museum).

NEW KINGDOM (Dynasties 18–20: c.1550–1069 BC)

The final expulsion of the Hyksos and the reunification of Egypt by Ahmose mark the beginning of the New Kingdom and **18th Dynasty** (c.1550–1295 BC). Thutmose I began the expansion of Egyptian power as far as the Euphrates and Fourth Cataract of the Nile. There was a strong emphasis on Thebes as the royal burial place and ancestral home of the family, but the city did not replace Memphis as the capital. The great expansion of Karnak temple as it stands today was begun by Thutmose I. Hatshepsut, Thutmose I's daughter, was not the only woman to ascend the Egyptian throne as king, but her reign is the most significant of the female rulers. Thutmose III consolidated Egypt's position in the Near East with more than 16 campaigns in western Asia, and several in Nubia. After his death, diplomacy was used to maintain Egypt's position, which is detailed in the remains of an archive of clay tablets discovered at Amarna. The reigns of Amenhotep II, Thutmose IV and Amenhotep III were a period of peace in which Egypt enjoyed her pre-eminence in the Near East, with increasing opulence and luxury. Art reached a peak of refinement and delicacy, epitomized by the relief decoration of the tombs of Kheruef, Ramose and others at Thebes. Amenhotep III's building works combined elegance and fine craftsmanship with vast scale. Traditional historical interpretation sees a conflict between the kings and the Amun priesthood during the later years of Amenhotep III and in the reign of his son Akhenaten. These kings seem to have attempted to remodel the divine kingship along the Old Kingdom lines with its emphasis upon the solar cult. The reign of Akhenaten and his creation of a new city, Akhetaten (Amarna), for the worship of the sun disc and with the king as sole intercessor, remains one of the most controversial periods of Egyptian history. The last kings of the dynasty, Tutankhamun, Ay and Horemheb, had to re-establish royal authority along more conventional lines. At this time the rising power of Hittites in Asia Minor became a threat to Egyptian influence in north Syria and the Levant.

The **19th Dynasty** (c.1295–1186 BC) began with the brief reign of Ramesses I, appointed as his successor by Horemheb. Sety I established the dynasty firmly on the Egyptian throne and displayed his power by campaigning in western Asia. He continued the building of Karnak temple and founded new temples at Abydos and in Nubia, as well as a new Delta residence city, later to be called Per-Ramesses. The Hittite threat continued to grow and the early years of Ramesses II's 67-year reign saw him campaigning in Syria–Palestine, culminating in the indecisive Battle of Qadesh in year five. Eventually in year 21, a treaty was signed between the two powers, which

EGYPTIAN DYNASTIES

Egyptian chronology is secure from the accession of the 25th-dynasty pharaoh, Taharqo in 690 BC. All dates before 690 BC are approximate. The internal order of kings in the major phases of the Middle and New Kingdoms is secure. The lengths of their reigns are also fairly certain. The order and reign lengths of the pharaohs of the Old Kingdom are also relatively certain, but greater allowances must be made. In the Intermediate Periods some pharaohs or dynasties were contemporary with each other. The recently revised lower dates for the 12th Dynasty (1963–1787 BC, rather than c.1991–1782 BC) show the degree of latitude in the earlier periods: this becomes even greater in the Early Dynastic–Old Kingdom. This list includes all the major rulers who are referred to in the guide, but a number of rulers who had very short reigns or left no major monuments are not included.

PRE-DYNASTIC PERIOD	c.5000–3100 BC	FIFTH DYNASTY	c.2498–2345 BC
DYNASTY '0'	c.3150–3050 BC	Userkaf	c.2494–2487 BC
King 'Scorpion'		Sahure	c.2487–2475 BC
		Neferirkare	c.2475–2455 BC
EARLY DYNASTIC PERIOD	c.3100–2686 BC	Neferefre	c.2448–2445 BC
FIRST DYNASTY	c.3050–2890 BC	Neuserre	c.2445–2421 BC
Narmer	c.3100 BC	Djedkare-Isesi	c.2414–2375 BC
Aha	c.3080 BC	Unas	c.2375–2345 BC
Djer	c.3050 BC		
Djet	c.3000 BC	SIXTH DYNASTY	c.2345–2181 BC
Den	c.2985 BC	Teti	2345–2323 BC
		Pepi I	2321–2287 BC
SECOND DYNASTY	c.2890–2686 BC	Nemtyemsaf	2287–2278 BC
Hotep-sekhemwy	c.2890 BC	Pepi II	2278–2184 BC
Peribsen	c.2700 BC		
Khasekhemwy	c.2600–2686 BC	FIRST INTERMEDIATE PERIOD c.2181–2040 BC
		SEVENTH/EIGHTH DYNASTIES c.2181–2125 BC
OLD KINGDOM	c.2686–2181 BC	
THIRD DYNASTY	c.2686–2613 BC	NINTH DYNASTY	c.2160–2130 BC
Sanakhte	c.2686–2613 BC	TENTH DYNASTY	c.2130–2040 BC
Netjer-khet Djoser	c.2667–2648 BC	
Sekhemkhet	c.2648–2640 BC	ELEVENTH DYNASTY	c.2125–2040 BC
		(at Thebes)	
FOURTH DYNASTY	c.2613–2498 BC	Intef I	2125–2112 BC
Sneferu	c.2613–2589 BC	Intef II	2112–2063 BC
Khufu	c.2589–2566 BC		
Djedefre	c.2566–2558 BC	MIDDLE KINGDOM	c.2040–1795 BC
Khafre	c.2558–2532 BC	ELEVENTH DYNASTY	(continued)
Menkaure	c.2532–2503 BC	Nebhepetre-	
Shepseskaf	c.2503–2498 BC	Menthuhotep II	2060–2010 BC
		S'ankh-ka-re	
		Menthuhotep III	2010–1998 BC

Neb-tawy-re	
Menthuhotep IV	1998–1991 BC
TWELFTH DYNASTY	c.1991–1782 BC
(revised dates: 1963–1787 BC)	
Amenemhat I	1991–1962 BC or
	1963–1934 BC
Senusret I	1971–1928 BC or
	1943–1899 BC
Amenemhat II	1929–1895 BC or
	1901–1867 BC
Senusret II	1897–1878 BC or
	1869–1862 BC
Senusret III	1878–1841 BC or
	1862–1844 BC
Amenemhat III	1842–1797 BC or
	1843–1798 BC
Amenemhat IV	1798–1786 BC or
	1797–1790 BC
Sebekneferu	1785–1782 BC or
	1789–1787 BC

SECOND INTERMEDIATE	
PERIOD	c.1782–1550 BC
THIRTEENTH DYNASTY	c.1782–1650 BC

FOURTEENTH DYNASTY
(Minor rulers contemporary with parts of
Thirteenth and Fifteenth dynasties)

FIFTEENTH DYNASTY	
(Hyksos)	c.1650–1550 BC
Apepi	c.1585–1550 BC
Khamudy	c.1550 BC

SIXTEENTH DYNASTY
(Local rulers contemporary with
Fifteenth Dynasty)

SEVENTEENTH DYNASTY	c.1580–1550 BC
(at Thebes)	
Seqenenre Tao	c.1560 BC
Kamose	c.1555–1550 BC

NEW KINGDOM	c.1550–1069 BC
EIGHTEENTH DYNASTY	c.1550–1295 BC
Ahmose	1550–1525 BC
Amenhotep I	1525–1504 BC
Thutmose I	1504–1492 BC
Thutmose II	1492–1479 BC
Thutmose III	1479–1425 BC
(sole reign from 1456)	
Hatshepsut	1472–1458 BC
Amenhotep II	1427–1400 BC
Thutmose IV	1400–1390 BC

Amenhotep III	1390–1352 BC
Akhenaten	1352–1336 BC
Tutankhamun	1336–1327 BC
Ay	1327–1323 BC
Horemheb	1323–1295 BC
NINETEENTH DYNASTY	c.1295–1186 BC
Sety I	1294–1279 BC
Ramesses II	1279–1213 BC
Merneptah	1213–1203 BC
Amenmesses	1203–1200 BC
(or entirely within the reign of Sety II)	
Sety II	1200–1194 BC
Siptah	1194–1188 BC
Tawosret	1188–1186 BC
TWENTIETH DYNASTY	c.1186–1069 BC
Ramesses III	1184–1153 BC
Ramesses IV	1153–1147 BC
Ramesses V	1147–1143 BC
Ramesses VI	1143–1136 BC
Ramesses VII	1136–1129 BC
Ramesses VIII	1129–1126 BC
Ramesses IX	1126–1108 BC
Ramesses X	1108–1099 BC
Ramesses XI	1099–1069 BC

THIRD INTERMEDIATE	
PERIOD	c.1069–656 BC
TWENTY-FIRST DYNASTY	c.1069–945 BC
Pa-seba-kha-en-niut	
(Psusennes)	1039–991 BC
Osorkon the Elder	984–978 BC
Siamun	978–959 BC

TWENTY-SECOND AND TWENTY-THIRD	
DYNASTIES	c.945–715 BC
Sheshonq I	945–924 BC
Osorkon I	924–889 BC
Osorkon II	874–850 BC
Takeloth II	850–825 BC
Osorkon III	c.730 BC

TWENTY-FOURTH DYNASTY	
(in Sau, or Sais)	
Bakenranef	c.716–711 BC

TWENTY-FIFTH DYNASTY	c.750–656 BC
Kashta	c.750–736 BC
Piye (Piankhy)	c.736–712 BC
Shabaqo	c.711–695 BC
Shebitqo	c.695–690 BC
Taharqo	690–664 BC
Tanwetamani	664–656 BC

LATE PERIOD	664–332 BC
TWENTY-SIXTH DYNASTY	664–525 BC
Psamtik I	664–610 BC
Nekau II	610–595 BC
Psamtik II	595–589 BC
Wahibre (Apries)	589–570 BC
Ahmose II (Amasis)	570–526 BC
Psamtik III	526–525 BC
TWENTY-SEVENTH DYNASTY	
(Persian Kings)	525–404 BC
Cambyses	525–521 BC
Darius I	521–485 BC
Pedubast III (rebel Egyptian dynast)	
Xerxes	485–465 BC
Artaxerxes I	465–424/423 BC
Darius II	423–404 BC
TWENTY-EIGHTH DYNASTY	404–399 BC
Amyrtaios	404–400/399 BC
TWENTY-NINTH DYNASTY	399–379 BC
Nefaarud I	c.399/398–394/ 393 BC
Hakor	393/392–381/ 380 BC
Pshenmut	380/379 BC
Nefaarud II	379 BC
THIRTIETH DYNASTY	380–341 BC
Nakhtnebef	c.379/378–362/
(Nectanebo I)	361 BC
Djedhor	361/360–360/
(Djeho/Teos)	359 BC
Nakhthorheb	359/358–342/
(Nectanebo II)	341 BC
SECOND PERSIAN DYNASTY	343–332 BC
Artaxerxes III	343–338 BC
Khabbash (Egyptian independent	
pharaoh)	c.338 BC
Darius III	336–332 BC
MACEDONIAN KINGS	332–305 BC
Alexander III the Great	332–323 BC
Philip Arrhidaios	323–317 BC
Alexander IV	323–305 BC
THE PTOLEMIES	305–30 BC
Ptolemy I Soter	305–282 BC
Ptolemy II Philadelphos	285–246 BC
Ptolemy III Euergetes I	246–222 BC
Ptolemy IV Philopator	222–205 BC
Ptolemy V Epiphanes	205–180 BC
Ptolemy VI Philometor	180–145 BC
Kleopatra II	180–116 BC

Ptolemy VIII Euergetes II	169–163 and 145–116 BC
Kleopatra III	145–101 BC
Ptolemy IX Soter II	116–107 BC and 88–80 BC (restored)
Ptolemy X Alexander I	107–88 BC
Kleopatra Berenike III	80 BC
Ptolemy XI Alexander II	80 BC
Ptolemy XII Neos Dionysos	
(Auletes)	80–58 and 55–51 BC
Kleopatra VI (58–57 BC)	
and Berenike IV	58–55 BC
Ptolemy XIII	51–47 BC
Kleopatra VII	51–30 BC
Ptolemy XIV	47–44 BC
Ptolemy XV Kaisarion	44–30 BC
ROMAN EMPERORS	30 BC–AD 395
Augustus	30 BC–AD 14
Tiberius	AD 14–37
Caius (Caligula)	AD 37–41
Claudius	AD 41–54
Nero	AD 54–68
Vespasian	AD 69–79
Titus	AD 79–81
Domitian	AD 81–96
Nerva	AD 96–98
Trajan	AD 98–117
Hadrian	AD 117–138
Antoninus Pius	AD 138–161
Marcus Aurelius	AD 161–180
Lucius Verus (co-emperor)	AD 161–169
Commodus	AD 180–192
Septimius Severus	AD 193–211
Caracalla	AD 211–217
Geta	AD 211
Macrinus	AD 217–218
Elagabalus	AD 218–222
Alexander Severus	AD 222–235
Philip	AD 244–249
Valerian	AD 253–260
Gallienus	AD 253–268
Claudius II Gothicus	AD 268–270
Aurelian	AD 270–275
Diocletian	AD 286–305
The Tetrarchy: Diocletian, Maximian,	
Constantius, Galerius	AD 293–305
Constantine I	AD 306–337
Maxentius (rival emperor)	AD 306–312
Julian	AD 361–363
Valens	AD 364–378
Theodosius I	AD 379–395

BYZANTINE EMPERORS	AD 395–c.639
Justinian I	AD 527–565
Phocas	AD 602–610
Heraclius	AD 610–642
Persian occupation	AD 619–629

ISLAMIC EGYPT

Islamic dates are calculated from the *hijra* (migration) of Mohammed from Mecca to Medina in AD 622. Because the Islamic calendar is slightly shorter than the Christian calendar, and moves forward by about 11 days each year, the Islamic year normally falls over parts of two Christian years. Only the most significant rulers are listed.

Conquest of Egypt by Amr ibn al-As	AD 639–642
The Khalifs (ruling from Medina)	AD 642–661 (H 21–40)
The Umayyad Khalifs (ruling from Damascus)	AD 661–750 (H 41–132)
The Abbasid Khalifs (ruling from Baghdad)	AD 749–869 (H 131–255)
The Tulunids (ruling in Egypt)	AD 868–905 (H 254–292)
Ahmed ibn Tulun	AD 868–884 (H 254–270)
The Ikhshidids	AD 935–969 (H 323–358)
Mohammed ibn Turghj al-Ikhshid	AD 935–946 (H 323–334)
The Fatimids	AD 969–1171 (H 358–567)
General Gawhar captures Fustat	AD 969 (H 358)
al-Muizz	AD 969–975 (H 358–365)
al-Hakim	AD 996–1021 (H 386–411)
al-Mustansir	AD 1036–1094 (H 427–487)
al-Mustali	AD 1094–1101 (H 487–524)
The Ayyubids	AD 1169–1252 (H 564–650)
Salah-al-Din (Saladin)	AD 1169–1193 (H 564–589)
Najm-al-Din Ayyub	AD 1240–1249 (H 637–647)

The Abbasid Khalifs	AD 1261–1517 (H 659–923)
The Bahri Mamluk Sultans	AD 1250–1390 (H 648–792)
Aybak	AD 1250–1257 (H 637–647)
Baybars I	AD 1260–1277 (H 658–676)
Qalaun	AD 1280–1290 (H 678–689)
Kitbugha	AD 1295–1297 (H 694–696)
The Burgi Mamluk Sultans	AD 1382–1517 (H 784–922)
Barquq	AD 1382–1389 (H 784–791) and AD 1390–1399 (H 792–801)
Qaitbay	AD 1468–1496 (H 872–901)
The Ottomans	AD 1517–1805 (H 923–1220)
Selim I the Grim conquered Egypt	AD 1517 (H 923)
Sulayman II the Magnificent	AD 1520–1566 (H 926–974)
The House of Mohammed Ali	(AD 1805–1953) (H 1220–1372)
Mohammed Ali Pasha	AD 1805–1848 (H 1220–1264)
Ibrahim Pasha	AD 1848 (H 1264)
Abbas I	AD 1848–1854 (H 1264–1270)
Said Pasha	AD 1854–1863 (H 1270–1280)
Ismail	AD 1863–1879
(khedive from 1867, H 1284)	(H 1280–1296)
Tawfiq	AD 1879–1892 (H 1296–1309)
Abbas II Hilmi	AD 1892–1914 (H 1309–1333)
Husayn Kamil	AD 1914–1917 (H 1333–1335)
Fuad	AD 1917–1936
(king from 1922, H 1340)	(H 1335–1355)
Faruq	AD 1936–1952 (H 1355–1371)

ensured peace and drew their spheres of influence. The treaty was later confirmed by the king's marriage to a Hittite princess. The treaty brought the military activities of the reign to a close, and Ramesses' remaining years were devoted largely to building activities. The later 19th Dynasty was perhaps not as inglorious as it is usually painted, although there were certainly succession disputes among the many descendants of Ramesses II. During the 19th and 20th dynasties increasing numbers of Libyans settled in Egypt, mainly in the Delta, but also in Upper Egypt. Merneptah, 13th but eldest surviving son and successor of Ramesses II, had to face a joint invasion by the Libyans and Sea Peoples, an ethnically mixed group. Scholars have identified Merneptah as the pharaoh of the Exodus but there is little to support this, although to his reign belongs the only reference to Israel in Egyptian texts. The reign of his son, Sety II, was interrupted by that of the usurper Amenmesses, perhaps himself a royal prince. Sety II was succeeded by his son, Siptah, whose mother, Queen Tawosret, acted as regent. Tawosret continued to rule after Siptah's death, and assumed the style of a ruling king.

Earlier scholars thought that the 19th Dynasty closed with a civil war lasting for ten, or even 20 years, but if there was any disturbance it lasted a few months at most. A new pharaoh, Sethnakht, assumed power. Sethnakht may have belonged to the extended family of Ramesses II, but, like the first pharaoh of the 19th Dynasty, he ruled for just one year. It was his son, Ramesses III, who established the authority of the 20th Dynasty (c.1186–1069 BC). Large-scale foreign invasion confronted Ramesses III who had to repel three forces of Libyans (years five and 11) and Sea Peoples (year eight). These conflicts are depicted in detailed scenes in the king's temple at Medinet Habu. The later years of the 20th Dynasty are usually characterized as a period of decline, with increasingly elderly princes ascending the throne in the Delta city of Per-Ramesses, and never exerting the authority of the kingship in the south of the country. The power of the priests of Amun continued to grow and eventually led to the division of the country with Thebes under the High Priest of Amun, who assumed the title of king. However, while late New Kingdom Egypt certainly underwent some major changes, it was probably not the period of decline that is usually described.

MAJOR SITES

Many of the most imposing of Egypt's standing monuments are of New Kingdom date, particularly those in the Luxor region. This is partly accident of survival; Memphis and the Delta would have possessed equally imposing monuments, but only vestiges of these remain.

Eighteenth Dynasty: Karnak, Chapel of Amenhotep I, Red Chapel of Hatshepsut, Chapel of Thutmose IV (all in the Open Air Museum); Karnak, central part of Amun temple; Luxor temple; Temple of Hatshepsut at Deir el-Bahari; Colossi of Memnon; Valley of the Kings; Tombs of the Nobles; Amarna, city and tombs. **Nineteenth Dynasty**: Memphis: Colossi of Ramesses II; Karnak, Hypostyle Hall, chapel of Sety II; Luxor temple, first court; Luxor, west bank: Temple of Sety I; the Ramesseum; Merneptah temple museum; Deir el-Medina village and tombs; Abydos, temples of Sety I and Ramesses II; Abu Simbel, temples of Ramesses II and Nefertari. **Twentieth Dynasty**: Karnak, first court, Temple of Ramesses III, Temple of Khonsu. Luxor, west bank, Temple of Medinet Habu; Valley of the Kings and Valley of the Queens.

MONUMENTS

The New Kingdom is well represented in all major museum collections: notable objects in the Egyptian Museum are discussed below (Egyptian Museum), and key pieces in other museum collections are referred to in descriptions of the various sites.

THIRD INTERMEDIATE PERIOD (Dynasties 21–25: c.1069–656 BC)

Dynasties 21 and 22 had Tanis and Bubastis in the eastern Delta as their chief residence and burial place. Dynasty 24 originated at Sau (Sais) in the western Delta. These, and the 23rd Dynasty, were all of Libyan origin. The kings installed their sons variously as high priests of Amun at Thebes, high priests of Ptah at Memphis and governors of Herakleopolis, and their daughters as God's Wives of Amun at Thebes, thus maintaining a controlling presence in the southern parts of the country. Other Libyan dynasts held fiefdoms in the Delta, whilst acknowledging the crowned pharaohs. In Upper Egypt, the nobility held offices in an almost feudal fashion. Eventually the Kushite kings from Nubia conquered Egypt (25th Dynasty) but the Libyan dynasts continued to rule under them. The activities of the 25th-dynasty kings in western Asia brought them into conflict with the expanding power of the Assyrians who invaded Egypt three times, besieging Memphis and eventually sacking Thebes.

MAJOR SITES

Tanis: the Temple of Amun and tombs of the 21st and 22nd dynasty kings. Bubastis: Temple of Bastet with Festival Hall of Osorkon II. Karnak: first court, Bubastite Portal and Kiosk of Taharqo; chapels of Osiris built by God's Wives of Amun. Luxor, west bank: tomb-chapels of God's Wives of Amun at Medinet Habu, tombs of high officials near Deir el-Bahari.

Tutankhamun, Egyptian Museum, Cairo

Pyramid at night

MONUMENTS

Coffins and jewellery of Pa-seba-kha-en-niut and others from Tanis (Cairo, Egyptian Museum). Statues of the God's Wives, Amenirdis I and Shepenwepet II, and of the Mayor of Thebes Montjuemhat; black granite head of Taharqo; stele of Piye (Aswan, Nubia Museum).

LATE PERIOD (Dynasties 26–30 and Second Persian: 664–332 BC)

Assyrian invasions undermined the authority of the Kushite pharaohs. The Assyrians supported Psamtik I (Psammetichus), the ruler of Sau (Sais) in the western Delta, who gained control of the northern part of Egypt. The Saite king removed the Libyan dynasts from office and, in the ninth year of his reign (656 BC), concluded a treaty with Thebes, which still acknowledged Kushite rule. This resulted in the reunification of the whole of Egypt under one pharaoh. Psamtik's successor, Nekau II, attempted to reassert Egyptian authority in western Asia, confronting the rising power of Babylon, but failed. Psamtik II was unsuccessful in regaining Nubia. Egypt nevertheless remained a leading political power under Wahibre (Apries) and Ahmose II (Amasis). The art of the 26th Dynasty copied much from earlier periods, but produced much notable and individual statuary. There were many mercenary troops from the Greek cities of Anatolia, and from Caria (in southern Anatolia).

The invasion of Cambyses in 525 BC brought Egypt under Persian rule (27th Dynasty). Although the Persians adopted Pharaonic style and endowed temples, their rule became unpopular. A Saite prince (28th Dynasty) threw off the Persian yoke heralding the last period of native Egyptian kings. These pharaohs supported the ambitions of the Greek city-states, notably Athens, in their conflicts with the Persian Empire, sending grain and ships. The 30th Dynasty, particularly the reign of Nakhtnebef (Nectanebo I) witnessed a period of some peace and prosperity and the pharaohs began work on many large temples throughout the country. Egypt again fell to the Persians for a brief period before the Persian Empire itself was conquered by Alexander III of Macedon. Alexander entered Egypt in 332 BC, and was recognized as pharaoh in Memphis. He visited the Oracle Temple at Siwa and founded Alexandria, before continuing his campaigns in Asia.

MAJOR SITES

Luxor: Karnak temple, various Late Period additions and restorations; el-Kab, temple (Hakor); Aswan, Temple of Khnum on Elephantine (30th Dynasty); Philae, earliest parts of temple (Shrine of Ahmose II, Chapel of Psamtik II, Gate of Nakhtnebef); Kharga Oasis, Temple of Hibis (Darius-Nakhthorheb); Bahariya Oasis; Siwa Oasis; Dendera, *mammisi* of Nakhtnebef.

MONUMENTS

All major Egyptian collections have some fine examples of sculpture of the Late Period. Many faïence amulets and bronze votive figures (notably of cats) were made at this time.

MACEDONIAN AND PTOLEMAIC DYNASTIES (332–30 BC)

Ptolemaic Egypt focused on Alexandria as the capital of an empire that stretched around the eastern Mediterranean, from Cyrenaica in Libya, through Palestine, along the coast of Anatolia, and included important islands such as Cyprus and Rhodes. There were many Greek and Macedonian settlers in Egypt, and new towns were built for them in the Faiyum and Middle Egypt. These towns followed the Greek education system and social structure and introduced Greek art and architecture. The Ptolemies also continued building many typically Egyptian-style temples throughout the country. The Egyptian cults, particularly those of Isis, Osiris and Serapis, became popular all over the Mediterranean. The country suffered from the dynastic squabbles of the later Ptolemies, and the increasing threat posed by Roman expansion. Nevertheless, Egypt remained the richest and most powerful country in the region.

MAJOR SITES

The sanctuary of the Temple of Luxor was renewed in the name of Alexander the Great, and a chapel in the Akh-Menu of Thutmose III at Karnak was also restored in this reign. The names of Alexander IV of Macedon are found on the grantite gateway of the Temple of Khnum at Elephantine, and a chapel at Speos Artemidos. The red granite sanctuary of the Temple of Karnak was dedicated in the name of Philip Arrhidaios. The Ptolemies built large-scale temples in the Egyptian style at Dendera, Edfu, Kom Ombo and Philae. There are many smaller Ptolemaic temples throughout the country. The major monuments of the Hellenistic tradition are to be found in Alexandria, but note also the Circle of Philosophers at Saqqara; the tombs in Hellenistic style and with mixed Graeco-Egyptian decoration in the necropolis of Tuna el-Gebel. In recent years many large monuments from Ptolemaic Alexandria have been located in the harbour.

MONUMENTS

Statues depicting the Ptolemaic family in both Egyptian and Hellenistic styles can be found in many museum collections, notably Alexandria and Paris. A head in Berlin is now generally recognized as an image of Kleopatra VII.

ROMAN AND BYZANTINE PERIOD (30 BC–AD 639)

T he defeat of Kleopatra VII and her suicide brought Egypt finally under Roman rule. The province held a unique position in the empire, as it was regarded more or less as the personal property of the emperor. Prosperity for the Greek settlers and the Graeco-Egyptian middle class continued until the fourth century AD, after which there was economic crisis. The temples begun by the Ptolemies were completed and decorated in the names of the emperors, and many new temples were constructed. Hadrian founded a new commercial city, Antinoöpolis, in Middle Egypt. Christianity became established early, and monasticism developed in the Egyptian deserts, notably in the Wadi el-Natrun. The latter part of this period is known as the Late Antique (Coptic) Period (c.AD 300–639).

MAJOR SITES

The last Egyptian-style temples were built at Dendera (gate and Hypostyle Hall), Esna, Philae (Trajan's Kiosk; Gate of Diocletian) and Kalabsha. A chapel of the Imperial Cult was incorporated into the Luxor temple. Late classical town sites at Antinoöpolis (Sheikh Ibada) and Ashmunein; Cairo, the fortress of Babylon. Monasteries at Sohag and Wadi el-Natrun.

MONUMENTS

Amongst the most notable archaeological finds of the Roman Period are the objects of daily life (Karanis Museum and Alexandria Museum). Statuary of the emperors (Alexandria Museum) is fairly conventional, more interesting are the painted wooden mummy portraits from the Faiyum (Cairo, Egyptian Museum; London, British Museum; Berlin).

ISLAMIC EGYPT

W hen Amr ibn al-As, commander of Caliph Omar, entered Egypt from Syria in AD 639, he was welcomed by the Coptic population which was sympathetic to the Arab conquerors because of the help they had given in ridding the country of the Greek Melkites (Byzantines), the last of whom were finally ousted from Alexandria in AD 642. The conquerors established themselves in a fortified encampment, later called Fustat, the first capital of Muslim Egypt. Fustat remained the capital under the Umayyads who ruled from Damascus, and later under the Abbasids who ruled from Baghdad. A slow Arabization process began, and Islam was gradually embraced by many of the Copts as the popularity of the Arabic language increased. As the power of the caliphate waned, Ahmed ibn Tulun, the Turkish Governor of Egypt, proclaimed himself an independent sultan in about 870 and transferred his residence to the hill of Jechkar, northeast of Fustat. This stronghold later grew into the city of el-Qata'i, which witnessed years of growth and development under Ahmed ibn Tulun. With his demise, however, Egypt underwent a period of political dissension and uncertainty which continued until the Abbasids were finally able to return in 905. They dominated the country from 939 to 969, and during this period, Fustat regained its prestige while el-Qata'i was completely destroyed.

FATIMIDS (969–1171)

The Fatimids, who claimed descent from Fatima, the daughter of Mohammed, came originally from Syria and settled in Kairowan in modern Tunisia. They had made several unsuccessful attempts to conquer Egypt, but in 969, Gawhar, commander of the forces of the Caliph al-Muizz, entered Fustat and met with little resistance. Upon its conquest, he deemed it a worthy enough place in which to establish a new city that would rival Baghdad, the capital of the Abbasids. Thus was conceived the city of Cairo, originally known as el-Qahira ('the Victorious').

The early Fatimids also brought a period of economic stability to Egypt. Foreign trade expanded in Europe and India, and the complex tax system was abolished. By 1079, the First Crusade entered Syria from the northwest, aiming to free Jerusalem from Muslim control. Jerusalem was captured in 1099 and the Crusaders then turned their attention to Egypt in 1168. The Crusaders' forays into Egypt were thwarted by the Kurdish general Salah al-Din, better known as Saladin, who set out to extend his power in Egypt, thus beginning a new period in Egypt's history which lasted until 1252.

After consolidating his power in Egypt, Saladin turned his attention to Syria, leading several campaigns against the Crusaders which finally led to the recapture of Jerusalem in 1187. Egypt, in the meantime, witnessed a period of prosperity and cultural growth and became a centre of theological studies. Saladin also fortified Cairo and built a citadel over a ramp of the Muqattam Hill, whose architectural features, though remotely of oriental derivation, are also strikingly typical of Crusade construction prevalent in Syria and Palestine.

BEDAZZLED

S o here we are in Egypt, 'land of the Pharaohs, land of the Ptolemies, land of Cleopatra' (as sublime stylists put it). Here we are and here we are living, our heads more hairless than our knees, smoking long pipes and drinking coffee on divans. What can I say about it all? What can I write you? As yet I am scarcely over the inital bedazzlement. It is like being hurled while still asleep into the midst of a Beethoven symphony, with the brasses at their most ear-splitting, the basses rumbling, and the flutes sighing away; each detail reaches out to grip you; it pinches you; and the more you concentrate on it the less you grasp the whole. Then gradually all this becomes harmonious and the pieces fall into place of themselves, in accordance with the laws of perspective. But the first days, by God, it is such a bewildering chaos of colours that your poor imagination is dazzled as though by continuous fireworks as you go about staring at minarets thick with white storks, at tired slaves stretched out in the sun on house terraces, at the patterns of sycamore branches against walls, with camel bells ringing in your ears and great herds of black goats bleating in the street amid the horses and the donkeys and the pedlars. As soon as night falls, everyone goes about with his cloth lanterns, and the pashas' grooms run through the city brandishing great lighted torches in their left hand. There is much jostling and arguing and fighting and rolling on the ground, much cursing of all kinds and shouting in all languages; the harsh Semitic syllables crack in the air like whiplashes. You brush against all the costumes of the Orient, elbow all its peoples (I now speak of Cairo); you see the Greek papá with his long beard riding his mule, the Albanian soldier in his embroidered jacket, the Copt in his black turban, the Persian in his fur pelisse, the desert Bedouin with his coffee-coloured face walking gravely along enveloped in his white robes.

Gustave Flaubert, 'Letter to Dr Jules Cloquet from Cairo on January 15, 1850',
from Flaubert in Egypt, translated and edited by Francis Steegmuller,
Penguin, 1996

Gustave Flaubert, 1821–1880, French novelist best known for pioneering the realist school of French literature and for his masterpiece *Madame Bovary* (1857), which he wrote after his return from the Orient.

MAMLUKS (1250–1517)

The Mamluks were originally an army of Turkish slaves (mainly Kipchaks) brought from the region north of the Black Sea and installed by one of Saladin's brothers on the island of Roda in the Nile near Cairo. They came to power through the marriage of the chief Mamluk, Aybak, to Shajar al-Dur, the wife of Sultan Ayyub who was herself proclaimed sultan after his death. The Mamluks ruled for almost three centuries—centuries often marred by political turmoil.

REIGN OF THE OTTOMANS (1517–1805)

In 1517, a Turkish dynasty (the Ottomans) occupied Cairo after having crushed the weak military opposition of the Mamluks. The Ottoman governors (pashas) never enjoyed great popularity in Egypt; they were frequently recalled by the central government in Istanbul in order to prevent them gaining undue personal prestige. Throughout this period, Egypt declined as a cultural centre though it retained its importance as a religious fountainhead.

NAPOLEON'S EXPEDITION

Napoleon, who cast himself as the bearer of the ideals of the French Revolution, mounted his expedition to Egypt in 1798, landing at Alexandria. But while the French army was trying to gain control of Cairo in what came to be known as the Battle of the Pyramids, England's Admiral Horatio Nelson destroyed the French fleet at Abu Qir. As a result, the French were forced into retreat, finally leaving Egypt three years later.

During this period of French interest, a national awakening of sorts occurred in Egypt. The country emerged from the darkness and was revived by the discovery by French scholars and archaeologists of the great heritage of Egypt. The discovery of the Rosetta Stone in 1799 allowed Champollion to decipher Egyptian hieroglyphic script in 1822.

MOHAMMED ALI AND THE DAWN OF MODERN EGYPT

After the departure of the French, Egypt was again plunged into chaos and was only saved by an army revolt led by Mohammed Ali, a young Albanian officer in the Turkish army, in 1805.

Though he acknowledged the Ottoman sultan as ruler, Mohammed Ali took control and remained in power as viceroy of Egypt for 40 years, during which the country witnessed the modernization of its institutions and a wide-scale building program, including the construction of canals. By the time of Mohammed Ali's death, Egypt had attained international status and had begun attracting the attention of Western powers.

SUEZ CANAL AND THE BRITISH

Mohammed Ali's successors, who won for themselves the title of 'khedive', continued his policies and, in 1875, took on total responsibility for the government of Egypt. During the rule of Khedive Ismail, the Suez Canal, linking the Red Sea with the Mediterranean, was opened in 1860 amid great celebrations. The project, designed by the French engineer Ferdinand de Lesseps, was so costly that an international fund was created to support it. Forty-four per cent of the shares went to Egypt. Six years later, Ismail was forced to sell his own interests in the canal company to British subscribers and, the following year, faced with bankruptcy, he agreed to the setting up of a French–British consortium to manage his finances. In 1882, Britain sent an expeditionary force to Alexandria to quell disturbances caused by the economic situation, thus beginning a period of increasing British influence in Egypt.

DAWN OF NATIONALISM

The British presence in Egypt did not stall the country's development, and with the founding of the Institute of Archaeology by Auguste Mariette in 1880, the Egyptians slowly became aware of their heritage. With the outbreak of World War I, Britain became conscious of the threat posed to the Suez Canal by the alliance between Germany and Turkey and so turned Egypt into a fully fledged protectorate by law. In 1919, the king of Egypt attempted to win independence from Britain. This was granted in 1922 under a treaty that left the responsibility for the defence of the country and the Suez Canal with the British. Egypt was given a constitution and the Wafd Party, which had negotiated independence, obtained the reins of government though the king retained his position.

In 1936, Egypt and Britain signed a treaty that later allowed the British forces to carry out their North African campaign and to halt the advance of the Germans and Italians on Suez at el-Alamein in 1942. In March 1945, the Arab States of the Middle East met in Cairo and signed a pact creating the Arab League, which aimed at forming a unified front to pursue the aims of the Arab world.

Meanwhile, the internal situation in Egypt worsened and the monarchy was attacked because of the extravagance of King Faruq, who had assumed power in

(following pages) Cairo, the magnificent Mosque of Sultan Hasan (left), and the 19th-century Mosque of al-Rifa'i, which was designed using the best medieval models.

1936. The creation of the state of Israel in 1948 and the emergence of a militant Islamic group (the Muslim Brotherhood), which advocated only Islamic rule, further discredited the monarchy. In 1949, the Israelis entered the Sinai Peninsula after defeating the Arab armies, which tried to regain Palestine. This defeat angered the people and led to violent riots in Cairo. In July 1952, after three years of disturbances, Faruq was toppled by a revolt of army officers led by Gamal Abdel Nasser. He was forced to abdicate and seek exile in Italy. The Egyptian Republic was proclaimed in June 1953.

Nasser's main concern was to rid Egypt of Western influence and he successfully concluded an agreement with Britain that called for the evacuation of the British from the canal zone. Nasser also replaced the heads of foreign companies with Egyptians and, in 1956, he nationalized the Suez Canal, provoking armed intervention by Britain and France. This situation was resolved by a US ultimatum that won the Egyptian leader great prestige in the Arab world. In 1967, Nasser attempted an ill-fated attack on Israel that resulted in the seizure by the Jewish state of the West Bank and Gaza. He offered to resign, but crowds in Cairo forced him to stay. Nasser died in 1970 and his successor, Anwar Sadat, yet again changed the course of Egypt's history.

Sadat's major policy move was the scrapping of Nasser's treaty with the Soviet Union and the expulsion of Soviet experts. He turned to the West for help to alleviate the country's economic problems and poverty, thus paving the way for an increased American involvement in Egypt, which began with the construction of the oil pipeline from Suez to Alexandria.

Conscious that the long-term success of his program depended on the removal of the threat of Israel, Sadat launched a surprise assault across the Sinai in 1973. This was the turning point in Egypt's turbulent relations with Israel, leading to peace talks in 1978 and the signing of the Camp David Accords and the peace treaty of 1979. Sadat was assassinated in 1981. He was succeeded by Hosni Mubarak, who has since sought to continue Sadat's policies while trying to reinstate Egypt in the Arab fold from which it was expelled in 1979 on account of its peace treaty with Israel.

RELIGION OF ANCIENT EGYPT

R eligion permeated Egyptian life, but for the ordinary people this was not temple-orientated. During the New Kingdom the temple functioned as a part of the state administration, being a place for the storage of commodities and their distribution as wages. In its religious capacity, the temple functioned rather like a monastery, with the rituals performed by the priests on behalf of the king in order to ensure the maintenance of divine order. The people prayed mainly in their homes, at altars to household deities and ancestors. These household deities were those concerned with day-to-day affairs, protectors against disease, scorpions or snakes, of women in childbirth. It was only on major feast days (which were mainly local rather than national) that the people and priests would celebrate together as the images of the gods were carried in procession. The lay-people could go to the temple to pray, but were permitted only in the outermost parts. Here they would make prayers to statues of the kings (living and dead) or high officials which acted as intermediaries between the people and the deities within the temples. Certain statues were particularly venerated: at Thebes, images of Amenhotep I and his mother Queen Ahmose-Nefertari were the centre of a popular local cult. In many of the temples of the later periods, a place on the back wall, directly behind the sanctuary, was accessible for lay-people to communicate directly with the gods. The most notable example is the huge aegis of Hathor on the back wall of Dendera temple. Ruthlessly hacked out in Christian times, this face of the goddess would probably have been covered in gold, but hidden from the eyes of worshippers by veils. Similar shrines can be found at Kom Ombo, where carved ears conduct the prayers to the gods, and the Ptah temple at Karnak, where the popular intercessors Amenhotep son of Hapu and Imhotep are represented.

Every temple had its calendar of festivals, the most important usually being the visit of the chief deity of the town to his or her consort. Occasionally the consort was resident in another town, so Hathor of Dendera made a three-day voyage to join her husband, Horus, at Edfu for the Feast of the Beautiful Meeting. The national festivals were those associated with the seasons, for example the New Year or Harvest. Although most of the festivals were local celebrations, some of them attracted visitors from all over Egypt or were of such importance that the king officiated in person. Such was the Opet Festival at Thebes, when Amun sailed from Karnak to consummate his marriage in the Temple of Luxor. This festival was often used by the king to appoint new priests. The celebration of the resurrection of Osiris at Abydos, with its passion play, was particularly popular, attracting pilgrims from all over Egypt. The festival of Bastet at Bubastis is described by Herodotos as a time of much drunkenness, which brought thousands of worshippers to the Delta city.

EGYPTIAN GODS

T he Egyptian pantheon is extremely complicated. We have to remember that Egyptian religion developed over a period of some 5,000 years, and that there were attempts to rationalize contradictions, in the Ptolemaic and Roman periods particularly. So, for example, the stories about Seth and Osiris, and the conflict between Horus and Seth, originally existed in various forms, and belonged to two different Horus gods—Horus-the-Elder, the brother of Seth, and Horus son of Isis. The most complete version of the cycle is in the work of Plutarch (*On Isis and Osiris*), writing in the second century AD. This combines elements known from earlier Egyptian texts, but smoothes out many of the contradictions. Similarly, there were numerous local gods who had the same name (Horus, Khnum, Hathor etc) and were originally separate entities, who were later thought of as aspects of one deity.

The Egyptian gods are often known by the Greek forms of their names. Here the Egyptian forms are preferred except in the cases of the most familiar, such as Osiris. Variant spellings of names are given in brackets, with Greek forms in italics.

Amun ('The Hidden One') Rising to become the principal god of Waset (Thebes) in Upper Egypt, Amun was first depicted in the early Middle Kingdom when he appears as a form of the fertility god, Min, an aspect of his nature that remained important. He was usually depicted as human with a tall double-plumed crown and blue skin, reflecting his role as a sky god. From the 18th Dynasty he was also shown with the head of a ram. He rose to national importance as the patron deity of the 18th-dynasty pharaohs and merged with the sun god Ra, as Amun-Ra. Those pharaohs enlarged the god's Theban temple (Ipet-sut, Karnak), and made Thebes a southern counterpart to Iunu (*Heliopolis*). Amun gained Mut as his consort and Khonsu as his son.

Anubis The god Anubis (Inpu) is usually depicted as human with a jackal's head, but he can also be entirely canine. Anubis was the protector of the cemetery and was accredited with the invention of embalming. He presided over mummification and was important in the judgment of the dead.

Tomb painting showing jackal-headed god, Anubis, Western Thebes

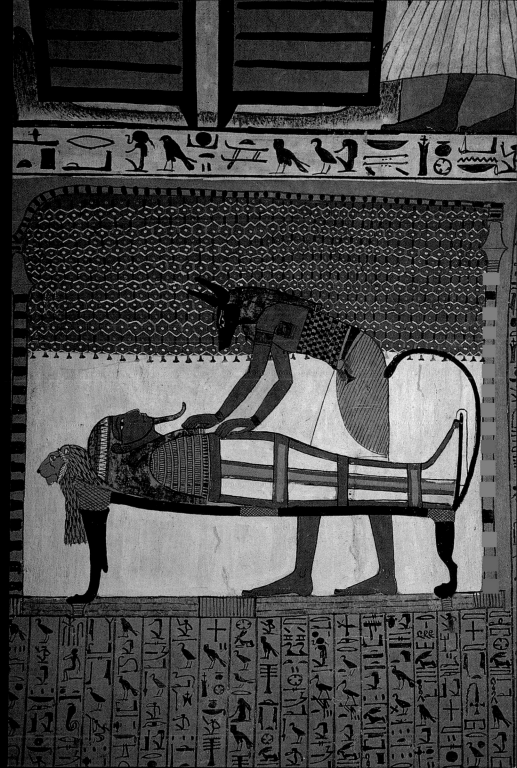

Apis One of the chief deities of Memphis, Apis (Hep) was a living bull believed to be the earthly manifestation of Ptah. During life, he resided in a palatial enclosure near the great Temple of Ptah, and after death and mummification was buried in the Serapeum of Saqqara, when a search was conducted for a replacement. Apis was a black bull distinguished by a number of white markings, notably a triangle on the forehead.

Aten Represented as the sun disc with its rays ending in hands, the Aten was not strictly a god, but the visible form of the sun god Ra-Harakhty of Heliopolis. Aten formed the focus of the sun-cult established by Akhenaten at Akhetaten (Amarna), where the temples were large open courts filled with altars, rather than dark sanctuaries of the other Egyptian cults. This form of worship emphasized the role of the king as the living intermediary between god and the people.

Atum The self-creating solar god of Iunu (*Heliopolis*), Atum existed in the watery primeval chaos, Nun. He came into being by thought, and then created Shu (air) and Tefnut (moisture). He was regarded as the elderly form of the sun god Ra, and ancestor of the gods.

Bastet The goddess of Per-Bastet (*Bubastis*) in the Delta, Bastet was both a lioness and a cat. Her great annual festival was a time of much drunkenness, deriving from the myth in which the violent lioness was pacified by making her drunk with beer coloured red to look like blood.

Bes Bes was a protector of the household, particularly of women, whom he helped in childbirth. A bearer of good fortune, he was shown as a bandy-legged dwarf wearing a lion skin and often carrying a tambourine. He is usually shown full-face, with his tongue out.

Geb Geb, son of Shu and Tefnut, is the god of the earth and married to his sister, Nut, goddess of the sky. Their children were Osiris, Isis, Seth and Nebet-hat (*Nephthys*).

Hapi The Nile in flood, and therefore shown as corpulent, often blue, with the plants of Upper and Lower Egypt on his head.

Harakhty (Hor-akhty; 'Horus of the Horizon') is represented with a falcon's head surmounted by the solar disc. He is the sun appearing on the eastern horizon. Usually assimilated with Ra as Ra-Harakhty.

Harpokrates (Hor-pa-khered; 'Horus-the-Child') Isis gave birth to Horus and hid him from Seth in the marshes of the Delta. Horus-the-Child (*Harpokrates*) is often depicted seated on his mother's lap, being suckled by the goddess. He was worshipped as a protector against dangerous animals, and on protective objects known as *cippi* was shown standing on the back of two crocodiles grasping snakes, scorpions, gazelles and lions.

Hathor The principal female deity, Hathor (Hut-Hor; 'House of Horus') could be depicted as fully human or as a cow. Her sacred instrument, the sistrum, usually carried her image combining a female face with cow's ears. Hathor was worshipped throughout Egypt as a goddess of female sexuality, music and dance. Her largest surviving temple is at Dendera, where she was a creator goddess. Elsewhere, she was a goddess of the West and of the necropolis, notably at Thebes and at Memphis. Hathor was the daughter of the sun god Ra, and could represent his burning eye. In this violent aspect she assumed the form of a lioness and was known by the names Sakhmet or Tefnut.

Heqet The frog-headed midwife goddess.

Herishef Herishef was the local god of Nen-nesut (*Herakleopolis*) near the entrance to the Faiyum. Herishef (*Arsaphes*; 'He who is upon his Lake') was a ram-headed solar and creator god. In Greek times Herishef was identified with Herakles (Hercules).

Horus Horus, meaning 'The One who is Far Off' (ie high in the sky), was the name of many falcon deities. There were local gods with the name, such as Horus of Nekhen (*Hierakonpolis*), and Horus Khenty-Irty (of Ausim, *Letopolis*, in the Delta), but the most significant forms were Horus-the-Elder, and Horus (Hor), the son of Isis and Osiris. The pharaoh was closely identified with Horus, and regarded as his living manifestation. Horus was usually depicted as human with a falcon's head surmounted by the double crown. He was also shown as a winged sun disc (*behdet*), a form he assumed in his battles with Seth. Horus was also the god associated with foreign lands. His consort was usually the goddess Hathor.

Horus-the-Elder (Harwer, *Haroeris*) In one tradition, Horus was the brother of Seth, not the son of Isis and Osiris. This form of the god was worshipped at Kom Ombo, where his consort is a form of the goddess Hathor.

Horus son of Isis (*Harsiese*) The son of Isis and Osiris came to be the most important form of the god, and assimilated many of the others. He was born after Seth had murdered and dismembered Osiris, and Isis had collected the pieces, which were skilfully mummified by Anubis. In the conflict with Seth for the throne of Egypt, Horus was eventually recognized by the council of gods as the legitimate heir to Osiris. The child forms of Horus, such as Harpokrates, were worshipped as protectors against illness and dangerous animals.

Hor-sema-tawy (*Harsomtus*) 'Horus the Uniter of the Two Lands' was the son of Hathor and Horus, notably at Edfu. He is usually depicted as a child standing as the emblem for unification: the hieroglyph of lungs and windpipe with the plants of Upper and Lower Egypt bound to it. He could be assimilated with Ihy, the son of the same divine couple at Dendera.

Ihy The son of Hathor and Horus at Dendera. Ihy was the god of music and joyfulness. He is usually depicted naked, with the plaited side-lock of hair denoting a child, and shaking a sistrum (a rattle used in the worship of Hathor).

Isis Sister and wife of Osiris, and mother of Horus, Isis is crowned with a throne, the hieroglyph for her name. The cult of Isis became immensely popular in the later phases of Egyptian history. She was revered as a mother, a magician and a protector. She absorbed many of the characteristics of Hathor, and could appear in cow form. Her cult spread throughout the Mediterranean and became one of the most important in the Roman Empire. Her principal consort in Ptolemaic and Roman times was Serapis.

Ius-aas The wife of Ra-Atum at Iunu (*Heliopolis*). She is the personification of the hand by which he created the first gods.

Khepri is the sun at dawn: 'He who Comes into Being'. Depicted as a winged scarab or a ram-headed scarab, or anthropomorphically with a scarab for a head.

Khnum According to Esna's theology, Khnum was the lord of creation. As an artisan god with the head of a ram, Khnum is shown seated at his potter's wheel forming humans from clay. At Esna his consort was the lioness goddess Menhyt. Another ram-headed Khnum was worshipped in the Aswan region where he controlled the Nile flood from his cave beneath the island of Bigga. Here Khnum was associated with the goddess Anuket (*Anukis*) and Satjet (*Satis*).

Khonsu A lunar god with a falcon's head, son of Amun and Mut, Khonsu was believed to be responsible for healing and driving out demons.

Maat Daughter of the sun god, Maat is shown with an ostrich feather on her head. She represents the perfection of the world at the moment of creation, and embodies the concepts of truth and divine order.

Min Min is the ithyphallic god of fertility and regeneration. He also protects the mining region of the Eastern Desert and the incense countries. Min and his emblem are amongst the earliest identifiable representations of the divine in Pre-Dynastic Egypt.

Montju (Monthu, Mont) The falcon-headed solar god of Waset (Thebes), Armant,

ANCIENT EGYPTIAN ETHICS

T he multiplicity of gods, and the imagery to be found in temples and tombs, tends to perplex most visitors. What exactly did the Egyptians believe in? Certainly the temple-based cults were more to do with the maintenance of divine order than private personal concerns. Yet there is also an Egyptian tradition of texts with a strong ethical and moral content. This 'wisdom literature' survives in copies of parts or whole texts, many of these copies being scribal exercises. These texts, often titled 'Instructions', are set out as a series of maxims relating to the order of society and modes of behaviour. Some of them are attributed to sages of the Old Kingdom, such as Prince Hardjedef, a son of Khufu, or the vizier Kagemni, who served Huni and Sneferu (3rd–4th dynasties), but it is likely that they were composed at a later date and attributed to a personality of the past, a common literary device in Egypt. A similar group of texts survives from the New Kingdom, and expresses fundamentally the same ideas. Here is a selection of the maxims which show us some of the concerns of the (upper class) Egyptian man.

- *Take a wife while you are young, so that she may provide you with a son; it is right to make people and happy is the man whose children are numerous.*
- *When you prosper and establish your house, love your wife, fill her belly and clothe her back, give her ointment to soothe her body. Gladden her heart as long as you live, she is a fertile field for her lord. But keep her from power.*
- *Make good your resting place in the necropolis, make a worthy station in the West.*
- *A respectful man prospers, the modest one is praised.*
- *When sitting in company shun your favourite food; restraint takes only a moment, gluttony is base and is reproved. When you sit with a glutton, eat when his greed is sated; when you drink with a drunkard, take only when his heart is content. He who is blameless in matters of food, no word can prevail against him.*
- *If you are the guest of a social superior, take what he gives as it is set before you; do not speak until he addresses you, then your words will satisfy him.*

- Do not be proud of your knowledge, consult the ignorant and the wise; the limits of art are not reached, no artist's skills are perfect; good speech is more hidden than greenstone, yet may be found among maids at the grindstones.
- If you meet a disputant in action—a poor man who is not your social equal—do not attack him because he is weak ... wretched is he who injures a poor man.
- If you are a man who leads, who controls the affairs of many, seek out all good deeds so that your conduct is blameless. Great is justice, lasting its effect.
- Do not scheme against people, because the god punishes accordingly. If a man says 'I shall be rich' later he will have to say 'My cleverness has snared me'.
- If you are sent by one dignitary to another on an errand of trust, stick to what he who sent you wants, give his message as he said it, keeping to the truth, not exceeding it.
- Do not malign anyone, great or small.
- If you are poor, serve a man of worth, but do not remind him if he was once poor and don't be arrogant toward him because you know his former position; respect him for what he has achieved.
- If you are in the antechamber, stand or sit according to your rank, do not push yourself forward: it is the god who gives advancement, he who uses his elbows is not helped!
- If you are a man who leads, listen calmly to a plaintiff: a man in distress wants to pour out his heart more than to win his case.
- If you seek perfect conduct, avoid the vice of greed. It is a grievous sickness without a cure, there is no treatment for it.
- Do not be greedy in the division of family property, nor covet more than your share.
- Do not listen to calumny, nor repeat it.
- Useful is hearing to a son who hears; if hearing enters a hearer, the hearer becomes a listener, hearing well is speaking well; hearing creates good will; he who hears is beloved of god; he who loves to hear is one who does what is said.
- Be deliberate when you speak, so as to say things that count; then the officials will say 'What he says is good'.
- Observe the feasts of your god; ... god is angry if neglected.
- Do not raise your voice in the house of god. Offer to your god, beware of offending him. Do not jostle him in order to carry him (in processions).
- Do not enter the house of a person of consequence until he admits you and greets you; do not snoop around his house.
- Do not indulge in drinking beer, lest you utter evil speech and don't know what you're saying.

- *Guard against fraud, against words that are not true; conquer malice in yourself; keep away from a hostile man, do not let him be your comrade.*
- *Do not depend on another's wealth, lest he become master in your house.*
- *Do not sit when another who is older than you, or of greater rank, is standing.*
- *Stand according to your rank, rank creates its rules.*
- *Attend to your position, be it low or high; it is not good to press forward.*
- *Do not reveal your heart to a stranger, he might use your words against you.*
- *Double the food your mother gave you, support her as she supported you.*
- *Do not eat bread while another stands by without extending your hand to him.*
- *Do not control your wife in her house, when you know she is efficient; don't say to her: 'Where is it? Get it!' when she has put it in the right place.*
- *Do not falsify the temple rations, do not grasp and you'll find profit.*

All of these show quite clearly that there were strict codes which governed behaviour in Egyptian society; that the wealthy and high ranking in society had obligations to those less privileged. Other documents, both legal and literary show that these injunctions also reflect the crimes of the Egyptian bureaucracy.

The goddess Maat, wearing the single ostrich plume. She personifies the central tenet of Egyptian religion, which we can only summarize as 'truth', 'divine order': the state of perfection of the moment of creation.

Tod and Medamud. Montju was a warlike god, and protector of the king in battle. From the Middle Kingdom on, Amun became the dominant deity in Thebes, but Montju remained significant and regained popularity in the Libyan and Late periods. In a parallel to the Apis, the sacred bull of Memphis, the *Buchis* bull was dedicated to Montju from the 30th Dynasty to Roman periods. The bulls travelled between the god's cult centres, and after death their mummified remains were buried in the Bucheum at Armant.

Mut The goddess Mut was probably invented in the New Kingdom to provide a consort for Amun. Her name means 'mother', and is written with the vulture hieroglyph. Mut thus easily absorbed characteristics of other vulture and maternal goddesses. She also became associated with the 'Eye of Ra' and the lioness goddesses Tefnut and Sakhmet. She was the mother of the king, and of the god Khonsu.

Nefertum Nefertum is the primordial lotus from which the sun emerged at the creation. He is the son of the lioness goddesses, Sakhmet at Memphis and Bastet at Bubastis.

Neith A creator goddess who wears the red crown of Lower Egypt, she was revered in the Delta city of Sais. Her symbol was the shield with crossed arrows, indicating her warlike nature. Later she was regarded as the wife of Seth and mother of Sobek.

Nekhbet Vulture goddess of Upper Egypt worshipped at Nekheb (el-Kab). She is a protector of the king and appears on his forehead. Nekhbet was also a goddess of childbirth.

Nephthys (Nebet-hat) Although married to Seth, the murderer of Osiris, Nephthys helped her sister Isis in the search for Osiris's body. She is shown mourning over the body with Isis, and is later a protector of the sarcophagus and canopic jars, along with Isis, Selket and Neith.

Nepri The corn god, son of Renenutet.

Nun The primordial ocean, chaos, in which life emerged in the form of the creator god.

Nut Usually represented by a thin, arched human body sprinkled with stars, Nut represents the sky (perhaps specifically the Milky Way) and was the wife of Geb, god of the earth. Each day it was believed the sun and the stars followed the curve of her body. Her image was frequently carved inside sarcophagi to protect the deceased. She was the mother of Osiris, Isis, Nephthys and Seth. Nut could also be depicted as a cow, with her legs as the four pillars of heaven. Amulets depict her as the 'Great White Sow' suckling numerous piglets (the stars).

Osiris Osiris was a king, the son of Geb and Nut. He was credited with inventing civilization and agriculture. Murdered by his jealous brother Seth, Osiris was resurrected through the intervention of Isis and Anubis, but he was confined to the nether world where he ruled. As supreme judge of the tribunal of the dead, Osiris was a very popular god and his cult flourished until the end of paganism in Egypt. He was pictured as a mummy with the white crown of Upper Egypt. He usually held a sceptre and a flail in his hands. In Ptolemaic times the characteristics of the god were assumed by Serapis.

Ptah According to the Memphite Theology, Ptah spoke and all things came into existence. Ptah is also associated with creation through fashioning by hand, and was therefore the patron of goldsmiths and craftsmen. He was usually represented wearing a skullcap, enveloped in a tight robe, and holding a sceptre comprising the symbols *was* (dominion), *ankh* (life) and *djed* (stability). He formed a triad with Sakhmet and Nefertum. In the New Kingdom he formed part of the state triad of Egypt alongside Amun-Ra and Ra-Harakhty. He could be assimilated with Tatjenen, a local Memphite god who represented the land as it emerged from the floodwaters, and with Sokar, the god of the Memphite necropolis.

Ra (Re) The principal form of the sun. In Egyptian 'Ra' is the word meaning sun, as well as the god. He appears in numerous different forms: Ra-Harakhty, the sun on the horizon; Atum, the creator sun god, and god of the evening; Khepri, another form of the creator. The main centre of sun worship was Iunu (*Heliopolis*) where there were vast temples, mainly open courts, with obelisks and mounds representing the sacred mound on which the sun god alighted at the creation. Ra was usually shown with a falcon head, but could also be depicted with a ram's head (particularly during the night journey of the sun barque) and as a scarab. His consort was Ius-aas, and his daughters Maat and Hathor. In the New Kingdom a state triad was created comprising Ptah, Amun-Ra and Ra-Harakhty. In the Late Period many locally important gods were assimilated with Ra in their aspects as divine creators: Khnum-Ra, Sobek-Ra.

Renenutet The goddess of harvest, Renenutet was depicted as a woman with a cobra head and flared hood emerging from her body, or as a coiled cobra. She often suckles her son, Nepri.

Sakhmet A ferocious lioness goddess, the manifestation of divine rage, her name means 'the Powerful One'. She was the daughter of Ra, and represented his burning eye, which he sent forth to destroy mankind. Sakhmet was believed to be the cause of epidemics, which she spread with the help of her loyal genies. As the cause of

(following pages) *Mosque of Mohammed Ali, Cairo*

plagues she also controlled healing, and amulets of the goddess became popular as a means of warding off illnesses. She became the consort of Ptah of Memphis. As 'Eye of Ra', Sakhmet was associated with a number of other goddesses: Bastet, Hathor, Mut and Tefnut.

Selket (Serqet, *Selkis*) The scorpion goddess, one of the protectors of the sarcophagus and canopic chest.

Serapis Serapis (Sarapis) was reputedly an invention of Ptolemy I, who sought to bring his Egyptian and Greek subjects together. The name of the god combines those of Usir (*Osiris*) and Apis. His image was in the Greek style, bearded, with a *kalathos* (grain measure) on his head, carrying a long sceptre and often accompanied by Cerberus, the three-headed canine guardian of the underworld. Serapis combined elements of the gods Zeus, Helios, Dionysos, Hades (Pluto) and Asklepios (Aesculapius), representing divine sovereignty, fertility and agriculture, the underworld and healing. Serapis became popular throughout the Hellenistic and Roman worlds, and he was worshipped alongside his consort, Isis, his son Horus, and the god of embalming, Anubis.

Seth The deity responsible for all the chaotic and hostile forces: thunder, desert, dangerous wild animals. In the Osiris myth, he was the brother and murderer of the god. Seth was especially revered in some parts of Egypt (northeast Delta) and also at certain times (the Second and 19th dynasties).

Shu was the personification of the air, as the atmosphere and sunlight that streams from the sun disc. He was an emanation of Atum. From his union with Tefnut (moisture) came the earth (Geb) and sky (Nut). Shu is often depicted on coffins and papyri as a human with his arms raised supporting the sky (in human or cow form).

Sobek The crocodile god Sobek (*Suchos*) was a creator and solar deity, son of Neith. He was the patron of the Faiyum region, and also important in parts of Upper Egypt (Kom Ombo).

Ta-weret (*Thoueris*) The protectress of women in childbirth, Ta-weret was depicted as a pregnant hippopotamus with the legs and paws of a lioness and the spine of a crocodile. Despite this fearsome appearance she was benevolent, and very popular. She was particularly worshipped in household shrines, and amulets in her form were used as protection, particularly by women and children. She was associated with Hathor and Bes.

Tefnut An emanation of Atum, Tefnut was the personification of moisture. Through her union with Shu, she was mother of Geb and Nut. Tefnut could also be the fierce lioness, the 'Eye of Ra'.

Thoth (Djehuty) The god of the moon, and of wisdom, time, weights and measures, inventor of writing and mathematics. His major cult centre was Hermopolis. Thoth is usually pictured with the head of an ibis and a combined disc and crescent moon on his head. He holds the scribe's tools in his hands. The baboon was also sacred to Thoth. In Ptolemaic and Roman times Thoth was equated with Hermes (Mercury) and his principal cult centre, Khemenu (Ashmunein) in Middle Egypt, became *Hermopolis*.

Wadjet ('The Green One') was the cobra goddess of the twin cities of Pe and Dep in the northwest Delta. Both the town and goddess were called *Buto* in Greek times. Wadjet was the patroness of the red crown and protector of the pharaoh as the uraeus, or rearing cobra that spat fire at its enemies.

COPTS AND MUSLIMS

Inspired by profound religious fervour and impassioned by the desire to spread the message of Allah, the Arabs entered Egypt in AD 639, took Babylon (Old Cairo) in AD 640 and expelled the last of the Byzantine forces from Alexandria in AD 642. The expression 'Copts', which the Arabs originally used to identify the entire population they encountered in their newly conquered land, later came to define only that part of the population which remained Christian. The Coptic Church does not differ from the Greek Orthodox Church except in the dogma concerning the nature of Christ. The Copts do not recognize the authority of the Pope nor the validity of ecumenical councils; instead, the Patriarch of Alexandria governs. From the 11th century, Egyptians—aware of the immense material advantages of assimilation—converted en masse to Islam; the Patriarchate has had its seat in Cairo since this time. Even so, the Egyptians retained the deep-rooted cultural qualities of their age-old nationalism. Thus, the country preserved a characteristic national identity as well as a certain political and cultural autonomy within the context of the Muslim religion. It was also an ideal starting point for the spreading of Islam across Africa.

Art and Architecture

Egyptian art has great aesthetic appeal and can be appreciated as any other art, but art for art's sake did not exist in ancient Egypt, where everything was governed by religious conventions. Even painting in houses, which appears to be purely decorative, is usually made up of religious and protective symbols. Nevertheless, the Egyptian artist was capable of great imagination in the combination of these elements to create remarkably attractive effects. Equally, the Egyptian artist's individuality was usually subordinated to the required conventions.

The principles of Egyptian art were defined by the beginning of the First Dynasty, as can be seen on the Palette of Narmer (Egyptian Museum, Cairo), where the figures are shown in the conventional way that was to continue until the Roman Period. Egyptian relief and painting is essentially two-dimensional, the subject matter being arranged without reference to time or space. Objects and people can be shown on a different scale according to their importance. Figures are laid out according to a 'canon of proportion'. Sometimes the grid squares used for this can be found in tombs (for example, the tomb of Horemheb in the Valley of the Kings); more often a few key heights are indicated. Slight changes in the canon of proportion account for the distinctions in style of different periods. Figures were not taken directly from life, but built up from components which showed the typical aspect of each part. For example, the eye and eyebrow are shown as if viewed full on, but the face is drawn in profile; the shoulders are full on, but the front of the torso is in profile. Objects were also shown in their most characteristic way, without use of perspective, so boxes and chairs were viewed from the side so as to be instantly recognizable. Sometimes two views are combined to make the object more intelligible: so, for example, the contents of a box could be depicted as if standing on top of it.

Architecture

Although mud-brick was always a major building material in Egypt, stone was employed in funerary structure of the Archaic Period, and facility in construction developed rapidly. By the Third Dynasty the enormous complex of the Step Pyramid at Saqqara was built, the first large-scale stone architecture in the world. Here all of the elements of mud-brick, wood and reed architecture are translated into stone. Within a relatively short time, the control of materials and techniques

Floodlit carving, Temple of Karnak

UNAS EATS THE GODS

The chambers of the great pyramids of the Fourth Dynasty at Giza, Dashur and Medum are undecorated, as are those of the Fifth Dynasty at Abusir. It was only in the reign of Unas, the last king of the Fifth Dynasty, that the burial chambers were covered with religious texts. These **Pyramid Texts** are found in the tombs of Unas and his Sixth-dynasty successors, Teti, Pepi I, Nemtyemsaf and Pepi II, all at Saqqara. Altogether there are 759 separate 'utterances'. Many of the 228 utterances which appear in the tomb of Unas were reused and modified in later tombs, but some were dropped and many new ones added. The texts deal with the rebirth of the king, his ascent to the sky to join the gods and the perpetuation of his food offerings. One of the most distinctive of the Unas utterances, used only by his successor, Teti, is 'The Cannibal Hymn'. It probably dropped from use in the Sixth Dynasty because it reflects an ancient tradition that was no longer felt to be appropriate. This translation, adapted from Miriam Lichtheim's *Ancient Egyptian Literature*, extracts some of the most striking parts of the text that would have been recited or chanted in the echoing chambers at the time of the king's burial.

Sky rains, stars darken,
The vaults quiver, earth's bones tremble,
The planets stand still
At seeing Unas rise in power,
A god who lives on his fathers,
Who feeds on his mothers!

Unas is the bull of heaven,
Who rages in his heart,
Who lives on the being of every god,
Who eats their entrails
When they come, their bodies full of magic,
From the Isle of Flame.

Unas is he who eats men, who feeds on gods.
It is Khonsu, slayer of lords, who cuts their throats for Unas,
Who tears their entrails out for him.
Unas eats their magic, he swallows their spirits:
Their big ones are for his morning meal,
Their middle ones for his evening meal,
Their little ones for his night meal.

Unas has encompassed the two skies,
He has circled the two shores;
Unas is the great power that overpowers the powers,
Unas is the divine hawk, the great hawk of hawks.
Those whom he finds on his way he devours whole.
Unas is god, oldest of the old,
Thousands serve him, hundreds offer to him.

Unas has arisen in heaven,
He is crowned as Lord of Light-land.
He has smashed bones and marrow,
He has seized the hearts of the gods,
He has eaten the Red Crown, swallowed the White Crown.
Unas feeds on the lungs of the wise.
He lives on hearts and their magic.
Unas abhors licking the coils of the Red Crown,
But delights to have their magic in his belly.

He has swallowed the knowledge of every god;
Unas's lifetime is forever, his limit is eternity.
Lo, their power is in Unas's belly,
Their spirits are before Unas as broth of the gods,
Cooked for Unas from their bones.

allowed the construction of the stupendous pyramid complexes at Medum, Dashur and Giza. Yet all of this was achieved with simple technology.

In the Old and Middle Kingdoms, the largest building works were the royal funerary complexes, consisting of pyramids and attached temples. In the New Kingdom and later periods the temples of the gods became the focus.

FUNERARY ARCHITECTURE

Much of our knowledge about Egypt comes from the burials, the decorated tomb-chapels and the objects found in the tombs. Wherever it was possible, cemeteries were located on the edge of the desert because of the importance of the agricultural land. Of course, the dry sand was also a good preserver of the body and goods buried with it. Thus, in Upper Egypt, most of the cemeteries are either along the desert edge or in the cliffs. In the Delta region this was impossible.

The mastaba (from the Arabic word meaning 'bench') was the form adopted in the Archaic and Old Kingdom for some royal and many noble burials. Originally, a simple pit grave was at the centre of a large mud-brick enclosure wall, which was then filled with sand and gravel. This developed into a solid brick (and later, stone) structure of rectangular plan, with battered walls. Offering niches, originally small (as at Medum), developed into multi-roomed chapels, the largest examples being of the late Old Kingdom at Saqqara (Mereruka). The early royal mastabas at Saqqara and Abydos were decorated with elaborate recessed brickwork called the 'palace façade'. This can also be seen in the Step Pyramid complex, where the outer enclosure wall is of this type, but built in stone. In the New Kingdom cemeteries at Saqqara and similar sites, the mastaba was replaced by a freestanding tomb-chapel which took the form of a small temple, with pylon entrance, courtyards and a small pyramid. This type of tomb was decorated with relief sculpture.

Rock-cut tombs are found throughout Egypt, but often at sites with imposing cliffs; they are thus common in Middle and Upper Egypt and notable cemeteries are at Aswan and Beni Hasan of the Old and Middle Kingdoms; Amarna and Thebes (Luxor) of the New Kingdom. The rock-cut tomb is strictly the funerary chapel. It usually comprises a courtyard (sometimes serving several chapels), a hall and statue-niche with offering place; the actual burials were made beneath the floor of the hall, or sometimes in the outer courtyard. In the Middle Kingdom, at Beni Hasan and Aswan, these burials were usually a simple vertical shaft, with a niche or small chamber at the bottom for the coffins and other goods. New Kingdom tombs, such as those at Amarna and the tomb of Ramose at Thebes, often have a sloping corridor or staircase leading down to the burial chamber. In only a few instances, for example Sennefer at Thebes, are the burial chambers decorated. The chapels were decorated with scenes of the activities of official life, private life, funerary ritual and later, with the 'Book of the Dead'. The decoration of this type of tomb could be either painted or sculpted, the choice often depending on the quality of the stone in the district. At Thebes the stone was generally poor and so the technique of painted decoration on plaster developed. Many New Kingdom tombs at Thebes also had a brick pyramid, with a limestone pyramidion. In the side of the pyramid there was a niche with a small kneeling statue of the tomb owner supporting a stele with a hymn to the sun (reconstructed pyramids at Deir el-Medina).

RELIGIOUS ARCHITECTURE

Most of the temple architecture that survives is of the New Kingdom and later periods. The classical form of the temple (as exemplified by Edfu) is actually a relatively late development, probably from the time of Amenhotep III. Few temples of the Old and Middle Kingdoms survive, but it is clear that they were much smaller in scale. Of course, it should be remembered that a temple as it survives today is only a vestige of what it was. The walls were painted in bright colours (still well-preserved in some places, for example Abydos, temples of Sety I and Ramesses II); the gateways were fitted with massive wooden doors covered with bronze and copper and decorated with engraved and inlaid figures. The temple furnishings, wooden statues and shrines have all vanished. Also, there would have been many other structures built of wood: kiosks, resting places for statues, smaller shrines and so on. It is known that one of the great gateways of Karnak had a porch of gilded wood attached to it. There are rarely any traces of the gardens which surrounded the temples either, although some tree-pits may be found at Deir el-Bahari.

Not all temples and chapels were built of stone, there were many of mud-brick, certainly in the earlier periods, and in lesser village and town sites. Indeed, temples like Karnak would have had large structures, such as pylons, of mud-brick: many kings claim to have replaced that which was built in brick with fine limestone. Pylon gateways of colossal scale have been preserved, showing that they too could be of brick. Decorated in just the same way as a stone pylon, all plastered and painted, with reliefs of the king smiting his enemies, brick pylons would have been difficult to distinguish from stone structures.

DOMESTIC ARCHITECTURE

The best-preserved monuments are, of course, those of stone, either built or rock-cut. These are the things designed for eternity: temples and tombs. Domestic architecture was of unburned mud-brick, wood and plaster. This was not, however, unsophisticated, and the few surviving examples of palace and house architecture show that they were large and elaborate complexes magnificently decorated. Mud-brick was ideally suited to the Egyptian climate: it can be warm and cool, and was also easy to come by, the Nile flood depositing a thick layer every year. Only the important features such as door jambs and lintels, and column bases, were made of stone.

Remains of private houses exist at Deir el-Medina and Amarna, and of large palace complexes at Malkata (Luxor, west bank) and Amarna, among other places. The massive mud-brick fortresses guarding the Second Cataract in Nubia, now submerged beneath Lake Nasser, were splendid examples of military architecture.

The houses at Deir el-Medina are all of similar plan, built between the street and the village wall, with a step down into the first room which was lit through the roof. This room seems to have been the place where the women of the family worked. Most of these rooms have a large brick structure which is now thought to be a shrine, although earlier Egyptologists thought that it was a place where women retired to give birth. The main room of the house lies beyond, up a step. This room usually has the stone base which supported a wooden column, and the remains of a dais against the back wall. The room was higher than the surrounding ones and lit by windows just below ceiling height. Remains of a brick-built stele and offering niche can often be found against the wall, sometimes with traces of the original decoration. Here the family would make offerings to the household gods and the ancestors. From this room a door led to the main bedroom, and another to a passage. From the passage the stairway led to the roof, which was used for storage and also a place to sleep in hot weather. The courtyard at the back of the house served as a kitchen and was partly roofed in the corner, and a deep shaft led to a storage chamber. Houses in the larger towns were probably of two or more storeys in height. The houses of the officials at Amarna were large villas, mostly of one storey, square in plan, inside an enclosure containing granaries, stables, servants' quarters, a household shrine and gardens.

PAINTING AND STATUARY

P ainting and sculpture formed an integral part of the conception of Egyptian buildings. Avenues were lined with sphinxes and temple entrances flanked by statues. Nearly all architecture, statuary and relief decoration was painted. Until the Ptolemaic Period most painting was done directly onto the stone, but from then on a thin layer of plaster (as at Kom Ombo) was often applied to the stone before painting. Painted decoration in tombs also varied, in some regions being applied directly onto smoothed stone, in others onto thick layers of plaster. Certain conventions were observed: whilst limestone and sandstone could be painted all over, using the whole palette, granite statuary was usually painted only on the mouth, eyes and crowns. The colours used were blue in hieroglyphs, and red and yellow. Some periods favoured certain stones—diorite from Nubia in the reign of Khafre, hard stones in the Middle Kingdom and Late Period. Quartzite was particularly favoured in the reign of Amenhotep III. Composite statuary was also made, notably in the Amarna Period, with costumed bodies in crystalline limestone; the heads, hands and feet in quartzite or jasper; the crowns of faïence; and the jewellery inlaid.

The art of Egypt is often seen through the official works, temple reliefs and decoration in the tombs of king and nobility. However, large numbers of sketches have survived, usually on *ostraca*, flakes of limestone. These include superb line drawings, sometimes featuring caricatures of fellow villagers and, occasionally, royalty. By the nature of the medium, painting on papyrus tended to be more spontaneous; although it is remarkable how easily the Egyptian artist could draw classically formal figures without the aid of grid lines. A good display of *ostraca* and papyri can be found in the Egyptian Museum in Cairo.

Many examples of royal jewellery have survived in the caches and burials. That from the Old Kingdom and Middle Kingdom is generally more appealing to modern taste than the New Kingdom pieces (best exemplified by Tutankhamun's jewellery). While Tutankhamun's jewellery is technically excellent, it is extremely, some might think excessively, elaborate and heavy. Much of it is complex, made up of hieroglyphs of the royal name. The jewellery of the queens and princesses of the 12th Dynasty found at Dashur is, by comparison, delicate and elegant. Technically it equals, if not surpasses, Tutankhamun's. The treasure of the Libyan kings from their burials at Tanis is often considered to be inferior in quality. However, the Libyan period was one of technical virtuosity in bronze-working, and many large images have survived, with elaborate decoration of inlaid gold and silver wire (the finest example is the God's Wife of Amun, Karomama, in the Louvre).

Good quality wood for sculpture was far less easily available than stone, and much had to be imported from western Asia. Nevertheless, there are many examples of superb wood-carving. Early examples vary in scale from the delicately carved wooden panels from the tomb of Hesire at Saqqara (Third Dynasty; Egyptian Museum), to the splendid barque of Khufu at Giza (Boat Museum). Wooden statues of high quality survive from all periods, as well as furniture and smaller objects such as cosmetic spoons. Furniture is usually decorated and carved with amuletic motifs. Some of it is strikingly simple and elegant (Hetepheres), but other examples are carved, gilded and inlaid with stained ivory, coloured glass and paste (Tutankhamun). The most appealing pieces are usually those which are simply decorated with inlays of ebony and ivory.

Opaque glass paste (usually, but incorrectly, termed faïence) was developed very early on in Egypt and was used for the mass production of cheap jewellery and amulets. The favoured colour was blue, which was regarded as having amuletic properties: this can vary from bright turquoise to dark ultramarine. Faïence was used for *shabti* figures and vessels, often painted with texts and decoration in black glaze. By the New Kingdom many different colours of glass paste were being used, and the Amarna Period particularly saw it used in inlays in furniture, jewellery and relief decoration. Much of Tutankhamun's jewellery includes glass paste. It could also be used for the figures and hieroglyphs which decorated shrines and coffins (as in the coffin of Petosiris, Egyptian Museum). True glass appears during the Amarna Period, with characteristic, drawn decoration.

REDISCOVERY OF EGYPT

N apoleon's expedition to Egypt in 1798 is generally regarded as the beginning of modern Egyptology. A host of scholars had joined the Napoleonic expedition in order to make a systematic study and publish any and all records of ancient and contemporary Egypt. But the most famous and important event was the accidental discovery of the Rosetta Stone (now in the British Museum in London), which contained the text of a decree made in 196 BC by a conclave of priests in Memphis in honour of Ptolemy V. It was written in two languages and three scripts: Egyptian hieroglyphic and demotic, and Greek. The attention of scholars was immediately focused on it, and the decipherment of the hieroglyphic script by Jean-François Champollion opened up ancient Egypt to study.

At the start of the 19th century, Mohammed Ali, as part of modernization and economic recovery programs for his country, opened Egypt to Europeans, many of whom established themselves around the court in Alexandria and in other major cities. Since it was not difficult to obtain an excavation permit, the newly appointed European consuls, diplomatic agents, engineers and businessmen also became archaeologists and antique dealers overnight. The treasures they accumulated became the nucleus of dazzling collections in European museums, and 'finds' made while digging major temples and pyramids out of the encroaching sands became the source of new excitement and impetus for the students of Egyptology.

The rich collection of Bernadino Drovetti, French Consul-General to Egypt, was bought by Carlo Felice of Savoy and found a permanent home in Turin in 1824. A second collection of Drovetti's went to the Louvre in Paris. Giuseppe di Nizzoli of Trieste, Chancellor of the Legation of Austria, collected fine pieces from Lower Egypt which were later divided between the museums of Vienna and Florence. The English Consul, Henry Salt, along with Giovanni Battista Belzoni and Giovanni Caviglia, put together two impressive collections of Egyptian treasures, one of which was later sold to the British Museum, the other to the Louvre. Other antique collectors continued their excavation operations in Egypt during the early 1800s and their magnificent finds enriched the museums of Berlin, London and Paris.

The work of Bonaparte's French Expedition continued with the arrival of more scholars. Jean-François Champollion and Ippolito Rosellini headed the joint Franco-Tuscan Expedition in 1828–29. They had a detailed plan for the study of the monuments, and made numerous drawings of the reliefs and paintings in the temples and tombs. The result was an enormous synthesis completed by Rosellini after the sudden, early, death of Champollion in 1832. Other expeditions, some publicly and others privately funded, copied inscriptions, reliefs and paintings. The last major work of this type was that of the Prussian Expedition of the Imperial Academy of Berlin, led by Karl Richard Lepsius. From 1842 to 1845, Lepsius and his assistants travelled the entire valley of the Nile far into Sudan, and the deserts surrounding it, surveying monuments and copying inscriptions and scenes in temples and tombs. The publications resulting from all of these expeditions excited considerable interest and rapidly increased knowledge of Egypt and Sudan and their monuments. These volumes still remain important as a record of preservation at the time, and of some monuments that have been completely destroyed since.

A significant development came with the career of the French Egyptologist Auguste Mariette, who began working in Egypt in 1850. Having seen the irreparable damage that antiquities dealers and art collectors were causing, Mariette urged the establishment of a national service for the care and conservation of standing monuments, and the creation of a museum. As a result, he was appointed Director of Egyptian Monuments in 1858, and a house at Bulaq was set aside to serve as a museum and storage place for excavation finds. This represented a major step towards the eventual formation of the Egyptian Museum of Cairo. Mariette conducted clearing, consolidation and excavation operations all over Egypt. After Mariette's death in 1881, Gaston Maspero succeeded him as Director of the Office of Antiquities

ALEXANDRIAN KINGS

An Alexandrian crowd collected to see the sons of Cleopatra,
Cæsarion and his little brothers Alexander and Ptolemy,
who for the first time were brought to the Gymnasium,
there to be crowned as kings amidst a splendid display of troops.

Alexander they named king of Armenia, of Media, and of the Parthians.
Ptolemy they named king of Cilicia, of Syria, and Phœnicia.
Cæsarion stood a little in front, clad in silk the colour of roses,
with a bunch of hyacinths at his breast. His belt was a double line of
sapphires and amethysts, his sandals were bound with white ribbons
embroidered with rosy pearls. Him they acclaimed more than the small ones.
Him they named "King of Kings!"

The Alexandrians knew perfectly well that all this was words and empty pomp.

But the day was warm and exquisite, the sky clear and blue,
the Gymnasium of Alexandria a triumph of art, the courtiers' apparel magnificent,
Cæsarion full of grace and beauty (son of Cleopatra, blood of the Lagidæ!),
and the Alexandrians ran to see the show and grew enthusiastic, and applauded
in Greek, in Egyptian, and some in Hebrew, bewitched with the beautiful
spectacle, though they knew perfectly well how worthless, what empty words,
were these king-makings.

C P Cavafy, 'Alexandrian Kings', translated by J Mavrogordatos,
Hogarth Press, London, 1951

Constantine Peter Cavafy (1863–1933) was born in Alexandria. Between 1872 and
1877 his family lived in England where English became his primary language. Upon
returning to Alexandria, he became a Greek poet. He lived most of his life in
Alexandria, loved English and French literature, and generally spoke English; even
his Greek had a British accent. Cavafy published about 200 poems and with some
justification he called himself a 'poet of old age'. He is well-known to English readers
from the many references to his work in Lawrence Durrell's *Alexandria Quartet*.
Cavafy's work earned him international recognition as one of the most important
poets of the 20th century.

The central panel of this window is a fine example of the complex geometric patterns of
Islamic design.

and of the museum. Maspero was instrumental in acquiring for the national collection important antiquities that had been found by professional tomb robbers and were being gradually fed onto the antiquities market. Most notable was the so-called Royal Cache at Deir el-Bahari, containing the bodies of some of Egypt's most famous New Kingdom pharaohs.

Numerous foreign expeditions worked in Egypt in the late 19th and early 20th centuries. Some of these was funded by wealthy amateurs, and others by foreign institutions. Notable amongst the latter was the Egypt Exploration Fund (now Society), which had Eduard Naville and Flinders Petrie as its chief excavators and Howard Carter amongst its artists. Petrie later worked for his own organization, the British School of Archaeology in Egypt. The Metropolitan Museum of Art in New York conducted excavations at Deir el-Bahari, and was particularly important in copying reliefs and paintings in the Theban tombs. Most European countries established institutes in Cairo, the oldest being the French Institute founded in 1881.

It was normal practice for the finds from excavations to be divided between the excavator and the Egyptian Museum, with any particularly important pieces remaining in Egypt. This policy considerably enriched museum collections abroad. It also had the effect of preserving material that had previously been ignored or discarded. The wily Flinders Petrie found that there was considerable benefit from saving a range of artefacts that could then be given to his sponsors (many of these have eventually made their way into museum collections), thereby encouraging their future generosity. Petrie himself was interested in pottery and other types of artefact that had previously received little scholastic attention. He was also pioneering in his work on the prehistoric phases of Egyptian archaeology.

Post-war archaeological operations brought rich rewards, with, especially, the uncovering of the largely undisturbed tomb of Tutankhamun by Lord Carnarvon and Howard Carter in 1922. The countless quantities of precious objects that made up the pharaoh's funerary equipment rightly remained in Cairo. In Saqqara, Cecil Firth and Jean-Philippe Lauer undertook the methodical excavation of Djoser's funerary complex and Lauer later continued the important work of reconstructing the monuments using the original blocks. From 1952, Egypt's archaeological efforts were focused on ways to save the ancient sites of Nubia, chiefly Abu Simbel and Philae, which would be flooded by the construction of the High Dam at Aswan. Excavations in Lower Egypt and the Delta, made difficult because many historic sites had been buried by silt deposited by the Nile, also resumed with much more rigorous methodology, though to date few spectacular finds have been unearthed.

CAIRO AND SURROUNDINGS

C airo, once dubbed the 'Mother of the World', is the largest city in Africa and the Arab world, and has a daytime population of some 15 million people, when workers from the nearby Delta flock to the city for employment. Cairo has always attracted people from the Delta and surrounding villages, but it owes its recent growth to the damage inflicted on the city of Suez during the 1967 Arab–Israeli war and the later conflict in 1973.

During rush hour, Cairo appears to be gasping for breath. Buses threaten to collapse under the weight of people scrambling through doors and windows or clinging on outside. Stations are crowded and streets are an endless cacophony of blaring horns and shouting people, interspersed with the call for prayer of the muezzin. Even as early as AD 1360, the celebrated Arab traveller Ibn Batuta described an overcrowded Cairo: 'There are but so many inhabitants, so much that the multitude seems to move itself in waves, making the city appear almost in such desperate straits and anguish to contain all this, like a sea in perpetual agitation.'

Present-day Cairo has its roots in el-Qahira ('the Victorious', an allusion to the planet Mars), built by the Fatimids in 969. You can still trace the city's history from the east bank of the Nile opposite Roda Island, where the Romans built a fortified camp for the Mamluks, Turkish slaves brought to serve in the Egyptian army who eventually came to power in the 13th century.

Opposite the walls that now enclose the old Coptic quarter was the city of Fustat. The first Islamic capital of Egypt, built in AD 639, it was destroyed in a 54-day fire in 1168, which was deliberately started to prevent its occupation by the Crusaders.

The route from the airport, the usual entry point for most tourists, passes through the residential area of Heliopolis with its modern luxury villas and apartments. Cairo is now undergoing considerable change in a bid to improve transport and its complex road system. A multimillion dollar project for an underground railway (metro) is one of the biggest projects in the city. Even the scenic Nile corniche has not escaped modernization; huge multistorey buildings now dot the river's banks. But you can still see graceful feluccas sailing along the river in the early mornings or afternoons, bringing a sense of tranquillity and images of the past.

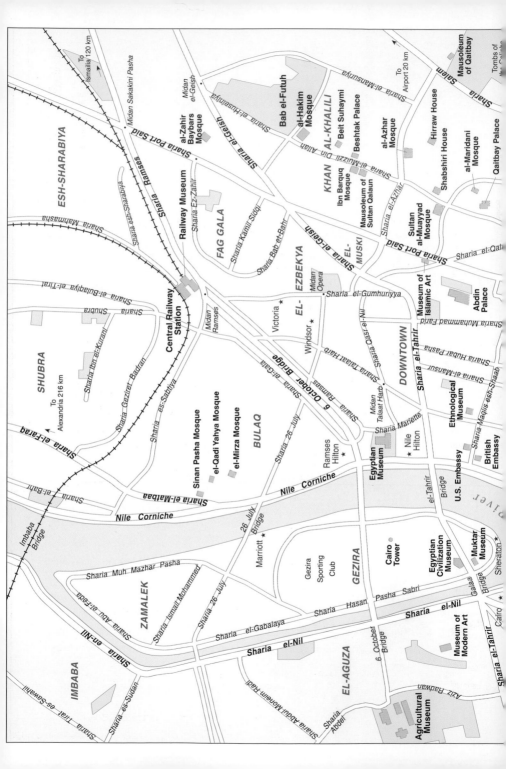

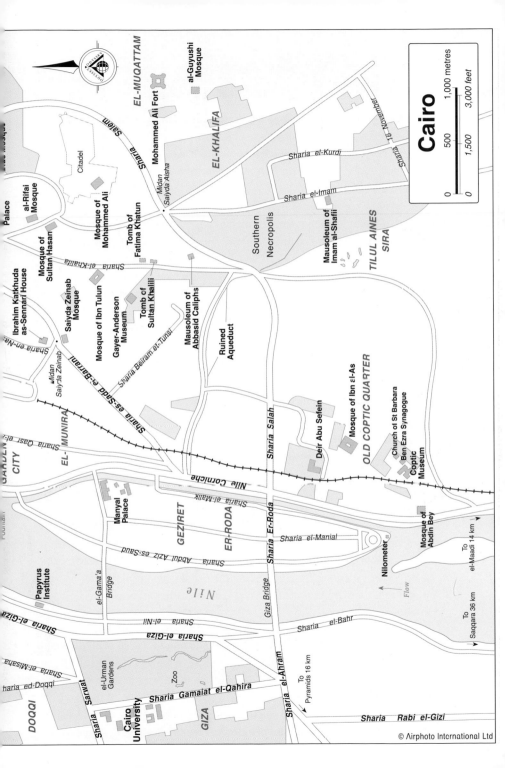

EGYPTIAN MUSEUM

Champollion and others had urged the foundation of a national Service des Antiquités de l'Egypte to preserve Egyptian objects and monuments, and to prevent the wholesale plundering of ancient sites which had characterized the earlier years of the 19th century. Objects from this first national collection were, however, given as gifts by the pasha to visiting foreign dignitaries, and, in 1855, the remainder was given to the Austrian Archduke Maximilian. In 1858, Auguste Mariette was appointed Director of the Service des Antiquités, and he created a museum to house the Egyptian collections in a warehouse at Bulaq. His determination to keep objects in Egypt was demonstrated when, in 1867, he refused the Empress Eugénie's request for the best of the collection. The flooding of the Bulaq Museum in 1878 caused the loss or damage of many objects, and in 1890, the collection was transferred to the Giza Palace of the Khedive Ismail. The present museum, to a design by Marcel Durgnon, was opened in 1902. Mariette himself is buried in the garden, in the exedra at the west end. His statue is flanked by busts of other eminent Egyptologists.

The museum is open daily from 9.00 am to 4.00 pm, except Fridays when it is open from 11.15 am to 1.30 pm. During the month of Ramadan the museum closes at 3.00 pm. It may also close or have restricted hours on certain national holidays.

The enormous exhibition—of over 120,000 objects—has vastly outgrown the space and is consequently somewhat congested. The museum is arranged on two floors, with the ground floor devoted mainly to statuary, sculpture and large architectural stonework in a chronological order clockwise from the entrance hall. The upper floor comprises the Tutankhamun galleries, other royal coffins, furniture, jewellery and many categories of smaller objects.The rooms of the museum are numbered across from west to east, beginning at the north side (furthest from the entrance), which is slightly confusing. The museum basically comprises a central hall with a gallery on each of its four sides, and an additional series of numbered rooms off both the West and East galleries. The galleries themselves are also divided into numbered rooms. As with all museum collections, objects are moved or lent to exhibitions elsewhere.

GROUND FLOOR

Facing the entrance is the **Central Hall**, comprising rooms 13, 18, 23, 28, 33, 38 and 43, which is dominated by the colossal limestone dyad of Amenhotep III with Queen Tiye. Heavily restored, but still an imposing monument, it came from the king's temple on the west bank at Luxor, behind the Colossi of Memnon. In the centre of the hall are the remains of one of the painted plaster floors from the palace at Amarna, with birds flying from the swamp. Also of note are some royal sarcophagi: Hatshepsut,

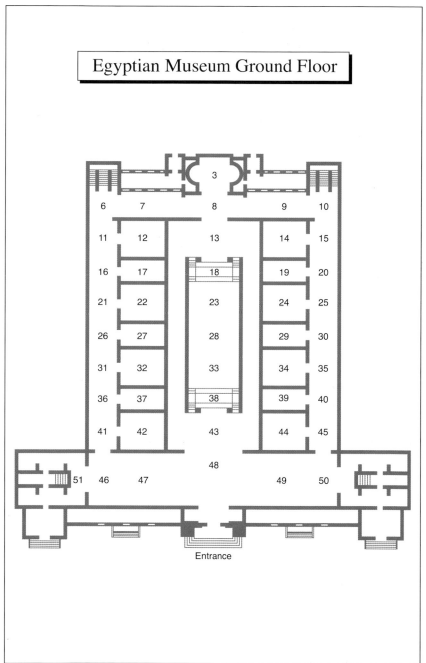

Egyptian Museum Ground Floor

Source: Robert Morkot

Tales Collected in Cairo:
One Thousand Nights and a Night

O ne of the most celebrated works of Islamic literature in the West is the collection of tales now known as *Alf Laylah wa Laylah* (*One Thousand Nights and a Night*). However, in the Arabic-speaking world this has not been ranked amongst the classical literature due to the colloquial style of the language and the nature of the tales themselves.

Many of the tales have become popular nursery and pantomime stories in the West, notably *Ala al-Din and the Magic Lamp, Ali Baba and the Forty Thieves* and *Sinbad the Sailor*. But all of the earlier European editions were sanitized for a nursery or drawing room audience: the original stories are far earthier.

The collection is framed by the narrative of Shahrazad who, to avoid being executed, tells her husband, King Shahriyar, a series of tales, carefully stopping at a crucial moment so that he spares her for another day. The result is an elaborate series of tales within tales.

The origins of the collection lie in a book of Persian tales called *Hazar Afsanah* (*A Thousand Tales*) that was translated into Arabic in the mid-ninth century AD. This Persian book is now lost, but a later synopsis suggests that, along with versions of some of the stories, it furnished the framework of Shahrazad's narrative, which appears to have its own origins even further away, in Indian folklore. The scheme of story-within-story was certainly developed in the 12th century.

The individual stories fall into three main geographical groups. The first group is Indian and Persian: these stories have all but disappeared through adaptation to more westerly locations and the addition of local colour. A second major group of tales comes from Baghdad: these are identified by their references to the reign of the Abbasid Caliph Harun al-Rashid (ruled AD 786–809, H 170–193). The last group reflects the city and time in which the whole collection was eventually welded together, that of Cairo in the Mamluk period. As the collection developed, the stories were altered and given a local flavour, and more were added. Modern research has shown that, as well as stories deriving from the folklore of a wide region, there are elements in some stories, notably that of Sinbad, that have parallels in, and perhaps reflect some familiarity with, Greek epics such as the *Odyssey*.

One Thousand Nights and a Night, or *Arabian Nights*, reached something like its present form in 14th-century Cairo. The standard modern text of the tales was put together in Cairo in the 18th century and published there in 1835. Another major edition of the Arabic text was prepared and published in Calcutta (1839–1842): this has formed the basis for most later translations. By then, some of the stories, and the name of the entire collection, were already popular in western Europe. A French version—adapted and selected by the Orientalist Antoine Galland—appeared in 12 volumes between 1704 and 1717. Parts of this were pirated and translated into English and published in 1706–1708. By the end of the century, many of the tales had become highly popular.

The 19th-century translations tended to be both archaic in language and genteel in content, omitting the explicitly sexual episodes and references, and taming the bawdiness. The most famous translation, published in 1885–1886, by the traveller and Orientalist Sir Richard Burton was rendered in an archaic style, made even more difficult by his tendency to invent words. The modern editions are not so coy, and several complete translations, or collections of the best-known tales, are available.

The tales combine romance and high adventure, the erotic and the farcical. There are satires on bureaucratic corruption ('The Tale of the Young Woman and Her Five Lovers'), and the awful repercussions of overindulgence ('The Historic Fart'). The tales have the whole range of characters from caliphs, viziers and cadis to barbers, cobblers, merchants, fishermen, sailors and shopkeepers, as well as large numbers of black eunuchs. Women make fools of men, playing on their weakness for beauty; they take secret lovers and discuss their merits. The world of the magical and fantastical is often close: afreet and jinn abound, helping and hindering the characters; winged horses and giant birds carry off the narrators. The whole is set against a backdrop of the great cities of Baghdad, Damascus and Cairo.

It is hardly surprising, then, that the tales fed the Western Orientalist fantasy with their descriptions of elaborate feasts, costumes and jewels. We read of chickens and lambs stuffed with walnuts, almonds and pistachios; of stuffings of shredded lamb with chick peas, pine kernels, cardamom, nutmeg, cloves, ginger and pepper; of rose jam; of moist jam of dates stuffed with almonds and cloves; of almond cakes soaked in honey and dusted with cinnamon; of houses built of white marble with mosaic floors, fountains, and walls covered with silks 'of as many colours as there are flowers in spring' ; of gardens filled with jasmine, rose, violet, carnation and tulip; of swords damascened in gold with hilts of rubies and jade; of carpets woven with gold thread; of jade vases, alabaster beds and diamonds the size of ostrich eggs.

Thutmose I and the God's Wife Nitoqert; and the black granite pyramidion of Amenemhat III.

Room 43, at the entrance to the Central Hall, contains some of the most important Early Dynastic objects, including a fine collection of stone vessels. Most notable is the Palette of Narmer. Of greywacke (schist), it was discovered at Hierakonpolis in 1894 and shows the king wearing both the white crown of Upper Egypt and the red crown of Lower Egypt, the first ruler to do so. The palette records campaigns which led to the unification of the two kingdoms and establishment of the united monarchy. Here, on one of the earliest royal relief sculptures, the conventions of Egyptian art are already clearly developed. The statue of King Khasekhemwy (Second Dynasty), also from Hierakonpolis, is important as one of the earliest royal statues. In hard green schist, the statue is quite small, but of good work. The king wears the white crown of Upper Egypt and the long *sed*-festival robe. The statue of Djoser, from the serdab attached to the Step Pyramid of Saqqara, is one of the most splendid and austere of royal statues, the image of a god-king. Although badly damaged as the inlaid eyes have been gouged out, the statue still commands attention. The heavy wig and beard focus attention on the head; the pronounced cheekbones and the downturned mouth give an individuality to the stern features; and the monumental effect is emphasized by the slim body enveloped in the *sed*-festival robe.

Gallery 47: Old Kingdom statuary and sarcophagi. There are many fine pieces here, but the most splendid pieces are the three triads depicting Menkaure. They were excavated at Giza (and have companions in the Boston Museum of Fine Arts). The king is flanked by the goddess Hathor (on the king's right side) and a deity who represents one of the nomes of Egypt. A notable feature of these statues is the king's physique, with broad shoulders, narrow waist and pronounced musculature.

Gallery 46: The greywacke head from the sun temple of Userkaf at Abusir continues the tradition of the Menkaure sculptures, but has an extraordinary delicacy. Note the way the red crown (itself unusually tall and broad) continues the line of the face. There are traces of a moustache, which was common in the Old Kingdom.

Gallery 41: Limestone slabs from the tomb of Nefermaat at Medum (Third Dynasty), with figures hollowed in silhouette, which was then filled with coloured paste. This technique was unsatisfactory as the paste soon cracked, and was used only here and in the tomb of Nefermaat's son at Giza. One block shows a fowling scene, with inlaid geese strikingly similar to the painted geese from the same tomb.

Face of Ramesses II at the Ramesseum

Room 42: Some of the most important Old Kingdom sculpture. The diorite seated figure of Khafre (Chephren) from the valley temple of the second pyramid at Giza is one of the triumphs of Egyptian sculpture. With remote gaze, the Horus-falcon hovering behind his head, this icon of Khafre expresses the ideal of god-like majesty. Fragments of the other diorite statues can be found here and elsewhere in this section. A number of superb wooden statues are also displayed here, of which the most impressive is the complete figure of Ka-aper, known as the Sheikh el-Beled, the village headman. Dating from the reign of Userkaf, this remarkable image was discovered in the tomb of Ka-aper, near his sovereign's pyramid at Saqqara. The sycamore wood lends realism to the fleshy figure, emphasized by the inlaid eyes of quartz and rock crystal set in copper. A wooden female figure, without arms and broken at the hip, is also from Ka-aper's tomb and perhaps represents his wife. The striking, slim young man, also broken at the hip, is possibly Ka-aper again, but shown in the vigour of youth.

Galleries 36 and 31: Relief fragments from the pyramid temple of Sahure of Abusir (Fifth Dynasty). The panels from the tomb of Hesire at Saqqara (Third Dynasty) are rare examples of wood decorated with low relief. There is a pronounced slenderness in the figures, a subtle modelling of the surfaces and large hieroglyphs.

Room 32: The painted panel of the Medum geese from the tomb of Nefermaat. The silhouette and colouring is accurate, but the feather patterns are highly stylized. It is interesting to compare this painting of feeding greylag geese with the inlaid ones from the same tomb (**Room 42**). Dominating the room are the statues of Rahotep and Nofret, also from Medum. These are particularly expressive. An important piece of a type less frequently found is the life-size copper statue of Pepi I from Nekhen (Hierakonpolis). The copper was hammered over a wooden frame with crown and kilt in other materials (gilded wood or plaster). The idealized male physique is well demonstrated in the serdab-statue of Ti, from his mastaba at Saqqara. Not as technically excellent as the other works in this room, it is nevertheless a fine piece and worthy of note for those who intend to visit the tomb.

Gallery 26: Statue of Nebhepetre-Menthuhotep, painted black and wearing the *sed*-festival robe and red crown. The statue was found at Deir el-Bahari, ritually buried and wrapped in a linen cloth. Its squat proportions and massive limbs are a striking contrast to the attenuated figures characteristic of this period (see sarcophagi of his wives upstairs).

Gallery 21: Granite dyad with king in the form of two Nile gods bringing offering tables with lotus flowers, birds and fish. The statue is notable for the archaic style of the hair and beards. One of the most striking images is the broken colossus of Amenemhat III from Krokodilopolis (Faiyum). Wearing a heavy ringleted wig of archaic design and a panther skin, the king appears in his role as a priest.

Room 22: Ten statues of Senusret I from Lisht. Well-preserved, because they were, for some reason, left unfinished and carefully buried near the mortuary temple. These classic images show the king in the royal headcloth (*nemes*) seated on the block throne. The sides of the throne have scenes of the unification of the Two Lands performed by Horus and Seth, and by Nile gods. Good, large, painted wooden figure of Senusret I in white crown (its companion with red crown is in the New York Metropolitan Museum), also from Lisht.

Gallery 16: Black granite sphinxes from Tanis. They were carved for Amenemhat III, removed to Per-Ramesses and recarved for Ramesses II and Merneptah, and again moved to Tanis, where they were excavated, by Pa-seba-kha-en-niut (Psusennes). The heavy lion's mane, which replaces the *nemes*-headdress, and the rather stern features of the king make these sphinxes more awe-inspiring than the rather bland New Kingdom sphinxes.

Room 12: Chapel of Thutmose III from Deir el-Bahari containing good, painted relief with bright colours. There is a large statue of the Hathor cow with speckled body, her head breaking through a thicket of papyrus. On the side is carved a suckling king, whilst a standing figure of the king is beneath her head. The name of Amenhotep II is carved on the statue. There are many other good 18th-dynasty sculptures in this room. The larger-than-life-size mummiform statue of the moon god Khonsu has the features of Tutankhamun. A black granite statue of Isis, mother of Thutmose III, has the remains of a gold headdress. The lovely kneeling statuette of Thutmose III offering jars is unusual as it is carved in marble. The large, green basalt statue of Thutmose III in white crown has the strong aquiline nose typical of this king (but also of Hatshepsut). The greywacke statue of Amenhotep II is charming, but lacks the vigour of his father's images. A black granite pair of statues from Karnak depicts Sennefer, Mayor of Thebes, and his wife. Sennefer is shown with the heavy gold collars around the neck and the double-heart amulet that he usually wears in the paintings in his tomb at Thebes.

The **North Gallery** (rooms 6–10) is filled with statues, sphinxes and sarcophagi. The walls are covered with New Kingdom reliefs, many from the tombs at Saqqara.

Room 3: The Amarna Room. Dominated by the bizarre colossi of Akhenaten from the Karnak temple, this is, to many visitors, one of the most fascinating rooms in the museum. The more refined Amarna style is represented by a group of important sculptures, including the unfinished quartzite head of Nefertiti, which is generally regarded as one of the finest portraits of her to have survived. It would have formed part of a composite statue, with inlaid eyes, the body and crown made in different stones and coloured glass. Many people prefer this head to the more famous painted head of Nefertiti in Berlin. A second quartzite head, although damaged, is in a finished state, the stone polished and the eyes and brows cut for inlay. This piece is notable for the subtlety of the carving around the mouth.

The **East Gallery** (rooms 10, 15, 20, 25, 30, 35, 40, 45) and the rooms off it are often unfairly neglected. At the entrance to the corridor stands a colossal black granite figure of Horon with a squatting child in front; the various emblems carried make up the name of Ramesses II. Room 15 has a case containing two remarkable sculptures: the head of Nakhtmin, and the upper part of the figure of his wife from a double statue. These two superb pieces are carved in hard crystalline limestone, but were smashed in ancient times. Nakhtmin was probably a member of the family of King Ay, successor to Tutankhamun.

Gallery 25: The middle of the gallery has many fine examples of Late Period sculpture. Some of the important 25th-dynasty works have been transferred to the Nubia Museum in Aswan.

Room 24. Two statues of Montjuemhat, Mayor of Thebes in the 25th Dynasty. These statues are splendid examples of the 'archaizing' style that began in the very late Libyan period, developing under the Kushites and continuing into the 26th Dynasty. The complete standing statue of Montjuemhat with wig is of a very similar style to those of the contemporary pharaoh Taharqo, made in the same workshop (perhaps by the same sculptor). These recall the physique and musculature of Old Kingdom statues, such as those of Menkaure, and certainly betray a Memphite influence on this style. Similar emphasis on musculature is found in the magnificent reliefs on the black granite shrine of Shabaqo from Esna.

Gallery 49: Sarcophagi and late statuary, including some interesting Roman sculptures. The interior coffin of Petosiris from Tuna el-Gebel is of pine wood (now blackened), with inscriptions inlaid in multicoloured glass-paste hieroglyphs.

As well as being one the world's greatest treasure houses, the Egyptian Museum in Cairo is also a magnificent example of the late-19th-century concept of a museum, reflected in its architecture.

Upper Floor

The major exhibition in the North and East galleries contains the treasures from the tomb of Tutankhamun. The collection is vast. Attention is paid here to the remainder of upstairs.

It is often forgotten that other tombs were discovered almost intact in the Valley of the Kings. **Room 13** contains some of the furniture from the tomb of Yuya and Tjuyu, the parents of Queen Tiye, wife of Amenhotep III. Here the charming, small thrones for the child princess, Sitamun, are particularly noteworthy. Less spectacular, but more human, are the woven papyrus sandals of Yuya.

Other royal treasures can be found in **Room 2**. Less opulent than the New Kingdom treasures, but perhaps more appealing to modern taste, is the furniture from the burial at Giza of Queen Hetepheres, mother of Khufu, and the jewellery of the 12th-dynasty princesses from Dashur and Illahun. Although the wood had disintegrated, it was possible to restore Hetepheres' furniture from its inlays and gold sheaths. An elegant, gilded wooden canopy, probably once hung with linen mosquito nets, covers the queen's throne and bed. Her carrying chair was sheathed in gold and inlaid with ebony. Note also the gold vessels, elegant and simple in form. The two caches recovered from the tombs of royal women buried at Dashur and Illahun are amongst the finest survivals of ancient jewellery. The crown of Princess Khnumet, daughter of Amenemhat II, is one of the most delicate and unusual pieces of Egyptian goldwork, consisting of gold wires dotted with star-shaped flowers and held at four points with crosses formed from four papyrus flowers set around a central disc. Also in this room are some of the treasures from the royal tombs at Tanis (22nd Dynasty).

Room 12: Amongst the many royal *shabti* figures is a remarkable collection of extravagant, ringleted wigs dating from the 21st Dynasty. Also displayed are some of the foodstuffs buried with Tutankhamun, including dishes of *dom*-palm nuts.

Room 17 contains important collections of funerary objects. One comes from the intact tomb of Maiherpri in the Valley of the Kings. This young Nubian prince died in the reign of Thutmose IV. His papyrus shows him black. It is an interesting collection of objects, particularly the chariotry and archery equipment. The tomb of the family of Sennedjem at Deir el-Medina is one of the best known, and beautifully decorated, so it is worth looking at the burials. Note that much of the painting on these objects appears to have been done by the same artist as the tomb. The coffin of Isis, wife of Sennedjem, shows the deceased with its mummy-board wearing festival garments, a style favoured in the 19th Dynasty.

Room 27: Many fine wooden models from Middle Kingdom tombs. Particularly

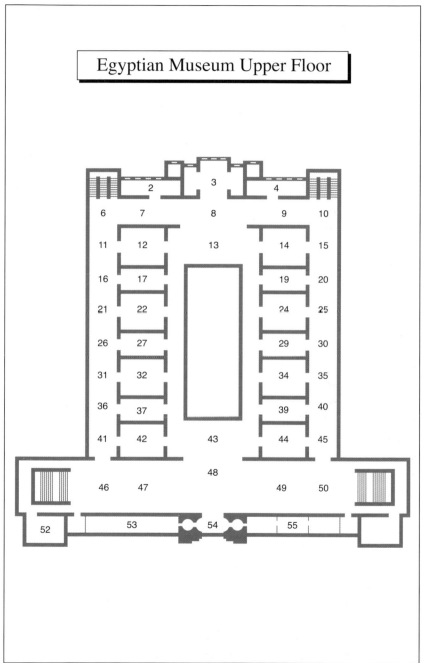

Egyptian Museum Upper Floor

Source: Robert Morkot

AT THE END OF THE SILK ROAD:
THE BAZAAR OF KHAN AL-KHALILI

S ilk first appeared in Egypt in any quantity during the Byzantine Period, a luxury controlled by the Sassanid Empire of Persia (AD 226–651). That empire fell to the expanding power of Islam, and the early centuries of Muslim civilization, particularly the eighth to the 11th, saw the empire of the caliphs emerge as a major world power and as leader of international trade. With their principal centre at Baghdad, the caliphs controlled much of the Silk Road from China, their rule also extending westwards to Morocco and Spain. Egypt had its own direct connections with the East by sea along the Red Sea routes to India and Ceylon that had been developed in the late Ptolemaic and Roman periods. Those connections brought pepper and spices that were then sold through the markets of Alexandria to European merchants, most importantly those from Venice.

Egypt became largely independent of the caliphs under dynasties of sultans and so avoided some of the political turmoil that engulfed other regions. With a population of 250,000, medieval el-Qahira (Cairo) was one of the largest and most splendid cities of its day. Surrounded by walls and filled with mosques and palaces, Cairo was the 'Mother of cities... peerless in beauty and splendour. The meeting place of comer and goer, the halting place of feeble and mighty', as the traveller Ibn Battuta described it in the 14th century.

At the heart of Mamluk Cairo lay the great *khan* (caravanserai) built by Sultan Barquq's Master of the Horse, the emir Jarkas al-Khalili in 1382. It attracted merchants from all over the Islamic world, especially Armenians, Jews and Persians. Merchants and craftsmen from Syria specialized in swords inlaid in gold and silver, the typical work of Damascus. From further away the merchants of Persia brought brocades, carpets, precious stones, cotton and silk. Rebuilt in 1511 by Sultan al-Ghawri, the Khan al-Khalili later expanded into the huge market area (including the adjacent Muski quarter) that still serves Cairo today with meat, fruit and vegetables, as well as the gold, jewellery and exotics that were its original purpose.

It was this trading centre of medieval Cairo that partly lies behind the tales of the *One Thousand Nights and a Night*, although it is grafted on to the Baghdad of Harun al-Rashid (ruled 786–809) and probably the world of the earlier Sassanid Empire. A few of the tales are specific in their setting in the Khan al-Khalili, but the whole sequence is filled with references to the Muslim trading world of the Silk Road from Baghdad to China (*Ala al-Din and the Magic Lamp*) and the sea routes from the Gulf to the islands of the East (*Sinbad the Sailor*). The *Tale of the Christian Broker* tells of a Cairene Copt and his encounter with a merchant from Baghdad who narrates his own story, involving a silk merchant and white silk woven with gold thread. In the complex interweaving of tales within tales comes another story of merchants from Mosul, who travel to Cairo via Aleppo and Damascus, where they sell their goods and buy the products of Damascus to take on to Cairo. The tales show the complex ways in which merchants travelled, selling and buying, and are obsessed with the huge profits that could be made. These merchants brought raw materials and finished goods—silks and carpets, Chinese porcelain and Damascus metalwork—which can now be found in the Coptic Museum and Museum of Islamic Art. From Cairo some of these trade goods made their way to Europe; others travelled up the Nile to places as remote as the Ottoman fortress at Qasr Ibrim in Nubia, where some early 17th century Chinese porcelain was excavated in the late 1990s.

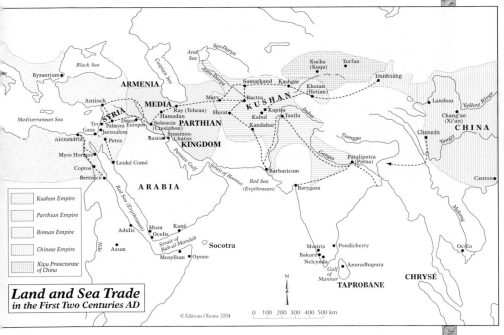

Land and Sea Trade
in the First Two Centuries AD

Kushan Empire

Parthian Empire

Roman Empire

Chinese Empire

Xiyu Protectorate of China

© Editions Olizane 2004

0 100 200 300 400 500 km

striking are those from the tomb of Meket-re at Thebes: two large servant figures, boats, the counting of cattle, fishing, carpentry, weavers etc. These are three-dimensional versions of the painted scenes at Beni Hasan. The two contingents of soldiers were found in the tomb of Mesehti at Asyut: Nubian archers and Egyptian spearmen. Nubians were important in many of the armies of the nomarchs during the late First Intermediate Period and are depicted in tombs of that period.

At the western end of the South Gallery (**Room 46**) can be found many of the coffins from the royal caches at Deir el-Bahari. Most notable here is the enormous cedar-wood coffin of Queen Merytamun, wife of Amenhotep I. The face of this coffin is particularly beautiful.

In the middle of the South Gallery (**Room 48**), by the circular opening, are the sarcophagi of two wives of Nebhepetre-Menthuhotep from Deir el-Bahari. They are amongst the finest examples of relief of this period. Technically sophisticated, they display the attenuated figures typical of the provincial Theban tradition. On the sarcophagus of Kawit, the queen is having her hair dressed whilst drinking a bowl of milk; note the elegant fingers of the queen and her hairdresser. The milking of the cow is also shown; beautiful figures, with the calf bound to the cow's foreleg. The cow sheds a tear. Here, at the entrance to the central hall there are sometimes special exhibitions. Lodged in a small case are some of the diminutive treasures of the museum, including the only known statue of Khufu and a superb head of Queen Tiye from Sinai.

The rather dark aisles overlooking the central saloon have some good pieces, notably (**Corridor 32**) the statue of King Auib-re Hor from Dashur. The king appears to be naked, but when discovered was overlaid with a fine layer of stucco. Traces of belt and kilt can be seen. The raised arms on the head indicate that this is an image of the *ka*. The rooms on the east side, off the main gallery (Tutankhamun), are often neglected but worth investigating, time permitting.

Room 14: Faiyum portraits, many from Hawara. Painted in wax, on thin panels of wood, these funerary portraits were attached to the mummy, or coffin, in place of the earlier type of death mask. Some of the faces are painted in a naive style, with large staring eyes, but others are remarkably realistic. The people represented formed the mixed Greek–Egyptian middle class, whose lives are well-documented by hundreds of letters and official records discovered in excavations in the Faiyum towns. There is a particularly fine tondo of two 'brothers'.

Room 19: Thousands of amulets and small figures of gods; stelae from the Serapeum at Saqqara, recording the Apis bulls.

Room 24: Papyri and *ostraca*, with some splendid line-drawings.

ISLAMIC CAIRO

I slam in Egypt began at Fustat, the first Arab city in Egypt, and later mushroomed into a great civilization with its most beautiful monuments in Cairo. Egypt was one of the first countries to be conquered by the Arabs after the death of Mohammed. Facing minimal resistance, the army of Amr ibn al-As conquered the weak fortress city of Pelusium by siege. Its location was crucial: posted at the extreme east of the Nile Delta, this gateway city opened the rest of the land to subjugation. Large numbers of the local population, dissatisfied with Byzantine rule, were converted to Islam so that Christianity was slowly reduced to a minority faith, thereby losing importance and secular influence in politics, economics and culture. The skilled Christian craftsmen and artists, however, did not hesitate to offer their services to the new rulers; they contributed to the embellishment of old structures, sometimes changing the style to conform with the distinctive Islamic use of arches and clear, open geometric courtyards.

On the site of Amr ibn al-As' encampment, which later became Fustat, rose the Mosque of ibn al-As, which has lost some of its original features because of continuous remodelling and embellishment over the years. Nonetheless, the present structure is considered Cairo's oldest mosque.

MOSQUES OF CAIRO

The mosque is the place where the Muslim community gathers for the ritual prayers on Fridays; they are the only prayers that are recited in public or in communion. From the beginning, the mosque has always had a political as well as a religious importance. In fact, before reciting prayers, the faithful engage in political discourses. This encourages social integration since each locality has only one main mosque. The function of the mosque may be compared to that of the Christian cathedral in history. The main difference, however, is that the mosque is not considered by Muslims as a house of God, as the Christians believe the church to be, but rather as a house of believers, a haven where people gather in observance of the rites of prayer.

The mosque as an original architectural form is derived from the house of Mohammed in Medina. In its most traditional form, it is composed of an open interior court off which are located various rooms and chambers, at times also adorned with elegant porticoes. Under the rule of the Umayyads and Abbasids (between AD 661–869), Fustat occupied itself with the enrichment and embellishment of its structures, erecting new monuments and buildings, all of which are unfortunately lost today. Outside its fortifying walls grew the suburbs of el-Askar, meaning 'the Army'.

In about 870, Ahmed ibn Tulun, the Turkish Governor of Egypt, proclaimed himself an independent sultan and transferred his residence to the hill of Jechkar northeast of Fustat where, after having destroyed both the Christian and Hebrew cemeteries, he constructed a citadel, the primitive stronghold which then grew into the city of el-Qata'i. This city witnessed glorious years of growth and development under Ahmed ibn Tulun. In its ancient splendour, it is said to have had 100,000 houses under its protective wing. It counted among its most resplendent and impressive buildings the palace of el-Maidan and the hospital, or *maristan*, of el-Askar. Today, not a trace of these splendid buildings remains. Aside from battered vestiges of private homes and palaces, only ruins of the aqueduct and the great Mosque of ibn Tulun still stand.

Designed and built by a Christian architect, the beautiful **Mosque of ibn Tulun** follows the lines and style of the Abbasid type, which is generally characterized by pilasters on which slightly pointed arches are applied. Soaring gracefully in front of the mosque is a minaret that originally had the same spiral characteristics as those of Samarra found in Mesopotamia. It was transformed into its present form in 1297 by the sultan, Lagin. The stucco-work which adorns the mosque is a revival of the style and technique found in Samarra. It is interesting to note, however, that certain designs and motifs are taken from Coptic art.

The first Fatimid monument in Egypt was the **Mosque of al-Azhar**, along the southern edge of Cairo, constructed by General Gawhar in 970. It has undergone so many restorations and reconstructions, especially after the devastating earthquake of 1303, that today it is impossible to make out its original structure. The mosque was entirely built on columns which were part of older monuments, and its style was strongly inspired by the cult edifices already existing in Tunisia and Spain.

The Mosque of al-Azhar, a highly regarded and respected centre of theological studies, immediately gained prestige in the Arab world. Its university is in fact still the most prestigious centre of learning for a devout Muslim; its students are highly esteemed and, having been educated in the most traditional Koranic disciplines, are then sent out to spread the revelations of Mohammed.

The second-most important mosque of the Fatimid epoch in Cairo, the **Mosque of al-Hakim**, was founded by al-Aziz in 990. The project was continued by his son al-Hakim between 1003 and 1012, following not only the planimetry but also the artistic forms of Mesopotamian styles which also characterize the Mosque of ibn Tulun. The name of al-Hakim (996–1021) is associated with some rather grotesque

The Turkish architecture of the Alabaster Mosque with its glittering aluminium-covered domes dominates Cairo, standing on the medieval Citadel.

scandals, such as the prohibition of numerous drinks and dishes, some particularly dear to the Egyptian palate; the imposition of a strict ban which forbade women to loiter in the streets; and the slaughter of dogs because their howling disturbed his solitary promenades around the city. In a fit of rage, he ordered an entire quarter of Fustat burned and pillaged.

The Kurdish general, **Salah al-Din**, better known as Saladin, supplanted the last of the Fatimids. This brilliant sovereign was a generous and honoured patron of the arts and culture; he brought about the elevation of Cairo to the most respected intellectual capital of the Islamic world. Testifying to this was the foundation of a *madrasa*, a theological school which followed strictly the disciplines of the Sunnis, the main sect of Islam.

Saladin also proved himself to be an invaluable innovator in the city's architectural and urban planning. The city walls, which enclose both the old and the new sections of Cairo, provided a sense of security for its inhabitants. His most important work, however, was the **Citadel**, constructed in 1179 over a ramp of the Muqattam hill. Many of the architectural features of this edifice are of remotely oriental derivation, but they are also strikingly typical of the Crusade construction prevalent in Syria and Palestine. The primitive fortress has undergone various expansions and transformations in the course of the centuries. A Turkish-style mosque was built within its walls by Mohammed Ali, who demolished the ancient palaces that once stood on the site.

A new impetus for architectural and artistic development in Cairo came from the Mamluk sultans who held the country for almost three centuries. Under their patronage, Cairo was enriched and beautified with a number of monuments, including the vast architectural complex consisting of a mausoleum, mosque with *madrasa* (school) and *maristan* (hospital) of Sultan Qalaun, and the splendid Mosque of Sultan Hasan, erected between 1356 and 1362—one of the masterpieces of Islamic art.

Cairo found new stimuli for growth and development in the vitality and force of Mohammed Ali. Through his initiatives a new city sprang up, with residential sections and zones delineated for administrative buildings patterned on European cities. Among many other architectural works constructed was the **Mosque of Mohammed Ali**. Also referred to as the Alabaster Mosque (its walls are covered entirely by a splendid alabaster finish from Beni Suef), its style is greatly influenced by the mosques of Istanbul. There is a panoramic view of the city from the terraces behind. The large number of splendid artefacts collected from various mosques and other ancient buildings in Cairo led, in 1880, to the foundation of the modest Museum of Arabic Art in the court of the Mosque of al-Hakim. With generous art donations from the private sector, it was necessary to build a new museum, and Bab el-Khalq was inaugurated in 1902. In 1952, its name was modified to the more appropriate **Museum of Islamic Art**, since numerous pieces from non-Arab nations such as Turkey and Persia were also exhibited.

The 23 halls are organized according to type of exhibit and in chronological order. It is most rewarding to follow the defined routes and not to miss any part of the exhibition. Recent archaeological excavations (some in the vicinity of Cairo) have provided, amongst other treasures, precious examples of figurative art from the Fatimid and Tulunid eras. Other excavations around Cairo have also yielded many ceramic fragments and even some exceptional vases and plates in an excellent state of preservation, which reveal the high level of refinement attained by artisans of the ninth and tenth centuries. Amongst the most beautiful examples of Islamic ceramics here are those finished with the characteristic technique of metallic lustre, which is probably of Egyptian origin. There are also some rare examples of Hispanic-Moorish ceramics.

Near the bazaar of Khan al-Khalili in south Cairo rises the imposing Mosque of al-Azhar, the renowned centre for worship and study for the whole Muslim world. Other monuments located along Sharia el-Muizzli Din Allah to the north are the **Mosque, Mausoleum and Maristan of Qalaun**, a sultan who lived in the second half of the 13th century. Of particular beauty are the mausoleum and the tomb, the latter rich with a colourful play of light on the magnificent structure and splendid wall decorations; its mosaics are amongst the most celebrated in Cairo.

Not far away are the **Madrasa of Mohammed al-Nasser** (son of Qalaun), with its beautiful façade, and the **Madrasa of Sultan Barquq**, an elegant building dating back to 1386. Towards the Mosque of al-Hakim is **Beit Suhaymi**, the ancient manor of a 17th-century sheikh, situated on a minor side street to the right. The mosaics, *mushrabiya* (wooden lattice-work screens) and the fountain are very interesting. Past the square containing the Mosque of al-Hakim and the Museum of Islamic Art is **Bab el-Futuh**, or Conquest Gate, a portion of which is buried four metres (13 feet) underground. The vault decorations are clearly of Byzantine influence. Rising on the other side of the mosque is **Bab el-Nasr**, or Victory Gate, which is built in the Graeco-Roman style.

A short distance to the west of al-Azhar is the complex of **el-Ghuri**, consisting of a *madrasa*, a mausoleum and a caravanserai, which today houses a school of traditional arts and crafts. A visit to this pleasant and interesting school is highly recommended.

The house of **Gamal Eddin al-Dahabi** is a remarkable example of civilian architecture of the 1600s. Going on along Sharia el-Muizzli Din Allah, one reaches the gate of **Bab Zuwayla**, also called Bab el-Mitwalli, which once marked the southern boundary of el-Qahira. Legend has it that a very famous healer who performed miracles used to live here.

The **Mosque of al-Muayyad** (15th century), the two minarets of which are incorporated within the towers of Bab Zuwayla, is one of the most beautiful in Cairo. Its portal in black and white marble and doors of thick wood are richly embellished with bronze plaques. The interior is also splendidly adorned, though some of the friezes have been replaced with modern copies.

From the Bab Zuwayla, the main road, Sharia Darb el-Ahmar, runs southeast (becoming Sharia el-Tabbana and then Sharia Bab el-Wazir). It passes many notable buildings, including the mosque and tomb of the emir, Qagmas al-Ishaqi (also known as the **Mosque of Abu Huraybah**), the **Mosque of Altunbugha al-Maridani** and the **Mosque of Aqsunqur**. This last, built in 1346–47, was partly destroyed by an earthquake and restored in 1651, when it was decorated with tiles, hence its most common name, the Blue Mosque.

Another area rich in interesting buildings is that enclosing the mosques of Sultan Hasan and ibn Tulun, and the Citadel, extending towards Old Cairo. The mosques are east of Midan Saiyda Zeinab at the bottom of Sharia Bur Said or west of Midan Salah al-Din below the Citadel. The Mosque of ibn Tulun (876–879) is not only endowed with rich and splendid decorations, but also holds the distinction of being the most ancient of the mosques still in a good state of preservation. Adjacent to it is the beautiful **Gayer-Anderson Museum**, an annex of the Museum of Islamic Art. It consists of two former houses restored and refurbished by an Englishman before World War II. The museum has irregular levels, winding corridors and galleries with *mushrabiya*.

To the northeast is the magnificent **Mosque of Sultan Hasan** (built 1356–1362), representing the most vigorous period of the Muslim Middle Age. Its decorations are austerely applied on bare surfaces, creating a noble and mighty complex overlooked by imposing minarets. The gate is majestic and leads to a cross-shaped vestibule. In the central court is a fountain crowned by a great cupola that was once painted blue. Notwithstanding the passage of time and human negligence, which have stripped it of part of its original beauty, the mosque stands unique in the panorama of Islamic art. Nearby stand mosques of minor importance (all of which face Midan Salah al-Din), and **Bab el-Azab**, the entrance gate into the Citadel, which encloses mosques and a military museum within its mighty walls.

On the same level as the southern tip of Roda Island is the ancient district of Qasr el-Shama, or **Old Cairo**, where the main Christian religious buildings and the Coptic Museum are clustered. Also included within the Roman walls are numerous Christian cemeteries belonging to the various orthodox sects of the Orient (predominantly Greek), Roman towers, and the ancient **Mosque of ibn al-As**, built in 642 by Amr ibn al-As, which has many legends revolving around it. The column enclosed by a grill is said to have been miraculously transported from Mecca by the order of Mohammed himself. In addition to the most famous Coptic churches, one can admire the walls surrounding the Christian cemeteries. There are also some less famous convents and churches which have both charm and spiritual intensity. Amongst these are the Convent and Church of Abu Sefein and the Church of Amba Shenuda.

East of the Citadel are two large Muslim necropoli, also called the **City of the Dead**. Following a tradition which was certainly influenced by the creeds of ancient Egypt and very uncommon in the Islamic world, tombs and burial places were built and furnished as if they were proper homes. On feast days, it is customary for entire families to visit the tombs of their loved ones, enjoying picnics or even spending a few days in and around the tomb. The richest tombs also provide the housing of servants and keepers, stables etc, and at a glance the cemetery looks like a normal residential area. However, it is distinctly gloomy and colourless on closer inspection. After the Arab–Israeli wars of 1948 and 1967, many people from the war zones found refuge in the cities of the dead and only a small portion of the necropoli are visited by tourists.

The northern cemetery, or **Tombs of the Caliphs**, is located east of Sharia Saleh Salem, between al-Azhar and the Citadel, and comprises many mosques and sultans' tombs. Among the most interesting is the **Mausoleum of Sultan Barquq**, built by his son between 1400 and 1411. It has twin minarets in the Mamluk style and two beautiful cupolas with a zigzag decoration (probably the first in Egypt to be built in stone). At the entrance, a stone with mutilated hieroglyphics is used as a doorstep, allowing the symbolic act of trampling on paganism before entering the house of worship. A real masterpiece is the *minbar* (or pulpit) in sculpted stone and also particularly beautiful are the decorations of the two domes. The second-floor porch offers an impressive view of the vast necropoli.

The **Mausoleum of Barsbay** on the left-hand side of Sharia Gawhar el-Qa'id (el-Muslim) as you go northwest, is more modest, but has a very beautiful minaret made of ivory-inlaid wood forming arabesques, and a beautiful dome.

The **Mausoleum of Qaitbay** is a 15th-century masterpiece of Arabic art, delicate and harmonious in proportion and decoration. The southern cemetery or **Tombs of the Mamluks** is a large expanse stretching from the Citadel to Maadi. Its most interesting monuments are the mosques of **Imam al-Layth** and **Imam al-Shafii**, and many tombs of the Abbasid caliphs. Most of the other mosques are inaccessible to non-Muslims and are badly preserved.

COPTIC CAIRO

T he fortress of Babylon, probably originating in the Persian period (525 BC) but rebuilt by the Romans, stands at the centre of the Coptic district. Within these ancient walls the Copts enjoyed relative protection. Throughout the centuries, the Copts have generally lived peacefully alongside the Muslim majority. The Coptic churches were occasionally subjected to the religious intemperance of fanatic adversaries however, but the Copts were never actually persecuted by the Muslims in Egypt. In the quarters of Qasr el-Shama, better known as Old Cairo, Muslim houses may be found interspersed with Coptic homes and buildings. There is an old synagogue here, too, although very few of the once-large Jewish population remain.

The most ancient and interesting of the remaining Coptic churches are situated in the heart of Old Cairo. The early Coptic churches of Egypt were usually constructed according to a Roman basilica plan comprising a central nave with two side aisles separated from it by a colonnade; at one end was an apse. Today, all traces of the original churches have disappeared. The traditional Coptic church normally consists of the narthex, the choir, the sanctuary and a baptistry, almost always situated at the far end of the north wing. The north aisle is reserved for women. At the end of the nave is the choir, separated by a chancel screen. The sanctuary almost always consists of three chapels, each of which has its own altar. Placed exactly behind the principal altar is the tribune, marked by a throne for the bishop and seats of the officiating clergy. The typical early Coptic church, devoid of columns and paintings (elements introduced much later), was extremely simple and rather plain. The entrance façade often, if not always, had only one narrow doorway, in order to conceal the presence of a religious building in a sea of houses.

Constructed over the ruins of two towers of the Roman fortress of Babylon, the **Church of St Mary**, dating back to the fourth century, was called el-Moallaqah, meaning 'overhanging' or 'suspended', owing to the peculiarity of its construction. Laid out on a basilica plan with a single nave, it has a splendid baptistry. Destroyed in the ninth century, el-Moallaqah was later restored and, after numerous renovations, it was chosen as the seat of the Coptic patriarch in 1039.

The original **Church of St Sergius** (Abu Sarga) dedicated to St Sergius and St Bacchus, two soldiers who suffered the agonizing trials of martyrdom under the reign of Maximian, probably dates back to the fifth century. It was destroyed in the fire of Fustat in the reign of the last Umayyad caliph, Marwan II, in around 750. It is based on a basilica plan, but is made more beautiful by an elegant narthex that takes devotees into a vast central hall, divided by two lines of pillars. The Church of St Sergius brings to mind religious structures in Rome and Constantinople. The crypt, definable as another church, is situated right under the centre of the choir and dates back to the fifth century. This is certainly amongst the

An example of Coptic ecclesiastical art

most interesting parts of the entire complex of buildings which belong, for the most part, to the Fatimid era of the tenth and eleventh centuries.

Although the **Church of St Barbara** in Old Cairo was dedicated to St Cyrus and St John, the church is now known as the Church of St Barbara after the chapel which contains her remains. St Barbara was the young martyr of Nicomedia who died at the hands of her own father whom she tried to convert to Christianity. Of basilican type, the church probably dates back to the fifth century, and, like the church of St Sergius, it was reconstructed in about the 11th century. Particularly interesting and pleasing is the wooden architrave running over the capitals, which is one of the more characteristic features of Coptic architecture. In the 15th century, the Arab historian, Maqrizi, celebrated this particular church in his writing, describing it as the largest and most beautiful Coptic church of his time.

Of the other Coptic churches in Old Cairo, three are worth a special mention. The **Church of the Virgin** (Haret Zuweila), constructed in 350 and destroyed in

1321, was later restored and became the seat of the patriarch until 1860. The **Church of the Virgin** (Haret el-Rum) built in the sixth century, has undergone countless alterations. The **Church of St Peter and St Paul** was built in 1910, following the wishes of the family of Boutros Ghali Pasha. It has the typical features of primitive Egyptian churches.

The building which currently houses the **Coptic Museum** is situated to the south of the southernmost walls of Old Cairo, rising over one of those places identified by tradition as the setting of legendary battles between Horus and Seth. It is a site which is particularly fascinating and evocative even for modern Egyptians as it contains the world's richest collection of Coptic art and treasures. Founded in 1908 with treasures and materials mostly from private collections, the Coptic Museum has witnessed a notable rise in importance. It has been designated a state institution, and was granted the dazzling collection of Coptic documents once held in the Egyptian Museum. The Coptic Museum is well lit and well ordered. There are also excellent funerary stelae from ancient churches and monasteries here. The textile industry of the Copts has real artistic value both for its technique and for its mastery of design. It drew admiration from Muslims who later used Coptic models in their work. The superb murals and the vast series of icons on wooden tablets deserve special attention.

CENTRE OF CAIRO

Midan el-Tahrir, or **Liberation Square**, just north of Old Cairo, is the focal point of the modern tourist town, surrounded by the Egyptian Museum, a large number of the main city hotels, airline offices, ministries and government offices. Close to the Nile, the square is linked to **Gezira Island**, where numerous museums and sports clubs are located. The northern part of the island is occupied by the modern residential area of **Zamalek** where wide, well-lined avenues offer a change from the crowded centre of the city.

Not far from the Midan el-Tahrir, northwards along Sharia Soliman Pasha (its official name, though little used, is Sharia Talaat Harb), is **Midan Talaat Harb**, another square dense with traffic, shops and offices. It is crossed by **Sharia Qasr el-Nil**, an avenue full of luxury shops, and branch offices of international companies and banks. Sharia 26 July, a main road link, crosses the river at two points and passes through Gezira Island before following the left bank.

At the opposite end, the avenue leads eastwards to the **Ezbekiya Gardens**, which are often packed with people. The gardens retain their charm, nonetheless, and there are numerous little stands selling second-hand books. Adjacent to the gardens is the **Midan Opera**, in the square where the Opera Theatre stood until 1971, when it was destroyed by fire. To get to Khan al-Khalili, the bazaar area, cross the old, interesting quarter of **Muski**, which is full of markets and colourful commercial establishments.

With a character all its own, the bazaar of **Khan al-Khalili** is exactly what an oriental bazaar should be and more. It is laden with various kinds of goods, crowded with tourists, craftsmen and local people and filled with exotic odours. Its alleys, so narrow that the roofs block most of the sunshine, form a labyrinth in which it is easy to get lost. If the atmosphere approximates that of the past, the goods on sale cater for the tourist with a taste for cheap souvenirs and imitations of ancient models. However, the shops still resound with the hammering of coppersmiths and old-style sewing machines with which competent tailors can fashion every conceivable kind of garment within a few hours.

Bargaining is a must and is widely practised by foreigners and residents alike. Plan at least a half-day visit to the bazaar, and before purchasing anything compare prices amongst the different shops. A relaxing respite from shopping can be found at Fishawi, an authentic and characteristic café close to the Mosque of Sultan Hasan.

OUTSKIRTS OF CAIRO

HELIOPOLIS

Heliopolis (or Masr el-Gadida, which means 'New Town' in Arabic) is 20 kilometres (12.5 miles) from Cairo, on the road to Suez. Today, it is a modern residential quarter, but in ancient times it was one of the most famous cities of Egypt. Though without great political significance, it was of major religious importance.

The Egyptian name of the city was Iunu, meaning 'the Pillar', alluding to the pillars that supported the heavens. It appears in the Bible as 'On' suggesting the Egyptian pronunciation. Heliopolis, as the Greek name indicates, was the main centre of the worship of the sun. Here Ra was worshipped in his different forms: as Khepri, the scarab creator god; as Harakhty, the rising sun; as Ra, the falcon god of the midday sun; and as Atum, the dying sun of the evening. The great temple housed a sacred stone, the *ben-ben*, upon which the solar god had alighted at the moment of creation. This stone was the origin of the obelisk form. Excavations have revealed some monuments, now displayed in a small park near the metro station.

The classic view of the Pyramids of Giza: the pyramids of three queens and the pharaohs Menkaure and Khufu are dominated by the central pyramid of Khafre, built on slightly higher ground and still retaining some of its casing.

The temples of Heliopolis were vast, but little survives. It is likely that the temples that Akhenaten constructed at Amarna and Karnak were based on those of Heliopolis. These were open courts with hundreds of altars and a central raised sanctuary with the *ben-ben* as its focus. The temples of the Fifth Dynasty at Abu Ghurob north of Abusir may also give us an idea of the Heliopolitan sanctuaries. These too have open courts, *ben-ben* and altars, with places for sacrifice. One notable feature of the Fifth Dynasty temples is the relief sculpture decoration, with scenes depicting the natural world, 'all that the sun disc encircles'. Similar scenes occur in Amarna art, and both may reflect the decoration of the solar temples of Heliopolis. Many statues and obelisks were removed from Heliopolis to Alexandria and to Rome.

Heliopolis is supposed to have been a resting place of the Holy Family during their escape into Egypt. Here you can see an age-old sycamore called the Virgin's Tree which, according to legend, gave shelter to Mary (in reality, the tree was planted in the 17th century to replace an older one).

Desert horsemen, Giza

HELWAN

Helwan is about 25 kilometres (15.5 miles) south of Cairo on the eastern bank road of the Nile. North of the town are the residential quarters of Maadi and the Tura Hills, the source of the stones used to face the pyramids of Memphis. Helwan is renowned for its thermal sulphurous waters, which are believed to have curative powers for rheumatism, kidney problems and skin infections. Among the local attractions is the **Wax Museum**, which illustrates scenes from Egyptian life from the time of the pharaohs until the last century. It also holds a collection of traditional dolls from all over the world. A **Japanese garden**, the only one of its kind in the Arab countries, strikes an odd but welcome note for the visitor, with its Buddhas, artificial lakes and small pagodas. The **Residence of King Faruq** (1936–1952) is now a museum open to the public. Nearby is the **Astronomic Observatory**, founded in 1903, which is used for housing meteorological records. Helwan is also well known for its industrial installations.

GIZA

The pyramids of Giza, standing on the desert plateau 11 kilometres (6.8 miles) southwest of Cairo, were once surrounded by desert. Today, Cairo has spread to the very foot of the plateau, and the whole archaeological site has lost the mystery for which it was once famous. Indeed, many people find it a disappointing place. There are plans to restrict traffic and keep construction at a suitable distance, which will go some way to protecting the monuments and perhaps restore a little of the atmosphere.

Dominating the site are the pyramid complexes of the kings of the Fourth Dynasty (c.2613–2498 BC), Khufu (Cheops), Khafre (Chephren) and Menkaure (Mycerinus), surrounded by the tombs of their families and courtiers. Each pyramid complex comprised a number of features: pyramid temple, causeway and valley temple, which changed in design and scale, but were essential. The pyramid stood within a paved court and enclosure wall, with the temple on the eastern side, and a statue of the dead king in the adjacent shrine. The entrance to the pyramid was situated on the northern side. Subsidiary or satellite pyramids, thought to have been burial places for queens, were also located within the complex. Boat pits are found adjacent to the pyramids; one next to the Great Pyramid still contains the dismantled boat. A causeway connected the pyramid temple with the valley temple, which stood at the edge of the flood plain. Used to bring the casing stone from the river during construction, the causeway was afterwards enclosed, to serve as the corridor between the two temples.

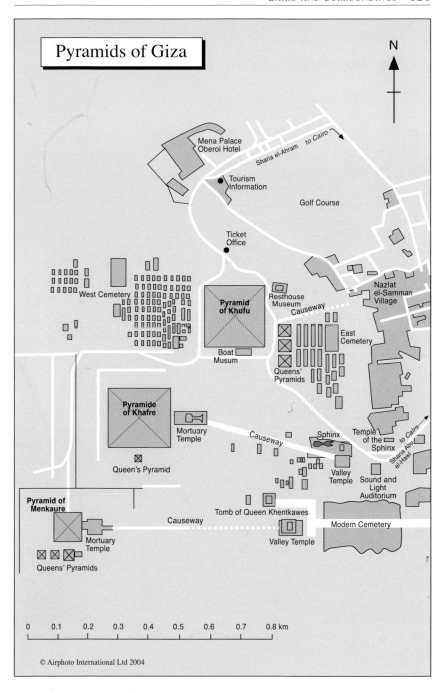

Pyramids of Giza

N

Mena Palace
Oberoi Hotel

Sharia el-Ahram   to Cairo

Tourism
Information

Golf Course

Ticket
Office

West Cemetery

Pyramid
of Khufu

Resthouse
Museum

Causeway

Nazlat
el-Samman
Village

East
Cemetery

Boat
Musum

Queens'
Pyramids

Pyramide
of Khafre

Mortuary
Temple

Causeway

Sphinx

Temple
of the
Sphinx

to Cairo

Sharia Abu
el-Hawl

Queen's Pyramid

Valley
Temple

Sound and
Light
Auditorium

Pyramid of
Menkaure

Causeway

Tomb of Queen Khentkawes

Modern Cemetery

Mortuary
Temple

Valley Temple

Queens' Pyramids

0   0.1   0.2   0.3   0.4   0.5   0.6   0.7   0.8 km

© Airphoto International Ltd 2004

Pyramid of Khufu (Cheops) (c.2589–2566 BC)

Only survivor of the Seven Wonders of the ancient world, the Great Pyramid has retained its fascination. Identified in the Middle Ages with the Granaries of Joseph, even more extreme ideas were developed by the 'pyramidiots' of the 19th century. They believed the pyramid, to put it simplistically, to be the repository of Divine Wisdom which could be understood through its measurements. One of the most influential proponents of these ideas was Charles Piazzi Smyth, whose disciple, Flinders Petrie, came to make a careful survey of the pyramids in 1880. Finding that Piazzi Smyth's theories were based on inaccurate measurements, Petrie rapidly abandoned the theories and devoted himself to a life in scientific archaeology, becoming the first Professor of Egyptology in Britain, at London University, in 1892. Even today, many wild theories are still proposed for the alien origin and function of the pyramids, but Egyptologists have no doubt that they were nothing more than royal tombs. In recent years there has been renewed excitement with the 'discovery' of a sealed doorway in one of the 'air shafts'. Initial investigations were followed-up in September 2002, making a hole in the door, only to reveal a second one a little way further on. Egyptologists suspect that the shaft was sealed when changes were made in the design of the pyramid, moving the burial chamber from the so-called 'Queen's Chamber' to the burial chamber ('King's Chamber') at the heart of the pyramid. This would have made the old shafts redundant.

The Great Pyramid, covering 13.1 acres at its base, had an original height of 140 metres (481 feet); the top 31 feet are now missing. Each side was originally 230 metres (755 feet) long, which is 440 Egyptian cubits. The sides incline at an angle of 51° 50' to the ground. The pyramid was originally faced in fine white limestone from the quarries at Tura on the opposite bank of the river; parts of this can be found at the base on the west side, but most was stripped away and used as building material for medieval Cairo. The visit inside the pyramid is rather an anticlimax, the most impressive feature being the Grand Gallery, an inclining corridor 8.5 metres high and 47 metres long, with a corbel vault. The burial, or King's Chamber, is built entirely of granite, with an empty and unadorned black granite sarcophagus. The ceiling of the burial chamber, of nine slabs, weighs about 400 tons. The construction, with five relieving chambers above the burial chamber, is a splendid feat of engineering, but cannot be seen.

Desert graveyard with pyramids in the background, Giza

Of the temple annexed at the eastern side of the pyramid, only the basalt flooring remains, though its actual layout and plan have been reconstructed. The processional causeway has also been largely destroyed, although some sculptured blocks have been recovered from it. The valley temple lies beneath the modern village and is unlikely to be cleared. Three small pyramids along the eastern side belonged to queens and princesses.

In 1925, a cache was discovered on the eastern side of the pyramid. This contained the coffin and burial furniture of Queen Hetepheres, wife of Sneferu and mother of Khufu. The coffin proved to be empty, leading the excavator, George Reisner, to speculate that the queen's original burial at Dashur had been disturbed, but that no one dared to tell the king that her body had been destroyed. So the pretence of the reburial remained until modern times. The furniture is now reconstructed in the upper galleries of the Egyptian Museum, and reveals an elegance and simplicity which can also be noted in the architecture of the Giza temples. Stylistically, this period is probably more appealing to modern taste than the extravagant and opulent products of the later New Kingdom, exemplified by the treasures of Tutankhamun.

The Boat Museum on the south side is more interesting, to most visitors, than the pyramid itself. The boat was excavated from a pit in 1954 and reconstructed. In cedar wood from Lebanon, the boat, 43 metres (140 feet) long, is of extraordinary grace, with high prow and sternposts. It would have ridden very high in the water, and was probably towed by other barges. A second boat pit is adjacent to the museum, with its dismantled boat still inside. They were at first believed to be the solar barques in which the king would cross the sky. However, they may actually have been used to take the king's mummified body to Abydos and bring it back to Giza for burial.

Pyramid of Khafre (Chephren) (c.2558–2532 BC)

The pyramid gives a false impression of being larger than its neighbour, which is achieved by its being built on slightly higher ground. Although considerably smaller at the base than the Great Pyramid, the steeper inclination of its sides (52°) increased its height. Today, it stands 136.5 metres high and measures 214.8 metres square at the base. The court surrounding the pyramid is the original area from which stone was quarried for its construction. Red granite was used for the lowest course of the casing, the remainder being Tura limestone, still preserved towards the apex. The internal arrangement of the pyramid is far simpler than that of the Great Pyramid, with the passage and chamber cut from the bedrock and the pyramid raised over them.

The complex of the second pyramid is better preserved than that of the Great Pyramid, with much more of the pyramid temple and causeway surviving and the valley temple (also known as the Granite Temple) almost intact. Constructed of massive blocks of limestone, faced inside and out with enormous blocks of red Aswan granite, the interior strikes the visitor as surprisingly small. One feature of construction is the way that the blocks have been fitted into position: rather than regular blocks just piled up, some are rabbeted to the adjacent block, others have the corners carved into them. The entrance leads to a long hall from which a door opens onto the second hall, T-shaped, with monolithic granite piers. The work here is of excellent quality, and the design is elegant if austere (compared with the pyramid temple of Sahure at Abusir). The floor is of alabaster and around the walls stood 23 statues of the king in schist, diorite and alabaster. The best-preserved, and rightly famous, image is now in the Egyptian Museum, with fragments of the others. Slits at the top of the walls allowed light to be reflected onto the statues from the alabaster floor and piers. There was neither relief sculpture nor painted decoration.

Sphinx

The Sphinx (Greek, from the ancient Egyptian *shesep-ankh*, 'Living Image') is carved from an outcrop left after quarrying stone for the Great Pyramid. It measures some 20 metres (65.6 feet) in height and 57 metres (187 feet) in length. The deterioration of the Sphinx in recent times is due, at least in part, to the poor quality of the stone, which is why it was left by the Egyptians in the first place. Further damage has been caused by time, pollution and a rising water table. The Sphinx has the features of Khafre, the body is that of a lion. Later worshipped as an image of the sun god Harakhty (Horus of the Horizon), a solar crown was added to its head. Between the paws, Thutmose IV erected his 'Dream Stele' recording his accession as king and the clearing of sand from the Sphinx. Later restoration was carried out in the Roman period. The temple of the Sphinx is of the same construction as the valley temple of Khafre and was probably also built by him: it seems to form part of the same complex. In the New Kingdom another temple was built close by.

(following pages) *The Great Sphinx at Giza. Part of the funerary complex of Khafre, the Sphinx combines the king's head with a lion's body, representing him as the celestial ruler.*

There have been claims that the weathering visible on the Sphinx was caused by water erosion and that it must therefore have been carved around 10,000 BC when climatic conditions were different. These speculations obviously question our general interpretation of the development of society and 'civilization', but are generally dismissed by Egyptologists as ludicrous.

Pyramid of Menkaure (Mycerinus) (c.2532–2503 BC)

This is the smallest of the three main pyramids at Giza, being 66.5 metres high and 108 metres square at the base. The lowest 16 courses are covered in red granite from Aswan, but the upper parts are unfinished. It is unknown whether they too would have been granite, or limestone. The blocks are un-smoothed, except around the entrance, where there is a large restoration inscription by Khaemwaset, son of Ramesses II. A basalt sarcophagus with panelled decoration was discovered in the burial chamber but was lost at sea while being transported to England. A wooden coffin, a 26th-dynasty restoration of the burial, is now in the British Museum. Three satellite pyramids, one cased in granite blocks, were probably for Menkaure's wives.

The funerary temple of Menkaure, situated on the east side of the pyramid, was completed, like the rest of the complex, by his successor, Shepseskaf. Mud-brick with a limestone facing was used instead of the intended black granite. The valley temple was completed in mud-brick with only the thresholds and paving in stone. A series of splendid sculptures was found here depicting the king and his consort, with the goddess Hathor and the nome deities. In alabaster and schist, they are now in the Egyptian Museum and the Boston Museum of Fine Arts.

ABUSIR

The first and last kings of the Fifth Dynasty chose to be buried near the Step Pyramid of Djoser at Saqqara, but the intervening rulers selected a site a little to the north of Saqqara, at Abusir. For those with enough time, it is an interesting site for a visit on the return from Saqqara. Most of the pyramids are in poor condition, having been constructed of rubble with a facing of Tura limestone. The pyramid of Neferefre is badly ruined, and that of Neferirkare was never finished. The causeway leading to Neferirkare's complex was altered so that it could serve the pyramid of Neuserre. The most significant monuments are the northernmost pyramid, of Sahure, and the mastaba of Ptah-shepses. To the north of the pyramid area were the sun temples of Abu Ghurob. The monuments here attracted the attention of Egyptians of the New Kingdom and Late Period. There is a record in the first hall of a visit to the mastaba

CLIMBING THE PYRAMIDS

At the distance of a few miles the Pyramids rising above the palms looked very clean-cut, very grand and imposing, and very soft and filmy, as well. They swam in a rich haze that took from them all suggestions of unfeeling stone, and made them seem only the airy nothings of a dream—structures which might blossom into tiers of vague arches, or ornate colonnades, maybe, and change and change again, into all graceful forms of architecture, while we looked, and then melt deliciously away and blend with the tremulous atmosphere.

A laborious walk in the flaming sun brought us to the foot of the great Pyramid of Cheops. It was a fairy vision no longer. It was a corrugated, unsightly mountain of stone. Each of its monstrous sides was a wide stairway which rose upward, step above step, narrowing as it went, till it tapered to a point far aloft in the air.

Of course we were beseiged by a rabble of muscular Egyptians and Arabs who wanted the contract of dragging us to the top—all tourists are. Of course you could not hear your own voice for the din that was around you. Of course the Sheiks said they were the only responsible parties; that all contracts must be made with them, all moneys paid over to them, and none exacted from us by any but themselves alone. Of course they contracted that the varlets who dragged us up should not mention bucksheesh once. For such is the usual routine. Of course we contracted with them, paid them, were delivered into the hands of the draggers, dragged up the Pyramids, and harried and be-deviled for bucksheesh from the foundation clear to the summit. We paid it, too, for we were purposely spread very far apart over the vast side of the Pyramid. There was no help near if we called, and the Herculeses who dragged us had a way of asking sweetly and flatteringly for bucksheesh, which was seductive, and of looking fierce and threatening to throw us down the precipice, which was persuasive and convincing.

Each step being full as high as a dinner-table; there being very, very many of the steps; an Arab having hold of each of our arms and springing upward from step to step and snatching us with them, forcing us to lift our feet as high as our breasts every time, and do it rapidly and keep it up till we were ready to faint, who shall say it is not a lively, exhilarating, lacerating, muscle-straining, bone-wrenching and perfectly excruciating and exhausting pastime, climbing the Pyramids? I beseeched the varlets not to twist all my joints asunder; I iterated, reiterated, even swore to them that I did not wish to beat anybody to the top; did all I could to convince them that if I got there the last of all I would feel blessed above men and grateful to them forever; I begged them, prayed them, pleaded with them to let me stop and rest a moment—only one little moment: and they only answered with some more frightful springs, and an unenlisted volunteer behind opened a bombardment of determined boosts with his head which threatened to batter my whole political economy to wrack and ruin.

Twice, for one minute, they let me rest while they extorted bucksheesh, and then continued their maniac flight up the Pyramid. They wished to beat the other parties. It was nothing to them that I, a stranger, must be sacrificed upon the alter of their unholy ambition. But in the midst of sorrow, joy blooms. Even in this dark hour I had a sweet consolation. For I knew that except these Mohammedans repented they would go straight to perdition some day. And they never repent—they never forsake their paganism. This thought calmed me, cheered me, and I sank down, limp and exhausted, upon the summit, but happy, so happy and serene within.

Mark Twain, Traveling with the Innocents Abroad, 1869 (Mark Twain's Original Reports from Europe and the Holy Land), *edited by Daniel Morley McKeithan, University of Oklahoma Press, 1958*

Mark Twain (1835–1910), distinguished American writer, was born Samuel Langhorne Clemens. Halley's comet was visible at the time of his birth, making his arrival an even more momentus occasion. From June to November 1867, Twain travelled throughout Europe aboard the *Quaker City* steamship.

of Ptah-shepses by two scribes in year 50 of Ramesses II. The same pharaoh had the obelisk in the sun temple of Neuserre restored. Artists copied the scenes in the temple of Sahure, and one was replicated in a temple built by the Kushite pharaoh Taharqo at Kawa in the northern Sudan (*c*.680 BC).

The pyramid of Sahure (*c*.2487–2475 BC) is badly ruined and is dangerous inside. It is sometimes possible to enter, but requires torches and a short crawl on the stomach. Arriving in what at first sight appears to be the burial chamber, it is a shock to find that you are actually standing above the blocks of the pointed roof to the burial chamber. This is one of the few opportunities to see the construction of a pyramid. The most interesting and significant feature of the complex is the temple attached to the pyramid. Far more elaborate in design than those at Giza, the open court was floored in polished basalt, surrounded by a colonnade of red-granite date-palm columns which supported a ceiling of white limestone originally painted blue with gold stars in low relief. The excavator, Ludwig Borchardt, calculated that there were originally 10,000 square metres of relief decoration, of which only about 150 square metres survive (good collections in Cairo and Berlin).

If open, the mastaba of Ptah-shepses has some interesting features, although the decoration is ordinary. Ptah-shepses was a high official of the reign of Neuserre, and married a member of the royal family. Most notable are the rooms off the southwest corner of the court, shaped to take full-size boats. Care should be taken here as the floor can give way. Also off the court, a smooth, sloping passage leads to the burial chambers which are open to the sky. Here the sarcophagi are impressive.

Abusir has recently been the focus of excavations and conservation by the Czech Institute. Amongst the many significant discoveries they have found mastabas of the Fifth Dynasty, and tombs of the New Kingdom and Late Periods. One of the most important finds is the intact tomb of Iufaa, a high official at the end of the 26th Dynasty.

MEMPHIS

T he unification of Upper and Lower Egypt and the foundation of the city of Memphis by Meni (Narmer; Greek: *Menes*) mark the beginning of Egyptian dynastic history. In fact, Meni was probably a half-mythical king, a composite of a number of rulers who brought about the unification of the country. Nevertheless, the Egyptians regarded Meni as the founder of the state, and Memphis was to remain Egypt's major administrative city throughout its history. Situated close to the junction of the Delta and the Nile Valley, it was in a prime position to govern the two lands.

The original name of Memphis was Inbu-hedj, the 'White Walls' (or the 'White Castle'), from its fortress enclosure. In later times it was referred to using the name of the pyramid of Pepi I, meaning 'Established and Beautiful' (in Egyptian, *Men-nofer*, pronounced *Menfi* by the 7th century BC, becoming *Memphis* in Greek).

During the Old Kingdom, Memphis was the chief administrative city, while Iunu (Heliopolis), not far away on the eastern bank of the river, was the major centre for the worship of the sun. Ancient Egyptian cities were not like modern ones; each king built himself a new palace and the government buildings gathered around this. Surveys and excavations of the past decade suggest that the earliest settlement was to the north of the major remains, near Abusir. In the Fourth Dynasty, the royal city of Memphis was probably near Giza, moving further south to the valley below Saqqara in the Fifth and Sixth dynasties. Of course, the major temples of Ptah and the other local gods, as well as shipyards and harbours, remained in the same place. The mounds of the ruins of ancient Memphis today cover a huge area, but much of what can be seen dates from the New Kingdom and the Late Period.

The rulers of the Middle Kingdom chose the southern districts of Memphis, standing between the river valley and the entrance to the Faiyum, as their residence and burial place. These kings did much to expand the agricultural potential of the Faiyum region, cutting canals and extending irrigation, so that from this time on it was one of the most important parts of Egypt.

Memphis lost some of its importance during the periods of disunity (the First and Second Intermediate Periods), but with the advent of the New Kingdom it again became a major city. From here, the kings of the 18th Dynasty set out on their campaigns to Asia, and to the city's ports came the products of the conquered lands. The Temple of Ptah was probably as big as that of Amun at Karnak, but much of the stone in the city's ruins was carried off in the medieval period in order to build Cairo. The Alabaster Sphinx and the Colossus of Ramesses II hint at the now lost glories of Egypt's first city.

In the Late Period, Memphis had large foreign communities, each with their own district: Jews, Phoenicians, Syrians and Greeks all resided here, with their own temples and cults. The city continued to flourish under Ptolemaic rule and some of the kings were crowned in the Temple of Ptah. With the Mediterranean as the centre of the Hellenistic and Roman worlds, Alexandria's position on the sea inevitably gave her pre-eminence and Memphis, whilst remaining an important religious centre, declined in commercial and military significance.

The chief deity of Memphis was Ptah, a patron of crafts, and himself a creator god at whose word all things came into being. He was usually shown mummiform. He became associated with another god of the region, the falcon Sokar, a god of death and fertility; later both Ptah and Sokar were assimilated with Osiris. Ptah's consort was the lioness goddess, Sakhmet, the violent daughter of the sun god, Ra, but also a healer. Their child was the blue lotus flower, Nefertum. By the New Kingdom, there were also temples to Amun and many other deities in Memphis, including the Syrians Baal, Astarte and Reshep.

The ruin-field of Memphis is vast, but much of it is now covered by agriculture; other parts are not generally accessible. Altogether, the remains of Egypt's most important city are not impressive due very largely to the destruction of many of the temples and stone buildings for the construction of medieval Cairo. The monuments visited are close to the remains (usually inaccessible) of the temple built by Ramesses II. Here, in an **Open Air Museum**, a number of statues and stelae have been re-erected near two monuments *in situ*. The **limestone colossus of Ramesses II** lies prone, with a viewing gallery built around it. This splendid statue is some 10.3 metres (33.8 feet) in height, despite the loss of its feet. These images of the god-king must be visualized in a setting like that of Karnak, dominating the entrances to the temple. Also in the enclosure is the **Alabaster Sphinx**, for many years lying on its side in water, hence the damage to the surface. Actually of crystalline limestone, this unusually large sphinx predates the Ramesside temple, having been erected by an 18th-dynasty monarch. Although uninscribed, the facial features suggest an attribution to Hatshepsut or Amenhotep II.

Close to the Ptah temple was the precinct of the god's earthly manifestation, the Apis bull. As Herald of Ptah, the Apis acted as intermediary between god and people. Near the museum, on the north side of the road to Saqqara, are the remains of the embalming house, built in the Late Period, with some of the embalming tables on view. From this area a great avenue ran to the Serapeum at Saqqara, lined with sphinxes and ascending the escarpment in a series of terraced temples. Of this processional route, only the Circle of Philosophers near the Rest House at Saqqara is now visible.

Excavation and survey work have been carried out in the Memphis region for over a century, vastly increasing our knowledge of this great city, but it is only by comparing the vestiges with the much better-preserved monuments of Thebes that we can gain any real impression of ancient Memphis. The temples of Ptah must have rivalled those of Amun at Karnak in size and splendour. The main Temple of Ptah was connected by canal with the Temple of Hathor, Lady of the Southern Sycamore, cutting a ceremonial route through the city. Ptah sailed along this canal on his annual visit to his neighbour, as Amun sailed to Luxor during the Opet Festival. Other canals and processional ways, some leading to the necropolis, divided the city into sections; they were probably lined with sphinxes and trees, statues and shrines, as at Thebes. To the north of the Ptah temple lay the district of the royal palaces—remains of a 26th-dynasty structure, known as the Palace of Apries, survive near a modern military camp—and farther north still were the harbours and dockyards. While the remains of the city of Memphis may be disappointing, the monuments of its necropolis are numerous and splendid.

Saqqara

The great necropolis of Memphis stretches for some 30 kilometres along the desert plateau, from Dashur in the south to Abu Rawash, north of Giza. While these northern and southern limits were favoured in the Fourth Dynasty the central part of the cemetery, Saqqara, was in regular use from the First Dynasty to the Graeco-Roman Period. The name Saqqara may derive from that of the Egyptian god of this region, Sokar.

Although the elegantly decorated tomb-chapels of the New Kingdom are currently the object of excavation and restoration, it is the monuments of the Old Kingdom that form the focus for the visitor. The massive mud-brick mastabas of the First and Second dynasties lie along the edge of the escarpment, but are presently inaccessible. The central and most important monument on site is the Third-dynasty **Step Pyramid of Djoser**. The earliest large-scale stone building in the world, the complex comprises courts and halls surrounding the pyramid itself, all within a vast enclosure wall. Many of the buildings are in fact dummies: rubble structures faced in polished stone, but without internal chambers. Although the use of small blocks of stone did not allow for the massiveness we now associate with Egyptian architecture, this edifice was a turning point. Here we can see the mud-brick, wood and reed architecture of early Egypt translated into stone. Such was its impact that Imhotep, the architect of this revolutionary monument, was later worshipped as a god. The site has been excavated and sensitively restored over a period of many years by the French Egyptologist J P Lauer.

The complex can be reached from the pyramid of Unas by the steps over the southern wall, but is more easily understood if entered through the gateway in the east wall. This gate, the only ancient entrance to the complex, leads into a columned hall: note that the great doors are carved of stone, standing permanently open. The columns of the hall are restored, but not to their full height; they are reed bundles, each engaged to a wall, creating a series of niches. The ceiling blocks of this hall were carved to resemble palm logs. The hall leads directly to the great court. Rather than entering the court, it is best to follow the narrow passage out of the colonnade hall (near the main entrance) to the north. This twists and emerges onto the *heb-sed* court where the most impressive buildings are found. The court has a dais at the southern end and a series of chapel façades. The southernmost is a pylon-shaped 'tent-shrine'. The rest are pavilions modelled upon the archaic Shrine of Upper Egypt, with three narrow reed columns supporting a curved roof. Large holes at the top of each column probably held elephant tusks or flagstaves, or some means of identifying which god resided in the chapel. A winding passage leads to the doorway of each of these chapels; at the entrances to the passages can be found a carved stone door and an imitation wooden fence in stone.

Coming to the east side of the pyramid, you can see the original mastaba construction (emphasized by the restoration). Two more buildings, the House of the North and the House of the South, are here. They have twisting passages and a suite of cruciform chapels, some containing later graffiti. The chapels were similar, being larger versions of those in the *heb-sed* court with four instead of three slender columns. The façade was screened with a low wall reaching just above the height of the door and surmounted by the *khekher* frieze. The buildings are restored to this height, which is less than a third of their original size. Near the House of the North are some fine, engaged papyrus columns. The entrance to the pyramid was on the north side where, adjacent to the remains of the temple, can be found the serdab, with a cast of the splendid statue of the king (the original is in the Egyptian Museum). Here, also, one can see the pyramids of Abusir and Giza in the distance. Beneath the pyramid is a series of galleries and chambers, some decorated with stelae showing the king performing the rituals of the *sed*-festival and with blue faïence tiles imitating reed matting (inaccessible, but one of these has been restored and is now in the Egyptian Museum). Huge quantities of stone vessels were also discovered here.

The main court can be reached either by continuing around the west side, or by returning around the east side. The great court had two B-shaped structures which probably represented the bounds around which the king had to run during the *sed*-festival. On the south side of the pyramid, restoration has clearly marked the various stages of construction. The first building was a mastaba which was then enlarged,

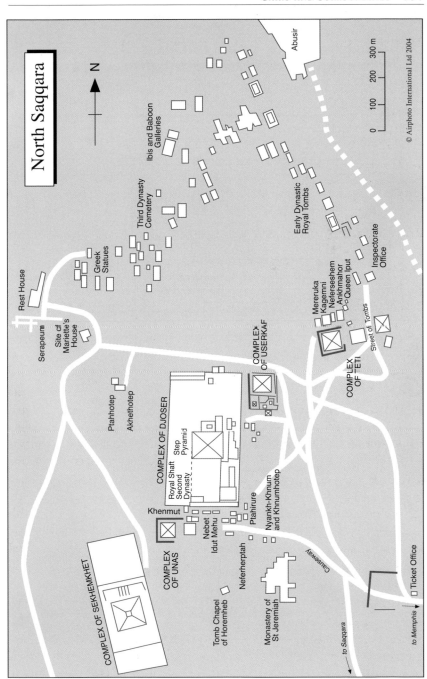

North Saqqara

N

Abusir

© Airphoto International Ltd 2004

0   100   200   300 m

Ibis and Baboon Galleries

Third Dynasty Cemetery

Early Dynastic Royal Tombs

Greek Statues

Inspectorate Office

Rest House

Mereruka
Kagemni
Neferseshem
Ankhmahor
Queen Iput

Serapeum

Site of Mariette's House

COMPLEX OF USERKAF

Street of Tombs

COMPLEX OF 'ETI

Ptahhotep

Akhethotep

COMPLEX OF DJOSER

Step Pyramid

Royal Shaft
Second
Dynasty

Khenmut

Nebet
Idut Mehu

Ptahirure

Nyankh-Khnum
and Khnumhotep

COMPLEX OF UNAS

Neferherptah

COMPLEX OF SEKHEMKHET

Tomb Chapel
of Horemheb

Monastery of
St Jeremiah

Causeway

to Saqqara

to Memphis   □ Ticket Office

Saqqara: Step Pyramid of Djoser

N

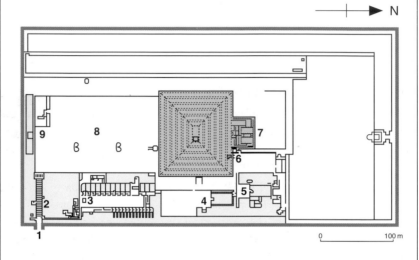

0   100 m

1 Entrance: Note the stone gate that stands permanently open.
2 Hall with engaged pillars. This hall leads directly to the open court in front of the pyramid, and by the winding passage to the *heb-sed* court.
3 The *heb-sed* court with throne dais at the southern end, surrounded by 'dummy' chapels.
4 The House of the South, representing the shrine at Nekhen (Hierakonpolis) with lily capitals. The passage leads to a room with statue niches. New Kingdom graffiti in ink identify the builder of the complex as Djoser, confirming his identification with Netjer-khet.
5 The House of the North, representing the shrine at Buto with papyrus capitals.
6 The serdab, with a replica of the seated statue of the king (original now in the Egyptian Museum, Cairo).
7 Badly ruined temple, unusually on north side (views of Abusir and Giza pyramids).
8 The great court with a throne dais in front of the pyramid, and the two B-shaped boundary markers around which the king ran in the jubilee rites.
9 The south tomb (not usually accessible), with galleries covered in blue tiles, in imitation of reed matting, and relief panels showing the king performing the rites of the *sed*-festival (comparable panels in Egyptian Museum, Cairo). Around the wall is a fine reconstructed area showing the panelling and uraeus frieze. From the top of the enclosure wall, good views south towards south Saqqara and the Dashur pyramids.

Source: Robert Morkot

later raised to a four-stepped pyramid, and finally to one of six steps. Opposite the pyramid stands the south tomb with its deep shaft. Perhaps used for the burial of the king's viscera, its exact function remains uncertain. Notice here the section of restored wall with uraeus frieze. Modern steps lead out over the enclosure wall. Looking from the wall to the south, one sees beyond the pyramids of South Saqqara to Dashur, with the **Mastabat al-Faraun** in the middle distance. Taking the shape of a sarcophagus, the Mastabat al-Faraun (Pharaoh's Bench), is the tomb of Shepseskaf, successor to Menkaure and last king of the Fourth Dynasty. This unusual structure is built of limestone, with chambers of granite.

A second step pyramid complex, built by Sekhemkhet a little to the south and west of Djoser's was never completed. It was excavated by the Egyptian archaeologist, Zakaria Goneim, who dubbed it the Buried Pyramid. Inside he found an alabaster sarcophagus with an unusual sliding end instead of a lid.

The pyramid of Unas (c.2375–2345 BC), last king of the Fifth Dynasty, lies to the south of the Step Pyramid. The pyramid itself is in poor repair, but the burial chambers are worth visiting. The low corridor descends steeply and passes under a series of portcullises, ending in a suite of rooms. The burial chamber itself is covered with inscriptions in sunk relief filled with blue pigment. These are the Pyramid Texts, prayers and utterances to effect the resurrection of the king. They include the 'Cannibal Hymn' in which the king gains power through eating the gods. The end of the chamber, surrounding the basalt sarcophagus, is faced in alabaster and decorated with a beautiful 'palace façade', delicately carved and painted.

On the south face of the pyramid are the remains of a large inscription of Prince Khaemwaset, High Priest of Memphis and a son of Ramesses II. He had antiquarian interests and was responsible for the restoration of many monuments in the Memphite necropolis. Khaemwaset was later made the hero of a tale in which he discovers a magic book in one of the tombs. The historical Khaemwaset died before his father so never became king; he was buried in the Serapeum.

On the south side of the Unas pyramid, one of the Persian tombs is accessible. Entry is via a very long (modern) spiral staircase (25 metres deep). The three small chambers have enormous sarcophagi and some simple, but technically excellent, relief. They are the burial places of the chief physician Psamtik, his son, Pediese, and the admiral, Djenhebu, and are worth visiting if you have time.

It is possible to look down into another of the deep Persian shafts on the east side of the pyramid (taking care of hats and other items that may drop down). Here also are the remains of the Unas' pyramid temple, largely destroyed but for a few

fragments, and the narrow granite door which marks the entrance to the temple from the causeway leading up from the valley temple. Between the causeway of Unas and the Step Pyramid are avenues of mastaba tombs, some of which are open. Whilst typical and nicely decorated, they are not the most important or impressive at Saqqara. The mastaba of Princess Idut, a daughter of Unas, was originally built for an official but taken over by the princess. It has some attractive fishing scenes.

The **causeway of Unas** has been excavated (for about 700 metres) and in places restored, roofed-over as it would have been. Fine relief decoration covers the walls and the star ceiling has a narrow slit to admit light. Descending the causeway, you can see some of the boat pits on the right. The valley temple itself is visible on entering the Saqqara site, directly opposite the modern ticket office. A number of tombs, which were buried when the causeway was built, have been cleared. Of these, the double tomb of the royal manicurists, Nyankh-Khnum and Khnumhotep, is the most interesting, with some excellent relief decoration. A freestanding tomb, it lay directly in the path of the Unas causeway, which was built over the top of it. Although they were depicted with their respective wives and children, it is the two officials who dominate the tomb. In several places they are shown in the sort of close embrace usually reserved for husband and wife, or king and deity. They are suggested to have been brothers.

South of the Unas causeway, over the ridge, lies the New Kingdom cemetery where, in the past two decades, some important tombs have been rediscovered by the joint Egypt Exploration Society–Leiden Museum and University expedition. These tombs were known in the 19th century, but their precise positions lost. They include the tomb of Horemheb, who was the leading army general under Tutankhamun, and later became pharaoh himself; the tomb of Tia and his wife, also called Tia, who was a sister of Ramesses II; and the tomb of Maya, treasury official to Tutankhamun. The relief decoration of these chapels is superb, but they are currently a restricted area. Many statues and blocks of relief sculpture were removed from these tombs to European museums in the 19th century (notably Berlin, Leiden, London and Bologna).

The road from the parking area by the Step Pyramid passes the ruined **pyramid of Userkaf** (c.2494–2487 BC), first king of the Fifth Dynasty. Now little more than a pile of rubble on the east side of the Djoser complex, it was unusual in having its temple on the south side. A portico covered with exquisite relief decoration, unfortunately shattered into fragments, surrounded the court. Particularly notable

Although the camel is everywhere in modern Egypt, it did not appear there as a domesticated animal until some two thousand years after the pyramids of Giza were built.

of the surviving reliefs is the fragment with birds in a papyrus thicket, now in Cairo (Egyptian Museum). Also from the court, a magnificent, colossal granite head of the king was recovered, a part of his cult image (Egyptian Museum). Close to the pyramid was the tomb of one of Userkaf's officials, Ka-aper, whose splendid wooden statue is a fine example of this medium (Egyptian Museum).

The most impressive group of mastabas lies to the north of the Step Pyramid complex, near the **pyramid of Teti**, first king of the Sixth Dynasty. This pyramid also has texts in the burial chamber, not as well preserved as those in the Unas pyramid, but easy of access and less visited. The courtiers of Teti were buried in the Street of Tombs near the pyramid. For those with little time, the **mastaba of Mereruka** is probably the most worthwhile. The largest at Saqqara, this mastaba contains 32 chambers, with some fine reliefs. In the entrance hall a scene of hunting in the marshes has a typical Old Kingdom device of birds, animals and people laid against a rippled background of papyrus reeds, an effective and pleasing technique. Note here the hippopotamus and crocodile conflict. Notice also the frog; it is easily spotted due to the greasy black patch, caused by countless tourists who have felt obliged to rub the relief. This type of damage is difficult to repair, and regrettably all too common in these tombs. The next two small rooms have scenes of agriculture and crafts, and the punishment of tax defaulters. A large room to the right is less finely decorated, but has interesting scenes of dancing and of Mereruka's wife playing the harp. The pillars of the large hall have splendid large figures of Mereruka in various costumes. A painted statue of the tomb owner emerges from the shrine, with the offering table beneath. Note his stylized athletic body, compared with the rather plumper figure in the reliefs. To the right, a door leads into a suite of chambers for Mereruka's son, Mery-Teti: these are unfinished. To the left of the shrine is a famous scene of force-feeding animals, including various antelopes and hyenas. Interpretations of this differ, some seeing it as an animal hospital, others as them being fattened for the table. A splendid group of Mereruka supported by his two sons and Mereruka carried in a palanquin follow. The next wall has fine ships. Going through the small door in the corner of the room brings one into another series of rooms, eventually connecting with the first chambers. A further suite of rooms lies off the entrance hall. This was for Mereruka's wife, Watet-khet-hor, a daughter of King Teti.

The relief decoration in the **mastaba of Kagemni** is generally thought to be finer than that of Mereruka. The tomb itself is less complex. Some other mastaba in the Street of Tombs may on occasion be open. Of these, the most renowned is that of the vizier, Ankhmahor, with its scenes of circumcision and other operations.

Saqqara: Mastaba of Mereruka

Mereruka

Vizier, Overseer of the Town, Inspector of Prophets in the Pyramid of Teti (Sixth Dynasty)

1 Mereruka sits at his easel painting the four seasons.
2 Gardening; fowling; leading cattle across a canal.
3 The hippopotamus hunt. A splendid example with the carved papyrus stems forming a fine background to the life in the marsh. The hippos, with large tusks, are hunted with harpoons: frogs and grasshoppers in the plant behind.
4 Carpentry; making stone vessels.
5 Desert hunt; craft scenes, including metal-workers heating a furnace by blowing through pipes, weighing metal, dwarves as jewellers, and large images of jewellery, including collars with heavy counterpoises and a diadem with streamers.
6 Fishing; preparing fish; caged birds.
7 Estate managers come to give the accounts of their farms to Mereruka and his scribes who are seated beneath a porch with lotus bud pillars.
8 The serdab (statue chamber).
9 Feeding birds.
10 Fishing.
11 Mereruka sits on his bed, his wife plays the harp.
12 Dancers and musicians.
13 Butchers.
14 Granaries and viticulture.
15 Funeral ceremonies.
16 Mereruka's pets and dwarves.
17 Mereruka carried in a palanquin; a large group with high relief showing Mereruka supported by his sons; a large figure of Mereruka watches the feeding of cattle, gazelles and ibex; force-feeding of hyenas; dwarves with pets; children's games.
18 The statue of Mereruka emerges from a door, with offering table in front.
19 Fishing; agricultural scenes; Mereruka and his wife play *senet*.
20 Unfinished suite for Mereruka's son, Mery-Teti, Vizier to Pepi I.
21 The suite for Mereruka's wife, Watet-khet-Hor, called Sesh-seshet, daughter of King Teti.
22 Shaft to burial place.

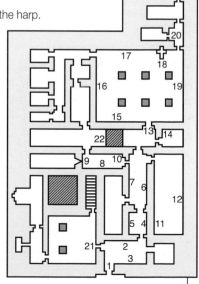

Source: Robert Morkot

A large double mastaba can be visited on the way to the Rest House. Built for Ptahhotep and his father, Akhethotep, in the late Fifth Dynasty, the scenes are of the usual type, but of excellent quality. Note particularly the various fowl from the estate.

A short walk from the Rest House is the **mastaba of Ti**. This important Fifth-dynasty tomb has an open court with a shaft leading to the burial chamber. A narrow passage leads into the mastaba past a narrow hall, all superbly decorated. The main pillared hall has a serdab running along one wall, with three spy holes. Inside is a cast of the statue of Ti (the original is now in the Egyptian Museum).

The **Serapeum** is one of the most extraordinary sites at Saqqara. Originally, the Avenue of Sphinxes led up from the Temple of Ptah in Memphis and crossed the desert, turning at the Circle of Philosophers. This was excavated by Auguste Mariette in 1850 and comprised statues of peacocks and leopards (animals associated with the cult of Dionysos) with figures of philosophers and poets including Homer. The avenue then led to the Serapeum itself. The earliest known burials of the Apis bulls, from the late 18th Dynasty, were in individual tombs, but Khaemwaset, son of Ramesses II, began a catacomb, the so-called Lesser Vault (inaccessible to visitors). This continued in use until the 26th Dynasty when Psamtik I inaugurated the Greater Vault, which is the site visited. All Apis bulls from the reign of Psamtik I until the Ptolemaic Period were buried here, each in a massive sarcophagus of granite, limestone or basalt, inside a chamber excavated from the corridor. These chambers were open only during the burial, then sealed with blocks. The walls near the entrance are filled with small niches which originally contained votive stelae left by visitors (most of these are now in the Louvre). The whole place has a marvellously eerie quality, especially when there are few visitors. The scale of the sarcophagi is quite stupendous.

The region surrounding the Serapeum appears to be a desolate area, but excavations have shown that in the Late Period it was a major site of temples. Here the mothers of the Apis bull (a cow associated with the goddess Isis) had their own catacombs, and there were also vaults for sacred ibises, baboons and falcons. Literally thousands of mummified creatures still fill these catacombs. The many temple ruins associated with these underground complexes have, like the Archaic- and Third-dynasty necropolis, which also covers this region, been buried again by the sand.

Washing near Saqqara

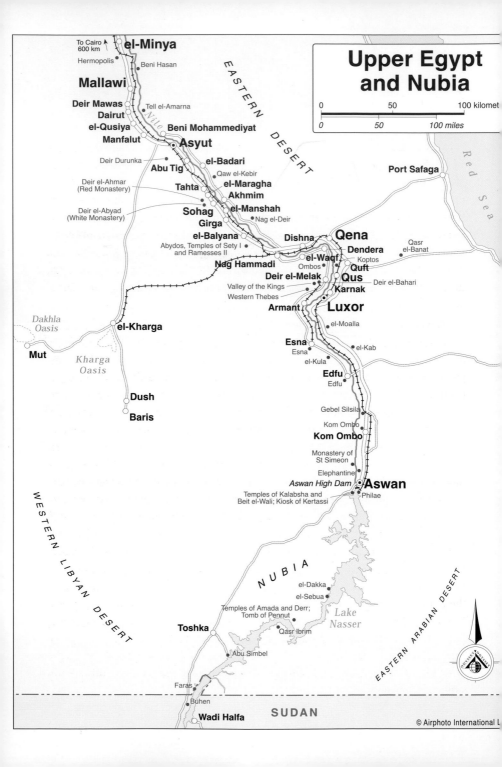

CAIRO TO LUXOR

Middle Egypt is a rich agricultural land and there is much of archaeological interest. Some of the major organized tours visit the sites here, but the area can become a restricted zone at times of political tension. El-Minya provides a good base for visits to Beni Hasan, Ashmunein and Amarna. There are hotels in Asyut and Nag Hammadi, which allow for longer visits to Abydos. Dendera can be visited en route from Nag Hammadi to Luxor. For those unable to spend time in Middle Egypt, both Abydos and Dendera can be visited in a day-trip from Luxor. Boats doing the full Cairo–Aswan cruise visit all of the major sites, but in recent years the regular operation of these has been affected by political and other factors.

Travelling south from Cairo along the main road, a number of sites are visible on the desert edge. The pyramids of **Dashur** are imposing, and the site, formerly a military zone, has recently been opened to tourists. Both built by Sneferu, the pyramids are comparable in size with those of Giza. They are easily visible from the main road. The northern pyramid, also known as the Red Pyramid, is actually the second most massive pyramid, exceeding that of Khafre in volume. It is, however, not as tall due to the shallow inclination of the faces, 43° 40'. The southern pyramid is generally known as the Bent Pyramid because of the change in angle of the slope from 54° 31' to 43° 21', at a point about half its height. The reason for this change is unknown, although a number of theories have been proposed. One suggested that the collapse of the Medum pyramid whilst this one was being built caused a rapid change of plan (not likely: see pyramid of Medum on the following page). It still retains much of its facing of Tura limestone. Pyramids of the 12th-dynasty kings, Amenemhat II, Senusret III and Amenemhat III, are also located at Dashur. Although the monuments themselves are not as imposing as their Fourth-dynasty antecedents, two caches of exquisite jewellery were discovered in subsidiary burials. From near the pyramid of Senusret III came the jewels of Princess Sat-Hathor and Queen Mereret, including some superb pectorals and a gold crown with foil streamers and falcon plumes. Princess Khnumet, daughter of Amenemhat II, was buried with an exquisite diadem of gold wires spangled with flowers. Now displayed in the Egyptian Museum, these are among the most perfect examples of the jeweller's art to have survived from ancient Egypt.

A little further south are the early 12th-dynasty pyramids of Amenemhat I and Senusret I at **Lisht**. The pyramids, in fact, have little to offer, although there was a large quantity of fine quality relief and sculpture recovered (a good selection of which is in the Egyptian Museum). The tomb of Senusret-Ankh, High Priest of Ptah at Memphis, may be accessible. The entire superstructure of the mastaba has been destroyed and a rather unpromising trap door opens onto a steep shaft (11 metres). This leads down to a finely decorated burial chamber.

Easier to reach (by a clear road from Rikka) and more worthwhile to visit is the extraordinary **pyramid of Medum**. Standing on the edge of the desert, its isolation makes it in many ways more impressive than the pyramids of Giza. The pyramid was originally a stepped structure, enlarged at least twice. Finally the steps were filled in, and the addition of a smooth outer facing turned it into a true pyramid. Its collapsed state emphasizes the phases of the pyramid's construction. It has been suggested that it collapsed while the southern pyramid at Dashur was being built, causing a rapid change in angle of inclination by the later builders. It now seems that Medum may have remained intact until Roman times or even the Middle Ages. It is thought that the Medum pyramid was built by Huni, the last king of the Third Dynasty, and probably completed by his son-in-law and successor, Sneferu. The pyramid is not difficult to enter. A long descending passage is followed by a short corridor; ascending a short vertical shaft brings one to the small burial chamber which is situated beneath the apex of the pyramid. The chamber has an impressive corbelled roof and the ancient construction timbers are still visible.

On the east side of the pyramid are the remains of the causeway, running down to the edge of the cultivation, and the temple. This is a remarkably small structure compared with those of the Fourth-dynasty pharaohs at Giza, or the elaborate complexes at Abusir and Saqqara. It is built of large blocks, the entrance opening onto a passage that turns back on itself and leads to the court in front of the pyramid. Here there are two enormous stelae, uninscribed. The passage has a number of graffiti in ink left by visitors in the New Kingdom.

The cemetery near the pyramid contained some large and important mastaba tombs, including those of the royal prince and High Priest of Heliopolis, Rahotep, in which the magnificent statues of the owner and his wife, Nofret, were discovered (now in the Egyptian Museum); and the tomb of Nefermaat and Atet, an important landmark in Egyptian tomb art, source of the 'Medum geese' and decoration of sunk relief figures filled with paste (Cairo, Egyptian Museum). One large mastaba near the pyramid is accessible through the robbers' passage. Although this is a little difficult, it is worth the bruises to see the undecorated burial chamber and the massive blocks sealing the real entrance still in position.

More Middle Kingdom pyramids lie to the south, accessible from the Beni Suef to Medinet el-Faiyum road (they may also be included as part of a visit to Faiyum). At Illahun the road runs along a large dyke built to divert the Nile flood into the Faiyum basin. The ruined brick pyramid of Senusret II stands on the desert edge close by. In the tomb of Princess Sit-Hathor-Iunet, a cache of jewellery was discovered (divided between Cairo and New York, Metropolitan Museum).

A little further south, the mud-brick **pyramid of Hawara** stands at the entrance to the Faiyum. One of the great tourist sites of antiquity, its vast temple complex was known as the Labyrinth, and was a wonder that surpassed the pyramids of Giza. Alas, nothing has survived to give any impression of its splendour. The pyramid is itself impressive, with its thousands of large mud-bricks, and the area occupied by the temple is easily discerned on both sides of the irrigation canal. A few fragments of architecture in granite and other stones litter the site. To the north of the pyramid are the remains of the large Graeco-Roman cemetery from which came many of the finest examples of the funerary paintings known as 'Faiyum portraits' (good collections in Cairo, Egyptian Museum; London, British Museum; and the Petrie Museum, University College London). These give a fine impression of the appearance of the Graeco-Egyptian middle class, and recent study of the skeletal material associated with one painting shows that it was an accurate likeness.

BENI HASAN

Beni Hasan is 23 kilometres (14.3 miles) south of el-Minya; the turning is signposted in el-Fikriya. After the river crossing there is a pleasant walk through the fields, where bee-eaters are usually to be seen in some numbers. The ascent to the tombs is quite steep, but aided by the staircase. Here is the best-preserved and only easily accessible group of late 11th- and early 12-dynasty noble tombs. Carved halfway up the cliff face, there are 39 rock-cut tombs, of which only the four finest are usually open. Numerous shaft graves are also to be found in the vicinity. The chief family buried here were the rulers of the Oryx nome. Although the rooms are large and hewn with great skill, the tombs are quite modest compared with those built by the other nomarchs in Middle Egypt, notably those at Qaw.

Beni Hasan: Tomb of Khety

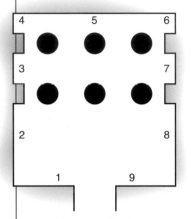

Khety (11th Dynasty)

The walls are divided into registers, number from top to bottom.

1 Hunting in the swamp with harpooning of fish and netting birds.

2 (i-ii), Hunting scene; (iii) barbers and linen workers; (iv) spinning and weaving; (v) dancers and musicians, with statue of Khety dragged on a sledge; (vi) woodworking, painting statuary, men playing the *senet* board game.

3 (i) Hunting in the desert continued; (ii) musicians; (iii) Khety and his wife.

4 (i-ii) Offering bearers; (iii) metal-workers; (iv-vii) animals and birds brought to Khety.

5 An unusual 'action' sequence of wrestlers; attack on a fortress.

6 Vintage and bird trapping.

7 Khety under a sunshade with his entourage.

8 Dancers and cattle before a statue of Khety in a shrine; butchers and offering bringers; agricultural scenes.

9 Rural life; boats in funeral procession; butchers and offering bearers; false door.

Beni Hasan: Tomb of Baqet III

Baqet III (11th Dynasty)

Very similar to Tomb of Khety.

1 (i) Hunting in the desert, including some strange imaginary beasts; (ii) barbers and linen weaving; (iii) spinning and weaving, games and dancing; (iv) cattle count; (v) musicians, goldsmiths, sculptors; (vi) fishing with boatmen fighting.

2 (i-vi) wrestling; (vii-ix) as in Khety, attack on fortress and battle.

3 (i) funeral procession with statue and offering bearers; (ii-iii) cattle count; (iv-v) potters; metal-workers; desert scenes; flax harvest, granaries and boats.

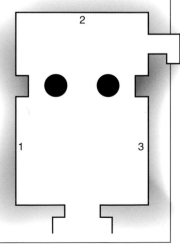

Source: Robert Morkot

Architecturally, the tombs form two groups. The earlier are large halls divided into two sections by lotus bundle columns; in the tomb of Baqet there are only two columns, in that of Khety, six. The columns are painted in bands, usually blue and red. This type of column is found in the tomb models of this period, notably the house of Meket-re (Egyptian Museum), and clearly imitated the architecture of elite houses. The later tombs comprise a portico, with so-called proto-Doric columns of eight or 16 sides, and a large square hall divided into three aisles by four columns, also proto-Doric. At the rear of this hall is a shrine with a statue of the tomb owner. Some of the scenes have been copied from one tomb into another, others are of stock types, showing agriculture and crafts, fishing and fowling. At times unsophisticated, the painting in the tombs, notably that of Khnumhotep, is lively and vigorous, and shows careful observation on the part of the artist, especially in its rendering of animals and birds.

TOMB OF KHETY (TOMB 17, 11TH DYNASTY)

One of the most important scenes here is to be found covering the whole of the back wall, where wrestlers are shown in a series of frozen positions in a clever action sequence; beneath, military activities, with the siege of a walled town. The whole reflects the disturbed political situation of the early Middle Kingdom, when local rulers maintained their own armies and there was conflict between different dynasties.

TOMB OF BAQET III (TOMB 15, 11TH DYNASTY)

This has very similar decoration to the preceding tomb. In this tomb, the desert animals also include some strange mythological creatures. The back wall again shows wrestlers and a military campaign. This tomb is important for the collection of unusual birds depicted, which include the coot, snipe, plover, bittern, a rare depiction of a night heron and a unique one of a black stork. Another rare bird is the roller shown with outspread wings which, with a golden oriole, is about to land in a fruit tree.

TOMB OF KHNUMHOTEP (TOMB 3, REIGN OF AMENEMHAT II)

Khnumhotep contains some of the most famous paintings at Beni Hasan. Amongst the agricultural scenes are men collecting figs, with baboons in the fig tree (notice here the way the shoulders are folded forward approximating a profile) and force-feeding of oryx. Also a group of Bedouin or Asiatics with distinctive costumes. Over the doorway to the statue shrine, Khnumhotep sits behind a hide, trapping waterfowl in a clap-net. Part of this scene contains the justly famous group of birds in an acacia tree: these include hoopoe, wagtail, shrike, redstart and spoonbill.

Beni Hasan: Tomb of Khnumhotep

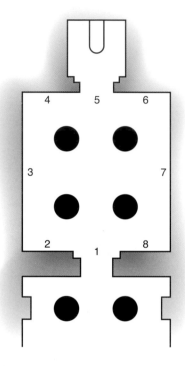

Khnumhotep
(12th Dynasty)

1   'Autobiographical' text on jambs and along base of walls; over door *muwu-*dancers and men dragging shrine with statue.

2   (i-iii) Agricultural scenes with harvesting and ploughing; men feeding oryx; (iv) the voyage to Abydos; (v) men collecting, and baboons stealing, figs from a tree.

3   (i-iii) Hunting in the desert with a group of Asiatics in brightly coloured robes bringing trade goods; (iv-vi) snaring birds, cattle count.

4   Khnumhotep fowling in the marshes.

5   Over the door to the chapel, Khnumhotep seated behind a hide with a clap-net catching waterfowl, and a justly famous scene of birds in an acacia tree, including hoopoe and grey shrike.

6   Khnumhotep spearing fish in the marshes.

7   Khnumhotep and his wife receive offerings.

8   Crafts, including (i) carpentry, (ii) boatbuilding, (iv) weaving and cookery, (v) sculptors; (iii) the journey to Abydos.

Source: Robert Morkot

TOMB OF AMENEMHAT (TOMB 2, REIGN OF SENUSRET I)

The columns, architraves and the panelling around the base of the wall have all been painted to imitate red granite. The hieroglyphic inscriptions on these features have been painted in blue, which is conventional for real granite. The paintings include some copied from the 11th-dynasty tombs.

SPEOS ARTEMIDOS

Speos Artemidos (also known as Istabl Antar) can be reached from Beni Hasan by donkey or boat. A walk through the village and across the desert brings the visitor to the wadi entrance. Dedicated to the lioness goddess Pakht, 'She who Scratches'. The wadi narrows and the ground rises as it penetrates the hills. The cliffs are covered with signs of quarrying and pierced with doorways. Some of these belong to New Kingdom tombs; one is the entrance to an unfinished chapel dedicated on behalf of Alexander IV of Macedon (son of Alexander the Great). The speos of Hatshepsut is the severed end of a rock spur. Outside, the Hathor-headed columns are unfinished. Inside, the decoration was largely recut for Sety I. It is quite attractive but damaged. The unfinished inner chamber has a niche high in the wall for the image of the goddess Pakht, and a relief depicting her at the side. Above the façade is the important, long inscription of Hatshepsut recording her restorations of temples throughout Egypt—the beginning of propaganda against the Hyksos rule. The wadi continues after the speos of Hatshepsut, and in a right-hand fork is another, much smaller rock-cut shrine. This is badly damaged, but there is an image of Hatshepsut's daughter, Neferure, with other figures.

ANTINOÖPOLIS

Cross the river to el-Sheikh Ibada on the local ferry from el-Roda. This vast, desolate ruin-field is all that remains of the splendid Roman city; even at the end of the 18th century, when visited by the Napoleonic expedition, the column-lined streets still stood, as did a triumphal arch and the magnificent gateway of the theatre. Occasionally, in the mountains of pottery, a broken capital or a fragment of a pillar can be found to attest to the splendours of this city. A small town had existed here long before the Roman city and the columns of a temple of Ramesses II still stand north of the village. Founded by the emperor Hadrian on 30 October AD 130, the city was dedicated to his lover, Antinous, who had drowned in the Nile near here a few days previously. The circumstances surrounding Antinous'

Beni Hasan: Tomb of Amenemhat

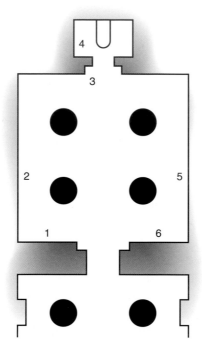

Amenemhat
(12th Dynasty)

1   Crafts, including (i) leather workers; (ii) bows and arrows, stone and woodworking; (iii) metalworking; (iv) potters; (v) flax cultivation and manufacture of linen; (vi-vii) agricultural.
2   (i) Hunting in desert; (ii) dancers with statue procession; (iii-vi) animals and birds being brought, cattle count, deceased with his dogs.
3   (i-iii) Wrestlers; (iv) attack on fort; (v) voyage to Abydos.
4   Shrine with destroyed statues of Amenemhat, his wife and mother, scene of offering bearers and an offering list.
5   Offering bearers; harpists.
6   (i) Wine making; (ii) brewing; (iii) fishing; (iv) storerooms; (v) musicians and false door.

Source: Robert Morkot

death remain unknown, but its closeness to the festival of Osiris (24 October) and its method, as well as the emperor's wishes, ensured that he was immediately deified. His cult spread throughout the Roman Empire, but Egypt, particularly Antinoöpolis, remained its main centre. Many statues were later sculpted showing Antinous in Egyptian kilt and royal headdress. Standing at the Nile end of the new Via Hadriana, which crossed the Eastern Desert to the Red Sea ports, Antinoöpolis, or Antinoë, continued to flourish during the Byzantine period.

ASHMUNEIN

Khemenu (the ancient Pharaonic name for Ashmunein) was the capital of the Hare nome whose governors were buried at el-Bersha. This was the centre of the worship of the god Djehuty (Thoth), the inventor of writing. Depicted as an ibis-headed man, Thoth was a lunar deity and usually depicted with the crescent and disc of the moon on his head. In Ptolemaic times the town was known as Hermopolis, from the equation of Thoth with the Greek god Hermes. At Khemenu, the Ogdoad (the eight creator gods; in Egyptian 'khmun' means 'eight') accompany Thoth, and here belongs one of Egypt's most important creation legends.

Today the granite columns of the Basilica dominate the huge site of Ashmunein. Excavated parts show the fluted column drums and Corinthian capitals of dismantled Ptolemaic temples. A German expedition (G Roeder 1929–1939) found over 1500 *talatat* brought from Amarna by Ramesses II to use in his pylon entrance to the Thoth temple. Twelve columns of the hall built in the reigns of Alexander the Great and Philip Arrhidaios still stood when the French expedition was here in 1820, but were destroyed in 1822. Among the few monuments of the earlier pharaohs amid the scrub is the Temple of Amun, begun by Merneptah and completed by Sety II. Vestiges of massive mud-brick walls surround the site. The most significant remains are the two colossal baboons (and fragments of others). Superbly carved in quartzite, these enormous figures were originally set up at the entrance to the Thoth temple in the reign of Amenhotep III. They probably carried large moon discs and crescents on their heads. At the south of the site there are two seated colossi of Ramesses II and a small temple dedicated in the reign of Nero.

TUNA EL-GEBEL

During the Late and Graeco-Roman periods, the cemetery of Hermopolis was at Tuna el-Gebel, some seven kilometres west of the town. Before reaching the cemetery, one of the Amarna boundary stelae may be visited. Carved on the cliff face, the large stele has two group statues of Akhenaten and Nefertiti with some of their daughters. The hieroglyphic text carries the king's narrative of the construction of the new city of Akhetaten. The scene above shows Akhenaten and Nefertiti, unusually in full profile, with two of their daughters, worshipping the sun disc.

The architecture and decoration of the tomb-chapels at Tuna el-Gebel display a fascinating blend of classical and Egyptian elements, with painted marble panels and mixed Hellenistic and Egyptian figures. But a note of caution: it can be dangerous wandering off alone as the sand is deep and there are reputedly many horned vipers.

The first chapel seen, and certainly the most important, is the **tomb of Petosiris**, High Priest of Thoth, probably in the period from the second Persian conquest to the very beginning of the Ptolemaic Period (roughly 345–300 BC). The relief decoration is remarkable, and prettily coloured. The chapel is in the form of a small temple, with a portico of floral columns and screen walls, opening onto a small hall supported by four square piers. The tomb shaft descends from the middle of the hall (the coffin with inlaid coloured glass is in the Egyptian Museum). The scenes are in the Egyptian tradition, with crafts and agricultural activities in the portico, and religious rites and offerings in the hall, but there is a considerable influence from Greek art in the style of the reliefs (particularly notable in the portico). The autobiographical inscription of Petosiris, carved on the façade, details the restorations to the temples of Khemenu following the reconquest by Artaxerxes III.

There is a number of other freestanding chapels close to that of Petosiris, with the streets of tombs leading off behind. The one immediately behind Petosiris takes the form of a chapel on a podium. Note here the carved windows of the façade. Close by is the tomb of Isadora, of the second century AD. Unfortunately, the body of Isadora is subjected to public gaze in the first room. Of the other tombs, the 'Oedipus tomb' had paintings of the Greek mythic cycle, but these have been removed to Cairo.

The great Roman waterwheel with its 34-metre-deep shaft is worth investigating. It is sometimes possible to enter: a spiral staircase winds around the outside of the shaft. Column bases in the windswept sand indicate an enclosure where the sacred

Tuna el-Gebel: Tomb of Petosiris

Petosiris

The Greatest of Five, the title of the High Priest of Thoth (c.Second Persian Period–Early Ptolemaic)

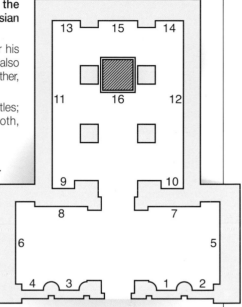

A family tomb, built by Petosiris for his father Sishu (or Nes-Shu), who was also High Priest of Thoth, and his elder brother, Djed-Thoth-ef-ankh.

Façade: autobiographical text and titles; scenes of Petosiris offering to Thoth, Sokar-Osiris, Osiris and Isis.

1-2 Jewellers and metal-workers.

3-4 Incense-makers and carpenters.

5   Cattle and vintners.

6   Farming scenes including harvesting and winnowing.

7-8 Family before Petosiris and his wife; sub-scenes of butchers and offering bearers; in recesses biographical inscriptions of Sishu, Djed-Thoth-ef-ankh and Petosiris.

9   Hymn to Osiris (door jamb); tree-goddess with Sishu and his wife, Nefer-renpet; Petosiris and Sishu; sub-scene of cattle in swamp.

10 Petosiris stands before brother, Djed-Thoth-ef-ankh, with offering table; Petosiris before Djed-Thoth-ef-ankh; sub-scene leading cattle across a canal or river.

11 Offering bearers; funeral procession with coffin on a bier with wheels; shrine and canopic jars on sledges; priest purifies mummy in front of pyramid; sub-scene of offering bearers, including three Nubians.

12 Sishu before the nine 'gods who adore Ra'; Djed-Thoth-ef-ankh and family before Sishu; sub-scene of cattle in swamp.

13 Djed-Thoth-ef-ankh adoring, then led to Osiris, worshipping four groups of gods; sub-scene of offering bearers.

14 Djed-Thoth-ef-ankh adores nine gods; Petosiris and Djed-Thoth-ef-ankh; sub-scene of crocodile and hippopotamus fighting.

15 Sishu and Djed-Thoth-ef-ankh before Osiris, Isis and Nephthys; scarab elaborately crowned rises above the palace façade flanked by winged goddesses.

16 Shaft to burial chamber.

Source: Robert Morkot

ibises were raised. The ibis and baboon catacombs are similar to those near the Serapeum at Saqqara. Both creatures were sacred to Thoth and were mummified so that pilgrims to the shrine could offer them to the deity. The ibises were buried in pots (as at Saqqara), and the side aisles are still crammed full of these. The winding corridors eventually lead to a chamber where a high priest of Thoth was buried. A short ladder leads to the sarcophagus, which almost completely fills its chamber. The earliest of the galleries is apparently of the 19th Dynasty. One of the most significant discoveries here was a group of letters intended for the Jewish garrison based on Elephantine during the Persian period.

TELL EL-AMARNA

No other period of Egyptian history has attracted as much speculation and romancing (and nonsense) as the Amarna Period. In its broadest use, the term embraces the latter part of the reign of Amenhotep III, with those of his successors Akhenaten, Smenkhkare, Tutankhamun and Ay (c.1360–1320 BC). Understandably, the religious aspects and the extraordinary artistic productions of this period led scholars to emphasize the ways in which it differs from the earlier 18th Dynasty, and to romance about Akhenaten as the 'first individual in history'. Indeed, he has been claimed as the tutor of Moses, the establisher of monotheism and an influence upon the 'Psalms of David'. Sigmund Freud was particularly important in the development of this view, which has continued to be influential through romantic novels about this period. Today, scholarly opinion is moving towards a very different perception: instead of a dreamy monotheist and pacifist who let his empire crumble away through inaction, Akhenaten is seen as authoritarian and reactionary. It is certain that, whatever the current academic view, the popular image of Akhenaten will retain its spell.

Although little survives *in situ* of the stone monuments of the city of the 'Horizon-of-the-Sun-Disc' (Akhetaten), these having been dismantled probably by Ramesses II for his building works at Hermopolis (Ashmunein), excavation has told us more about the structure of this city than any other of ancient Egypt. The first excavations were those of the British archaeologist Sir Flinders Petrie (in 1891–92), which were followed by major German excavations led by Ludwig Borchardt and a series of British digs by the Egypt Exploration Society that still continue under the direction of Barry Kemp. These excavations have uncovered the plans of the major ceremonial and residential buildings, as well as the houses of the nobility and ordinary people.

Woman carrying a jar, Beni Hasan

Although much of the major stonework has been removed, thousands of fragments of statuary, relief work and architectural fragments, painted plaster, and faïence inlay and tiles allow us to build up an impression of the original appearance of the city. Amongst the most notable discoveries was the house of the royal sculptor, Dhutmose, from which came the red quartzite head of Nefertiti (Cairo, Egyptian Museum), the celebrated painted limestone head (Berlin) and the remarkable series of plaster portraits of members of the royal family and court (Cairo; Berlin). Petrie excavated here because local farmers had turned up thousands of inscribed clay tablets, many of which were destroyed before their importance was recognized. These are the 'Amarna Letters', correspondence sent to Amenhotep III and Akhenaten from the rulers of western Asia. What survives reveals the complexity of international diplomacy in the later 18th Dynasty.

Boundary stelae cut in the cliffs defined the limits of the city. Only one of these is easily accessible, but it is one of the best preserved. It marked the northwest of the city, at Tuna el-Gebel. The area of the city thus spread over the two banks of the river, the actual town on the arid east bank and the farmland of its temples and officials on the west bank.

The **Northern Tombs** are easily accessible, but less architecturally impressive than the southern group. The plan of a typical tomb is the inverse of those at Thebes (Luxor), with a long hall followed by transverse hall and shrine. In the more elaborate examples both halls can be expanded into columned rooms (for example, the tombs of Panehesy and Ay). Most of the tombs are unfinished and many have suffered damage, caused either maliciously or through the conversion of the tomb into a house, or in one case a church. At the entrance there is usually a life-size figure of the tomb owner, and sometimes his wife, in prayer to the sun. The most notable feature of the decoration of the Amarna tombs is the dominance of the king and royal family. Most tombs have scenes from the life of the tomb owner, often including his reward by the king. In all of these scenes, the king is shown on a scale far larger than the tomb owner and the rest of the court.

Two tombs are apparently later than the main group, and are carved into an isolated spur of the cliffs.

Huya (tomb 1) was the Steward of Queen Tiye at Akhetaten. This tomb is interesting as Akhenaten's mother, Tiye, dominates the scenes. Tiye, accompanied by the princess Baketaten are shown dining with Akhenaten, Nefertiti and their daughters. The elder queen daintily picks at her food, while Akhenaten munches on a kebab and Nefertiti tackles a whole small bird. The meal is accompanied by

Amarna: Tomb of Meryre I

Meryre, Greatest of Seers of the Aten in the House of the Aten in Akhetaten

Meryre carries the same title as the High Priest of Ra-Harakhty at Heliopolis, but specific to the great temple at Amarna.

1 Carved floral bouquets, with central sheaf of papyrus and alternating bands of lotus, cornflowers, mandrakes and leaves.

2 Meryre and Tinro, probably his wife, worship the rising sun.

3 Meryre, carried on the shoulders of his friends, is rewarded by Akhenaten and Nefertiti at the Window of Appearances. The canopy extending in font of the window is visible, giving shade to those honoured by the king. Beneath is a damaged sub-scene showing the rejoicing by Meryre's family and retainers.

4 Akhenaten and Nefertiti in their chariots going to the temple of the sun disc. They drive along the royal road from the great riverside palace in the north of the city to the temple and central city. A schematic palace is shown at the top-left, with attendants sweeping the floor and sprinkling water. Contingents of the army, officials, and at their head, the viziers, run with the chariots. At the temple, cattle with decorated horns wait to be sacrificed. This scene is framed by borders and extends around the corner onto the adjacent wall. This is an innovation of the Amarna artists; in earlier scenes, for example, in Theban tombs, each wall is defined by borders and scenes do not break out from them, or around corners.

5 Akhenaten and Nefertiti make offerings to the sun disc. Emanating from the sun are what appear to be broad collars: these are thought to be rainbows. In the sub-scene is a fine group of blind singers and a harpist.

6 A large scene, again extending around two walls. Upper: Meryre accompanies Akhenaten and Nefertiti and four of their daughters on a visit to the temple. Although a schematic depiction, this does give some idea of the enormous offerings laid out on the hundreds of tables in the outer court. The main offering point (also in scene 7 in the tomb of Panehesy) is behind the main pylon. The butcher's yard is shown near the rear of the temple. Lower: Meryre is appointed to his office by Akhenaten accompanied by Nefertiti. Interesting scenes of the town, with extensive cattle sheds, and the harbour with ships. Further along are the granaries and the temple storage rooms, which are particularly interesting: they contain amphorae and jars of wine and oil, bread, cakes, dried fish, chests containing the temple jewellery and gold, and elaborate vessels of the type that form the Asiatic tribute. Beyond is a complex with gardens with sunken pool. Here, the trees are particularly effective. This area contains an enigmatic complex, which appears to have lots of rooms and doors, but nothing in it.

Source: Robert Morkot

Amarna: Tomb of Panehesy

Panehesy, Chief Servitor of the Aten in Akhetaten

This tomb was converted into a church.

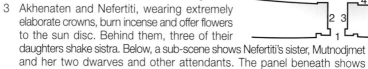

1   Lintel, Akhenaten and Nefertiti with three daughters adore the sun disc. Behind the daughters are two dwarves who accompany the small group shown above them. The principal person here is a young woman with a heavy side-lock, with fan bearers behind: she is Mutnodjmet, sister of Nefertiti.

2   Akhenaten and Nefertiti adore the sun disc, three daughters shake sistra. Below, a sub-scene shows the vizier and other high officials bowing to Mutnodjmet with her attendants. The panel beneath shows Panehesy adoring the sun, with a hymn in praise of the god and the king.

3   Akhenaten and Nefertiti, wearing extremely elaborate crowns, burn incense and offer flowers to the sun disc. Behind them, three of their daughters shake sistra. Below, a sub-scene shows Nefertiti's sister, Mutnodjmet and her two dwarves and other attendants. The panel beneath shows Panehesy adoring the sun, with a hymn in praise of the god and the king.

4   Panehesy stands before Akhenaten and Nefertiti and their four daughters. The centre of the scene has a group of offering tables, draped with vines and with burning incense. Unusually Nefertiti wears a wig rather than a crown.

5   Akhenaten and Nefertiti in their chariots with bodyguards who have to run to keep up. In the upper right a schematic view of the palace.

6   Stairs to unfinished burial chamber.

7   Akhenaten and Nefertiti reward Panehesy at the Window of Appearances. Their eldest daughter Meritaten is with them and three younger daughters stand behind. Scribes make quadruplicate records of the king's gifts, and foreign ambassadors look on. The sub-scenes show the rejoicing by Panehesy's family and retainers.

8   Akhenaten and Nefertiti celebrate religious rituals. The scene gives a schematic view of the main temple with pylons and courts and numerous offering tables. The king has mounted the steps to the principal offering point. Nefertiti stands by his side and is just visible as an outline. This way of superimposing two of the most important actors is found only in these tombs: normally they would be completely separate, even if to be understood as side-by-side.

9   The baptistry of the Coptic church, with another scene of Akhenaten and Nefertiti making offerings to the sun.

10   Panehesy with his son adore the sun disc.

11   Stairs to second burial chamber

12   Shrine with destroyed statue of Panehesy, offerings.

Source: Robert Morkot

music; the performers are Syrian, and some wear blindfolds. Other scenes show a state visit by the queen mother to the city, and the presentation of the foreign tribute in year 12. Beneath the scene showing the reward of Huya is another, showing activities in the royal workshops. Here the Chief Sculptor of Queen Tiye, Iuty, is finishing a statue of the princess Baketaten, while other sculptors make elements of composite statues and furniture. It is probable that Huya died during Akhenaten's reign and was buried (perhaps temporarily) in the tomb, since there are scenes of the funeral in the statue chamber.

Meryre II (tomb 2) Comptroller of the Household of Nefertiti. This unfinished tomb also has a scene of the presentation of the foreign tribute in year 12. There is a particularly fine scene showing the reward of Meryre and his joyful return to his house.

The main tombs in the northern group are scattered along the cliffs with a commanding view across the plain to the city and river beyond.

Ahmose (tomb 3) Fan Bearer on the Right Hand of the King. This tomb has a simple plan, like a classic Theban tomb, but in reverse. The scenes were not completed, but the cutting of the chambers is very fine. The scenes in the outer hall are partly carved, but the ink preparatory drawing is well preserved, and very elegant. There are very deep burial shafts in the transverse hall, and a colossal statue of Ahmose in the shrine.

Meryre I (tomb 4) was the High Priest of the Aten. This tomb is an elaborated tomb with two pillared halls, the second one unfinished. The first hall, with the typical, rather dumpy, ornate columns, has a splendid scene of the royal family driving in chariots along the royal road to the temple; note how the scene goes around the corner of the room, breaking normal convention. The other major scene shows the royal visit to the temple: there is good detail here of trees and the contents of the storerooms, and a flotilla of barges at the quay.

Pentu (tomb 5) was the King's Physician. Another simple tomb, with unfinished decoration.

Panehesy (tomb 6) was Chief Servitor of the Aten in Akhetaten. Two halls, each supported by four columns, lead to a statue shrine. Much of the decoration in the outer part is completed, and the tomb may have been used. There are stairs and passages from both halls leading down to the burial chambers. The tomb is important for the scenes in the doorway, showing the royal family adoring the sun, with, beneath, a narrow band where the sister of Nefertiti, Mutnodjmet, is shown accompanied by her two dwarves. The first hall was converted into a church, and the baptistry in the first hall survives.

The **Southern Tombs** are much more elaborate than the northern group, with large columned halls. They are mostly unfinished, although some of the relief sculpture is superior in quality to the northern group.

The most splendid of the group is the unfinished tomb of Ay (tomb 25), which would have had 24 columns in the first hall alone. Only the northern part of this, with the first row of columns in the southern part, was completed. Even though the first hall was not finished, and the inner parts not even begun, the decoration was started. Ay was one of the most important of Akhenaten's officials, and later ascended the throne as king, successor to Tutankhamun. Some Egyptologists think he was the father of Nefertiti. The tomb is important for the texts of the 'Hymns to the Aten' (in the hall), with splendid figures of Ay and his wife. Nefertiti's sister is also depicted in this tomb, again with her dwarves.

Tutu (tomb 8) is architecturally one of the most elaborate tombs, but is unfinished. The transverse hall had two rows of six columns, the rear columns having screen walls between them.

Maya (tomb 14) Fan Bearer on the Right Hand of the King. Another unfinished tomb with columns in the transverse hall. The scenes are conventional, although Nefertiti's sister, Mutnodjmet, again appears.

The **Royal Tomb**, if open, can be visited by those with sufficient time. It is situated a long way down the great central wadi, which is itself imposing. Surprisingly massive in scale, Akhenaten's tomb resembles that of Merneptah and later Ramessides more than those of his predecessors of the 18th Dynasty. The only well-preserved decoration is in a side chamber where the death of one of the king's daughters in childbirth is recorded. The princess lies on a bed, while the nurse carries away her newborn child; her parents stand at the foot of the bed, their arms raised in grief. In recent years various suggestions have been put forward as to the identity of the child, some scholars proposing that it may be Tutankhaten (later Tutankhamun). Other royal tombs were begun in the wadi.

The city, like most ancient Egyptian town-sites, is today badly denuded. The best-preserved building is the **North Palace**, the lower levels of the walls giving a clear idea of the scale and layout of this building. When surveying the bare remains of stone column bases and thresholds, a sunken pool surrounded by a colonnade and the audience hall on the main axis, remember the fragments of painted plaster in the Egyptian Museum which were found here. The palace is a large formal building with two enormous courts. There was a sanctuary and animal stalls in the first court, and it is clearly not a normal residence palace. It has been suggested that the king here appeared as the ruler of all living things (hence the animal enclosures). The palace stands at the northern end of the great Royal Road, and may have been the focus of rituals before the king proceeded into the central city.

In the **Central City** many mounds and fragments survive, but many buildings are difficult to identify. Much of the great **Central Palace** has been encroached upon by sand and cultivation. Recently, work in the smaller Aten temple has consolidated the remains, and a modern column has been erected to give an impression of the original style and size. Altogether, much imagination is needed to visualize the Horizon-of-the-Sun-Disc.

Good collections of sculpture and antiquities from Amarna can be found in many museum collections. Fine depictions, in stone and plaster, of Akhenaten, his family and courtiers from the workshop of Dhutmose are displayed in Cairo and Berlin. Other statues and fragments can be found in most major collections, notably London, British Museum; Paris, Louvre; New York, Metropolitan Museum; and Brooklyn Museum. Many slabs of relief sculpture found by Roeder at Ashmunein, but originally from Amarna, are in the Brooklyn Museum, others are in the Metropolitan Museum and Boston Museum of Fine Arts. The Petrie Museum at University College London has an excellent collection of small sculptural fragments, and much glazed tile and inlay from Petrie's excavations.

Between Mallawi and Asyut are a number of other important sites, but they are rarely visited and some need special permission. Opposite Mallawi, and north of Amarna, are the tombs of **Deir el-Bersha**. Here, situated high in the spectacular cliffs, earthquakes and quarrying have taken their toll and the tombs are now badly damaged. Similar in plan to those of Beni Hasan, with portico and hall, the most important was that of Djehutyhotep (reign of Senusret III). A famous scene in this tomb depicted the transport of a colossal statue from the alabaster quarries at Hatnub (southeast of Amarna), but was badly damaged in 1890. Fragments of the fine relief decoration are now preserved in the Egyptian Museum. Also from this site is the superbly painted wooden coffin of Djehuty-nakht, now in the Boston Museum of Fine Arts. **Meir**, near el-Qusiya, the ancient Qis (Cusae), was the burial place of the local nomarchs during the 6th and 12th dynasties. Architecturally unimpressive, in the low edge of the Western Desert, these tombs were splendidly painted. On the east bank of the river, a little north of Asyut, lie the tombs of **Deir el-Gebrawi**. Belonging to nomarchs of the 6th Dynasty, they too have been badly damaged.

ASYUT

A syut has long been an important centre because of its strategic position at the end of the road to/from Kharga. The road itself was the northernmost extension of the Darb el-Arbain, the 'Forty Days Road', which comes from Darfur in the highlands of western Sudan. In the medieval and early modern periods this was the main slave route and camel road connecting sub-Saharan Africa with the Nile Valley. The modern road to Kharga and Dakhla leaves the valley about eight kilometres north of Asyut.

Asyut is a large and important modern city, with a number of hotels. It is convenient for those who wish to break the journey to Luxor, or who are intending to visit Kharga. Little of the ancient town has been recovered, but there are tombs of the First Intermediate Period and Middle Kingdom in the cliffs close to the town. These are situated in a military zone and are presently inaccessible without special permission. Perhaps the most notable discovery was in the tomb of Mesehti, where the two groups of wooden soldiers, Nubian bowmen and Egyptian spearmen (Cairo, Egyptian Museum) were found. The tomb of the nomarch Hepdjefa had some important texts, but, more interestingly, statues of this man and his wife were later taken to Sudan, where they were found in a tomb at Kerma (now in the Boston Museum of Fine Arts). South of the town is an important monastery, Deir Durunka. Now a vast group of buildings halfway up the cliff face, its focus is an ancient quarry which is reputed to be one of the resting places of the Holy family on their flight to Egypt. It is a major pilgrimage centre for the Coptic community with a large number of hostels.

SOHAG

C lose to Sohag are two important monasteries, the Deir el-Abyad (White Monastery) and the Deir el-Ahmar (Red Monastery). The White Monastery is a large rectangular white limestone building, most of which is occupied by the church of St Shenouda. Founded in AD 440, it is a basilica structure, the columns mostly collapsed, with a triple apse covered by half-domes. The frescoes in the apsidal end have been cleaned. The stone for the monastery was brought from the nearby ancient site of Athribis (modern Wannina), and blocks with Pharaonic decoration can be found built into the walls. The Red Monastery is a complete contrast, built of fired brick. Today it stands in the winding streets of a modern village.

Crossing the river by the bridge at Sohag to the east bank of the Nile, it is not far (two kilometres) to **Akhmim**. An ancient cult centre of the fertility god, Min, excavations by the Egyptian Antiquities Organization in 1983 brought to light a temple of Ramesses II. In front of the gateway to the temple were fallen colossal limestone statues of the king and of one of his wives, Queen Merytamun. It is unusual to find statues of royal women on this scale, so this finely sculpted piece is particularly important. Another colossal statue thought to depict Merytamun has very recently been excavated at Tell Basta (Bubastis, modern Zagazig) in the Delta.

ABYDOS

The ancient town of Abydos (Egyptian: Abedju) was an important one from early times. The kings of the First and Second dynasties built large mud-brick tombs (or cenotaphs) here. By the end of the Old Kingdom the cult of Osiris was firmly established here, merging with that of the local god, Khenti-amentiu ('Foremost of the Westerners', ie ruler of the dead), and the city became a centre of pilgrimage. The voyage to Abydos is depicted in many New Kingdom tombs, and between the temples and cemetery many hundreds of stelae were set up by visitors hoping to partake eternally in the resurrection of the god. From the Middle Kingdom onwards, kings also erected temples here in which they became a manifestation of Osiris.

TEMPLE OF SETY I

One of the best-preserved New Kingdom temples in Egypt, it is renowned for the quality of its relief decoration. In some places the original colour and glossy finish have also survived. Ramesses II completed the outer parts of the temple, before constructing his own, much smaller, temple nearby.

The temple is entered through the remains of the pylon and first court. A stair-ramp rises steeply to the colonnaded terrace and entrance to the second courtyard. The design of this outer part of the temple is reminiscent of Hatshepsut's temple at Deir el-Bahari, with the steep rise in level and colonnades of square pillars, although it is on a much smaller scale. The walls flanking the entrance to the second court carry well-preserved processions of the numerous sons and daughters of Ramesses II. Another stair-ramp leads to the temple terrace with its portico of square pillars. To the south of these courts are the temple magazines, and the audience hall, corresponding to the small palaces attached to temples such as the Ramesseum and Medinet Habu at Luxor.

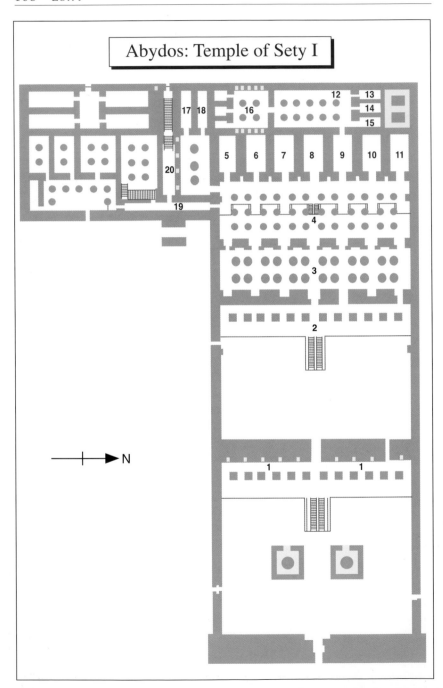

Abydos: Temple of Sety I

Temple of Sety I at Abydos

1 Procession of the sons and daughters of Ramesses II.
2 Façade completed by Ramesses II: note the blocked doorways on all except the central axis and route to the Osiris sanctuary.
3 First hypostyle hall with beautiful unpainted relief on the north wall.
4 Second hypostyle hall: more very fine relief sculpture. The scenes (many of suckling) between the doors to the sanctuaries are particularly handsome, well-coloured and retain a high polish.
5 Sanctuary of Sety I: the decoration differs slightly from the other sanctuaries. The scenes relate to kingship, and include the king carried in the sed-festival.
6 Sanctuary of Ptah.
7 Sanctuary of Ra-Harakhty.
8 Sanctuary of Amun.
9 Sanctuary of Osiris.
10 Sanctuary of Isis.
11 Sanctuary of Horus.
12 The rites of raising of the djed-pillar.
13 Sanctuary of Horus.
14 Sanctuary of Osiris-Sety I.
15 Sanctuary of Isis.
16 Osiris Suite.
17 Sanctuary of Nefertum.
18 Sanctuary of Ptah-Sokar.
19 Gallery of the Lists with scene of Sety I and the crown prince Ramesses offering to the cartouches of earlier kings, beginning with Meni. It is selective, with notable omissions such as Hatshepsut and the Amarna pharaohs. This hall leads to service quarters, including the Butcher's Hall, and the Hall of the Barques.
20 Corridor leading to the Osireion decorated with scenes showing the subjection of chaotic forces: catching waterfowl in a clap-net; the king accompanied by the crown prince lassoes a wild bull.

Source: Robert Morkot

The temple is unusual in design, with seven sanctuaries and, originally, seven processional ways and seven main doorways. Five of the entrances were blocked when the façade of the temple was completed by Ramesses II. This left only the central axis (leading to shrine of Amun) and that immediately to the north (to the shrine of Osiris) open. All seven routes remain obvious in the two, rather gloomy, columned halls. At the north (right) end of the halls the relief sculpture was completed, but never painted. To modern eyes this is, in many ways, more appealing than the fully coloured reliefs. The lack of paint allows a close examination of the delicate bas-relief. The artistic style adopted by the sculptors of Sety I recalls that of Thutmose III, rather than that of the immediately preceding late 18th Dynasty. The best of painted decoration is to be found in the chapels and in the Osiris suite.

The second of the columned halls gives access to the seven sanctuaries. This scheme placed the chief state gods of Egypt alongside the triad of Abydos. Thus, the chapel on the central axis is dedicated to Amun-Ra, with those of Osiris, Isis and Horus to the north and, to the south, the chapels of Ra-Harakhty, Ptah and Sety I himself. The chapels have splendid images of the presiding deities in their varied forms and attire, and of their sacred barques, which were housed here at the time of festival processions. Each sanctuary is divided into two parts, the back wall being dominated by a false door. The naos containing the divine statues presumably stood in the back part, and the barque in the front part when required. A hall off the Gallery of the Lists housed the barques when not in use. The scenes show episodes in the daily liturgy of the temple, although the order in which they appear varies in places from that in the surviving papyrus texts of such rites. The same elements appear in each chapel. The king, as High Priest, breaks the seals and opens the doors of the shrine. He then adores the god, performs the incense rite, an act of purification, and washes the god. The statue is anointed and dressed in coloured garments; then jewellery, crowns and sceptres are attached to it. The culmination of the daily is rite is the presentation of food offerings and incense, followed by sprinkling with pure sand and the king's backward retreat from the sanctuary, sweeping away his footprints as he goes.

A separate suite of rooms for the celebration of the mysteries of Osiris is reached through the Osiris chapel. The decoration of the three chapels and the columned hall is particularly fine. The suite is arranged north–south with a chapel for Osiris, flanked by those of Isis and Horus, at the north end. A columned hall leads to a square columned room lined with niches, and three more chapels at the southern end. It is certain that these rooms were used for the celebration of the mysteries of Osiris. In the central chapel of Osiris, it is Sety I himself who becomes the god. The west wall of the columned hall has a series of scenes showing Sety raising the *djed*-pillar, the emblem of Osiris, adorning it and dressing it in garments.

The Osiris suite behind the main sanctuaries, and the Osireion immediately behind this part of the temple, dictated that various other suites of rooms were placed to the south of the sanctuaries, resulting in an unusual L-shaped plan. A doorway at the south end of the line of sanctuaries opens onto a hall supported by three columns, and with two narrow chapels. These were dedicated to the gods Nefertum and Ptah-Sokar, both of whom had associations with rebirth and the afterlife in the Memphite region. The left door jamb of the entrance into the Ptah-Sokar chapel carries a particularly fine 'cryptic' writing of the names of Sety I in which the element 'men' of the king's throne name Men-maat-ra is written with an obelisk (this can also be found elsewhere in the temple). In the Nefertum chapel the god appears mummiform and with a lion's head surmounted by a falcon and lotus flower. The columned hall has four niches in the south wall to contain divine statues.

Adjacent to the entrance into the Nefertum and Ptah Sokar suite another narrow doorway leads into the Gallery of the Lists, which provides access to a number of other chambers. One of the most important historical reliefs in the temple is to be found here: the list of Egyptian kings from the unification to Sety himself. Sety I, and his eldest son, the future Ramesses II, are shown offering to the cartouches of the royal ancestors, beginning with Meni (Menes/Narmer). It is a selective list, with some notable omissions, such as Hatshepsut, Akhenaten and Tutankhamun, but is nevertheless a significant document for understanding the Egyptians' perception of their past. The rooms off this corridor included the hall where the barques of the temple's gods were kept, the temple storerooms and butchers' hall. This had a separate entrance so that the animals could be brought in. A Roman graffito on the wall opposite the entrance to the Hall of Barques shows the god Anubis (without wig) wearing a Roman military costume.

A second corridor leads at right angles from the Gallery of the Lists to a steep staircase and exit. The walls carry a splendid scene of the king lassoing a bull, with the aid of the crown prince. The staircase leads to the outside, and one of the most remarkable structures at Abydos, the **Osireion**. This stands directly behind the temple and on the same axis. Because of close similarities in its architecture to the valley temple of Khafre (Chephren) at Giza, it was once thought to date from the Old Kingdom, but is now recognized as an integral part of Sety I's temple. In design it follows the plan of a royal tomb in the Valley of the Kings. There is a long descending corridor, which has its entrance in the desert. This is decorated with reliefs of the 'Book of Gates' just as a royal tomb would have been. The corridor turns 90 degrees and, passing through two vestibules, enters the columned hall. Here the construction was of massive granite piers and architraves. In the middle of the room a sarcophagus and canopic chest were placed on an 'island', surrounded by a canal which was intended to be permanently full of water. Another chamber beyond the hall preserves its astronomical ceiling. It is probable that a hill was raised over the structure, planted with trees.

Temple of Ramesses II

North of the Sety I temple, a short walk across the desert, stands the remains of the **Temple of Ramesses II**. Comparable in plan to one of the mortuary temples on the west bank at Luxor, it is more conventional than the Sety I temple. A pylon and gateway gave access to the first courtyard, most of which is now destroyed. A second pylon with granite gatway lead into the second court, surrounded by square pillars with attached Osiride statues of the king. There are fine relief sculptures of religious processions, and lengthy lists with the 'name rings' of Egypt's foreign enemies. As is usual, a terrace and portico mark the entrance to the temple proper. On the main axis are two columned halls, the second with several sanctuaries. The temple is built in a fine-grained limestone, and there is much delicate relief sculpture. In places the colour is well preserved, despite being open to the sky. Of particular note is the procession of nome figures in the columned hall. On the exterior of the north and west walls are scenes of the Battle of Qadesh, which are worth examining for the details of the armour and weapons of the enemy and the foreign mercenaries in the Egyptian army. Of these, the Shardana warriors, with their horned helmets, round shields, sharp swords and distinctive facial features are easily recognizable. From this temple parts of a second list of kings were removed to London (British Museum).

A number of other sites are scattered over a vast area, but are of not great interest to most visitors. The main cult temple of Osiris (known as Kom el-Sultan) lies north of the Temple of Ramesses II, on the edge of the cultivation. Presumably the ancient city lay nearby. To the west are some important monuments of the Early Dynastic period. The Shunet el-Zebib ('Storehouse of Dates') has massive mud-brick walls still standing to a height of 12 metres, and 5 metres thick. It is a double enclosure, and, although generally referred to as a fort, is probably a cult complex associated with the

WOMEN IN ANCIENT EGYPT

T he female principle was a vital element to Egyptian religion, and men clearly feared female sexuality and power at the same time as revering it. The great goddesses, notably Hathor and Isis, were creator goddesses and gave birth to the sun (the ceiling in the chapel at Dendera shows this). They are also shown as the mother of the king and, through the act of suckling him, give him divine power.

Although she played a prominent role, the role of the Egyptian queen was directly related to that of the pharaoh. There was no word for 'queen' in our sense: they were either 'King's Great (Chief) Wife', 'King's Wife', or 'King's Mother'. Similarly there was no concept of a regnant queen, since the kingship was masculine. Those women who did assume sole rule therefore became female kings, wore the male regalia and, in the case of Hatshepsut, were actually depicted as men. Although kings did marry full or half sisters, this was less common than generally supposed, and most queens were daughters of officials. Egyptologists once thought that the right to the throne was through the female line, but we now know this was not the case except when there was no male heir.

Egyptian women generally had more rights than in other ancient societies. They could act in legal matters on their own behalf, without a male relative as their representative. They could own property, and bequeath it to their children or, as in the case of Naunakhte, leave a will disinheriting ungrateful children. In cases of divorce, women received their dowries back, and additional property, unless accused of adultery.

Even so, the ideal woman in Egyptian art and literature appears as the subordinate companion of man, either as mother, wife or daughter. That ideal beauty, found in many tomb paintings, is described in this love poem:

She looks like the morning star
Rising at the beginning of a happy year.
Shining bright, fair of skin,
Lovely is the look in her eyes,
Sweet is the speech of her lips,
She has not a word too much.
Upright neck, shining breast,
Her hair like real lapis lazuli;
Her arms are gold, her fingers like
lotus buds.

Heavy thighs, narrow waist,
Her legs parade her beauty;
With graceful step she treads the ground,
And captures my heart by her
movements.
She causes all men's necks to turn to
see her.
Joy has he whom she embraces.
When she walks abroad she is like the
Eye of the Sun.

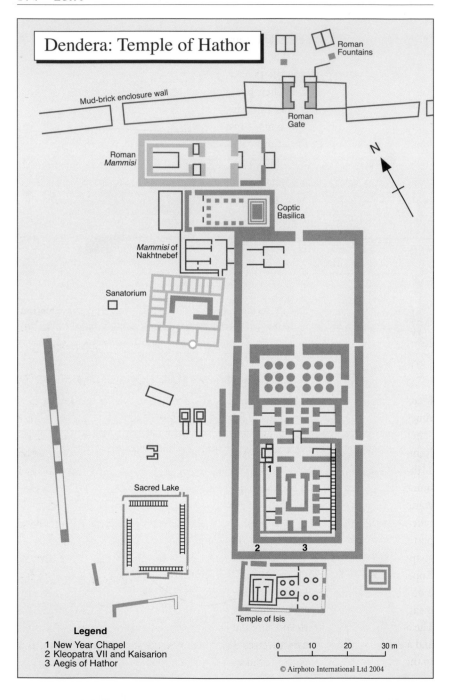

Dendera: Temple of Hathor

Roman Fountains

Mud-brick enclosure wall

Roman Gate

N

Roman Mammisi

Coptic Basilica

Mammisi of Nakhtnebef

Sanatorium

Sacred Lake

1

2   3

Temple of Isis

Legend

1 New Year Chapel
2 Kleopatra VII and Kaisarion
3 Aegis of Hathor

0   10   20   30 m

© Airphoto International Ltd 2004

burials of the early pharaohs 3 kilometres further west in the area known as Umm el-Qaab ('Mother of Pots'). The large mud-brick mastaba tombs of the late Pre-Dynastic and Early Dynastic rulers have been excavated here, although much has been covered again by sand. Their position appears to relate to the wadi entrance further off. This was perhaps thought of as the entrance into the underword. Important finds continue to be made here, most recently a group of Early Dynastic boat burials comparable with those adjacent to the Giza pyramids.

Some 2 kilometres south of the Temple of Sety I is a group of Middle and early New Kingdom monuments. They include a temple of Senusret III and a terraced temple of Queen Tetisheri, the mother of Ahmose, reuniter of Egypt (18th Dynasty). A pyramid, with chapel, commemorates Ahmose himself. The chapel has been excavated recently and yielded small fragments of relief sculpture recording Ahmose's military victories.

DENDERA

D endera strikes one by its vast scale, which is emphasized by its isolation. It is sometimes possible to visit in the evening when the temple is floodlit (silent with no unnecessary theatricals), which reveals the real majesty of Egyptian temples.

Dedicated to Hathor, greatest of Egyptian goddesses, the temple was once the focus of an important town, Iunyt, 'the Pillar'. A temple existed here from earliest times, and an ancient image of the goddess was preserved in the chapel behind the sanctuary, as was a statue of Pepi I. The temple as we now see it is of Ptolemaic–Roman date, although parts of earlier structures are to be found in the court, and an 11th-dynasty chapel has been re-erected in the Egyptian Museum. The sanctuary and inner parts of the temple are a Ptolemaic construction, the great hypostyle hall being completed in year 21 of the emperor Tiberius (AD 34). The columns of the hypostyle take the form of the naos-sistrum, a cultic object of Hathor. Here the ceiling is particularly noteworthy for its zodiac. The Ptolemaic part of the temple has a pylon-shaped façade (now forming the back wall of the hypostyle hall). The Hall of Appearances is supported by six Hathor-head columns, and flanked by six chambers. Two of these have doors leading to the outside, one for the food offerings (notably meat) to be brought in, and the other giving access to the nearby well, for pure water. The other rooms were for the preparation of perfumes and unguents, keeping statues, and a treasury. The last chamber gives direct access to the staircase to the roof, and to the inner parts of the temple (used when the main doors were not opened). The

Hall of Offerings has access to the stairs to and from the roof. Here the daily offerings to the goddess were made. The hall immediately preceding the sanctuary was the Hall of the Ennead, where the statues of the other deities that were in the temple were brought on festival days. The sanctuary, or 'Great Seat', is decorated with scenes of the daily ritual, with the naos and barque of the goddess.

The chambers for other deities that surround the sanctuary have some good reliefs. The first on the east is for the nome-gods of Dendera; the next for Isis; then Sokar. The dedication of the next chamber is unclear, either Hor-sema-tawy (son of Hathor), or (perhaps, with) 'Son of Earth', a serpent god. The two connected chambers at the angle of the building were for the gods of Lower Egypt and the sistrum. The central chamber on the rear wall contained statues of the goddess, and a particularly ancient one was preserved in the chamber high in the wall. This statue showed the goddess squatting, presumably in the act of giving birth. Directly behind this chamber on the exterior wall was the aegis of the goddess, and place where worshippers could communicate directly with the goddess. The chambers in the southwest angle were for the statue of Ra. From the first of these it is possible to descend to the crypts where there are large, superbly carved images of the sacred emblems of the goddess. These include a particularly imposing depiction of the *menat*-collar, which was housed in the next chamber on the west. The last shrine was for Ihy, Hathor's divine child, the remainder of the space being occupied by the small court and the elevated New Year chapel where the statue of the goddess was brought for that festival. The ceiling here shows the arched figure of the sky goddess giving birth to the sun whose rays illuminate the image of Hathor, which emerges like the sun itself between the hills of the horizon.

The staircase leading to the roof has large figures carrying the images, shrines and emblems for the rituals. On the roof are two suites of chapels dedicated to Osiris, of which the more distinctive is on the east. Of its splendid astronomical ceiling, divided by a high relief figure of the goddess Nut, the zodiac is a plaster cast from the original that was removed early in the 19th century (and is now at the Louvre, in Paris). The light, columned kiosk at the back of the temple was for the ritual of 'Union with the Solar Disc', when the statue of the goddess was revived by exposure to the sun's rays.

The reliefs on the exterior rear back wall depict Kleopatra VII and her son by Julius Caesar, Kaisarion. Although Kleopatra was the ruler of Egypt, her son, still a child, is given precedence and is shown as an adult. Note also the great aegis of Hathor in the centre of the wall, mutilated in Christian times. This image was covered in gold

(above left) *Girl at Beni Hasan;* (above right) *Washing water buffalo, Asyut;* (centre right)
Ox-driven water wheel, Qena; (below) *Pilgrim's home showing scenes from the Haj, Dendera*

foil and would have been a place for ordinary people to worship the goddess, although it would have been veiled from the eyes of the profane.

A small Temple of Isis, built by Nakhtnebef (Nectanebo I) of the 30th Dynasty, stands behind the main sanctuary, with a separate chapel (reign of Augustus) arranged at right angles to its axis. In this chapel, the centre of the back wall has a deeply carved series of emblems of Hathor (aegis, collar and sistra) and an unusual, full-face figure of the goddess giving birth. A gateway in the enclosure wall probably indicates a processional route between the birth house and the temple of Ihy, which can be seen across the fields.

Returning to the courtyard along the western side of the temple, there is a relief showing the pharaoh presenting all of the crowns of Egypt. In addition to the red and white crowns and the *nemes*-headdress, there are some extravagant confections of horns, serpents and scarabs which are typical of the Ptolemaic and Roman periods. The reliefs on the outer wall of the hypostyle hall depict the emperor Nero in Pharaonic guise.

Dendera is a good example of a temple complex, with its *mammisi*, sanatorium and sacred lake enclosed by massive walls. The mounds of brick and broken pottery that surround the temple conceal the remains, mostly unexcavated, of the priests' houses, temple storerooms and workshops. Note also the construction of the great enclosure wall, mud-brick in rising and falling waves; this is pan-bedding to permit the sections of the walls to rise and fall when the water table rose, so that it did not crack. It may also symbolize the watery chaos, Nun, from which the island of creation (ie the temple) rose.

The *mammisi* of Nakhtnebef (Nectanebo I) of the 30th Dynasty is the only earlier monument surviving *in situ*. Its ground level is much lower than that of the later temple. The interior rooms have some finely carved and well-preserved reliefs of the divine birth, over which the frog-headed goddess Heqet presides. These are a development of the scenes of the birth of the pharaoh found in the temples of Luxor and Deir el-Bahari. Adjacent to the *mammisi* is the Christian basilica. Probably of fifth-century AD date, it is very plain except for the niches with carved eagle (the Baptistry), and cross and foliage surrounds. The Roman *mammisi*, which replaced Nakhtnebef's, has some especially fine, crisply carved scenes on the intercolumnar walls of the colonnade. These depict the emperor Trajan (AD 98–117) making offerings to Hathor and her son Ihy. The emperor wears extraordinarily elaborate kilts and crowns. Against the outer enclosure wall, near the gateway, are arranged many blocks from earlier structures; some are of Middle Kingdom date, others Ramesside. There are also some broken New Kingdom statues, including part of a once-splendid colossal queen (probably Mutnodjmet, the wife of Horemheb).

The enormous gate in the enclosure wall was decorated by the Roman emperors Domitian and Trajan. The threshold is one massive block of granite. The lintels are decorated with a winged sun disc and a winged scarab pushing the sun. Although a common image, the winged scarab is not usually found on this scale, nor is it usually shown, as here, from below, with its legs visible. A large relief of Domitian presenting sistra to Hathor and Isis was originally covered with gold foil. Outside the gate stand the Roman fountains, used by worshippers for purification. The niches originally contained statues of the presiding deities, Hathor, Horus and Ihy. One of the most important festivals was that in which Hathor left Dendera and journeyed south to visit her consort, Horus in his main temple at Edfu.

The temple precinct of Hathor was certainly the largest and most important at Dendera, but there were other temples dedicated to Horus, and to their son, here called Ihy, who was shown as a naked child playing the sistrum. The gateway of one of these temples, probably that of Ihy, is visible across the fields. A short walk along a well-defined path allows a view of the outer enclosure wall of the Hathor precinct and the gateway to the Isis temple. Little, however, remains of the temple other than paving slabs and a few blocks in part of the village, usually the resting place of goats. The notable cemetery dates back to the Old Kingdom and stretches out in the desert, but is the home of packs of feral dogs.

(following pages) *The Temple of Luxor*

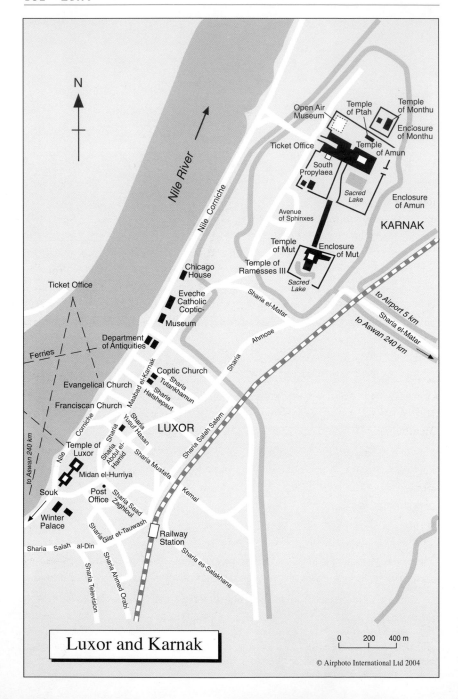

N

Nile River

Nile Corniche

Open Air Museum

Temple of Ptah

Temple of Monthu

Enclosure of Monthu

Ticket Office

Temple of Amun

South Propylaea

Sacred Lake

Enclosure of Amun

Avenue of Sphinxes

KARNAK

Temple of Mut

Enclosure of Mut

Temple of Ramesses III

Sacred Lake

Sharia el-Matar

Chicago House

Eveche Catholic Coptic-Museum

Ahmose

to Airport 5 km

Sharia el-Matar

to Aswan 240 km

Ticket Office

Ferries

Department of Antiquities

Sharia

Coptic Church

Sharia Tutankhamun

Sharia Hatshepsut

Maabad el-Karnak

Evangelical Church

Franciscan Church

Corniche

Sharia Yusuf Hasan

LUXOR

Nile

Temple of Luxor

Sharia Abdul el-Hamid

Sharia Mustafa Kemal

Sharia Salah Salem

to Aswan 240 km

Midan el-Hurriya

Souk

Post Office

Sharia Saad Zaghloul

Sharia Gisr et-Tauwash

Winter Palace

Railway Station

Sharia es-Salakhana

Sharia Salah al-Din

Sharia Ahmed Orabi

Sharia Television

Luxor and Karnak

0   200   400 m

© Airphoto International Ltd 2004

LUXOR AND KARNAK

T he town of Luxor (or in Arabic, el-Uqsur, 'the Palaces'), 676 kilometres (420 miles) south of Cairo, is the main tourist centre for the largest surviving concentration of ancient monuments in the Nile Valley: the temples of Karnak and Luxor on the east bank, and the Theban necropolis on the west bank.

Many names have been given to this region during its history, but the most commonly used as a general term is Thebes, which is Greek in origin. Why the Greeks took the name Thebes is uncertain, but today it is used to refer to the whole of the area, both east and west banks. The original Egyptian name of the town was Waset, derived from the *was*-sceptre, a symbol of divine power carried by the gods. In the later 18th Dynasty, the town was paralleled with Heliopolis (in Egyptian, Iunu) and called the 'Southern Iunu'. Biblical texts refer to it as No, or No-Ammon, from the Egyptian for 'city' (*niu*), and 'City of Amun', and in Ptolemaic–Roman times the name was Diospolis Megale (Magna). From the Middle Kingdom onwards one of the chief cities of Egypt, Thebes was a major residence city of the kings, as well as the burial place of the rulers of the 11th and 17th to 20th dynasties.

In the Old Kingdom, Thebes was a small town of little importance. Its rise to power began in the First Intermediate Period when the local princes extended their control over much of Upper Egypt and gradually northward against the rulers of Herakleopolis. After a lengthy civil war, Egypt was reunited by Nebhepetre-Menthuhotep II, who chose to be buried at Deir el-Bahari.

Although of Upper Egyptian origin, the 12th-dynasty kings chose the Memphis–Faiyum region as their major power base and burial site. Nevertheless, their building works and endowments in the Temple of Amun at Karnak established it as a shrine of national importance.

During the Second Intermediate Period, princes who claimed descent from the 13th-dynasty kings ruled Thebes. Their control extended over much of Upper Egypt. These were the rulers who began the campaigns against the Hyksos and the Kushites, most effectively under Kamose and his younger brother and successor, Ahmose.

Ahmose's campaigns brought the whole of Egypt, and Nubia as far as the Second Cataract, back under the control of one king. His successors expanded Egypt's power

(following pages) *The temples of Karnak grew over centuries, with complex additions and two main axes. The Hypostyle Hall stands at the centre of this view across the Sacred Lake, with the obelisk of Hatshepsut near the sanctuary rooms.*

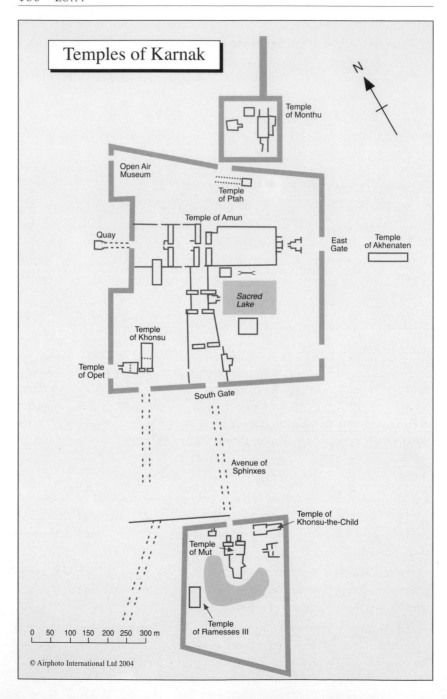

Temples of Karnak

Temple of Monthu

Open Air Museum

Temple of Ptah

Temple of Amun

Quay

East Gate

Temple of Akhenaten

Sacred Lake

Temple of Khonsu

Temple of Opet

South Gate

Avenue of Sphinxes

Temple of Khonsu-the-Child

Temple of Mut

Temple of Ramesses III

0 50 100 150 200 250 300 m

© Airphoto International Ltd 2004

even further afield, establishing her pre-eminence throughout the Near East, from the river Euphrates to the Fourth Cataract of the Nile. Although Memphis remained the major administrative city, the kings chose their native town of Thebes as their burial place and lavishly endowed the temples of its gods.

After Ramesses II made Per-Ramesses in the Delta his major residence, new building works at Karnak were much reduced in scale, although Thebes remained the royal burial place. The high priests of Amun and a group of noble families were the prime power during the Third Intermediate Period: the royal representatives were princesses who held the office of God's Wife of Amun.

The last period of large-scale royal building activity was during the 25th Dynasty, whose kings were especially devoted to the worship of Amun. With their sisters and daughters serving as God's Wife, and with royal princes as High Priests of Amun and Mayors of Thebes, the 25th Dynasty had a strong presence in the city, greatly important to their empire, which stretched from the Mediterranean to present-day Khartoum.

The Assyrian invasion of 664 BC drove Taharqo from Egypt and spelt disaster for Thebes. The city was sacked and looted of its treasure, a catastrophe that resounded throughout the world.

Restoration and building work continued throughout the Late and Ptolemaic–Roman Periods, but Thebes never regained its former importance. A rebellion, centred upon Thebes and encouraged by the priests of Amun, exacted the retribution of Ptolemy Soter II. Roman visitors, awed though they were by its monuments, found the city itself reduced to little more than a cluster of villages.

TEMPLES OF KARNAK

The temples lie some three kilometres (1.9 miles) north of Luxor. Although usually applied to the central enclosure, the Temple of Amun also embraces the southern enclosure of the goddess Mut and the northern enclosure of Monthu.

Karnak impresses the visitor less by the beauty and elegance of its buildings and sculptures (though these can be found) than by the vastness and complexity of the temples, and the massiveness of certain parts.

The Temple of Amun was built, enlarged and rebuilt over more than 1,000 years, a process which is still imperfectly understood. Today, the three groups of temples, the enclosures of Amun, Mut and Monthu, are surrounded by enormous brick walls erected by Nakhtnebef (Nectanebo I). In the New Kingdom, the Amun temple lay

inside a far smaller precinct, the wall of which is still visible in places. The Temple of Ptah, by the north gate, and the chapels of Osiris all originally lay outside the Amun precinct and within their own enclosures, probably along the roads of the city of Thebes which surrounded the Amun temple to the north and east.

In the Old Kingdom, the chief deity worshipped at Thebes was the solar and war god, Monthu. The earliest-known temples dedicated to Amun belong to the First Intermediate Period and the Middle Kingdom. The origins of Amun are obscure: in the earliest reliefs at Karnak he is worshipped as an aspect of Min. Little remains *in situ* of these earliest temples at Karnak (see Middle Kingdom Court, below), but many blocks and fragments of buildings and statuary have been recovered from the foundations of later works. Statues found here, of Senusret I as Osiris, and of Senusret III, are now in the Cairo and

The Nile at Luxor divides the temples of Luxor and Karnak on the east bank from the City of the Dead on the west bank.

Luxor museums and in the Court of the Cachette. A good impression of the early building works is conveyed by the reconstructed chapels in the Open Air Museum, situated to the north of the first courtyard (the admission price is additional to the temple entrance fee).

A visit to Karnak can be an exhausting experience, and, by the complex nature of the ruins involves a lot of walking and retracing of steps. The normal guided tour walks in a straight line through the first court to the sanctuary and then out to the Sacred Lake. A visit that attempts to include the whole range of monuments is best divided, with one or more breaks at the café by the Sacred Lake. The following description of the monuments begins with the main axis of the temple; the Temple of Thutmose III; the eastern and northern parts of the enclosure; the southern courts;

Obelisk at Karnak

and the Temple of Khonsu. Those with any strength left may choose to walk back to Luxor via the Processional Way and the enclosure of the goddess Mut.

OPEN AIR MUSEUM

A number of the monuments reconstructed in the Open Air Museum were found inside the Third Pylon of Amenhotep III (including parts of chapels he himself had built). They originally stood in the court (the 'Festival Court of Thutmose II') that occupied the meeting place of the north–south and east–west axes of the temple, which was later covered by Amenhotep III's massive new entrance.

The **White Chapel of Senusret I** was carefully dismantled and used as building material in the Third Pylon of Amenhotep III. A simple structure on a high platform with a peristyle of square pillars, the whole is covered in delicate low relief in the finest style of the Middle Kingdom. A ramp-staircase at both ends leads to the resting place for the statue or sacred barque. Built from hard white limestone, this small structure has a refinement and elegance lacking in many of the more massive monuments of the New Kingdom. The chapel's first use was probably for the celebration of the jubilee festival, but it was later a resting place for the divine statue in procession.

The building works of the early New Kingdom self-consciously continued Middle Kingdom artistic traditions. Amenhotep I had Senusret I's White Chapel copied, and the Middle Kingdom inheritance is clearly seen in the decoration of his own **Alabaster Barque Shrine**. The shrine, simple in design and with delicate relief (note the fine portraits of Amenhotep I) is made of Egyptian alabaster (properly calcite, or travertine) from Hatnub in Middle Egypt. It originally had doors of wood covered with bronze, both materials brought from Asia. One of the outer faces was decorated by Thutmose I. The barque shrine was dismantled by Thutmose III who built an almost identical shrine in the same place, the remains of which can be seen next to the Seventh Pylon (see below).

Whilst there is little earlier than the reign of Thutmose I *in situ* at Karnak, later constructions were also dismantled and used as building material. One of the finest and most important of these works, the **Red Chapel of Hatshepsut**, is also housed in the Open Air Museum. Of hard red quartzite with a base of black granite, it is thought that the shrine was to have served as the main sanctuary of Amun, although it may never have been completed. Hatshepsut included herself and Thutmose III in the decoration on the shrine, but after his accession as sole ruler, Thutmose III seems to have attempted alterations to remove Hatshepsut's name and figures. This attempt was abandoned, perhaps because the hardness of the stone rendered the alterations unsightly, and the structure was replaced with a shrine of Thutmose's own. Most of Hatshepsut's figures and cartouches remain undamaged and the blocks have many interesting scenes, including one of the earliest depictions of the Opet Festival.

A beautifully decorated shrine of Thutmose IV, constructed of calcite, was also found in the Third Pylon. Monuments of this ruler are rather rare, many having been dismantled by his son and successor Amenhotep III. However, surviving elements display the fine style of relief sculpture that we usually associate with the later king, and show the importance of Thutmose's reign in the development of 18th Dynasty art. The Franco-Egyptian Centre at Karnak rebuilt and cleaned the chapel in 1995–1996. The massive blocks average 30 tons each in weight, the ceiling blocks 35 tons. In form, the barque shrine is very similar to the chapel of Amenhotep I, near which it now stands. The shrine originally stood in the southwest angle of the festival court of Thutmose II, and had been built against a barque shrine of Thutmose III. Parts of this shrine have been reconstructed nearby. Another reconstructed monument of Thutmose IV (behind the Red Chapel) has square pillars covered in delicate low relief sculpture.

Also of interest in the museum is a relief of Amenhotep IV (Akhenaten) slaughtering his enemies. Originally decorating the gateway of the Third Pylon, this scene was carved before the change in artistic style and the emphasis upon worship of the Aten early in the king's reign. Many smaller architectural elements from buildings of the Middle Kingdom and early 18th Dynasty can also be seen. One of the earliest is a column of Antef II (with the earliest known reference to Amun from Karnak) found in the Middle Kingdom Court. Stone lintels and door jambs with the names of Senusret I and III, Ahmose and Amenhotep I belong to other buildings which are now lost.

TEMPLE OF AMUN: THE GROWTH OF THE TEMPLE

Any attempt to understand how Karnak developed should begin in the **Middle Kingdom Court** at the temple's heart. This 'court' is the site of the Middle Kingdom temple, the plan of which (or its later replacement) is visible in the few foundation courses surviving. The temple was oriented east–west, with entrance towards the river. Its plan was simple, comprising a sanctuary with side rooms and a hall in front. The relationship of the temple to the other Middle Kingdom buildings is very unclear, but in front of it, perhaps in the area of the Third Pylon and the junction with the southern courtyards, there may have been a jubilee court. It is certain that many of the Middle Kingdom monuments still stood until the mid-18th Dynasty.

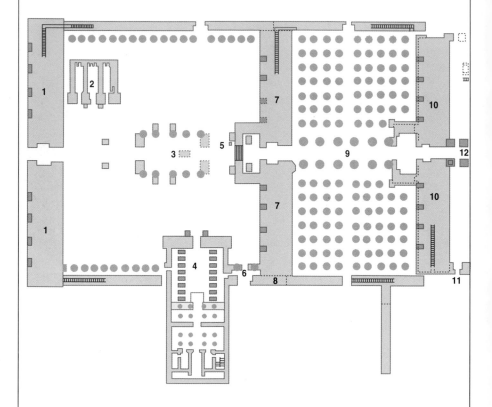

Karnak: Temple of Amun

1   First Pylon
2   Barque Shrine of Sety II
3   Kiosk of Taharqo
4   Temple of Ramesses III
5   Colossus of Pinudjem I
6   Bubastite Portal

7   Second Pylon
8   Scene of Sheshonq I
9   Hypostyle Hall
10 Third Pylon
11 Gate of Ramesses IX
12 Obelisks of Thutmose I

0   10   20   30   40   50 m

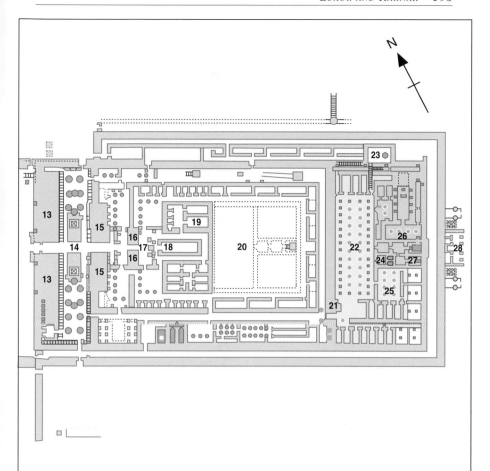

13 Fourth Pylon
14 Obelisks of Hatshepsut
15 Fifth Pylon
16 Sixth Pylon
17 Hall of Annals
18 Shrine of Philip Arrhidaios
19 Reliefs of Hatshepsut
20 The Middle Kingdom Court

21 Karnak Table of Kings
22 Festival Hall of Thutmose III
23 The Solar Chapel
24 Chapel of the Royal *Ka*
25 Chapel of Sokar-Osiris
26 The Botanical Garden
27 Reliefs of Alexander the Great
28 The Eastern Temple

Middle Kingdom houses have been excavated inside and outside the 30th Dynasty precinct wall, indicating that parts of the town then lay to the east where the Eastern Temple and Gate and the Osiris chapels now stand.

Few fragments of the building works of the 13th–17th dynasties have been recovered, but amongst them is one of Egypt's most important historical texts, the '**Stele of Kamose**'. Now in Luxor Museum, the stele was recovered from the foundations of the colossus (Pinudjem) in the first courtyard, in 1954. One of at least two such monuments, the text is the second part of the account of Kamose's victories over the Hyksos at their Delta capital of Avaris.

The 18th Dynasty and the New Kingdom are marked by the accession of Ahmose, Kamose's brother and successor, who finally drove the Hyksos from Egypt and reunited the country. Although he inaugurated the period of Karnak's greatest importance, Ahmose is represented here by only one fragmentary lintel (now in the Open Air Museum), which copies a monument of Senusret I.

Amenhotep I, a ruler later revered at Karnak and throughout the Theban region, certainly built many monuments to Amun, but again little survives *in situ*. A temple and gateway, oriented north–south, may have occupied the area of the Court of the Cachette. Here also may have stood the White Chapel of Senusret I, of which Amenhotep I commanded a limestone copy to be made. Further south still was the Alabaster Barque Shrine (now in the Open Air Museum) in which the god's sacred boat rested before being sailed on the Sacred Lake.

It is necessary to oversimplify the description of the Amun temple's expansion since many details are still uncertain, and it is not always possible to know whether the works of some individual rulers (eg Thutmose I and III) are the result of many additions and alterations during the reign, or part of a broader scheme extending over their whole reign. Indeed, just because a building carries the name of a king does not mean that he necessarily founded it; he may have merely been responsible for the decoration of a predecessor's unfinished work.

Thutmose I enclosed the Middle Kingdom temple (court) within a circuit wall which extended to the west, creating a courtyard in front of the older building. The wall enclosed the area now occupied by the shrine of Philip Arrhidaios and the rooms of Hatshepsut: its western limit is the Sixth Pylon. This court was probably lined with the colossal statues of the king as Osiris, which are now located in the halls between the Fourth/Fifth and Fifth/Sixth pylons. Thutmose I enclosed his building within a second circuit wall, creating a corridor around the northern, eastern and southern (where it is somewhat broader) sides. The temple was also extended further west with the construction of the Fourth and Fifth pylons and two narrow halls. Thutmose I may himself have had the Osiride statues removed to line these halls. The roof of the hall behind the Fourth Pylon was supported by a single line of columns, the foundations and bases of which are visible in excavated pits. The Fourth Pylon marked the main entrance to the temple, and continued to do so until the reign of Amenhotep III.

Hatshepsut's 22-year reign may well have seen the inauguration, or planning, of much of the work completed, decorated and dedicated in the name of Thutmose III. The monuments finished by her were either dismantled or altered by her successor. The magnificent barque shrine of Amun, the Red Chapel (now in the Open Air Museum), probably stood near the present site of the **Sanctuary of Philip Arrhidaios**, surrounded by the suite of rooms in red sandstone. The chambers which Hatshepsut built around the barque shrine abutted the Middle Kingdom temple on its western side. One wall has been removed from its original position to one of the side rooms, and although Hatshepsut's figures have been erased, the clear colour and handsome style of relief typical of this reign survive in the figures of Amun.

Hatshepsut's other building works at Karnak extended the temple to the east, where a chapel with two more obelisks (their bases still visible) was later developed by Thutmose III (see the Eastern Temple, below). To the south, Hatshepsut elaborated the southern courtyards and the Processsional Way to Luxor (see below).

The most striking feature of the building works of Thutmose III is that they enclose, develop within and expand to the east and south of those of Thutmose I, but do not extend further to the west. Thutmose I's pylon (the Fourth) remained the main entrance to the temple, although Thutmose III did set up his own pair of obelisks in front of those set up by his grandfather.

In the hall between the Fourth and Fifth pylons, Thutmose III encased the obelisks of Hatshepsut in stone to the height of the roof, hiding them from view from within the temple. Here also he erected two rows of pillars where there had been one. Gates attached to both sides of the now-encased obelisks created a corridor between the Fourth and Fifth pylons. More gateways between the Fifth and Sixth pylons and walls in front of the sanctuary turned the whole temple into a massive corridor with rooms to the north and the south.

Abutting the east outer wall of Thutmose I, Thutmose III built the Akh-Menu, a complete temple related in design and function to the mortuary temples of the kings (see below). Access to this temple was made by cutting a gateway in the Thutmose I wall at the east end of the broad southern corridor. Further east still, the king constructed the Eastern Temple.

Thutmose III also made alterations to the southern courtyards and pylons (see below), dismantling some of the buildings of Amenhotep I, replacing the king's barque shrine near the Seventh Pylon with an identical one in his own name. Thutmose III erected another barque shrine in the court in front of the Fourth Pylon, which served as a resting place when processions turned to the southern Processional Way. He also enlarged the Sacred Lake.

The main axis of the temple seems to have remained unaltered during the reigns of Amenhotep II and Thutmose IV, although buildings of theirs (later dismantled and used as fill in the Third Pylon) are known. Thutmose IV added a porch (in wood) to the Fourth Pylon, which remained the main entrance to the temple. He added a calcite barque shrine (now in the Open Air Museum) to the court in front in front of the Fourth Pylon. This abutted the barque shrine of Thutmose III.

It was Amenhotep III who began the expansion westward towards the river, removing everything that occupied the court at the junction of the north–south and east–west axes.

TEMPLE OF AMUN: THE MAIN AXIS

There are very few ancient depictions of the Karnak temple, but from the evidence available, we can be fairly sure that a large, T-shaped harbour lay in front of the temple, with a canal (following the line of the modern road) connecting it to the Nile. The course of the Nile has certainly changed since ancient times, but where it flowed in relation to the temples, whether closer or further away, is unknown. The present quay was built by Ramesses II and has small obelisks of Sety II at the foot of the ramp (also notice here how much lower the level of the temple is compared to modern ground level). On the front (western side) of the quay are many important Nile level texts recording the height of the river. The texts are a valuable addition to the historical sources as they give year dates for many of the kings of the Libyan and Kushite periods. They can be seen from the wooden footbridge which connects the quay with the road, or by walking down into the cleared area around the quay. South of the avenue can be seen a series of ramps (25th Dynasty) which led down to the harbour and were used for collecting water for temple rituals.

By the end of the New Kingdom, the area between the quay and the main entrance of the temple, the Second Pylon, was filled with gardens and the

The colossal pillars of the Great Hypostyle Hall at Karnak were originally brightly painted. They supported a solid roof, and with only clerestory windows, evoked the gloom of the primordial swamp.

Processional Way flanked by an avenue of ram-headed sphinxes. The sphinxes, each with a lion's body and a ram's head, protect figures of Ramesses II (recarved for Pinudjem I). Today the avenue runs only from the quay to the First Pylon and many of the sphinxes line the sides of the first courtyard. The present entrance to the complex, the massive and unfinished First Pylon was probably built in the 25th Dynasty (although some scholars suggest a 30th-dynasty date). Remains of the brick ramps used in the construction of the southern tower can still be seen in the court. Although 113 metres (371 feet) wide, 15 metres (49.2 feet) thick and rising some 40 metres (131.3 feet) high, the impressiveness of the pylon is somewhat reduced by its unfinished state.

The first stone building in the gardens in front of the temple was the barque shrine of Sety II, now contained within the first courtyard (north side). A resting place for the statues of Amun, Mut and Khonsu during the processional festivals, it contains three chapels decorated with scenes of the king making offerings to the sacred barques. Note also the niches in the easternmost chapel, which held statues of the king himself. The doorway to the central chapel was flanked by two statues of the king carrying staffs. The bases of these survive (one statue in the Louvre).

In the 20th Dynasty, Ramesses III built a second barque shrine, of far more elaborate design, on the southern side of the Processional Way. The shrine is actually a complete miniature temple. A pylon entrance, flanked by statues of the king, gives onto the festival hall, a courtyard lined with a colonnade of square piers with Osiride statues of the king. A short staircase leads to the terrace of the temple with its portico, columned hall and sanctuary rooms. The courtyard has scenes of the processions of Amun (east wall) and Min (west wall). A ramp leads to the terrace of the temple with a colonnade of four pillars. The hall beyond gives access to the main sanctuary. The decoration in the sanctuary is quite well preserved. The outer western wall (access through a small door behind the colonnade) has a large scene of the river procession to Luxor. The whole gives a good idea of the basic classic plan of a late New Kingdom temple (compare with the Khonsu temple).

The area of the first courtyard (103 metres by 84 metres, 336 by 276 feet) was enclosed with colonnades in the 22nd Dynasty, and between the Temple of Ramesses III and the Second Pylon, Sheshonq I built the gate known as the Bubastite Portal, with, on its outer face, a scene of the king presenting captured Asiatic cities to Amun. Sheshonq I is generally (but probably wrongly) identified with the biblical 'Shishak, King of Egypt', who captured Jerusalem (I Kings 14: 25–26) in 925 BC. The inner faces of the gate have reliefs depicting Sheshonq I being suckled by a goddess in the presence of his son, the High Priest of Amun, Iuwelot, who oversaw the construction works. An inscription at Gebel Silsila records the quarrying of stone for the work here.

In the centre of the courtyard stand the ruins of the immense Kiosk of Taharqo, one of the Kushite pharaohs, who was responsible for the last major additions to Karnak. Ten open papyrus columns in two rows formed a great colonnade, probably unroofed, which flanked a huge altar of alabaster. The screen walls are a Ptolemaic addition. Today only one of the columns is complete, having been restored to its original height of 26 metres (85.3 feet). It may have been the construction of this kiosk that necessitated the removal of the rams from the Processional Way to the side of the court. At the entrance to the kiosk is a fine calcite sphinx of late 18th-dynasty date, probably depicting Tutankhamun or Horemheb.

The Second Pylon, called 'Illuminating Thebes', was the main western entrance to Karnak for some 500 years. The great gateway is still flanked by royal statues, two striding figures of Ramesses II and the Colossus of Pinudjem I. Carved in pink granite, this rigid image of a ruler, his crook and flail crossed on this chest, is an impressive, but hardly beautiful, icon. Rather different is the graceful queen who stands on his feet and reaches just to his knee. The statue is usually thought to have been carved probably for Ramesses II towards the end of his reign, but may actually be a recarved statue of Amenhotep III. It was usurped by Ramesses VI and again later by the High Priest of Amun, Pinudjem I. The massive towers of the Second Pylon stand only to half of their original height. During restoration work many thousands of blocks of stone, known as *talatat*, were found inside them, the remains of Akhenaten's temples dismantled and used as building material. The Second Pylon was completed by Horemheb, and seems to have stood on the site of one of Akhenaten's structures. A Ptolemaic porch stands in front of the entrance to the celebrated Hypostyle Hall.

Amenhotep III may have laid the foundations of the central colonnade of the **Great Hypostyle Hall**. Perhaps he intended the open papyrus columns, like those of the Luxor temple colonnade, to have been flanked by high walls, creating a dark corridor before the temple; the king's other surviving temples at north Karnak (the Monthu temple), Luxor and Soleb (in the Sudan) all have enclosed porticoes or colonnades of this type, a feature of the last years of his reign. Even if the foundations were laid, the work can have been little advanced at the time of the king's death, and Akhenaten soon abandoned work on the Amun temple. When building work began again, in the reign of Tutankhamun, Akhenaten's temples were dismantled, the Second Pylon built, and the many-columned hall was created.

Occupying an area 102 metres by 53 metres (335 feet by 174 feet) the hall has a central nave of 12 open papyrus columns each 22 metres (72.2 feet) high, surrounded by avenues of bundle papyrus columns, 122 altogether, each nearly 15 metres (49.2 feet) high. The Hypostyle Hall is best seen when it is deserted, very early in the morning, or perhaps in the middle of the day, because only then can a true idea of its vastness be gained. Rather lacking in aesthetic charm, it needs silence and time to watch the light and shadow in this stone papyrus swamp. It is difficult to imagine this vast hall roofed in as it would have been: the massive stone window panels with their narrow slits filtering shafts of sunlight into the central aisle and illuminating the colour on the reliefs (some traces remain on the underside of the architraves), as well as the many statues, their offering tables piled high with food and flowers.

The relief decoration of the walls is mostly of religious ceremonies, including the processions of the sacred barques. In places the sculpture is of fine quality, and on a very large scale. The northern parts carry decoration of the reign of Sety I; the remainder was completed by Ramesses II. A number of later Ramessides had their names added on the columns. The outer wall north wall of the Hypostyle Hall was decorated by Sety I with scenes showing his military victories against the Libyans and in Syria–Palestine.

The monumental entrance to Karnak built by Amenhotep III, the Third Pylon, now forms the back wall of the Hypostyle Hall. This structure is badly ruined and gives little impression of its original massiveness. The pylon stands on the site of an earlier courtyard, the Festival Court of Thutmose II. Many of the buildings now in the Open Air Museum were recovered from inside the pylon, carefully dismantled. The gateway of the pylon was decorated by Amenhotep IV (Akhenaten) in the early years of his reign (see Open Air Museum).

Before Amenhotep III built the Third Pylon, the main entrance to the temple had been the pylon of Thutmose I (the Fourth Pylon), and this remained significant with the westward expansion of the temple. To the Egyptians 'Ipet-sut', the residence of Amun, began with the Fourth Pylon. The exact meaning of Ipet-sut is obscure, some Egyptologists understanding it as 'the Most Select of Places', others as 'the Gathering Place of the Thrones'.

The relatively small space between the Third and Fourth pylons was open to the sky, and formed an important junction. To the south lay the courts connecting with processional route to the Sacred Lake, the Temple of Mut and on to Luxor. The Gate of Ramesses IX now connects the two pylons at this point. To the north, the Kushite pharaoh Shabaqo added a columned porch. Amenhotep III's pylon covered a large part

Crossing a canal, Luxor

of the area of the earlier court and lies on the north–south axis of the temple. In building here the king effectively blocked the great Processional Way through the southern courts, and presumably had a cultic purpose in doing so. Formerly processions to the Sacred Lake had turned and passed through the double barque shrine of Thutmose III and Thutmose IV (see Open Air Museum) into the southern courts. Perhaps Amenhotep III wished to emphasize the solar east–west axis of the temple and increase the importance of the river processions to Luxor and the west bank.

The main entrance to Ipet-sut was flanked by the two obelisks of red granite set up by Thutmose I, their points covered with electrum (a natural alloy of gold and silver). Both were still standing 200 years ago, but now only the southern obelisk remains, 19.5 metres (64 feet) high. In front of them was another pair of obelisks erected by Thutmose III. Thutmose IV added a porch to the pylon. Called the 'Great Gate of Electrum' it had two wooden columns sheathed in gold and a pavement of silver. As we see it today, the gateway of the Fourth Pylon is a Ptolemaic restoration, but what is rather interesting is that it replicates the earlier inscriptions. So we can see texts naming Shabaqo and Thutmose IV, all carved by Ptolemaic sculptors.

The Fourth Pylon gave onto a strangely narrow hall, the *wadjyt*, or columned hall, of Thutmose I. This is now lined with large statues of Thutmose I as Osiris, which probably originally lined a court surrounding the Middle Kingdom temple. Hatshepsut removed the roof of this hall in order to raise two obelisks. Brought into the hall from its northern side, they are of granite quarried at Aswan. Hatshepsut's own words record the event:

> 'My majesty began to work on them in year 15; the second month of winter, day one, ending in year 16, fourth month of summer, last day, in total seven months of quarry work...'

The northern obelisk stands intact, 29.5 metres (97.8 feet) high, but of its southern companion only the broken stump remains in place; its upper part now lies near the Sacred Lake. A block (displayed in Luxor Museum) from the Red Chapel shows Hatshepsut presenting her two obelisks to Amun, having had the whole of their upper parts overlaid with electrum. Again, the event is recorded in her own words:

> 'I gave for them of the finest electrum. I measured it by the gallon like sacks of grain. My majesty summoned a quantity beyond what the Two Lands had yet seen. The ignorant and the wise know it...
>
> 'Seen on the two sides of the river, their rays flood the Two Lands when the sun disc rises between them at its appearance on the horizon of heaven.'

Thutmose III re-roofed the hall and encased the lower parts of Hatshepsut's obelisks with large stone blocks, thereby separating the two parts of the columned hall, and creating a new narrow hall between the Fourth and Fifth pylons. The standing obelisk carries a central column of text, deeply and crisply carved in the granite, with the titulary of Hatshepsut. It is flanked by alternating figures of Hatshepsut, designated by her throne name, Maat-ka-ra, and of Thutmose III, making offering to Amun. Although the royal images and names remain untouched, the figure of Amun and his names were partly erased in the reign of Akhenaten. It is obviously extremely difficult to erase carving on granite, especially in this location, and it is extraordinary how much was effected.

The southern part of the columned hall is slightly larger than the northern, having eight rather than six pillars. A gateway in the southern part of the hall gives access to the corridor leading to the Temple of Thutmose III, the Akh-Menu, at the eastern end of the whole complex. The reliefs in the gateway depict a processional statue of Amenhotep III, although the whole was recarved in the reign of Sety II.

The Fifth Pylon, built in limestone, is attributed to Thutmose I, and was called 'Amun is Great of Awe'. The area beyond, with the sanctuary, may originally have been a large court or hall, but was extensively remodelled. Thutmose III built a further pylon, the Sixth, and more building works turned this area into another narrow axial hall. The Sixth Pylon, and walls surrounding the sanctuary, carry the record of the king's victorious campaigns in Asia and the area is consequently known as the Hall of Annals. Here, Thutmose III presented to Amun the military successes which justified his rule.

Immediately before the sanctuary, Thutmose III set up the two square pillars of pink granite decorated in high relief with papyrus (north) and sedge plant or lily (south), the symbols of Lower and Upper Egypt. The crispness of the carving and the simplicity of the design mark these as two of the most handsome of Egyptian pillars. Flanking the doorway into the northern part of the divided hall are two colossal statues of Amun and Amunet. The god's image has the features of Tutankhamun (the shapeless body is part of the modern restoration). The statue of Amunet shows many Amarna characteristics, notably in the modelling of the breasts and belly.

The red granite sanctuary standing at the temple's heart dates from the reign of the Macedonian pharaoh Philip Arrhidaios, half-brother and joint successor of Alexander the Great. A sanctuary of Thutmose III (probably replacing Hatshepsut's Red Chapel) had stood here, although it is perhaps unlikely that it survived the reign of Akhenaten. The sanctuary is a double shrine, the eastern part having a large

The ram-headed sphinxes that flank the Processional Way at Karnak combine the solar lion with the ram sacred to the temple's god, Amun. Originally the rams were crowned with gilded sun discs.

window in it, originally fitted with double doors so that the rising sun could be admitted to shine in upon the god. The exterior shows that the sanctuary was conceived as two separate, but adjoining, elements. Standing on a platform the front part of the sanctuary is higher than the rear, shown by the cornices. The whole is covered with delicate relief sculpture, and much of the original colour is preserved. The coronation of the Macedonian pharaoh is shown on the exterior of the front chamber, and large figures of him making offerings to Amun decorate the rear. Stylistically, the relief carving continues that of the 30th Dynasty. The hieroglyphic texts are large and elegantly laid out.

The sanctuary is surrounded by a two groups of chambers built in sandstone by Hatshepsut. One hall of the group on the north has some well-preserved reliefs depicting Hatshepsut. The scenes were covered over in the reign of Thutmose III by erecting a new screen wall in front of them. Some of the lavish offerings given by Thutmose III to the Temple of Amun are shown on the wall immediately to the north of the sanctuary. Divided into registers, the wall has many different types of

Statues of Ramesses III in the form of Osiris line the courtyard of his temple in the first court of Karnak, one of a number of small temples that acted as resting places for the statue processions.

jewellery, chests and vessels. In the narrow banks separating the registers are given the number of each type presented. Also included are two obelisks and flag-posts for the temple's gateway. The king's annals record that he gave around 15 tons of gold to the temple during his reign.

The sanctuary brings the visitor to the centre of the temple, the so-called Middle Kingdom Court. In the open space, the remains of a temple structure have been planned. There was a sanctuary on the main axis, but how this building was incorporated, architecturally and cultically, into the temple as we now see it, is impossible to know. Looking across the open space, one now sees the colonnade of the main hall of the Akh-Menu of Thutmose III. The main axis of the Amun temple is clearly visible in the slightly wider spacing at the centre of the colonnade. The impression is, however, entirely false, since a solid enclosure wall once surrounded the whole of this area and access to the Akh-Menu was at the southern end, where a doorway is flanked by two standing statues. The ritual access to this door was from the *wadjyt*-hall of Thutmose I, along a direct corridor, avoiding the main axis of the temple.

Temple of Amun: The Akh-Menu of Thutmose III

The entrance to the Akh-Menu was cut in the enclosure wall of Thutmose I and is flanked by two broken standing statues of Thutmose III. The Akh-Menu is a complete temple that has much in common with the mortuary temples of the kings on the west bank. The main entrance leads into a small vestibule. First turn right into a corridor, which opens into chambers. Halfway along this corridor are reliefs showing episodes from the *sed*-festival (jubilee) of Thutmose III. In one scene the king wears the traditional short cloak and in another he shoots arrows, helped by the gods.

Return to the vestibule and enter the **Festival Hall**, oriented north–south. Immediately to the left are two small chambers, one of which contained the **Karnak Table of Kings**, showing Thutmose III making offerings to 61 of his predecessors. An important historical document, most of the blocks were removed to the Louvre and are now replaced by casts. The Festival Hall has a central nave of unusual tent-peg columns which represent in stone the slim wooden poles used to support light constructions such as tents. Many traces of paint are preserved, giving a good idea of the original decoration. The nave is surrounded on all sides by square columns, indicating that although it was built as a hypostyle hall, the room is actually conceived as an open courtyard. On the western side, the Middle Kingdom Court is visible, due to the destruction of the side wall of the hall and the enclosures of Thutmose I. The far (north) end of the hall has three sanctuary rooms. In one of these is a large statue which gives the initial (deceptive) impression of a crucifix; it is actually a very fragmentary group showing the king between two deities. Other pieces lie around it.

On the eastern side of the Festival Hall are various suites of rooms. In a more conventionally planned temple, these suites would have surrounded the hypostyle hall, behind the court and before the sanctuary. The southernmost is the suite of Sokar-Osiris, deity of the underworld. Next to it, a small chamber with two chapels was dedicated to the royal *ka* and contained cult images of the king. North of the door on the axis of the main Amun temple is a suite with a two-columned hall and two chapels, and from the northeast corner of the Festival Hall a staircase leads to the chapel of Ra-Harakhty. The main axis of the Amun temple has been used within the Akh-Menu and has a series of three rooms lying along it. From the second room, a doorway leads into a suite of two rooms, which were partially redecorated by Alexander the Great. The innermost room has a broken colossal statue of a falcon. A modern wooden staircase leads into a suite dedicated to Amun, the first hall of which is supported by elegant sandstone columns. The columns are good examples

The colossus in the first court of the Temple of Amun at Karnak. It was probably carved for Amenhotep III, but was recarved for Ramesses II and now carries the name of the High Priest Pinudjem I.

of the mid-18th-dynasty style. This room is know as the Botanical Garden because of its delicate reliefs of the plants, animals and birds recorded by the artist who accompanied the king on his Asiatic campaigns. As in the Punt scenes at Deir el-Bahari, the artist has shown great interest and skill in depicting the unusual and unfamiliar natural life of foreign lands.

A second modern staircase and bridge across the walls of the Akh-Menu and the outer enclosure wall of Thutmose III leads to the Eastern Temple.

TEMPLE OF AMUN: THE EASTERN AND NORTHERN AREAS

Immediately visible is part of the brick enclosure wall which encircled the Amun precinct in the reign of Thutmose III. Here, the north corner and east wall create a court in front of the **Eastern Temple**. Hatshepsut built a chapel here, probably in brick, with two obelisks, the bases and some shattered fragments of which can still be seen. A large alabaster statue of Hatshepsut with Amun, which formed the focus of this chapel, now stands in the room to the south of the shrine. Thutmose III's chapel comprises three chambers, in front of which is a portico of square columns with Osiride statues of the king. The small gateway opposite the central sanctuary room is of the reign of the emperor Domitian (AD 81–96). The focus of the chapel, the shrine, is an enormous hollowed block of calcite with seated figures of the king with the goddess Amunet. About half of the block survives, but even in this state it is impressive. The outer sides have delicately carved reliefs of all the manifestations of Amun. Originally sealed with wooden doors, this shrine is where Thutmose III was worshipped as the intermediary with, and manifestation of, Amun.

Nakhtnebef (Nectanebo I) of the 30th Dynasty added two small chapels at the northern and southern ends, which enclosed the bases of Hatshepsut's obelisks.

A courtyard, the 'Upper Court' of Karnak, lay in front of the temple, which was entered through the Eastern Gate from the town of Thebes. Here Thutmose IV set up a single obelisk, and its emplacement is still visible between the chapel of Thutmose III and the Temple of Ramesses II. The obelisk was quarried for Thutmose III at Aswan, but it lay in the workshops of the Karnak temple for 35 years until Thutmose III's grandson completed the inscriptions and set it in place. The single obelisk designated this a solar court; the carved figures of Amun-Ra and Amun-Atum associated Amun with the morning and evening sun. The obelisk was removed from Karnak in the reign of Constantine, who wanted it to adorn Constantinople. However, at the emperor's death in AD 337, it was still at Alexandria. Diverted to Rome, it was set up in the Circus Maximus in 357 as a companion to an obelisk erected by Augustus. In 1588, it was rediscovered and erected in the square of St John Lateran at the order of Pope Sixtus V. Today, at 32.18 metres (105.6 feet) high and weighing 455 tons, it is the largest of the standing obelisks.

Towards the east is the back of the Temple of Ramesses II. This temple, which was constructed in front of the Upper Court, served the same function as that of Thutmose III. The chapel itself comprised a pylon and a small hall with Osiride pillars of the king in the centre. The back wall had three doorways, which associated the king with Amun, Mut and Khonsu. Beyond lay a four-pillared hall, which effectively blocked direct access to the single obelisk and chapel of Thutmose III. Before the pylon lay a courtyard, extending probably as far as the huge Eastern Gate and brick *temenos* (a wall enclosing the whole area) of Nakhtnebef (Nectanebo I). The temple was dedicated to Amun and 'Ramesses-who-Hears-the-Petitions-of-the-People'. In front of the pylon are the columns of the portico built in the reign of Taharqo (690–664 BC). Within this temple was discovered the magnificent black granite seated statue of Ramesses II, one of the most famous images of the king, now in the Museo Egizio in Turin.

To the north is the overgrown area between the 18th Dynasty and 30th Dynasty *temenos* walls. The several chapels of Osiris here, which date from the 23rd to 26th dynasties, originally lay within their own small enclosures along the streets of the city of Thebes. Of these chapels, that of Osiris, Ruler of Eternity, is the best preserved. This was originally a two-roomed chapel fronted by a brick-walled courtyard, with its entrance on the northern side. A stone court was added to the chapel by the God's Wife of Amun, Amenirdis I, and her nephew, the 25th-dynasty king, Shebitqo. The reliefs are interesting for the regalia of the god's wife and the king, which display Kushite influences. There is now a lake in front of the chapel, making entrance risky.

Much of the area north of the main temple is unexcavated and overgrown with scrub. Cobras can be a problem here in certain seasons and the ground can subside. Unaccompanied exploration is therefore not recommended. Here lay the Treasury of Shabaqo and other chapels.

Immediately to the north of the court between the Third and Fourth pylons lay the gate through the 18th-dynasty wall and the northern entrance colonnade built in the 25th Dynasty (called the 'Golden Hall of Shabaqo').

A well-defined path runs from the gate in the north wall of the Great Hypostyle Hall to the North Gate of the precinct. Here are more chapels of Osiris dedicated by the God's Wives of Amun, as well as the important Temple of Ptah.

Now wedged against the enclosure wall of Nakhtnebef (Nectanebo I), the Temple of Ptah must originally have occupied a more spacious enclosure on the road leading from the North Gate of the 18th-dynasty wall into the city. In his foundation inscription, Thutmose III says that his stone temple replaced one of mud-brick with wooden pillars. There are now four gateways in front of the temple, perhaps excessive for such a modest shrine. The second and fourth gates were constructed in the reign of the Kushite pharaoh Shabaqo, and must have provided two courtyards in front of the temple. Ptolemaic rulers added the first and third gates, and a columned porch on the façade of the temple. The chief interest of the temple proper, a small building of Thutmose III, is in its complete state. The three chapels are roofed, and when the guardian closes the door, the headless cult image of Ptah and the large granite statue of his consort, the lioness-headed Sakhmet, are eerily illuminated by single shafts of light from above. It is difficult elsewhere to achieve such an impression of an Egyptian sanctuary. The rear wall of the temple carries figures carved in the Ptolemaic period depicting the revered sages Imhotep and Amenhotep son of Hapu. Imhotep was the architect of the Step Pyramid of Djoser, and Amenhotep an official of Amenhotep III. Both had popular cults in the Late Period, and here act as intermediaries with the deities in the temple.

TEMPLE OF AMUN: THE SOUTHERN COURTS AND THE SACRED LAKE

At the junction of the north–south and east–west axes, where the Third Pylon now stands, there may have been a Middle Kingdom temple. It is more certain that the White Chapel of Senusret I and Amenhotep I's limestone copy of it, and the barque shrines of Thutmose III and Thutmose IV (all now in the Open Air Museum) stood in this area. During the New Kingdom, a series of large courtyards and pylon gateways was built stretching south from this area towards the temple of the goddess Mut and the Processional Way to Luxor.

Leaving the narrow court between the Third and Fourth pylons through the **Gate of Ramesses IX**, the first courtyard entered is the **Court of the Cachette** where, in 1902–9, a pit containing over 750 stone statues and stelae and more than 17,000 bronze and wooden statues was excavated. Here the priests, probably in the early Ptolemaic Period, had carefully buried some of the many, now surplus, dedications to the temple. The east and west walls of the courtyard, built in the 19th Dynasty, carry reliefs of Ramesses II (Treaty with the Hittites, west wall, outer side) and Merneptah (the king as a child protected by the ram-headed sphinx of Amun, east wall, inner side, and a copy of the 'Israel Stele').

The doorway of the Temple of Ramesses III frames the only standing column of the great Processional Way of the Kushite pharaoh Taharqo.

The Seventh Pylon, built by Thutmose III, forms the southern wall of the court. Here, against its northern face, are ranged some of the largest statues from the cache, of the Middle and early New Kingdom periods. Note, when passing through the gateway of the pylon, the two niches in the western side which were used for royal statues. The southern entrance to the pylon is flanked by the emplacements for two obelisks and colossal statues. These obelisks are probably the same as those represented in the offering scene of Thutmose III on the wall north of the sanctuary of Philip Arrhidaios. The eastern obelisk is little more than a shattered fragment. Its western companion now stands in the Atmeidan in Istanbul. Made of red granite, its present height is 19.8 metres (65 feet), but probably one-third of it is missing from the lower part. In the early fourth century AD, it was removed from Karnak (the earthworks can still be seen on the western side of the court) to Alexandria, in order to ship it to Constantinople. It eventually reached that city and was raised on the *spina* of the Hippodrome in the reign of Theodosius (AD 379–395). Visitors to Istanbul can examine the sculpted base, with its imperial inscriptions and scenes showing the obelisk aboard its barge, in the Hippodrome.

The remainder of the southern courts is presently inaccessible, as they are closed for restoration work carried out by the Franco-Egyptian Centre. The area can be viewed, however, from the higher ground on the west side on the way to the Temple of Khonsu (see below), and from the east side, where some interesting reliefs are on the outer walls.

Leave the courtyard between the Seventh and Eighth pylons through the gateway in the northeast corner of the courtyard. This leads into the **Barque Shrine of Thutmose III**, a small platform surrounded by a broken colonnade of square piers. In the centre are the lower parts of the alabaster shrine which Thutmose III built to replace the shrine of Amenhotep I (now in the Open Air Museum). Here, after having been carried from the sanctuary, the barque of Amun rested before being sailed on the Sacred Lake. Now descend from the platform and turn right.

The outer wall of the courtyard, between the barque shrine and the door immediately north of the Eighth Pylon, carries three large and unusual scenes. These **reliefs of the High Priest Amenhotep** comprise two similar outer panels depicting the reward of the high priest in front of a statue of Ramesses XI and a central scene of the high priest with the king. These reliefs are important in the history of Karnak and Egypt in the later 20th Dynasty as they mark the rising power of the high priests, which culminated in Herihor's calling himself king in the Temple of Khonsu.

The Eighth Pylon is the work of Hatshepsut, but it was altered by Thutmose III and its decoration (south face) completed by Amenhotep II. Six colossal statues, one of which depicts Amenhotep I, flank the gateway. There is also the lower part of large femal statue, broken at the waist. The upper part was removed by Belzoni (who intended to take the lower part as well) and is now in the British Museum. It represents a royal woman of the early 18th Dynasty with the heavy curled wig of the goddess Hathor.

The southernmost courtyard is larger than the other courts, perhaps in order to bring the gateway opposite the entrance to the Temple of Mut, and to include the chapel of Amenhotep II on its eastern side. The court is bounded on the north by the Ninth Pylon, which carries a dedication text of Horemheb and a copy of the 'Marriage Stele of Ramesses II' (see also Abu Simbel). The stone pylon, completed by Horemheb and filled with *talatat* from the temples of Akhenaten, may have replaced an earlier brick gateway or pylon on the same site. Two colossi of Horemheb flank the entrance. There are interesting reliefs of Horemheb in the southern part of the court, including a Nubian campaign and the king with the chiefs of Punt. The eastern enclosure wall of the court incorporates the **Festival Chapel of Amenhotep II**, altered by Sety I to make it a resting place for the barque of Amun. Raised on a platform, the entrance façade is a long colonnade (more clearly seen from the western side, see below).

The southern gate of Karnak is the Tenth Pylon of Amenhotep III, its outer face and statues (which are worth visiting) can be inspected on the way to the Temple of Mut. The inner face has two colossi of Horemheb, accompanied by small statues of his queen, Mutnodjmet, thought to have been the sister of Nefertiti (these may be recarved from images of Amenhotep III).

The **Sacred Lake** was originally much smaller and the enclosure wall of the early 18th Dynasty probably came to where the Seventh Pylon now stands. The lake was enlarged by Thutmose III. On its southern edge largely unexcavated mounds conceal many buildings, including the **Fowl Pens** where the geese of Amun were kept (the tunnel leading to the lake can still be seen). It is not recommended to walk in this area. On the far eastern side of the lake, beneath the seating stand for the sound and light show, are the **Houses of the Priests**. A street can be made out, with houses leading off it. They seem to have occupied much of the area of the eastern part of the enclosure. Here also are remains of one of the earlier brick precinct walls. At the northwestern corner of the lake is the **Granite Scarab of Amenhotep III**. Brought from the mortuary temple of the king (behind the Colossi of Memnon), the scarab is an image of the solar god, Khepri. Nearby (next to the cafeteria) is the

Temple of Taharqo (690–664 BC). The present structure incorporates blocks from a building of Shabaqo (*c.*711–695 BC): notice the fine relief head of Shabaqo wearing the white crown, rebuilt into an otherwise plain area of wall on the east side. The king wears the double uraeus, a feature of the 25th Dynasty, and often erased by later rulers.

Taharqo's building was an elevated platform with subterranean rooms (inaccessible). The platform probably had a solar court where the image of the god was brought following rites in the chambers below. The decoration depicts obscure religious rites. The structure had a direct connection with the Sacred Lake, and the theology relates to the god's solar rebirth. The rites may have been part of the weekly journey of Amun to Djeme (Medinet Habu) on the west bank.

TEMPLE OF KHONSU

The Temple of Khonsu, situated on higher ground in the southwest corner of the Amun precinct, allows a good view of the southern courts. The seated colossi before the Eighth Pylon and the portico of the Amenhotep II jubilee chapel can be seen more clearly from here. The Temple of Khonsu is a good example of a well-preserved New Kingdom temple of the classic style. The temple is not included in the main tourist route, and is often empty: such quietness considerably adds to its charm.

Built by Ramesses III, the temple contains a number of reused blocks from the mortuary temple of Amenhotep III on the west bank. The later Ramessides and the High Priest of Amun, Herihor, completed the decoration of the temple. Herihor is well attested in the reign of Ramesses XI, a time of considerable political instability in the Theban region. He first appears in Thebes as High Priest of Amun, but also as a leading army general, and his original rank was certainly military. Within the confines of the temple, Herihor assumed royal style, writing his name and titles within cartouches. Herihor and his family appear in a large archive of contemporary documents that shed some light on the events of the latter years of the reign of Ramesses XI. Herihor and another High Priest, Paiankh, led the army into Nubia, against the Viceroy of Kush. Following the death of Ramesses XI, it was this family that eventually assumed royal style in Tanis.

As at many other places in Karnak, the 25th-dynasty kings built a columned portico in front of the pylon of the Khonsu temple. Little now remains but a few bases. More striking are the remains of the **Avenue of Rams** in front of the temple, which is punctuated by the precinct wall of Nakhtnebef and the **Gate of Ptolemy Euergetes**. A fine example of a Ptolemaic gateway, this carries good reliefs depicting the king before the various forms of Khonsu. The Avenue of Rams can be seen through the (usually closed) modern gate bordering the modern road through Karnak village towards Luxor. Although it is often said to have connected with the Processional Way to Luxor, this avenue probably led to a landing stage and canal.

The pylon of the Khonsu temple was left without formal sculptured decoration, although a couple of panels of relief may be seen on the eastern tower. The pylon leads to a colonnaded court (not lined with statues as in temples associated with the royal cult). Although modest in scale, it is rather attractive. The relief sculpture is of good quality, although badly damaged in places. It was executed in the name of the High Priest of Amun, Herihor, who here assumed royal style. His names and titles, written within cartouches, may be seen on the abaci of the columns. The scenes show the river procession during the Opet Festival. There is a large scene depicting Herihor with his extended family, clearly modelled on similar scenes of the children of Ramesses II and Ramesses III in their temples. Here we see Herihor with his wife Nodjmet, 17 'sons' and 19 'daughters'. These must include in-laws and grandchildren. Interestingly, some of the names are Libyan, indicating that Herihor had established connections with the rising Libyan military elite who were to seize the Egyptian throne a short time later.

The scenes in the small hypostyle hall show the transition of power; those on the walls depict Ramesses XI officiating, while those on the columns show Herihor, but only using the titles High Priest and Army General, without the royal aspirations he displays in the outer court.

The barque shrine and sanctuary rooms were decorated in the names of Ramesses III and IV. The relief sculpture surrounding the barque shrine is particularly crisp and elegant, showing that later Ramesside art can compete with the best of other periods. In one of the eastern side rooms, the painted relief is almost undamaged. Although it is forbidden, the guardian often allows visitors to climb to the temple roof from which fine views over the whole of Amun precinct are to be had.

On the external east wall of the temple is a large band of text with the cartouches of Djeho, second ruler of the 30th Dynasty: a must for collectors of obscure pharaohs!

At right angles to the Khonsu temple, oriented east–west, is the unfinished Ptolemaic **Temple of Ipet**, a hippopotamus goddess associated with childbirth and identified with Ta-weret, here worshipped as the mother of Osiris (who is here assimilated with Amun).

Karnak: The Precincts of Monthu and Mut, and the Processional Way to Luxor

For those those who have the time and interest, a walk around the outside of Karnak temple visiting the other temple precincts is a worthwhile experience. For those who cannot complete the full circuit, the southern gate and avenue leading to the temple of the goddess Mut is the more rewarding part.

Instead of entering the Amun temple at the First Pylon, turn left and follow the *temenos* wall of Nakhtnebef (Nectanebo I) to the north, to the village of el-Malqata. Continue following the precinct wall as it turns east and walk to the outer side of the North Gate. Here the unnaturalness of the Nakhtnebef precinct is most clearly appreciated. The massive brick walls of the Amun enclosure, with the Temple of Ptah inside, come strangely close to the *temenos* punctuated by the stone gateways of the temple of the goddess Maat and six chapels built by the God's Wives of Amun, all of which face directly on to the brick wall of the Amun temple. In ancient times there must have been a main road and perhaps a crossing here, with the small chapels lining the road to the north and the precinct of Ptah at the junction. To the north, an excavated area shows the complexity of the levels below the later wall. Here are a gateway of Thutmose I and some small chapels, along with many brick buildings. A few fragments of stone buildings stand in the open space in front of the village. Follow the precinct wall to the east to the Ptolemaic gateway and remains of the avenue, where the higher ground level allows a view of the **Temple of Monthu** (during the Old Kingdom, the chief god of Thebes). Little more than the foundations can be seen of this temple, which was founded by Amenhotep III and expanded by later rulers down to the Ptolemies. The avenue led to a quay and the temple may at one time have been connected by canal with the Temple of Monthu at Medamud, to the north.

A walk along the precinct wall to the east and then south provides a good view over the whole area. On the eastern side of the Monthu temple is a building dedicated to his son, Harpre. Along the same axis as the main temple with its entrance to the south is the temple of the goddess Maat, built by Ramesses II. Further to the east lie the excavated remains of the **Treasury of Thutmose I**.

Continue to follow the wall of the Amun temple as it turns south. There is little to see here, but the barrenness and desolation provide a stark contrast to the milling throngs inside the main enclosure. Halfway along the wall stands the Eastern Gate, with its bases of obelisks and statues of Ramesses II. For devotees of Akhenaten, a short detour should be made here. From the gateway, follow the track for a short distance due east to the bases of some of the colossi of Akhenaten, now in the Egyptian Museum. (Some of the heads are also in Luxor Museum.) Akhenaten built a temple here (one of perhaps four in the Karnak area), which he decorated with jubilee scenes. Like his other temples, it was dismantled (probably by Horemheb) and used as building material in the Second and Ninth pylons.

Return to the East Gate and follow the wall first to the south and then west to the outside of the Tenth Pylon, the great South Gate of Karnak. Visitors with less time or inclination can follow the shorter and more direct route from the First Pylon along the main road to the gateway of the Temple of Khonsu, then continue west to this point.

The Tenth Pylon is badly ruined, except for its gateway. To the left are the lower parts of a colossus of Horemheb (perhaps recarved), and to the right the stupendous base and feet of the **Colossus of Amenhotep III**. This was probably the largest standing statue ever set up by the Egyptians and the remains are impressive not only for their size, but also for the loveliness of the sculpture. Fragments of the statue are ranged along the precinct wall. Note particularly the buckle of the king's belt which gives the name of the statue, 'Neb-maat-ra [Amenhotep III] is Monthu of the Rulers'. This statue, which must have reached to the same height as the top of the gateway, remained standing until the Roman Period, when it was probably felled by an earthquake.

The Tenth Pylon marks the beginning of the **Processional Way** to Luxor. It is not known when this was established, but it was made considerably more elaborate by Hatshepsut, who built a number of chapels along its length. These way stations, a room on a raised platform, with statues of Hatshepsut flanking each door, are depicted on her Red Chapel. It has been suggested that a canal originally ran between the two temples and that this was later filled in and lined with ram-headed sphinxes. Behind each sphinx, or between them, was planted a tree. Until recently, the sandstone sphinxes, some shattered and eroded beyond recognition, were covered in drifts of sand, a few palms the only vegetation. But extensive restoration and clearance of the avenue, and rebuilding of the paved road, have tidied up the area considerably.

The South Gate faces the entrance to the precinct of the goddess Mut, where a number of temples, originally separate, are enclosed by one of the massive walls erected in the reign of Nakhtnebef. To the east of the entrance to the precinct are the barely visible foundations of the **Temple of Kamutef**, the 'Bull of his Mother', the fertility aspect of Amun. To the west, where the avenue turns, are the remains of the double barque shrine, built by Hatshepsut and extended by Thutmose III.

The main axis of the southern enclosure (not always accessible) is occupied by the **Temple of Mut**, which is largely ruined. Thought to date from the reign of Amenhotep III, the temple has 25th Dynasty and Ptolemaic additions. Of especial note are the large reliefs of Bes in the Ptolemaic entrance. The temple has been excavated and cleared in recent years; once it was an eerie site, overgrown with scrub and reeds, and littered with black granite statues of the lioness-headed Sakhmet. The statues line the main court, and others stand in the sanctuary areas. Each statue has a different name, the whole forming a litany in stone and an invocation of the different manifestations of this ferocious goddess. Some are standing, some seated, some whole, some broken. There were originally 730 such statues, carved for Amenhotep III and originally placed in his vast temple on the west bank. Like so much of the sculpture made for the celebration of the king's *sed*-festival, the Sakhmet statues were recycled. The lioness goddesses were believed to dwell within a **crescent-shaped sacred lake**, which can be seen at the back of the temple. Called Asheru, the lake gave its name to the goddess (Mut in Asheru) and to this region of Thebes. On the far side of the lake is the **Temple of Ramesses III**, close by the continuation of the Processional Way.

To the east of the main entrance is the **Temple of Khonsu-the-Child**, built by Amenhotep III with additions by later rulers. Here, as in the *mammisi* of Ptolemaic temples, the birth of the god to the divine couple was celebrated. Amongst the few surviving reliefs is a circumcision scene. Broken statuary and the massive broken fragments of an alabaster barque shrine lie amongst the reeds.

On leaving the Mut enclosure, turn left and follow the reconstructed avenue past the enclosure wall. By the modern main road there is a junction, where the **Avenue of Sphinxes** turns towards Luxor, and straight ahead the road continued to a quay. To the right is the Avenue of Rams leading to the Temple of Khonsu. It is not far to the junction with the main road from the airport, which can be followed the rest of the way into the city. Walking towards Luxor, small excavations have uncovered other parts of the avenue, but most lies beneath the town.

The Processional Way ends at the brick enclosure wall of Nakhtnebef which creates a huge court in front of the Temple of Luxor. A well-preserved section of the avenue can be seen, but notice that here the sphinxes have human heads.

The pylon entrance to the Temple of Luxor was completed by Ramesses II. The gate was originally flanked by two obelisks, but one was given to France in 1819 and now stands in the Place de la Concorde, Paris.

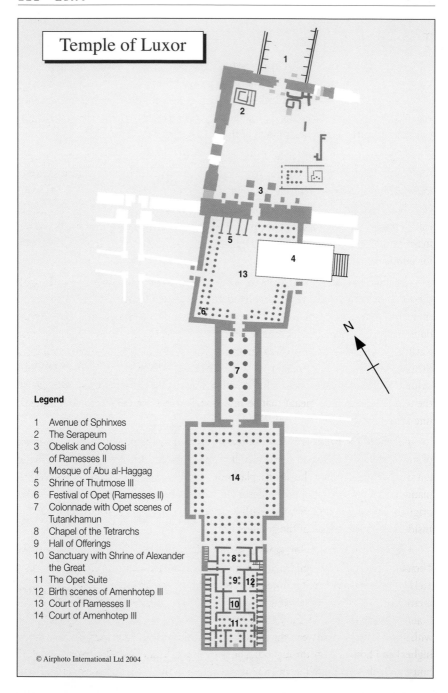

Temple of Luxor

Legend

1 Avenue of Sphinxes
2 The Serapeum
3 Obelisk and Colossi
   of Ramesses II
4 Mosque of Abu al-Haggag
5 Shrine of Thutmose III
6 Festival of Opet (Ramesses II)
7 Colonnade with Opet scenes of
   Tutankhamun
8 Chapel of the Tetrarchs
9 Hall of Offerings
10 Sanctuary with Shrine of Alexander
   the Great
11 The Opet Suite
12 Birth scenes of Amenhotep III
13 Court of Ramesses II
14 Court of Amenhotep III

© Airphoto International Ltd 2004

Temple of Luxor

T he Temple of Luxor, Ipet-resyt, is one of the most handsome in Egypt. Built of sandstone from the quarries of Gebel Silsila its great central court is particularly lovely at dusk when the stone deepens to orange. A late-afternoon visit has the advantages of seeing the building at sunset, as well as by the excellent lighting (without sound) which makes much of the relief sculpture easier to see.

Luxor was the venue of the Feast of the Opet, one of Thebes' main festivals. Although a local, rather than state, festival, it was normally attended by the king. Amun journeyed from Karnak to reside in Luxor, the 'Southern Opet' (Ipet-resyt) or 'Harem'. Here he consummated his marriage and symbolically fathered the king. In the reign of Hatshepsut, the divine statues were probably carried along the Processional Way, but in the later 18th Dynasty they came to Luxor by river. The whole event was an occasion for public celebration and rejoicing.

The main part of the temple as we see it today was built by Amenhotep III, with the first courtyard and pylon completed and decorated by Ramesses II. However, there was certainly a sanctuary here earlier in the 18th Dynasty, and Hatshepsut doubtless constructed a major temple here as the focus of her processional route from Karnak. That, or its successor was dismantled by Amenhotep III, and may well form the platform on which the main part of the king's temple stands, just as his enormous pylon (the Third) at Karnak was filled with dismantled structures. The expansion of the temple northwards meant that several changes were made in its axis in order to line it up with the Processional Way to Karnak.

In front of the pylon is a large courtyard, created by the precinct wall. A number of small structures have been excavated here, but only one, the Serapeum, is visible. It is a small, single-roomed chapel on a platform surrounded by a colonnade. This temple, inaugurated in the reign of the emperor Hadrian on 29 July AD 127, is built of brick, originally plastered and painted, with a stone doorway of typical Egyptian design. Inside is a Roman statue of the goddess Isis.

Also in front of the pylon are two seated colossi of Ramesses II, in black granite. Their four standing companions, in red granite, are in various states of restoration. Until 1831, two obelisks of red granite flanked the gateway. Now there is only one, 22.5 metres (73.8 feet) high and weighing 227 tons; Mohammed Ali gave the second to France. During the 19th century, the Temple of Luxor was occupied by part of the town, with streets running between the capitals of the columns (the ground level was much higher) and houses built throughout.The obelisk was lowered after the removal of 30 houses which surrounded it. In 1833 it was set up in the Place de la Concorde, Paris.

The western tower of the pylon has scenes of the Battle of Qadesh (best seen when lit in the evening) and, like the court beyond, it was probably built during the reign of Sety I, though decorated in the early years of Ramesses II.

Just through the gateway is the **Mosque of Abu al-Haggag**, the doorway of which is halfway up the wall, at the 19th-century ground level. Abu al-Haggag was a holy man whose relics are kept within the mosque, which is now used only for special services. His great feast, the date of which varies according to the lunar calendar, involves the towing of a boat around Luxor. Whatever its current symbolism, this feast is surely derived from the Opet Festival.

The **Court of Ramesses II** is lined by a double colonnade, with statues between the columns on the southern side. Although they prominently carry his names, not all of these were carved for Ramesses; some were the work of Amenhotep III. On the northwestern side of the court is the **Shrine of Thutmose III**, consisting of three chapels with a granite portico. This, the earliest surviving building at Luxor, was rebuilt and recarved when Ramesses II built the courtyard around it. The gate in the western wall of the court marks the old way to the temple quay. The gate in the eastern wall is the People's Gate, by which the ordinary people gained access to the courtyard in order to present their petitions to the royal statues, which then interceded with Amun on their behalf.

From the western gate, a fine procession moves south along the wall. The fat bulls are decorated for sacrifice; their hooves curve under their great weight, and between their horns, which have wooden hands attached to the ends, are the painted wooden heads of Asiatics or Nubians. The sacrifice of the cattle symbolizes the plundering of foreign lands. The Asiatic cattle have large humps over the shoulder whilst the Nubian ones have long twisted horns. Some cattle have large tasselled earrings. The procession is led by some of the sons of Ramesses II to the pylon of the Temple of Luxor. This is one of relatively few depictions of temples, and it is well preserved. The pylon is shown with its flag-posts, and the six statues in front of it (viewed from the side); but the standing statues are shown wearing the double crown whereas those that actually stand outside the pylon wear the white crown. An earlier, but less well-preserved, depiction of Luxor can be found on the back of the east tower of the pylon (in the corridor between the pylon and the mosque).

Two black granite seated statues of Ramesses II guard the entrance to the colonnade. The better-preserved statue is one of the finest surviving of the king. Particularly graceful is the figure of the queen at his side.

The statue of Ramesses II sits in the public court of Luxor temple at the entrance to the columned hall. It passed on the prayers of the ordinary people to the gods within the temple.

The colonnade, which was originally enclosed by high walls and lit only with shafts of light, had a small pylon entrance. This, and where it joins the wall of the Ramesside court, can best be seen from the central courtyard. Planned by Amenhotep III, the work was left unfinished at his death. Tutankhamun was responsible for the carving of the Opet scenes on the long walls, and Ay decorated the pylon, but the whole work was not finished and dedicated until the reign of Horemheb. For this reason, the names of Tutankhamun have everywhere been replaced by those of Horemheb. The western wall is the better preserved, depicting the Opet procession from Karnak to Luxor. The eastern wall has the return voyage to Karnak. The scenes are interesting for their content, and for their mixture of Amarna and classical styles. It is best seen when lit in the evening. On the short entrance walls, Tutankhamun makes offerings to Amun. The figures are large and carved in lovely low relief. These, particularly on the northwestern wall, are amongst the finest portraits of the young king. Marked by the return to a more classical style, they still show Amarna influence in the swelling stomach and large thighs. The figures of Amun, however, are dull and conventional.

The long wall begins with offerings made to the sacred barques inside the Temple of Karnak. Throughout the scenes the barque of Amun, shown on a larger scale higher up on the wall, has been lost, but the barques of Mut, Khonsu and the king himself can all be seen. The procession leaves the temple (it is unusual that the figures are shown superimposed on the temple's pylon—the Third Pylon, of Amenhotep III), with its knotted flagstaffs. Each barque is placed upon a river barge (a much larger, though almost identical vessel) and then rowed, while being towed by smaller barges. Soldiers help by pulling from the banks. It is obvious that this scene was designed and carved by artists who had been trained in the Amarna style, even to the technique used in carving the relief. Notice the tumblers, the Nubian drummers and stave fighters, the chantresses of Amun with their sistra, and the officials in their chariots. The arrival at Luxor is celebrated with offerings. (The small offering tables with their scenes of preparation are strikingly similar to reliefs in the tombs at Amarna, and from the Karnak *talatat*.) The short wall has a splendid scene of the king dedicating offerings by extending his sceptre. Notice here the superbly carved royal hand, which is emphasized in deep relief as the focus of the scene.

The 14 columns with open papyrus capitals, although not as massive as those of the Hypostyle Hall at Karnak, are somewhat more elegant. The effects created by the architecture must have been quite striking, as the procession of the sacred barques

(preceding pages) *The Temple of Luxor is one of the finest architectural survivals of the New Kingdom.*

passed through this hall, lit only by narrow shafts of light from the windows high in the side walls, and emerged into the dazzling sunlight of the central courtyard.

The **Courtyard of Amenhotep III** is one of the great achievements of Egyptian architecture. It is lined on three sides by a double colonnade, and on the southern side by a deep portico on a raised platform. Unfortunately, some of the effect is lost due to the destruction of the side walls and of many of the roofing blocks of the colonnades. In 1989 this was the site of one the most significant discoveries in Egypt for many years, a cache of statues, apparently deliberately and carefully buried during the Roman Period. These statues may now be seen in a gallery of the Luxor Museum.

The portico, or **Hypostyle Hall**, is the entrance to Amenhotep III's original temple, which is distinguished by its being set upon a terrace (clearly visible from outside). The changes in the axis of the temple are easily seen from here. At the back of the hall (note in passing the altar dedicated to the emperor Constantine) are the chapels used as resting places for the sacred barques of Mut and Khonsu.

The hall beyond the hypostyle is often, incorrectly, said to have been converted into a Christian church. Originally supported by eight columns, this room has two side chambers, probably used to keep the barque and portable statue of the king during the Opet Festival. The doorway into the chamber beyond was turned into an apse in the later Roman Period, and the reliefs were plastered over and painted. However, far from being a church, this was where the Roman emperors were worshipped and Christians would have been forced to make sacrifices to them. The painting in the apse shows Diocletian (AD 286–305) and Maximian with their two Caesars, Constantius Chlorus and Galerius. Immediately to the left of the apse is an Egyptian artist's error. Two almost identical scenes show Amenhotep III kneeling before Amun, who touches the back of his crown. Close examination of the lower scene shows that the artist put the wrong crown on this figure (though it is correct in the scene above). Traces of the alterations, which would have been disguised further with plaster and painting, are still visible.

A modern door has been cut in the apse, leading to the **Hall of Offerings**. The roof is almost complete, and a lot of paint survives on the splendid reliefs. Here Amenhotep III presents enormous offerings to Amun before being accepted by the god (on the south wall) and conducted into his presence in the sanctuary. The sanctuary of Amenhotep III was a hall with four large columns, but these were dismantled when the present **Shrine of Alexander the Great** (332–323 BC) was built in the room. Here Alexander, with all the regalia and attributes of an Egyptian pharaoh, is shown being accepted by Amun.

Beyond the sanctuary is the suite of rooms where Amun resided during the Opet Feast. In one of the rooms to the east of the sanctuary is a badly damaged cycle of reliefs depicting the birth of Amenhotep III. Similar to the Hatshepsut cycle at Deir el-Bahari, Amun visits the king's mother, Queen Mutemwiya, the god Khnum forms the king on the potter's wheel, and the child is born and presented to the gods.

Around the temple are the remains of the Roman fort and later churches, although, due to the changing course of the river, some areas have been lost.

Luxor Museum

Inaugurated in 1975, the Luxor Museum contains a splendid collection of sculptures and small objects mainly from the Theban region. The display is excellently laid out and time should be made for a visit. The museum is open during the afternoon and evening, times vary according to the season.

On entering the museum, the visitor is confronted by a colossal pink granite head of Amenhotep III. This comes from one of the standing statues in the court of his great temple behind the Colossi of Memnon on the west bank. The cosmetic lines of the eyes were originally gilded. Notice too the angle of the eyes viewed in profile; they were angled to look down on the people gathered in the court. There is also a magnificent, if sadly fragmentary, painting of Amenhotep III at the time of his accession. Seated beneath the triple canopy, the king appears in his full majesty accompanied by his mother, as, in myth, Horus appeared with Isis.

The main exhibition begins with sculpture of the Middle Kingdom. A statue excavated at Armant, a little to the south of Luxor, represents a king as Osiris. Although uninscribed, it should probably be attributed to Menthuhotep III. The statue is simple in its execution and the features have an unusual softness. The upper part of a similar Osiride statue of Senusret I from Karnak is more monumental, whereas the granite head of Senusret III in the fully developed 12th Dynasty style is, in comparison, forbidding.

As elsewhere in the Theban region, the majority of surviving monuments is of the New Kingdom. Here, a few particularly fine, or important, examples have been selected for display. The sandstone head of Amenhotep I is hardly handsome, but it is rare to find monuments of this king, despite his vast building works and the reverence attached to him by his successors. The most important historical inscription in the museum is the 'Stele of Kamose', discovered at Karnak. This details some of the campaigns against the Hyksos kings of the Delta, part of the struggle of the Theban

Freize from the Temple of Luxor

princes to reunite Egypt under their own rule. A block from the Red Chapel of Hatshepsut shows her offering two obelisks to Amun, perhaps the pair erected in the columned hall of Thutmose I, one of which is still standing.

The greywacke figure of Thutmose III is one of the most perfect of Egyptian images to have survived. The large alabaster group of Amenhotep III with the seated crocodile god Sobek is also quite splendid. The stone gives the king's features a delicate softness, whilst the god has sharp teeth and a malicious grin. The statue is marred by the heavily cut cartouches of Ramesses II. A lovely small group, also from the reign of Amenhotep III, has two small, chubby crocodiles with beautifully curving tails.

The upper gallery has a number of small objects from the tomb of Tutankhamun, and a group from the treasure found at Tod, a little to the south of Luxor. Found in a bronze casket with the cartouches of Amenemhat II, the treasure included ingots, collars and amulets of lapis lazuli and cylinder seals from Mesopotamia, together with a number of vessels of silver, perhaps of Aegean work. The whole was probably the gift of an Asiatic ruler to the pharaoh who then dedicated it to Monthu, the chief deity of Tod. Amongst the more arresting images to be found in the museum is the head of Akhenaten from one of the colossal statues of the king set up in his temples at Karnak (see also Egyptian Museum). Nearby is a large section of relief from one of these shrines. The thousands of *talatat* were used as building material by Horemheb and Ramesses II in their pylons at Karnak and Luxor, but it has been possible to reconstruct large areas of the decoration on paper: only this one section has been put together out of the actual blocks.

The lower gallery of the museum now contains one of the finest collections of Egyptian statuary discovered in recent years, excavated from the court of the Luxor temple in 1989. The most impressive are from the reign of Amenhotep III and are in black granite. Remarkably plain, they are of superb quality and have hardly been damaged. The star of the exhibition is certainly the pink quartzite cult image of Amenhotep III. The figure stands on a sledge and was originally decorated with collars and armlets of gold foil. The only damage is the alteration to the name of Amun, carried out during the reign of Akhenaten.

Amongst the statues and relief blocks displayed outside the museum, note the scene of Amenhotep II driving his chariot and shooting arrows through a copper target. The king had insisted on a copper, rather than wooden, target because he was so much stronger than other men that his arrows went straight through a wooden target.

THEBES: THE WEST BANK

he necropolis of Thebes lay on the west bank of the river, with the cliffs of the Western Desert providing a place for rock-cut tombs and a magnificent backdrop to the temples of the kings. The mortuary temples of the rulers of the 18th–20th dynasties lie along the edge of the cultivation: the northernmost is that of Sety I and the southernmost that of Ramesses III (Medinet Habu). Many have been plundered or destroyed in ancient, or more recent, times and are known only from their foundations and fragments recovered by archaeologists. Behind the temples, in the hills beneath the natural pyramid of the Theban Peak (known as el-Qurn), are the tomb-chapels of the elite of Thebes. Today these groups of tombs are named after the nearest village. The early local rulers of Thebes were buried in the northern part of the necropolis, at Dra Abu el-Naga, and nearby at el-Tarif. Their tombs are called *saff* tombs (from the Arabic meaning a 'row'), because of their multiple entrances. They are not well preserved, difficult to find, and, frankly, not worth the effort. From the 18th Dynasty onwards, the kings chose to be buried in remote desert wadis in an attempt to protect their tombs from robbery. There is currently an enormous amount of archaeological work on the west bank, with many tombs being excavated and restored, and temple sites being re-excavated.

To make a thorough visit of the west bank at least three days should be allowed, depending on the time of year: division of the monuments can be equally by area or type. By area perhaps has the advantage of a variety of monuments. As a suggestion, the temples of Medinet Habu, with the Valley of the Queens, Deir el-Medina and the area of the Colossi of Memnon would easily fill one day in the southern part of the region. A second day could be spent visiting the tombs of the nobles at Qurna, the Ramesseum, Deir el-Bahari and the tombs of el-Asasif and el-Khokha, and a day left for the Temple of Sety I and the Valley of the Kings. However the monument area is visited, it will be exhausting! Tickets should only be bought for the monuments to be visited on that day. The following describes the monuments by category, and from north to south.

TOMBS OF THE NOBLES

he necropolis of **Dra Abu el-Naga** lies in the low slopes of the hills between the entrance to the Valley of the Kings and the bay of Deir el-Bahari. This was the site of the royal necropolis of the 17th Dynasty. Some 18th-dynasty nobles were buried here, but it was particularly popular in the 19th Dynasty

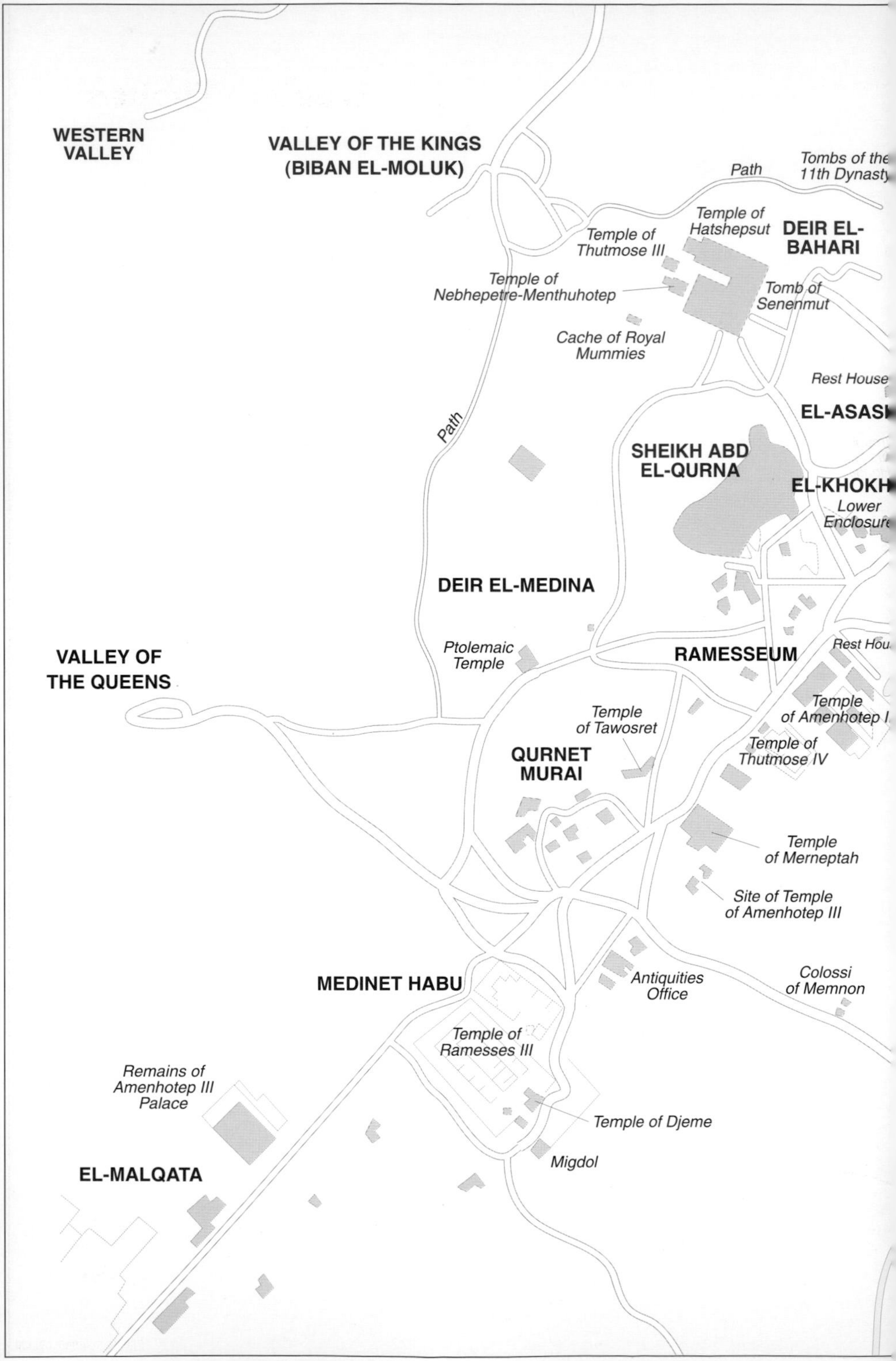

WESTERN VALLEY

VALLEY OF THE KINGS (BIBAN EL-MOLUK)

Path

Tombs of the 11th Dynasty

Temple of Hatshepsut

DEIR EL-BAHARI

Temple of Thutmose III

Temple of Nebhepetre-Menthuhotep

Tomb of Senenmut

Cache of Royal Mummies

Rest House

EL-ASASI

Path

SHEIKH ABD EL-QURNA

EL-KHOKH

Lower Enclosure

DEIR EL-MEDINA

VALLEY OF THE QUEENS

Ptolemaic Temple

RAMESSEUM

Rest Hou

Temple of Amenhotep I

Temple of Tawosret

QURNET MURAI

Temple of Thutmose IV

Temple of Merneptah

Site of Temple of Amenhotep III

MEDINET HABU

Antiquities Office

Colossi of Memnon

Remains of Amenhotep III Palace

Temple of Ramesses III

Temple of Djeme

EL-MALQATA

Migdol

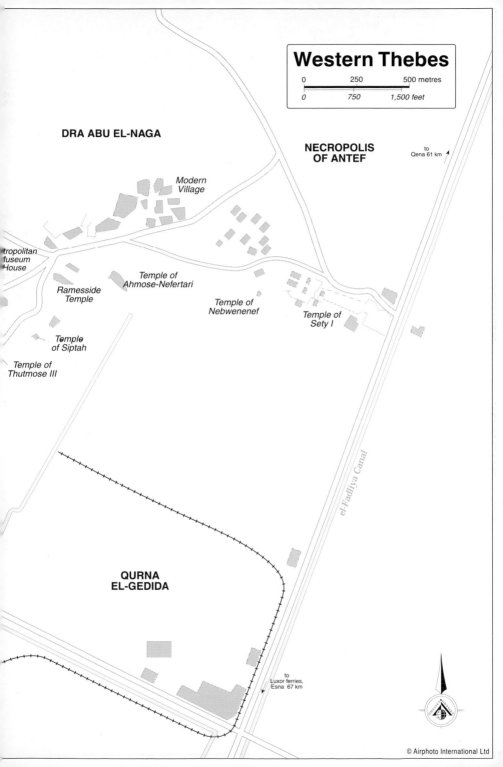

Thebes: Tomb of Pabasa

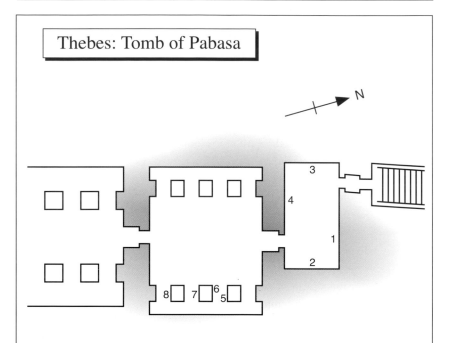

Pabasa
Steward to God's Wife of Amun, Nitoqert (26th Dynasty, Psamtik I)

Large Late Period tomb with good quality relief sculpture. A long staircase leads from the entrance, which looks out onto the processional way to Deir el-Bahari. This is a typical feature of the tombs in this area, enabling the deceased to join in the annual Feast of the Valley, which focused on the temple. As the staircase enters the chambers:

Lintel: two scenes depicting Psamtik I, his daughter Nitoqert, who officiated as God's Wife of Amun at Thebes, and Pabasa.

1-2 Pabasa receives offerings: a sub-scene depicts the pilgrimage to Abydos.

3-4 Pabasa receives offerings: sub-scene depicts the funeral procession.

    The open solar court is a feature of Late Period tombs. Compared with the nearby tomb of Montjuemhat, this is modest in scale and decoration. There are some unusual scenes on the pillars.

5   A bedroom.

6   Spinning; catching fish in a net.

7   Beekeeping; catching birds; picking fruit.

8   Viticulture.

Source: Robert Morkot

(when several high priests of Amun carved their tombs here), perhaps because it lies opposite Karnak. The tombs here are rarely visited.

On the northern slopes of the bay of **Deir el-Bahari** are tombs of the Middle Kingdom, whilst those occupying its central plain, **el-Asasif**, are mainly of the 25th and early 26th dynasties (*c*.700–600 BC). Their massive brick superstructures (with pylons and gateways) are clearly visible from the terraces of Hatshepsut's temple. Montjuemhat (tomb 34), was the most powerful of the Theban officials of the late 25th Dynasty, being the Fourth Prophet of Amun, Mayor of Thebes and Governor of Upper Egypt. This tomb is being restored and will be open to visitors in the future. **Pabasa** (tomb 279) and Aba (tomb 36) served the God's Wife of Amun, Nitoqert, daughter of Psamtik I. The tomb of the Steward Harwa, near that of Montjuemhat is currently being exacavated by an Italian team, and is proving to be one of the largest and most important of this group. The fine reliefs in these copy earlier tomb scenes from Thebes and elsewhere, and show the archaizing interest of artists of this period.

The hills on the southern side of Deir el-Bahari contain the cemetery of el-Khokha. The most notable tombs here are of the reign of Amenhotep III. The chapel of the sculptors, Nebamun and Ipuki (tomb 181), has fine painted decoration, but several other chapels are decorated in relief. The stone in which the Theban tombs are carved is not of the best quality for carved decoration, and so the usual method of decoration here was painting on plaster, which gave a better surface. During the reign of Amenhotep III, however, the best bands of stone were sought out for the tombs of his most important Theban officials. From the style and technique of the work it seems that they were decorated by artists brought from Memphis, where carved relief was usual. Amenemhat-Surero (tomb 48) was the Steward of Amenhotep III at Thebes. His large and finely decorated tomb is unfinished. The figures of the owner are hacked out, indicating that he fell from office. Some of the loveliest low relief and most interesting scenes are to be found in the tomb of the Steward of Queen Tiye (wife of Amenhotap III), **Kheruef** (tomb 192). These depict unusual episodes in the jubilee festivals of the king, including the setting up of the *djed*-pillar and the reward of the officials. Also decorated in low relief, and dating from the earliest years of Amenhotep IV (Akhenaten), is the tomb of the Steward Parennefer (tomb 188). There are also some interesting painted tombs of late 18th- and 19th-dynasty date. Neferhotep was the Chief Scribe of Amun, and his is one of few private tombs dated to the short reign of Tutankhamun's successor, Ay. The scenes are unusual, combining funerary scenes with some vestiges of Amarna influence, notably the reward of Neferhotep by Ay, and more unusually the reward

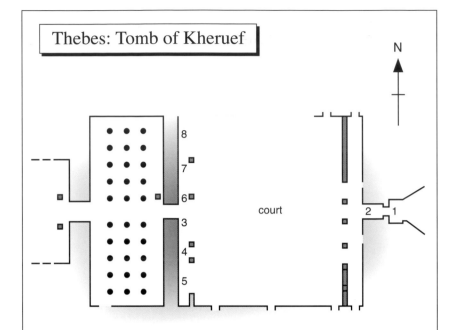

Thebes: Tomb of Kheruef

N

court

Kheruef
Steward of Queen Tiye (18th Dynasty, Amenhotep III)

A very badly damaged tomb, but containing very fine quality relief sculpture with extremely rare scenes of the *sed*-festival (jubilee) of Amenhotep III.

1   Damaged lintel scenes showing Amenhotep IV (Akhenaten) and his mother, Queen Tiye before Atum and Ra-Harakhty.

2   Amenhotep IV (Akhenaten) before Ra-Harakhty, Amenhotep III and Queen Tiye.

3   Kheruef before Amenhotep III in *sed*-festival costume, Hathor and Queen Tiye. A procession of princesses.

4   Amenhotep III and Queen Tiye leave the palace for the *sed*-festival accompanied by courtiers and dancers.

5   Amenhotep III and Queen Tiye appear as the solar deities, sailing on the lake during the festival.

6   Kheruef before Amenhotep III during the reward of officials during the festival. Behind Amenhotep III, Queen Tiye sits on a throne with female captives bound to it, and she is depicted in the panel as a female sphinx.

7   Amenhotep III erects the *djed*-pillar as part of the festival rites; sub-scenes show musicians, dancers, offering bearers and the slaughter of cattle.

8   Adoration of the *djed*-pillar.

Source: Robert Morkot

Thebes: Tomb of Si-Mut

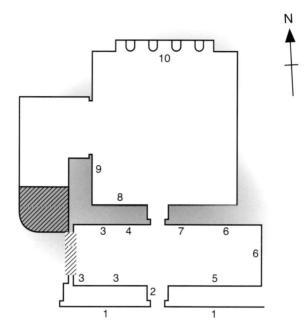

N

Si-Mut
Kyky, Chief Cattle Counter of the Estate of Amun
(19th Dynasty, Ramesses II)

A good example of a Ramesside tomb, with some unusual scenes.

1 Stelae.
2 Si-Mut and his wife, with a lute player.
3 Agricultural scenes; Si-Mut worships the goddess Mut.
4 Si-Mut makes offerings to deities including Amun.
5 Religious scenes from the 'Book of Gates'; Si-Mut inspects cattle.
6 Funerary banquet; funeral procession.
7 Judgement scene.
8 The raising of the *djed*-pillar; the tree goddess.
9 The mummy on a couch.
10 Statues of Si-Mut and his family.

Source: Robert Morkot

of Neferhotep's wife by Queen Tiy. The **tomb of Si-Mut**, known as Kyky, dates to the reign of Ramesses II and has some fine painting.

Sheikh Abd el-Qurna contains the largest and most important group of private tomb-chapels. On the plain and the hill directly behind the Ramesseum are a number of easily accessible tombs which are always open to visitors. The largest of these is the **tomb of Ramose** (tomb 55). A broad staircase leads down to the forecourt (from which a second tomb-chapel opens), with the smoothed façade of Ramose's tomb occupying the whole of the western side. Here the usual transverse hall has been expanded into a large chamber supported by four rows of eight columns (some of which are now restored). The finest series of reliefs is immediately to the left of the entrance. It shows the ritual banquet of Ramose's family, and includes people already deceased at the time of the tomb's decoration. Ramose, Vizier of Upper Egypt and Mayor of Thebes in the later years of Amenhotep III's reign, is shown with his wife and parents (his father had been Mayor of Memphis), his half-brother (the king's Chief Steward in Memphis) and a more distant relative (Amenhotep son of Hapu, one of the king's most important officials). This scene is amongst the finest works of the 18th Dynasty, its appeal to modern eyes doubtless increased by it being unpainted. The southern wall has a painted funeral procession with a fine group of female mourners. Servants carrying the burial equipment are followed by a procession of royal representatives and high officials, headed by the Viceroy of Nubia. A long sloping passage beneath this scene leads to the burial chamber, which is inaccessible. The back wall of the chamber is particularly interesting. The doorway leads to the second, ruined hall (supported by eight pillars) and the unfinished shrine beyond. Left of this doorway is a scene of the accession of Amenhotep IV (Akhenaten) in the classical style. The king is seated on a dais under the triple canopy, with the goddess Maat behind him (compare this with the painting of Amenhotep III in Luxor Museum). To the right of the doorway is one of the earliest scenes in the Amarna style. Although much of the scene is uncarved, the line drawing in black ink has great beauty. Akhenaten and Nefertiti are shown in the Window of Appearances, whilst Ramose is anointed with perfumes and rewarded with gold collars (compare this with the similar scene in the nearby tomb of Khaemhat). The figure of the vizier here is in striking contrast to those elsewhere in the tomb— Ramose is now shown with a long skull and jaw like the king. Also interesting is the action drawing of Ramose prostrating himself in the royal presence (Khaemhat bows only from the waist). Notice also the representatives of the Asiatic and African states with which Egypt had contact, brought here to witness the power of the pharaoh and the reward of loyal officials.

Thebes: Tomb of Ramose

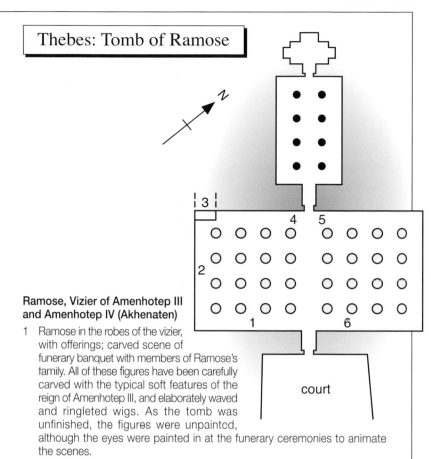

**Ramose, Vizier of Amenhotep III
and Amenhotep IV (Akhenaten)**

1   Ramose in the robes of the vizier,
    with offerings; carved scene of
    funerary banquet with members of Ramose's
    family. All of these figures have been carefully
    carved with the typical soft features of the
    reign of Amenhotep III, and elaborately waved
    and ringleted wigs. As the tomb was
    unfinished, the figures were unpainted,
    although the eyes were painted in at the funerary ceremonies to animate
    the scenes.

2   Painted scene of funeral procession with mourners and furniture that is to
    be buried, including Ramose's chair and bed, chests and vessels of ointments,
    his sandals and scribal palette and writing board.

3   Passage leading to the burial chamber.

4   Amenhotep IV seated under the triple canopy at his accession, accompanied
    by the goddess Maat, the remainder of the scene has not been drawn in.

5   Amenhotep IV (Akhenaten) and Nefertiti, in the 'new style', at the Window
    of Appearances with the sun disc (Aten) above. Ramose, in the new style,
    shown, like the king, fully in profile, addresses a group of officials, and is
    then seen again, in a remarkable action sequence, prostrating himself; a
    group of foreign ambassadors looks on. This scene is notable because of
    the dramatic change in artistic style from the conventional accession scene
    on the adjacent wall, and also the superb line drawing of the uncarved parts.

6   Offering scene.

Source: Robert Morkot

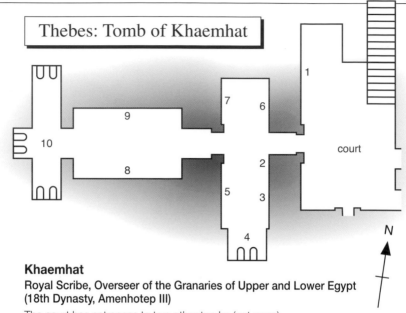

Khaemhat
Royal Scribe, Overseer of the Granaries of Upper and Lower Egypt (18th Dynasty, Amenhotep III)

The court has entrances to two other tombs (not open).

1 Stele.
2 Khaemhat with offerings.
3 Renenutet, the cobra-headed harvest goddess, in a shrine nurses the infant corn god, Nepri; Theban harbour with boats bringing grain.
4 Niche with large statues of Khaemhat and his wife.
5 The whole wall is a scene in which Khaemhat presents an account of the produce to Amenhotep III. It is superbly executed in delicate low relief. Amongst the notable elements are the rows of bulls shown on a diminutive scale, and the carefully carved wavy hair of the young scribes. The head of Amenhotep III is a cast (original in Berlin).
6 More agricultural scenes from Khaemhat's office of Overseer of the Granaries: measuring fields; cutting grain; gleaners; and a delightful vignette of the bored charioteer asleep but still holding the reins (note that the chariot appears to be drawn by mules rather than horses), while the groom dozes in the shade of a tree.
7 Khaemhat and other officials are rewarded in the presence of Amenhotep III at the time of the first *sed*-festival of the king's 30th year. The officials enter into the royal presence, have perfume ointment put on their hair and then have the gold collars tied around their necks. The head of Amenhotep III is a cast (original in Berlin).
8 Funerary scenes, mostly lost but for figures of Osiris and Hathor at far end.
9 The Fields of Yaru, and voyage to Abydos; offering scenes.
10 Statues of Khaemhat and his relatives, badly damaged and smoke blackened.

Source: Robert Morkot

The **tomb of Khaemhat** (tomb 57), close by that of Ramose, is also decorated in delicate low relief. The scenes are interesting to compare with those in Ramose's tomb, which is almost contemporary. Khaemhat is shown being rewarded by Amenhotep III on the occasion of one of the jubilees. The other scenes, which are of agricultural activities, are of a type often found in painted tombs, and their treatment in the differing media can be usefully compared. The statues of the deceased and his family in this tomb are unusually well preserved, both the large group in the transverse hall and the three highly polished groups in the shrine. Two fine relief heads of Amenhotep III from scenes in the transverse hall are now in the Berlin Museum (they have been replaced here with casts).

Almost adjacent is the **tomb of Userhat** (tomb 56), which is more typical of Theban tombs, being quite small and with lively painted scenes. The plan is a good example of the standard Theban type, with the doorway from the courtyard opening on to a narrow transverse hall, followed by a corridor-hall with a statue niche.

A steep climb up from this group of chapels leads first to the **tomb of Rekhmire** (tomb 100), who was vizier during the later years of Thutmose III. This is one of the most rewarding of the earlier 18th-dynasty chapels because of its fine painting and informative scenes. In plan it is typically Theban, with a transverse hall and corridor, but here the scale is greatly increased, with the roof of the corridor-hall sloping upwards to a great height. In the first hall, the presentation of the foreign tribute to Thutmose III (left of the doorway to the corridor) is particularly notable. As is so often the case elsewhere, the Egyptian artist has skilfully captured the characteristics of unfamiliar animals: from Africa, an elegant giraffe is followed by vicious dogs, their teeth bared, and long-horned cattle; and from Syria, a bear and an elephant. In this same room is an unusual panel showing a hunt in the desert. The flying animals in this scene show the influence of Aegean art (Aegean people are to be seen in the tribute scene). On the left side of the corridor-halls are scenes of workshops of the Temple of Amun, depicting many fascinating details such as the fashioning of statues, the casting of bronze doors, leather tanning and mud-brick making. The large banqueting scene on the right wall can be compared with that in the tomb of Ramose. Here, at the peak of the early 18th-dynasty classical style, the continuation of Middle Kingdom traditions is still visible. The tall, slim, female figures are painted a creamy yellow. Their tight-fitting white tunics and quite simple hairstyles seem austere when compared with the elaborate robes and coiffures of the later tomb. The whole style of decoration is more restrained, but equally delicate. Notice the servant girl shown (several times) with tresses hanging across her face, and once, unusually, from behind. In this delightful figure the artist has broken with convention, and has

Thebes: Tomb of Userhat

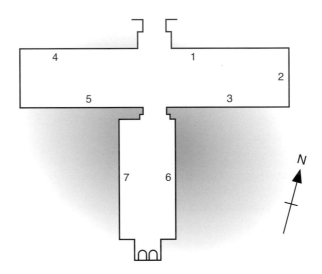

Userhat
Royal Scribe, Child of the Royal Nursery
(18th Dynasty, Amenhotep II)

A modest chapel with attractive painted scenes.

1 The inspection of cattle; agricultural scenes.
2 Stele; purification of statue and Opening of the Mouth ritual.
3 Funerary banquet.
4 Userhat and his wife make offerings.
5 Storehouses; the registering of army recruits; barbers cutting the hair of new recruits.
6 Hunt in the desert, with Userhat in his chariot; marsh scenes and wine production.
7 Funeral procession.

Source: Robert Morkot

Thebes: Tomb of Rekhmire

Rekhmire

Vizier (18th Dynasty, Thutmose III)

1   The duties of the vizier, with the law court, and collection of the Upper Egyptian taxes.

2   Rekhmire presents the foreign 'tribute' to Thutmose III. The five registers show the exotic produce of the empire and adjacent lands. The Asiatic tribute includes chariots, horses and wine jars, a bear and a rather small elephant: Thutmose III himself hunted elephants in the Orontes Valley during his Asiatic campaigns. The Kushite (Nubian) tribute includes fierce dogs and a giraffe along with the usual gold, ebony and tusks of ivory, and long-horned cattle. There is also a group from the Aegean, probably Crete, with distinctive kilts and long wavy hair.

3   The tax of Lower Egypt.

4   The temple workshops.

5   Agricultural scenes.

6   The family of Rekhmire.

7   The produce of the eastern border, with scene of the vintage with grapes being trodden.

8   Hunting in the desert and fowling.

9 -10 Rekhmire inspects the workshops of the Temple of Amun: there are detailed scenes of the carving and polishing of colossal statues and sphinxes; smelting of metal and casting of bronze doors; rope-making.

11   The voyage to Abydos.

12   Offering lists and the funerary deities: Anubis, Osiris and Hathor, Mistress of the West.

13   Rekhmire returns from audience with pharaoh.

14   Funerary banquet in several registers. The women wear the classic 'sheath-dress' typical of the Old and Middle Kingdoms, and squat on mats on the floor. This contrasts with the scenes in later 18th Dynasty tombs with their lion-legged chairs, and elaborate flowing and pleated costumes. Servant girls hang garlands of fresh lotus flowers around the necks of the guests. One servant is shown in an unusual three-quarter view from behind, although her feet are awkwardly positioned.

15   Rekhmire's garden with a large formal lake surrounded by trees: a boat is being towed on the lake. The funerary ceremonies with statues and the sarcophagus dragged on a sledge.

16   Niche for statues.

Court

N

Source: Robert Morkot

Thebes: Tomb of Sennefer

Sennefer
Mayor of Thebes, and Overseer of the Cattle of Amun

In the tomb Sennefer's wife appears with six different names, mostly variants with the element 'Senet', meaning 'sister', but most frequently she appears as Meryt ('Beloved').

1 Sennefer seated, with his daughter Mut-tuy, standing behind, receives offerings of food, and of the 'gold of honour'. Sennefer wears the collars of gold rings that are characteristic of the 'gold of honour' along with the double-heart necklace and large gold earrings. He wears this jewellery in many of the scenes. The earrings are unusual for grown men. Servants also bring furniture for the tomb, including the bed, the *shabti* figures and the mask to cover the mummy. On the adjacent wall, Sennefer's wife, Sent-nofret, who was the king's nurse, is shown standing, as if she has just risen from her chair.

2 Sennefer seated receives offerings. The ceiling is painted as a vine arbour.

3 Above the doorway, two jackals seated on shrines. Offering prayers above the door and on the jambs.

4 Large figures of Sennefer and Meryt walk towards the door 'in order to see the sun disc every day'; large seated figures of Sennefer and Meryt.

5 Funeral scenes with furniture being taken to the tomb; oxen slaughtered; and obelisks being raised outside the tomb.

6 Sennefer and Meryt make offerings to Osiris and Hathor.

7 Sennefer seated with wife, receives offerings.

8 Sennefer seated, with offerings; the journey to Abydos, with images of Sennefer and Meryt being towed across the river, and offerings being made.

9 Two scenes. Sennefer and Meryt, with her sistrum looped over her elbow, make offerings to a shrine in which Osiris and Anubis are seated. The body of Sennefer is mummified by Anubis, with Isis at the foot and Nephthys at the head, surrounded by religious texts and figures of the four sons of Horus, and *ba*-birds. Between the scenes a grape vine grows up the wall, spreading out onto the ceiling.

10 A priest in a leopard skin purifies Sennefer and Meryt with water. Sennefer wears the double hearts, one gold, one silver. On the silver heart, the name 'Alexandros' has been added neatly in hieroglyphics, presumably by a Graeco-Egyptian visitor in Ptolemaic or Roman times.

11 A priest wearing a leopard skin makes offerings and burns incense before Sennefer and his wife.

12 One of the finest of the pillar scenes: Sennefer sits in the shade of a tree, sniffing a lotus, wearing the gold of honour; Meryt kneels at his side on a much smaller scale; a circular alabaster table carries jars of wine.

13 Sennefer and Meryt seated. In front of them a tree on a standard from which a figure of Isis as the tree goddess would have given pure refreshing water and food (lost in damaged area).

Source: Robert Morkot

done so with great skill, except for the feet, which are unnaturally crossed. Between the banquet and the funerary scenes at the end of this hall, Rekhmire is shown being towed upon the lake in his formal garden. As well as the informative painted scenes in this tomb, one large text is especially significant. This records the appointment of Rekhmire by the king and the duties of the vizier. Not only does it tell the actual function of the office, it illuminates Egyptian morality.

A short distance further up is the **tomb of Sennefer** (tomb 96B), Mayor of Thebes in the reign of Amenhotep II. The tomb-chapel is badly preserved and is now used as a storeroom, but a stairway leads to the burial chamber, one of the jewels of the Theban necropolis. The first small room has an unsmoothed ceiling decorated with vine trellises and painted bunches of grapes (hence the name given by early visitors, the 'Tomb of the Vine'). A low door leads into the main chamber which is supported by four square pillars. The ceiling is decorated with abstract patterns and more vines. Although there is little that is striking in the content of the paintings, their clarity and execution are quite delightful. All the columns have large figures of Sennefer outlined in black and filled with flat washes of colour. Sometimes he is accompanied by his wife, Meryt. In nearly all of the scenes he wears the Gold of Honour, rewards from the king comprising necklaces of gold disc beads, double armbands and a heavy gold bracelet, its shape derived from an ivory ring. He also wears a double-heart amulet, one of gold and one of silver, which was a special favour from the king, whose names are sometimes written on it. In the scene of the purification of Sennefer and Meryt with water, a Greek visitor of the Ptolemaic or Roman period has neatly written the name 'Alexander' in hieroglyphics on the silver heart. In most scenes, Sennefer wears large gold earrings, which is unusual. (Men are often shown with pierced ears, but rarely with rings through them.) One of the loveliest column panels has Sennefer seated in front of a tree with Meryt (much smaller) at his side. The strength and simplicity of the painting, with its restful colour scheme, never fails to delight.

To the north of the tomb of Ramose are two of the most celebrated tomb-chapels in the necropolis, those of **Nakht** and **Menna**, recently restored. They are remarkably small, but their painted decoration is exquisite. They both date to the reign of Thutmose IV or early in that of Amenhotep III.

Behind the hill of Sheikh Abd el-Qurna, in a valley similar to, but not as grand as, Deir el-Bahari, King S'ankh-ka-re Menthuhotep III planned his temple and tomb. Little survives today, but opposite, in the back of the Qurna hill, lies the large tomb of Meket-re, the king's chancellor. Although the fine reliefs are now little more than fragments, an undamaged statue chamber was excavated by the New York Metropolitan Museum of Art. Here many fine wooden models were discovered, three-dimensional

A CURIOUS OBSESSION

D`uring this little expedition there occurred a painful incident between Flaubert and me, the only one of our entire trip: we did not speak to each other for forty-eight hours. It was both unpleasant and comical, for in this case Flaubert obeyed one of those irresistible impulses that sometimes overcame him. Besides, in the desert one is hypersensitive, as the story will show. We had left Koseir with three skins full of execrable water, which were to supply our needs on the way; all three skins were incautiously loaded on the same side of the same camel: on its other side was part of our baggage as counterweight. The desert is inhabited by a prodigious number of rats, who feed off dead animals and are troglodytes. They dig tunnels and hole up in them. The camel carrying our water supply put his foot down on a spot just above one of these tunnels: the earth gave way under its weight, the poor animal broke its leg, fell, and in falling tore all three waterskins. That happened the evening we left. We had three days to go before reaching the Nile, and two and a half before Bir 'Ambar, the only well on the way with water fit to drink.

On our way to Koseir we had found that Bir el-Hammamat (Well of the Pidgeons) was dry, and that Bir es-Sidd (Closed Well) had been ruined by falling rock. It was Thursday, 23 May, about eight in the evening; even assuming we were to have no accident, we could not be at Bir 'Ambar earlier than some time on Sunday the 26th; thus, a minimum of sixty-six hours without drink...

...Suddenly, about eight in the morning, while we were passing through a gorge— a furnace—between pink granite rocks covered with inscriptions, Flaubert said to me: 'Do you remember the lemon-ice at Tortoni's?' I nodded. He went on: 'Lemon-ice is a wonderful thing. Confess that you wouldn't mind eating a lemon-ice right now. ' I said 'Yes' rather gruffly. After five minutes: 'Ah, those lemon-ices! The white frost that comes on the outside of the glass!' I said: 'Shall we change the subject?' He replied: 'That would be a good idea; still, lemon-ice has much to be said for it. You fill the spoon: it's like a little mound. You crush it gently between your tongue and your palate. It melts—slowly, cooly, deliciously. It moistens the uvula; it flows over the tonsils; it goes down into the esophagus, which doesn't mind a bit, and passes into the stomach, which almost swoons with joy. Between you and me, there's a shortage of lemon-ice in the desert of Koseir!'

I knew Gustave. I knew that nothing could stop him when he was in the grip of one of his morbid obsessions, and I made no further reply, hoping that my silence would silence him. But he began again, and seeing that I didn't answer he began to shout: 'Lemon-ice! Lemon-ice!' I was at the end of my tether and had a horrible thought: 'I'll kill him!' I said to myself. I drew my dromedary up close beside him and took his arm: 'Where do you want to ride? Ahead or behind?' He answered: 'I'll go ahead.' I reined in my dromedary, and when our little troop was two hundred paces ahead of me I resumed my way. That night I left Flaubert with our men and lay down on the sand two hundred metres from the camp. At three in the morning we set out, still just as far apart and without having exchanged a word. About three o'clock the dromedaries speeded up and showed signs of excitement: water was not far off. At half-past three we were at Bir 'Ambar, drinking. Flaubert put his arms around me and said: 'Thank you for not putting a bullet through my head: in your place I couldn't have resisted.' The next morning we were enjoying something better than Tortoni's lemon-ices: we were drinking Nile water again, the equal of the most exquisite wines, especially when you have just left the desert where you punctured your waterbags.

Maxime Du Camp, Souvenirs Litteraires, 1883

Maxime Du Camp (1822–1894). Born in Paris, Du Camp was a traveller and soldier, as well as a writer, artist and editor. His adventurousness and outspoken opinions were thought to be representative of the progressive modernists who made up the younger generation of his day. Perhaps the earliest of the travel photographers, he learned photography from his close friend, the novelist Gustave Flaubert. Du Camp's calotypes started appearing from 1851. His book, *Le Nil, Egypte et Nubie*, containing 220 calotypes, was one of the first to be illustrated with original photographs.

Thebes: Tomb of Nakht

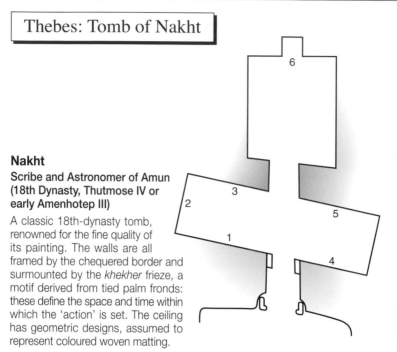

Nakht

Scribe and Astronomer of Amun (18th Dynasty, Thutmose IV or early Amenhotep III)

A classic 18th-dynasty tomb, renowned for the fine quality of its painting. The walls are all framed by the chequered border and surmounted by the *khekher* frieze, a motif derived from tied palm fronds: these define the space and time within which the 'action' is set. The ceiling has geometric designs, assumed to represent coloured woven matting.

1 Large scene of Nakht and his wife; Nakht oversees the agricultural activities of the year: ploughing, reaping, threshing and winnowing; a sub-scene with Nakht again, and a rather unusual 'landscape' with agricultural scenes.

2 Painted false door with servants making offerings; sub-scene with a large, beautifully detailed array of offerings, the tree-goddess (twice) presenting papyrus and offerings decorated with vines.

3 Funerary banquet which contains some famous vignettes: musician girls with harp, double-flute and lute; seated blind harpist, with young women sniffing lotus flowers and mandrakes.

4 Nakht with offering bearers and priests.

5 Fowling and fishing in the marshes. The large figures of Nakht accompanied by his wife and family, shown on a smaller scale, are arranged symmetrically, but the variants in the two groups avoid monotony. The background papyrus swamp is almost geometric: an area of green paint has been overlaid with rigid, formal papyrus. The lake or river at the centre has been reduced to a symbolic patch without perspective, and with two fish placed vertically. The birds, particularly the wings, are essentially hieroglyphic figures. The final detailing of this scene was never completed. Beneath is the scene of the vintage that usually appears as a pendant to the fowling and fishing. Birds caught in a clap-net are then prepared by drying or storing in jars of fat.

6 Statue niche, the remainder of the room is undecorated.

Source: Robert Morkot

Thebes: Tomb of Menna

Menna
**Scribe of the Royal Estates
(18th Dynasty, Thutmose IV or early
Amenhotep III)**

Very similar in style (same artists?) to Nakht.

1 Menna oversees agricultural activities. This scene contains some notable vignettes. Top register: measuring the fields to assess the harvest. Second register: six scribes counting the grain, with another sitting on top of a mound of grain. Third register: reaping; carrying the grain to the threshing floor; girls fighting over ears of corn; a girl taking a thorn from another's foot. Fourth register: threshing. Near the door, Menna and his wife are seated, with two of their daughters in front of them, both elaborately ringleted and attired in the headdress of the 'Royal Ornament', indicating a position in the palace.

2 Splendid large figures of Menna and his wife, elaborately dressed, making offerings to Osiris who is seated within a golden shrine. The sub-scene is much more informal, with offering bearers.

3 Funerary banquet, badly damaged.

4 Funeral procession.

5 Weighing of the heart and judgement by Osiris.

6 Pilgrimage to Abydos and funeral scenes. The Opening of the Mouth ritual using an adze, and a foreleg of beef: these were interchangeable due to their shape, both representing the constellation of the Great Bear. The texts are blank.

7 Fowling and fishing in the marshes: unfinished. Here the marsh is reduced to a clump of papyrus at the centre of the symmetrical scene. The figure of Menna's daughter is particularly charming. At the centre of the scene are two tilapia fish, symbols of rebirth. Beneath them an absurdly small crocodile grapples with another tilapia, although its jaws do not go round the fish. Sub-scene of offering bearers.

8 Niche with broken statues.

Source: Robert Morkot

versions of the painted tomb scenes found at Beni Hasan and el-Bersha. Now divided between the Egyptian Museum and the Metropolitan Museum, New York, these models are a delightful and informative document for the study of the Middle Kingdom. Particularly fine is the elaborate group of the cattle census (Egyptian Museum), with its wonderful spotted cows.

The most southerly part of the private necropolis is **Qurnet Murai**, a low hill between Deir el-Medina and the plain. The tombs here are of late 18th-dynasty to Ramesside date, and are rarely visited. The tomb of Merymose, who served as Viceroy of Nubia under Amenhotep III, was occupied as a house earlier this century. It is now inaccessible, but a fine black granite anthropoid coffin from here is displayed in the British Museum, which also possesses fragments of Merymose's two black granite sarcophagi. Close by is the tomb of Huy (tomb 40), the Viceroy of Nubia in the reign of Tutankhamun. This chapel is notable for its excellent paintings showing the appointment of Huy as viceroy, his arrival in Nubia, and the collection and presentation of tribute to the king. Amongst the objects presented are footstools, fans and shields, which are very similar to examples found in the king's tomb. The Nubian princes are shown in all their finery, and a princess is brought in a chariot which is drawn by cattle.

In a small valley behind the Qurnet Murai hill lies the village and cemetery of **Deir el-Medina**. This was the home to the workmen who carved and decorated the royal and private tombs, and, whilst in many ways not typical of ancient villages, it is one of few places where houses can be seen. At the northern end, a high brick wall surrounds the Ptolemaic temple. Raised over earlier New Kingdom buildings, this temple, dedicated to Hathor, is well preserved but unremarkable. In the New Kingdom, the chief deities of Deir el-Medina were Queen Ahmose-Nefertari and her son Amenhotep I, whose temple is just north of the Ptolemaic precinct. Adjacent is a Hathor chapel of Sety I and, opposite, the remains of a temple of Amun built by Ramesses II.

The village was entered from the north end. The main street is lined by terraces of houses, each long and narrow, running back to the village wall. The original 18th-dynasty village was the length of this main street. Where the street turns in a double bend is a later extension. In the southern part, the house plans are not as regular. Most houses follow much the same plan. A step goes down from the street into the first room, which usually has an enclosed high brick bench on one side. This is now generally thought to be a domestic shrine. A step up leads into the main room of the house. This room was higher than the others and lit by windows just beneath the ceiling. A dais marks the place where the owner and his wife sat, and often there is a stone column base (the column being of wood). The wall often has a false brick door and niche, which were used for the household cults, offerings being presented to favourite deities and ancestors. The walls were plastered (in some cases, patches survive) and the false door and birth room would have been painted. Beyond the main room are the master bedroom and a corridor with a staircase to the roof. At the back of the house, against the village wall, was a courtyard, which was probably partly covered. Here the cooking was done, and a deep shaft gave access to a storage room for foodstuffs.

More is known about the occupants of this village than any other single community in ancient Egypt. The paintings, and burials, in the tombs surrounding the village have enabled Egyptologists to reconstruct the genealogies of many of the families from the late 18th Dynasty to the end of the 20th. In addition, numerous stelae, *ostraca* and papyrus documents detail their lives. We even know in which houses in the village some of them lived. The documents also reveal the usual problems of village life: theft, adultery and attempted murder. There are also records of strikes and failure of the temple to pay their food rations on time. Although often treated as if they represent the 'ordinary' people of ancient Egypt, the villagers were palace employees, responsible for the work on the royal tomb, and hence far from ordinary.

The cemetery lies on the steep hill surrounding the village. Of the tombs, three are usually accessible, and are the finest, although many others have attractive and interesting paintings. The **tomb of Sennedjem** (tomb 1) is surprising in the brightness and freshness of its colour. As is typical of Deir el-Medina tombs, a steep staircase leads to a small vaulted burial chamber. Although the subject matter of the paintings is conventional, the execution is superb. A rich palette, a fine hand and perfect preservation make this one of the most rewarding tombs to visit. The coffins and other goods from this family tomb, which was cleared in 1886, are now displayed in the Egyptian Museum in Cairo.

Adjacent to the chapel of Sennedjem, and almost as well preserved, is the **tomb of Inherkhau** (tomb 359). A steep staircase leads to a small vaulted hall, which has good ceiling patterns (notice the motif of a cow's head with a solar disc between its horns), and a badly damaged scene of the tomb owner making offerings to royal statues. More steps lead into the burial chamber. Here the dominant colour is gold.

Thebes: Tomb of Sennedjem

Sennedjem

Servant in the Place of Truth, a title indicating that he was an artisan employed on the royal tomb (19th Dynasty)

A steep staircase leads to a particularly splendid burial chamber beneath the restored pyramid. The contents of the tomb, including the coffins, can be seen in the Egyptian Museum, with painting obviously by the same hand, perhaps Sennedjem himself. The painting is notable for its elegant line and rich colouring (including a strong red) on a gold background.

1   Door jamb has a fine scene of the cat of the sun killing the serpent Apep with a knife. The ceiling of the entrance has Sennedjem adoring the horizon goddess in the form of a pair of arms reaching from the horizon hieroglyph and grasping the sun disc. The ceiling of the chamber is vaulted, and is divided into panels by bands of hieroglyphic text. The scenes are religious, including: a large figure of Ra-Harakhty and Ra seated on a dappled cow, the sun disc rising between two trees; Sennedjem adores seated deities; Sennedjem and his wife, Nefertary, receive food and refreshing water from the tree goddess (note how Nefertary's hair, and the leaves of the tree, just extend over the boundary of the scene); Sennedjem and Nefertary adore gods of the night.

2   A series of panels. The mummified body of Sennedjem lies on a lion-shaped couch in a kiosk screened by a rather nice bead net. At either end are the goddesses Isis and Nephthys as kites. Below is the family of Sennedjem.

3   Sennedjem and Nefertary adore the gods of the underworld, who appear mummified, seated with a shrine. Only Osiris and Ra-Harakhty are distinguished by their heads and crowns. Above, two jackals seated on shrines face an offering table.

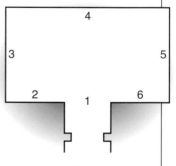

4   A series of panels: the mummified body of Sennedjem lies on a lion-shaped couch and is tended by Anubis; Sennedjem squats before Osiris; Sennedjem escorted by Anubis.

5   The wall is laid out as a map. In the upper lunette, baboons adore the barque of Ra. The god has a particularly large sun disc on his head, and in front of him is the instrument of justice. Below, water surrounds the Fields of Yaru. In the upper register, Sennedjem and Nefertary adore a group of deities including Ra-Harakhty, Osiris and Ptah; Sennedjem sails across the water; the Opening of the Mouth ritual. In the two registers below, Sennedjem and Nefertary cut corn in the Fields of Yaru, pull flax, and plough the fields and sow grain. They wear their festival garments, as befits the afterlife. Beneath are groves of palm trees of different types and flowers.

6   Sennedjem and Nefertary adore the fearsome guardians of the gates of the underworld. Beneath: members of Sennedjem's family.

Source: Robert Morkot

Thebes: Tomb of Inherkhau

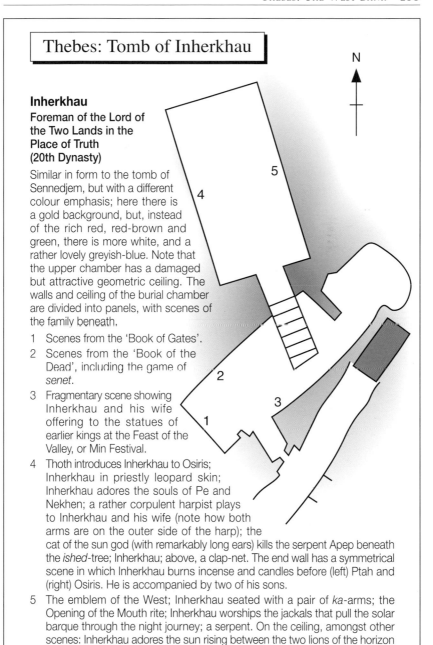

N

Inherkhau
Foreman of the Lord of the Two Lands in the Place of Truth (20th Dynasty)

Similar in form to the tomb of Sennedjem, but with a different colour emphasis; here there is a gold background, but, instead of the rich red, red-brown and green, there is more white, and a rather lovely greyish-blue. Note that the upper chamber has a damaged but attractive geometric ceiling. The walls and ceiling of the burial chamber are divided into panels, with scenes of the family beneath.

1 Scenes from the 'Book of Gates'.

2 Scenes from the 'Book of the Dead', including the game of *senet*.

3 Fragmentary scene showing Inherkhau and his wife offering to the statues of earlier kings at the Feast of the Valley, or Min Festival.

4 Thoth introduces Inherkhau to Osiris; Inherkhau in priestly leopard skin; Inherkhau adores the souls of Pe and Nekhen; a rather corpulent harpist plays to Inherkhau and his wife (note how both arms are on the outer side of the harp); the cat of the sun god (with remarkably long ears) kills the serpent Apep beneath the *ished*-tree; Inherkhau; above, a clap-net. The end wall has a symmetrical scene in which Inherkhau burns incense and candles before (left) Ptah and (right) Osiris. He is accompanied by two of his sons.

5 The emblem of the West; Inherkhau seated with a pair of *ka*-arms; the Opening of the Mouth rite; Inherkhau worships the jackals that pull the solar barque through the night journey; a serpent. On the ceiling, amongst other scenes: Inherkhau adores the sun rising between the two lions of the horizon (with beautifully stippled fur).

Source: Robert Morkot

The execution of the painting is superb, and includes some unusual mythological subjects: Inherkhau offering to the *bennu* bird (the Egyptian phoenix, a blue heron), which was a symbol of the sun god; and the cat of the sun god killing the evil serpent Apep (notice here the stippling on the cat's fur, and also on the two lions of the horizon, opposite).

Further off is the tomb of Pashed. The painting here is also very attractive, with scenes similar to those in the other tombs. One is unusual: Pashed is shown praying beneath a palm tree by water (a lake or the river).

ROYAL NECROPOLIS

VALLEY OF THE KINGS

A modern road runs northwards along the Dra Abu el-Naga hills, past Carter's dig house, then twists and turns back south into the wadi leading to the secluded Valley of the Kings. The more energetic may climb the paths from the north side of the bay of Deir el-Bahari and over the mountain ridge into the valley (about 45 minutes to one hour), an effort amply repaid with splendid views of the Theban region.

The Valley of the Kings contains 62 excavated tombs but not all of these were royal; some belonged to privileged members of the nobility and were usually undecorated (these officials have tomb-chapels in the main private necropolis). Several of these tombs have been discovered almost intact. There has been considerable archaeological activity in the valley in the past decade, with several teams clearing tombs, and a major excavation in the area between the tombs of Ramesses VI and Ramesses III. This work has produced numerous small objects and fragments of burial equipment, as well as houses built for the workers on the tombs. One of the major discoveries was in KV 5, a tomb constructed for the children of Ramesses II. Although this had been known for a long time, and previously entered, its vast scale and many burial chambers were a revelation. Kent Weeks has also completed his detailed survey of the valley.

Changes in the plan and decoration of the royal tombs from the earliest, that of Thutmose I, to the latest, Ramesses XI, are quite clear. The earliest tombs have staircases, corridors and a right-angle bend, a plan which becomes simpler until they are little more than huge, sloping corridors. The tombs can be divided into three main types. Of the tombs that are regularly open to visitors, the first phase is represented by those from Thutmose III to Thutmose IV; the second, by those from Horemheb to Ramesses III; and the third, by those from Ramesses IV to Ramesses IX. The earliest tombs (to Tutankhamun) are decorated with scenes taken from the 'Book of the Secret Chamber' (also known as the 'Amduat' or 'That Which is in the Underworld'), which details the journey of the sun through the underworld. This continued to appear in later tombs, but other texts were introduced. The 'Litany of Ra' first appears in the tomb of Thutmose III, but does not become a regular feature until the tomb of Sety I. From then on it is usually to be found at the entrance to the tomb, introduced with large figures of the dead king before the falcon-headed sun god. The 'Book of Gates' appears in most tombs from that of Horemheb onwards. It recounts the journey of the sun through the 12 gates that divides the hours of the night. Parts of other books appear in the later Ramesside tombs, they too relate to the solar journey.

The essential features of a royal tomb in the valley are descending corridors; a 'well room', which was a deep shaft, possibly to foil robbers or trap rainwater; a pillared hall; and a burial chamber. These elements were elaborated with additional chambers and corridors.

The tombs are described here in order from the entrance into the main part of the East Valley, the side road to the east, then from the main area to the west and south.

The **tomb of Ramesses IV** (KV 2) is a good example of the third type of king's tomb: essentially a large straight corridor plunging down to the burial chamber. The tomb was abbreviated, presumably because of the king's death, and the burial chamber is actually adapted from what should have been the well room and pillared hall. Nevertheless the decoration is good and typical of the 20th Dynasty, with the 'Litany of Ra' and the first appearance of parts of the 'Book of Caverns'. The colour is good, and the burial chamber contains a massive granite sarcophagus.

The **tomb of Ramesses II** (KV 7) is badly damaged and not open to visitors. It is currently being cleared and conserved by the Egyptian Documentation Centre under the direction of Christian Leblanc. A large tomb, its plan follows the bent axis plan of earlier 18th Dynasty tombs, rather than the nearly straight axis of his immediate predecessors' tombs. Opposite, on the east side of the valley is the tomb (KV 5) constructed for many of the king's sons. Although known since the time of early visitors, this enormous vault has been more thoroughly examined and cleared in recent years by Kent Weeks and the American University in Cairo.

The decoration and layout of the royal tombs, seen in its ultimate form most clearly in the tomb of Ramesses VI, actually dates back to the reign of Merneptah, the 13th son and successor of Ramesses II. The **tomb of Merneptah** (KV 8), despite its badly damaged decoration, is worth visiting. It lies at the end of the short road to the

The head of Ramesses II, Western Thebes

west. The design is simplified, with a single straight corridor rather than the 'jogged' type found in the tombs of Horemheb and Sety I. The massive corridor plunges 80 metres (262.6 feet) steeply downwards to the cavernous burial chamber whose ruinous state makes it all the more impressive. An immense outer sarcophagus in the room preceding the burial chamber was never taken further down. The king's red granite anthropoid sarcophagus lies in the burial chamber. A third sarcophagus (now in the Egyptian Museum) was appropriated by Pa-seba-kha-en-niut (Psusennes) for his own burial at Tanis in the Delta.

The **tomb of Ramesses IX** (KV 6) was never completed, and the corridor beyond the first pillared hall was enlarged to serve as the king's resting place. Nevertheless, the decoration is good and some of the figures of the pharaoh have a very distinctive profile, with rather hooked nose.

Next to the tomb of Ramesses IX lies the entrance to tomb KV 55, one of the puzzles of Egyptology. Undecorated and now inaccessible, this tomb was excavated by Theodore Davis in 1907. Some of the contents are displayed in the Amarna Room

Temple of Hatshepsut, Western Thebes

TRIBULATIONS OF VILLAGE LIFE

Although numerous papyrus documents survive from ancient Egypt, too few of them are of types which detail what life was like. There are letters, a few marriage contracts and land surveys, but the vast majority are religious and official documents. Our best sources for the study of provincial village life come from the Ptolemaic and Roman periods and are written in Greek. Of course, Egypt under the rule of the Ptolemies and the Roman emperors differed in many ways from the earlier periods, but the documents also reveal how much of the agricultural life continued as it had done for hundreds of years. One of the most vivid glimpses of rural life comes from the archive of a village scribe called Menkhes found at the Faiyum site of Tebtunis in 1900. The papyri, some over four metres long, had been used to wrap the mummified crocodiles, sacred to the local god, Sobek. The archive covers a period of ten years between 120 and 110 BC, and includes land surveys of the village, a place called Kerke-Osiris, near Tebtunis, records of the crops grown and amounts produced, and numerous incidents which had been reported to the scribe to be passed on to higher authorities.

One of the principal concerns of both government and people in Egypt has always been the control of irrigation. The land of any village was divided into quite small field plots, owned by different individuals and institutions, crisscrossed by irrigation channels, larger canals and dykes. The maintenance of the canals and dykes was essential to prevent flooding and waterlogging of land, or salination. The archive of Menkhes shows that this was one of the main causes of problems between villages whose land adjoined. There are complaints about farmers who, in flooding their fields, have also flooded neighbouring fields which had already been sown, thereby destroying the grain; failure to maintain boundary dykes had the same result, and there are regular complaints that fields have become salinated because of flooding from the fields of the neighbouring village.

The annual survey of the fields to assess rents and taxes and must have uncovered numerous attempts to gain land at the expense of one's neighbours. As far back the 'Instruction' texts of the Middle Kingdom we find the injunction:

Do not move the markers on the borders of the fields, nor shift the position of the measuring-cord. Do not be greedy for the cubit of land, nor encroach on the boundaries of a widow.

By the Ptolemaic period, certain commodities were a monopoly, which led to a thriving black market. The archive of Menkhes records a complaint from the official salesman, Apollonios, that contraband olive oil had been smuggled by a resident of the neighbouring village and was being sold illegally at dead of night. Apollonios called the police and they entered the house where the oil was being sold, but while they were making their search the smuggler took to his heels. On another occasion Apollonios tried to arrest black marketeers, only to be beaten up.

There were other tensions in the village, which sometimes led to violence. One resident complained that an armed gang had broken into his house, and into his mother's locked bedroom, and carried off the valuables, including two expensive garments and a jar of coins, even though he had done nothing to offend the gang leaders. Even the hospital wasn't a safe place: an unfortunate farmer who had gone to the hospital attached to the local temple of Isis was attacked while waiting for his cure. On one occasion the village scribe himself was arrested and accused, along with his brother and others, of an attempt to poison a visiting official. One of the most bizarre thefts was that of the village's 40 sacred sheep, stolen by a gang from a neighbouring village (who perhaps had less reverence for them).

What evidence we do have from earlier periods, notably from the artisans' village at Deir el-Medina (near modern Luxor), shows that many of the same troubles prevailed. These royal employees relied on having their wages and rations paid from the local temple, and when they were late, they had to go and demand them from the officials. In addition to theft and violence, the Deir el-Medina documents reveal more about another common feature of ancient village life, adultery. The foreman, Paneb, was accused of committing adultery with three married women of the village, as well as with the daughter of a fellow workman. This charge was filed along with several others of thefts from royal and private tombs, removing government tools for use in cutting his own tomb and taking government employees (other village workmen) to cut stone columns for his tomb (apparently during official work time). Paneb was also accused of murder; but he had his enemies in the village who were determined to bring him down. Village life in Egypt may have been difficult, but it was certainly eventful.

Tomb of Ramesses VI, Valley of the Kings

of the Egyptian Museum. These include a wooden coffin inlaid with coloured stones and glass paste. Its gold mask had been ripped off in antiquity, and the names of the owner had been cut out of the inscriptions. Four alabaster canopic jars with superb female heads had been drilled to add a royal uraeus to the brow. Gilt-wooden panels from a funerary shrine made by Akhenaten for Queen Tiye blocked the corridor. The skeleton has, at different times over the years, been attributed to Akhenaten, Queen Tiye and Smenkhkare, who was once thought to have been the brother and short-lived successor of Akhenaten. More recently some scholars have suggested that Smenkhkare may actually be the name adopted by Nefertiti as Akhenaten's co-regent and successor. Another view is that the burial was that of Kiya, the second wife of Akhenaten, and perhaps mother of Tutankhamun. Whoever it was, this is a reburial, probably by Tutankhamun, of one or more members of Akhenaten's family.

Directly opposite is the entrance to the **tomb of Tutankhamun** (KV 62), discovered by Howard Carter and Lord Carnarvon in 1922. There are often long queues to visit this small tomb, one of the least exciting in the valley. Most visitors leave wondering how the burial furniture was ever fitted into this cramped space. Probably carved not for the king, but for a high official (perhaps Ay), the rooms were hastily converted at Tutankhamun's early death. The paintings in the burial chamber are slightly unusual, including the dragging of the sarcophagus on a sledge by the high officials (notice the two viziers, with bald heads and loose white robes), and the Opening of the Mouth, performed by the king's successor, Ay.

Tutankhamun's tomb was concealed for many centuries beneath the mud-brick houses of the workmen who cut the **tomb of Ramesses VI** (KV 9), which is one of the largest tombs in the valley, with a vast corridor sloping down to the burial chamber. The tomb is decorated throughout with scenes from the books of the underworld. Decapitated figures marching along the walls, whole scenes which are upside down, and snakes with wings and human legs all contribute to the nightmarish vision. The burial chamber is dominated by the shattered remains of the massive granite sarcophagus, which is said to have been broken by thieves— but what sort of thieves have the means of destroying stone like this? The colonnade surrounding the chamber supports a vaulted ceiling, with its double figure of the goddess Nut in yellow against the dark sky. The sun can be seen passing through her body during the 12 hours of the night in the corresponding panels. The tomb has been open since Graeco-Roman times and there are many graffiti. The outer parts of the tomb are decorated in the name of Ramesses V, and the tomb was certainly begun for him, being completed by his successor. It seems that both kings were actually buried here.

The road to the east leads ultimately to the inaccessible tomb of Hatshepsut, in the cliff directly behind Deir el-Bahari. But other important tombs also lie in this direction. Because of the brevity of his reign, the **tomb of Ramesses I** (KV 16) is converted from the single small well room at the end of a steep corridor. It is, however, attractively painted with large figures of deities, brightly coloured on a blue-grey ground. The similarity of subject, style and colouring to the tomb of Horemheb is striking, and the two tombs were certainly executed by the same artists. Both tombs are distinctive in their use of a blue-grey background.

By contrast with that of his father, the **tomb of Sety I** (KV 17) is the largest and most elaborate of the royal tombs. It is usually closed because of rock falls and a lack of ventilation. Throughout the tomb, a delicate bas-relief, which is characteristic of many of Sety's other monuments, covers the walls with scenes from the 'Book of What is in the Underworld' and the 'Book of Gates'. The corridor descends to a well room, decorated with offering scenes. Beyond are two pillared halls, one a false burial chamber designed to deceive robbers. Here the decoration is unfinished, and the pillars have beautiful ink drawings of the king with various gods. To modern Western eyes, these are perhaps more satisfying than the finished painted reliefs. The corridor descends further from the floor of one of these chambers, passing over a second well, to an anteroom with the pillared burial chamber beyond. The king was destined to lie under the vault of heaven for eternity, its dark sky scattered with the constellations (note the pregnant hippopotamus). A number of decorated chambers surrounding this hall were used for storing the funerary furniture. Some large wooden statues of the king from here (similar to the black and gilt statues of Tutankhamun) are now in the British Museum. The tomb was first entered in modern times by Belzoni in 1817, and it was he who removed the alabaster sarcophagus and canopic chest, now in the John Soane Museum, London. A staircase descends a further 200 metres (656 feet) into the hill before being blocked by a rock fall.

The **tomb of Thutmose IV** (KV 43) is a good example of the first type with steeply descending corridors and 90-degree turns. The tomb descends to the burial chamber and is carefully finished in its basic construction, but is largely undecorated. There are some painted scenes in the well room and antechamber, showing the king with various deities against a background of golden yellow.

The **tomb of Prince Monthu-hir-khepeshef** (KV 19) is a simple large corridor, but beautifully decorated. The scale suggests that this was an unfinished king's tomb: a text indicates that it was intended for Prince Seth-hir-khepeshef, who later became the pharaoh Ramesses VIII. The incomplete tomb was later decorated for a son of Ramesses IX in the style of tombs in the Valley of the Queens. Unlike those tombs, the adult prince appears alone before the gods. The painted figures are in the best style of the 20th Dynasty, with exquisite line drawing and elaborate pleated costumes. The prince has the aquiline features typical of this family. The elegant figures against a white background and the unpainted ceiling offer a respite from some of the more overwhelming decoration of other tombs in the valley.

There is a wide variety in the decoration and date of the tombs that lie in the west and southern branches of the valley. The **tomb of Horemheb** (KV 57) is the first of the 'jogged' corridor tombs of the second type. Not quite as elaborate as that of Sety I, it has many of the same features. Staircases and corridors lead steeply down to the well room, painted with figures of the king and gods on a blue-grey ground and almost identical to the burial chamber of Ramesses I. Beyond lie the false burial chambers. As usual, the staircase continues from the floor of one of these rooms to an antechamber, which duplicates the paintings of the well room above. The large, pillared burial chamber is particularly interesting for its unfinished scenes. Here the Egyptian artist can be seen at work: the grid lines for laying out the design, the drawings and corrections in black and red ink, and various stages of the carving with figures abandoned half-cut. One of the small side chambers has a handsome painted figure of Osiris.

The **tomb of Ramesses III** was begun for his father, Sethnakht, but abandoned because the corridor cut into the adjacent tomb of Amenmesses. A small chamber allowed for the realignment of the axis and completion according to the typical 20th-dynasty layout. The finest and most interesting paintings are to be found in the small side chambers near the tomb's entrance. Here are elaborate pieces of furniture, boats and Nile gods. The blind harpist (fifth room on the left) was first published by James Bruce who visited the tomb in 1769 (hence the name 'Bruce's Tomb', or 'Harper's Tomb' given by early scholars). The large cartouche-shaped granite sarcophagus lid, removed by Belzoni, is now in the Fitzwilliam Museum in Cambridge. The lid carries an image of the king as Osiris, in very high relief, flanked by the goddesses Isis and Nephthys. The box of the sarcophagus is in the Louvre.

Situated at the southern end of another wadi, the **tomb of Amenhotep II** is strikingly similar to that of his father, Thutmose III, but regularized. The antechamber was never painted, but the burial chamber is extremely fine. Rectangular rather than oval in shape, it is divided into two sections, the first supported by six square pillars, the furthest end of which is sunk to take the sarcophagus (*in situ*). The paintings again imitate papyrus, although within the rectangular shape of the chamber it is perhaps less effective than in the tomb of Thutmose III. The pillars, unfinished, have large figures of the king with various deities. In many cases, only the headdress and a few details have been added in colour, but the ink drawing is elegant and its unfinished state appealing. (Compare with that of Sety I for differences in style.) Close inspection reveals some grid lines used in the layout, and occasional corrections to the figures. As in the tomb of Thutmose III, four small chambers for the storage of funerary furniture open off the burial chamber. In the southwest chamber, Victor Loret found, in 1898, one of the caches of royal mummies. The seclusion of Amenhotep II's tomb caused it to be used by the officials who collected nine royal mummies for reburial here in the 22nd Dynasty. They included Thutmose IV, Amenhotep III, Siptah and Sety II. Amenhotep II was found still lying in his own sarcophagus.

The **tomb of Siptah** (KV 47) is a fairly conventional corridor tomb. There is some very beautiful relief decoration near the entrance, showing the king, elaborately attired, before Ra-Harakhty against a rich background of golden yellow.

The **tomb of Sethnakht** (KV 14) is a grand ruin. In the entrance, the erased figures of Queen Tawosret, the tomb's original owner, can be seen. The corridor descends to the burial chamber of Tawosret with conventional columns and vaulted astronomical

(following pages) *Scene from a noble's tomb, Western Thebes*

ceiling. Another corridor continues to the almost identical burial chamber of Sethnakht. This has a wrecked majesty, with the king's red granite sarcophagus lying amidst the rubble.

The **tomb of Sety II** (KV 15) is a simple corridor descending to the well room and pillared hall, with the burial chamber adapted from the corridor. The decoration was completed quickly, changing from relief to painting. There are some good figures of the king, but the most interesting and unusual elements are the painted scenes showing statues within shrines. The statues are mostly painted in yellow, indicating gilt, and have close parallels in the gilt-wooden images from the tomb of Tutankhamun.

Of those that can be visited, the **tomb of Thutmose III** is the earliest, and certainly one of the most worthwhile. Situated at the end of one of the southern wadis, it can be reached by climbing a modern staircase, then passing through a short ravine to the entrance. The staircase and corridor, rough-hewn and undecorated, lead to the well, a deep shaft now crossed by a short bridge. The ceiling is painted with stars and the top of the walls with a simple ornamental frieze. The door into the rooms beyond would have been sealed and plastered over. The antechamber, supported by two square pillars, has walls covered with a textbook of 741 different divinities, its ceiling spangled with stars. Here the tomb takes a 90-degree turn, with the stairs to the burial chamber leading from one corner. Oval in shape, resembling a cartouche, this burial chamber is one of the loveliest in the whole valley. Far from grandiose, its decoration has an unrivalled elegance and simplicity. The painting is in the style of a funerary papyrus, with 'stick' figures in black. On one of the square columns (west pillar, north face), the king is shown with female members of his family, and in the scene below, sucking the breasts of the tree goddess. The whole is a delightful respite from the richness of the later tombs.

Several tombs belonging to officials were discovered more or less intact. Although undecorated and today inaccessible, their burial goods can be seen in the Egyptian Museum. Maiherpri was a Nubian prince who was educated at the Egyptian court with the royal princes, under one of whom, Amenhotep II, he later held office. Yuya and Tjuyu were the parents of Queen Tiye, the chief wife of Amenhotep III. Their tomb, discovered by Theodore Davis in 1905, contained many fine objects, including two chairs belonging to their granddaughter, Princess Sitamun.

There are further tombs in the West Valley, reached by a separate road near the Rest House, but only that of Ay is generally open. Transport is recommended. The tomb of Ay was probably intended for Tutankhamun; it was clearly decorated by the same artists only a couple of years after the young pharaoh's death. The most unusual feature of the tomb is the scene of Ay and his queen, Tiy, not Tutankhamun's widow, Ankhesenamun, hunting in the marshes. This scene is usually compared to the scenes in the tombs of the nobles, and invoked as a reference to Ay's non-royal origins. However, identical types of scene appeared on a gold shrine from the tomb of Tutankhamun and are later found in Ptolemaic and Roman temples.

VALLEY OF THE QUEENS

The earliest tombs in the Valley of the Queens belong to the late-18th or early-19th Dynasty. The finest of the tombs, that of Nefertari, chief wife of Ramesses II, has recently been extensively restored. It can now be visited with a special ticket. The Valley of the Queens is much smaller than the Valley of the Kings, but is fringed by impressive cliffs. Recent excavations have uncovered many previously unknown tombs. Although most are undecorated or badly damaged, some have beautiful decoration. The tombs presently accessible belong to the 20th Dynasty.

The **tomb of Queen Titi**, an otherwise unknown royal lady, has sunk relief in delicate colours, but not all of it is well preserved. One of the more interesting scenes shows Hathor as the goddess of the Western Mountain (i.e. the Theban necropolis) emerging from the hill. The golden cow, following Egyptian convention, is actually superimposed upon the hill, which is shown in bands of pink with stippling to represent the rock. The remainder of the tomb is decorated with mythological subjects and figures of the queen with various deities. In the first corridor, the figures are on a white background, but in the room beyond, a richer effect is achieved with a golden ground.

The painted relief in the **tomb of Prince Amen-hir-khepeshef** is notable for its vivid colouring. Whilst bright and fresh, the palette lacks some of the subtlety of earlier work; note the use of oranges, as well as very bright blues, turquoises and greens. The first chamber, the tomb's finest, has large figures of the prince being introduced to various gods by his father. Here the richly patterned and coloured robes of the prince and his father, Ramesses III, are well conveyed. One unusual feature is the way in which the individual scenes are allowed to ignore the corners in the room. In earlier tombs the individual walls were framed, but from the Amarna period onwards, scenes can sometimes occupy parts of two walls. Various scenes from the 'Book of Gates' fill the corridor beyond. The burial chamber has an uninscribed granite sarcophagus.

The decoration of the **tomb of Prince Seth-hir-khepeshef**, another son of Ramesses III, is very similar, but badly darkened by smoke. Also similar in decoration, though with a slightly more elaborate plan, is the **tomb of Prince Khaemwaset**, Ramesses III's eldest son. The first corridor again has scenes of the king introducing his son to the gods, and the second has scenes from the 'Book of Gates'. Two small rooms lie off the first corridor. The prince is shown making offerings to the funerary goddesses, Isis, Nephthys, Selket and Neith, who are all painted a rather bright turquoise.

Tomb of Nefertari

Nefertari was the chief wife of Ramesses II during the first two decades of his reign, and figures prominently in the temples of Luxor and Abu Simbel. Her tomb was the finest surviving in the Valley of the Queens, but had to be closed after becoming badly damaged by extrusion of salt caused by a rise in the water table. It has now been reopened following restoration by the Getty Foundation. Access is strictly limited, by numbered ticket (bought at the student ticket office near the Colossi of Memnon on the day of the visit). The decoration is in modelled and painted plaster. Although the scenes are of a conventional type, mostly of the queen making offerings to various deities, their elegant layout and the superb quality of their execution, combined with a rich palette, make this tomb one of the triumphs of Egyptian art. The images of the queen are especially fine, employing techniques of shading not generally found earlier. The hieroglyphs in the texts are notable for their large scale and their beautiful detailing.

WEST BANK: THE TEMPLES

The 'Houses of Millions of Years', usually, although incorrectly, called mortuary temples, were built along the edge of the cultivated land. In these the king became closely associated with Amun, and was worshipped during and after his death as a manifestation of the god. These temples were visited annually by the statue of Amun when it was taken from Karnak for the 'Beautiful Feast of the Valley'. Scenes in Theban tombs and at the Ramesseum show the royal statues accompanying the god's sacred barque. The focus of the festival was the Temple of Hatshepsut at Deir el-Bahari, where the statue of Amun resided overnight. The festival was a time when the people of the city came to the tombs of their families, where they celebrated. At dawn they brought the portable statues of their ancestors from the chapels to be reborn in the rays of the rising sun.

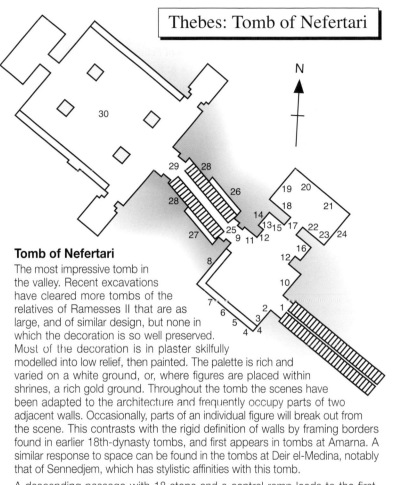

Thebes: Tomb of Nefertari

30

N

29 **28**

28 **26** **19** **20**

18 **21**

14 **13** **15** **17** **22** **24**

27 **25** **9** **11** **12** **23**

16

8 **12**

Tomb of Nefertari

10

The most impressive tomb in
the valley. Recent excavations
have cleared more tombs of the
relatives of Ramesses II that are as
large, and of similar design, but none in
which the decoration is so well preserved.

7 **6** **2** **1**
5 **3**
4 **4**

Most of the decoration is in plaster skilfully
modelled into low relief, then painted. The palette is rich and
varied on a white ground, or, where figures are placed within
shrines, a rich gold ground. Throughout the tomb the scenes have
been adapted to the architecture and frequently occupy parts of two
adjacent walls. Occasionally, parts of an individual figure will break out from
the scene. This contrasts with the rigid definition of walls by framing borders
found in earlier 18th-dynasty tombs, and first appears in tombs at Amarna. A
similar response to space can be found in the tombs at Deir el-Medina, notably
that of Sennedjem, which has stylistic affinities with this tomb.

A descending passage with 18 steps and a central ramp leads to the first,
square, chamber.

1   Damaged figures of Nekhbet and Wadjet. A rock-cut bench with cavetto
    cornice runs around two sides of the room. This carries the names and titles
    of the queen. Below, in the recesses, are paintings of shrines, and this is
    probably where the shrines containing funerary statues of Nefertari were
    placed. The walls above are covered in beautifully executed texts and scenes
    from chapter 17 of the 'Book of the Dead'. The hieroglyphs are large, elegantly
    laid out, finely detailed and coloured on a white ground. The vignettes above:

2   Nefertari plays the *senet*-game; 3 Nefertari as a *ba*-bird; 4 Nefertari kneeling
    in adoration of the twin lions of the horizon; 5 A *bennu*-bird—the heron
    ('phoenix') of the sun god; 6 The mummified body on a bier in a shrine with

Nephthys and Isis as kites; 7 A Nile god with potbelly and the udjat eye, symbol of health and completeness; the remaining figures are badly damaged.

8 The decoration of the wall is divided into two sections, with mummified figures, including Nefertari.

9 Above the door to the burial chamber are the fours sons of Horus: Imsety (human), Hapy (baboon), Qebehsenuef (falcon) and Duamutef (jackal), although the names of the last two have been transposed.

10 Nefertari adores Osiris, seated in a kiosk, with a standing figure of Anubis on the adjacent wall. The shrine has a richly coloured frame with bands and chevrons surmounted by a cavetto cornice and frieze of uraeuses against a red ground. Over the door into the side chambers is a kneeling figure with two *udjat* eyes within ovals, flanked by large uraeuses and ostrich feathers.

11 To the left of the door a splendid figure of Osiris stands within a shrine, flanked by the fetish of Anubis (a skin attached to a pole).

12 The entrance to the side chambers has large images of Selket (left) and Neith (right). The decorative scheme is united by the colouring, and by the coloured dado beneath the scenes.

13 A *djed*-pillar with human arms: note how the flail extends around into the next scene, behind Nefertari's sleeve.

14 A superb figure of the queen with her characteristic slim elegant figure and flowing costume, with long pleated sleeves, red crimped sash, and vulture headdress. She is guided by Isis, who wears the headdress and *menat*-collar of Hathor, and a splendid beaded sheath dress. The goddess leads her to...

15 the sun god Khepri, here a rather startling image with a human body and a scarab for a head.

16 Horus-son-of-Isis leads the queen to Ra-Harakhty and Hathor, Mistress of the West, the goddess who protects the Theban necropolis.

17 In the door, symmetrical images of the goddess Maat.

18 Nefertari presents cloth to Ptah.

19 Nefertari before the ibis-headed Thoth, between them a stand with scribal palette, water bowl and frog amulet. A double scene fills the entire wall.

20 Her arm extended with the *sekhem*-sceptre, Nefertari presents spectacular offerings to Osiris. On a bed of leaves, whole red and black dappled oxen lie side-by-side, each with the skinned foreleg placed on top of it, along with ribs and the heart; another mat supports loaves of bread and more forelegs, and the animals' heads; the offerings are surrounded by baskets of fruit and surmounted by bowls of incense, the smoke blowing towards the god. Osiris, wearing the *atef* crown, is coloured green for rejuvenation. In front of him the four sons of Horus are placed on a standard, and behind him is the lotus-leaf shaped fan.

21 Nefertari makes corresponding offerings to the elderly sun god Atum.

22 A splendid image of a ram-headed mummified god with large sun disc, flanked by Isis and Nephthys, who both wear the *afnet*-headdress. This scene shows the culmination of the sun god's nighttime journey through the underworld: it is the moment when he becomes Osiris, and thereby is able

to rejuvenate himself. The two lines of text tell us that: 'This is Ra when he has come to rest in Osiris', and 'This is Osiris resting within Ra'. The image and texts reveal that Osiris and Ra are, for a brief time, joined, but each retains his own identity.

23 Another superb figure of Nefertari, her arms raised in adoration of...

24 the seven cows and the bull, and the four oars. This is chapter 148 of the 'Book of the Dead'.

A steep corridor leads down to the sarcophagus hall, the decoration cleverly fitted to the shapes created by the sloping ceiling.

25 Large cartouches with Nefertari's name are protected by the uraeus goddesses. The goddesses Neith and Selket flank the door.

26 Nefertari wearing a heavy wig offers the globular *nemset*-vessels to the seated goddesses Isis and Nephthys and a squatting figure of Maat with outstretched wings.

27 A parallel scene in which Nefertari offers to the Theban form of Hathor, to Selket and to Maat. In these scenes the circular alabaster-topped offering tables, covered with leaves, carry an array of bread, fruit and vegetables, the incense carries the essence to the gods. The smoke is effectively rendered. Below both recesses are symmetrical scenes...

28 of Anubis on his shrine with a red sash around his neck, and supporting the flail with his back leg. The hieroglyphic texts carry his speech welcoming the queen. Above a winged cobra with the *shen*, symbol of eternity, enfolds the queen's cartouche. Beneath the figures of Anubis the goddesses Nephthys and Isis kneel on large hieroglyphic signs, the collar indicating 'gold'. The goddesses wear the *afnet*-headdress, with their names above (cutting across the baseline into the adjacent scene). They lean on the *shen*-symbol and welcome the queen into the afterlife.

29 The door is framed by the titles of 'the Osiris, the King's Great Wife, the Mistress of the Two Lands, Nefertari, Beloved of Mut'. The lintel carries a squatting figure of Maat with outstretched wings. More images of Maat in the doorway itself, with splendid coiled cobras representing Nekhbet and Wadjet.

30 The sarcophagus chamber is supported by four square pillars, with a rock-cut bench running around the outside. The decoration and texts relate to chapters 144 and 146 of the 'Book of the Dead'. The ceiling is covered with stars, and the tops of pillars and walls have a bold *khekher* frieze in green on a red ground. Beneath the scenes are bands of gold and red against black. The large images of queen and deities are all elegantly executed and coloured. Most of the images are the doorkeepers of the underworld, who have names such as 'The One who Eats the Excrement of his Hind Parts', and 'Hippopotamus-Faced, Raging with Power'. Having passed the gates, the queen adores Osiris, Hathor, Mistress of the West and Anubis. The pillars have scenes of Horus attired as the Iun-mut-ef priest in leopard skin and side-lock before Osiris in his shrine; Nefertari with Hathor and Anubis; large *djed*-pillars. The granite sarcophagus stood at the centre of the room, and a niche in the middle of the west wall held the canopic chest.

Source: Robert Morkot

Temple of Sety I at Qurna

The Temple of Sety I is the northernmost of the 'Houses of Millions of Years' and combines elements of both the 18th- and 19th-dynasty types. Entered through two pylons (now destroyed) the temple proper stood at the back of the second court, with a colonnaded portico. Along the main axis of the temple was the suite of rooms dedicated to Amun, with, on the southern side the chapel for the king's father, Ramesses I, and, on the northern side, the solar chapel. Ramesses I reigned for only one year, so his son included a suite of rooms in this temple for his worship. Here Sety can be seen anointing his father's image. The solar chapel consists of an open court with a large altar in the middle. It is to be found in a similar position in the other temples, although only that at Medinet Habu is well preserved.

The whole structure lacks the grandeur of the Ramesseum or Medinet Habu, but this is adequately compensated for by the relief decoration which, as in all of Sety I's monuments, is of very high quality. Amongst the more unusual scenes is one (chapel on the north side of the hypostyle hall) depicting Sety I seated, with a female figure behind him representing the temple personified.

Deir el-Bahari: Djeser-Djeseru

One of the most splendid examples of royal mortuary temples is certainly the **Temple of Queen Hatshepsut** which, due to its spectacular situation, its architectural design and the high quality of its execution, is one of the most notable monuments of Egyptian architecture. The modern name of the site is the 'Convent of the North', after the Coptic monastery later built within the same temple. First cleared by the Egypt Exploration Society under the direction of Eduard Naville, the temple has been for many years the focus of restoration work by the Polish Centre for Mediterranean Archaeology. They have been able to recreate the architectural and decorative elements of the upper terrace from the numerous surviving fragments.

The mountain range encircling the temple was consecrated to the goddess Hathor, often depicted as a cow with the typical crown formed by a solar disc between two lyre-shaped horns, here coming out from the mountain to the west of Luxor, seat of the necropolis. The place had been chosen by the sovereigns of the 11th Dynasty for their burials, and the remains of a majestic temple erected for Nebhepetre-Menthuhotep are still visible on the south side of Hatshepsut's building. A pathway on the ridge links Deir el-Bahari to the Valley of the Kings. A broad avenue led up to a valley temple. Remains of gardens may still be seen at the entrance to the complex. The temple itself rises in a series of terraces. The terraces, cut into the slopes of the mountain, rest on porticoes, the walls of which are decorated with high-quality reliefs showing various events which Hatshepsut felt were worthy of being recorded. Unfortunately, the reliefs have suffered extensive damage, both in ancient and more recent times. On the lower terrace (south side, far southern end) is a scene of the transportation of two obelisks from Aswan to Thebes on an enormous river barge. The short south wall of the lower terrace (the northern side) has a large figure of Hatshepsut as a sphinx trampling her enemies, erased in ancient times, but still just visible.

The reliefs of the main terrace are better preserved with, on the northern half, the divine conception and birth of Hatshepsut; the god Amun, in the guise of Thutmose I, visits Queen Ahmose; Khnum fashions Hatshepsut on the potter's wheel; and a pregnant Queen Ahmose is conducted to the birth-couch by the frog-headed goddess Heqet. At the northern end is the Chapel of Anubis, where the colour is particularly well preserved. Although the figure of Hatshepsut has been erased, there are superb hovering vulture and falcon deities.

On the south side of the terrace are depicted the expedition to the land of Punt, one of the most remarkable events of Hatshepsut's reign: the arrival of the Egyptian ships, the exchange of Egyptian handicrafts with local products, valuable materials, rare animals, resins, antimony for the eyes, gold, ivory, panther skins, monkeys, a giraffe and felines of various kinds for hunting. The Queen of Punt is depicted as enormously obese, but opinion is divided about whether this is elephantiasis, or, as in many African countries, an indication of her wealth. The original block (here replaced with a cast) is in the Egyptian Museum.

At the southern end is the **Chapel of Hathor**. Two columned halls precede the rock-cut rooms of the sanctuary. The capitals of columns have the full face of the goddess with cow's ears. The bas-reliefs depict the festivals, with river processions, and the accompanying contingents of soldiers with their weapons and divisional standards. The goddess Hathor is depicted as a cow nursing the queen. The architect Senenmut, designer of the entire temple, is himself represented by images concealed in various locations in the niches of the sanctuary.

The portico of the third terrace is formed by square pillars with the statues of the king as Osiris. This part of the temple suffered considerable damage at the hands of Thutmose III. The courtyard of the third terrace is surrounded by deep colonnades. On the north is the solar sanctuary, with its large open court and altar. On the south

are chapels for the cult of Hatshepsut and her father, Thutmose I. In the centre is the principal sanctuary, enlarged during the Ptolemaic age.

To the north of the avenue leading to the temple, the **tomb of the architect Senenmut** was discovered. The ceiling of one chamber has an astronomic decoration representing the constellations (see tomb of Sety I in the Valley of the Kings). This tomb remained unfinished, perhaps because Senenmut fell from the queen's grace and was buried in another tomb, at Sheikh Abd el-Qurna.

Between the upper terrace of Hatshepsut's temple and Nebhepetre-Menthuhotep II's temple (11th Dynasty) are the ruins of a temple of Thutmose III. This temple was almost completely destroyed, but is now being extensively (some think excessively) restored by the Polish team. When complete it must have dominated both of the earlier temples flanking it. It stood on a ledge of the cliffs with terraces and ramp-stairways built out in front.

The **Temple of Nebhepetre-Menthuhotep** is not open to visitors. It doubtless inspired the later architects, with its combination of terraces and colonnades. The central feature was either a pyramid or a flat-topped mastaba-like structure. This was surrounded by a colonnade. A columned hall gave access to the cult rooms at the back of the temple, and concealed the entrance to the king's tomb beneath. Eduard Naville excavated the complex for the Egypt Exploration Society, finding the burials of several of Menthuhotep II's wives, and numerous fragments of the painted relief sculpture that decorated the temple. The sarcophagi of queens Kawit and Ashayt are displayed in the Egyptian Museum, Cairo. The style of decoration of the temple and sarcophagi is elegant. The figures are crisply carved in the fine limestone that was used and have the rather slender proportions that are also typical of Theban art in the early 18th Dynasty. When the complex is viewed from the cliffs above, the remains of the garden that stood in front are clearly visible. A statue of the king (Cairo) wearing the robe of the *sed*-festival was found in one of the chambers in the deep trench in front of the temple. This cutting was probably intended as the king's tomb originally, but the plans were modified.

Southwest of the circle of Deir el-Bahari is the hiding place of the royal mummies (now in the Egyptian Museum) discovered by Maspero in 1881; these were gathered here, in the shaft tomb of Queen Inhapi, during the 21st Dynasty to protect them from tomb robbers. A second discovery took place in 1891, east of the tomb of Senenmut, where the sarcophagi of the high priests of Amun and Khonsu had been hidden.

Colossi of Memnon, Western Thebes

RAMESSEUM: 'UNITED WITH WASET'

The Ramesseum is one of the most romantic ruins surviving in the Theban region and is worth visiting for that reason. The pylon and first court are in a poor state, but the many trees give the place great charm. The second court is dominated by the broken colossus of the king as Osiris. The hypostyle has suffered less, but the sanctuaries and chapels are almost totally destroyed. An idea of the temple's plan and original appearance may be obtained from Medinet Habu, which was almost identical. The quality of the work at the Ramesseum was, however, superior. The temple has been the focus of restoration work by a French–Egyptian team from the Louvre and the Egyptian Documentation Centre, led by Christian Leblanc.

The most notable monument here is the shattered colossus of Ramesses II, which once dominated the first court. Its original height was probably about 17 metres (55.8 feet) and its weight more than 1,000 tons. It was still intact when Diodorus Siculus visited the site in the first century AD. The polish of the granite is still remarkable. This statue was the inspiration for Shelley's poem 'Ozymandias'. The name derives from the Greek form of the throne name of Ramesses II, User-maat-ra. The poet never visited the site, but the names of many other early 19th-century visitors are carved on the walls and columns.

There are remnants of other fine statues in the second court. The entrance to the hypostyle was flanked by two further statues, the superb black granite head of one remains here. This head, it has recently been discovered, was originally from a statue of Amenhotep III, but was recut for Ramesses II. The body of a larger seated statue remains here. The head and upper torso were removed from the site by Belzoni and now dominate the Egyptian sculpture gallery of the British Museum.

Beyond the hypostyle, the next chamber has a fine astronomical ceiling. Surrounding the temple are many vaulted brick buildings which formed the storage rooms and administrative office of the temple. There was also a school here. These temples were the main centres for the payment of rations to, for example, the workers of Deir el-Medina who were engaged on the cutting of the royal tombs.

COLOSSI OF MEMNON

These two isolated colossi originally flanked the entrance to the largest of the temples on the west bank, that of Amenhotep III. The temple was pillaged by later pharaohs for stone to build their own structures and for statues to decorate them. Some of its statuary may now be found in the Ramesseum and at Medinet Habu, and other pieces were moved to the Karnak precinct, notably the many statues of the goddess Sakhmet that adorn the Temple of Mut. The site was also ransacked by the early European collectors and a fine collection of statues from here now adorns the British Museum. Recent work has given some idea of the plan and vast scale of this temple, and excavations have uncovered more colossal statues and parts of the temple's architecture. A large stele and a few broken statues, including a rather bizarre image of a crocodile-tailed lion (a depiction of one of the Egyptian constellations), are the most significant monuments visible of what must have been one of the most spectacular of Egyptian temples.

The colossi themselves are 15.6 metres (51.2 feet) high on bases of 2.3 metres (7.5 feet). Originally they would have had double crowns (like the colossi at Abu Simbel). Amenhotep III, appearing as the sun god, is flanked by his mother, Queen Mutemwiya, and his wife, Queen Tiye.

The two statues enjoyed great fame in the ancient world, especially during the first two centures AD. They became identified as images of Memnon, a Trojan hero killed by Achilles. A crack in the northern colossus, caused by the earthquake of 27 BC, meant that in the early morning the statue emitted a strange noise, which, it was said, was Memnon greeting his mother, the goddess Eos (Dawn). The statues were a tourist attraction and the base of the northern colossus has many inscriptions carved on it. The emperor Hadrian came here to hear the singing, as did Septimius Severus. It was the latter emperor's restoration of the statue which silenced it.

MEDINET HABU: 'UNITED WITH ETERNITY'

Medinet Habu is one of the best-preserved complexes on the west bank. It comprises the **Temple of Ramesses III** with adjacent palace, surrounded by the remains of a town, the whole enclosed within a massive defensive wall. The complex is entered through the High Gate, or Migdol, which was built in the style of an Asiatic fortress. It has several windows from which the king could appear in splendour, seeming to stand on the carved heads of his enemies.

Originally an inner enclosure would have separated the temple from the town. Now, there is a large open space. On the south are the isolated chapels of the princesses who held the office of God's Wife of Amun in the 25th and 26th dynasties: Amenirdis I, Shepenwepet II and Nitoqert. Their tombs were beneath the chapels. That of Amenirdis I has very fine relief decoration.

The small Temple of Amun just to the north of these chapels was founded by Hatshepsut and Thutmose III and later enlarged by the 25th-dynasty and Ptolemaic

(following pages) The Ramesseum, Western Thebes

kings. This temple was the focus of the weekly festival (every ten days, an Egyptian week) during which the statue of Amun was brought from the east bank to reside here. The temple was believed to be the site of the first land to appear at the time of the creation. The Temple of Ramesses III suffered destruction at the close of the 20th Dynasty, but this small Amun temple continued, and even increased in importance in the following Libyan and Late periods. The original structure has a small group of cult rooms, with a large barque shrine on a platform standing in front of it. Pylons and halls were added in front of this, towards the quay. The gateway of the Ptolemaic pylon (stone facing on a now-destroyed mud-brick core) has a superb winged sun disc, which retains much of its original colour.

The main Temple of Ramesses III is impressive because of the state of preservation of the front part. Although technically less fine than earlier temples, its reliefs are interesting and historically important. The first court is oriented across the temple axis, focusing on the Window of Appearances from the palace. In this court the scenes show battles against the Libyans along with the slaughtering of various other enemies; the whole scheme extols the power of the king. On the back wall of the pylon (north tower) Libyan chiefs are brought and the king's officials count the severed hands and phalluses of the slaughtered foes.

A ramp leads up and through the pylon to the second court, where the scenes are religious. Here the great cycles are the Festival of Min (north wall) and the Festival of Sokar (south wall). In both, the colour is well preserved and the detail fascinating. A ramp leads up, between the bases of two colossi, to the terrace of the temple proper, with its portico. The decoration here has been cleaned and shows the vivid original colours. There are many fine images of the Egyptian gods on the pillars.

The back part of the temple is less perfect: three hypostyle halls had a series of chapels for various deities, including, on the south side, a suite for the cult of Ptah-Sokar-Osiris, and on the north, a solar court. The statue groups which are to be found here were brought from the Temple of Amenhotep III behind the Colossi of Memnon.

On the outer walls of the temple (north side) is the most important cycle of reliefs depicting battles with the Sea Peoples and Libyans. The most impressive scene is a large engagement, presumably in the Delta, with many boats. The small palace on the south side of the temple would have been used when the king came to perform rituals in the temple; it was not the major residence palace. On the back wall of the south tower of the pylon is a splendid scene of hunting bulls in the marshes. The palace has an audience hall on the axis behind the Window of Appearances, and near this can be found the king's shower room, with its stone tank intact.

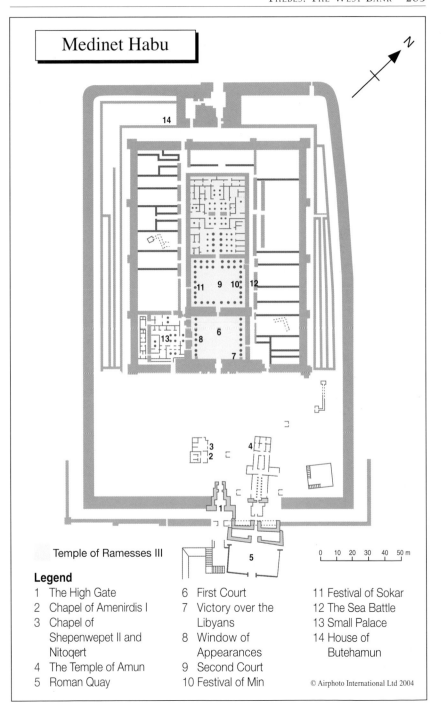

Medinet Habu

Temple of Ramesses III

0 10 20 30 40 50 m

Legend

1 The High Gate
2 Chapel of Amenirdis I
3 Chapel of
   Shepenwepet II and
   Nitoqert
4 The Temple of Amun
5 Roman Quay

6 First Court
7 Victory over the
   Libyans
8 Window of
   Appearances
9 Second Court
10 Festival of Min

11 Festival of Sokar
12 The Sea Battle
13 Small Palace
14 House of
   Butehamun

© Airphoto International Ltd 2004

The town surrounding the temple became important in the later 20th Dynasty, when Deir el-Medina village was abandoned. It continued to flourish into Coptic times. At the back of the enclosure there still stand four columns of the house of Butehamun, a well-known official from an old Deir el-Medina family, whose letters tell us much about the troubled times at the end of the reign of Ramesses XI.

UPPER EGYPT, SOUTH OF LUXOR

T he major monuments of Upper Egypt usually visited are the Ptolemaic and Roman temples of Esna, Edfu and Kom Ombo. The three are in many ways very similar, but closer examination of them highlights their differences. There are many other important sites in the region but most are not easily accessible or regularly visited. Although there have been no major incidents in this part of Egypt, security has been an issue in recent years, and tourists have often been obliged to join convoys from Aswan to Thebes or to make visits to Edfu and Kom Ombo. It is advisable to check in Luxor or Aswan what the present requirements are in order to visit the sites. A new bridge is being constructed to ease access to Gebel Silsila. The main road from Luxor to Aswan runs along the east bank of the river, and the major sites on the west bank are easily accessible using it. There is a road on the west bank, going as far as Edfu, but this is only needed if a visit to Armant is intended.

ARMANT

A rmant, 10 kilometres south of Qurna (Luxor, west bank), 43 kilometres north of Esna, has always been an important town, and in recent times was a major centre for sugar production. Armant (Egyptian: Iunu) was the chief town of the fourth nome of Upper Egypt, until eclipsed by Thebes in the 11th Dynasty. The chief god was the solar and war god, Monthu, whose name is preserved in the Greek city name, Hermonthis, and from that into the modern Armant. In the Late Period, Monthu had a sacred bull, Buchis, which during its life travelled between his four temples in the Theban nome. After death, like the Apis bull at Memphis, Buchis was mummified and buried in a special necropolis, the Bucheum. The site was excavated by the Egypt Exploration Society, which found burials from the 30th Dynasty continuing through the Ptolemaic period. The Bucheum lies to the north of the town, but is not presently accessible. The ruins of the main temple stand in the centre of the modern town, but are not well preserved and not of general interest. They date from the reign of Thutmose III and Ramesses II. There are scenes of Nubian tribute on the pylon (which stands only a few metres high), with drummers and a rhinoceros. In the remains of the inner parts of the temple reused blocks from earlier shrines can be identified.

On the east bank, the first site south of Luxor is the pretty Temple of Tod (the road to Tod is at Armant station 21 kilometres south of Luxor). The ancient site was called Djerty, Tuphium in Greek, and dedicated to Monthu. Excavated and restored by the French Institute, the temple stands in an enclosed area in the village but is not always open. There is a quay with an avenue of sphinxes and a way station of the reign of Thutmose III. The main structure of the temple is largely Ptolemaic and Roman, built in front of a temple of Middle Kingdom date. A chest with the name of Amenemhat II was found buried beneath the floor of the Middle Kingdom temple, containing a horde of silver vessels of western Asiatic origin (Luxor Museum). Superb blocks of relief sculpture from a monument of S'ankh-ka-re Menthuhotep (Cairo) were amongst many parts of early buildings found in the excavations: some are displayed at the site.

At Moalla, the tombs of Ankhtify and Sobekhotep are significant monuments of the First Intermediate Period. They have some good painting in the style typical of the period and important historical texts, but are perhaps of interest only to the specialist.

ESNA

Esna is first encountered in Egyptian records of the 18th Dynasty, although is doubtless of much greater antiquity. The Egyptian name, Ta-Sna, is preserved in the modern, but the Greek name, Latopolis, refers to the reverence of the Nile perch (*Lates niloticus*) here. The barrage, built in 1906, has a lock through which all river traffic must pass. Esna was an important terminus for the caravan routes to Sudan, and it was from here that Johann Ludwig (aka John Lewis) Burckhardt, the famous Swiss traveller and Orientalist, who rediscovered Abu Simbel after centuries of obscurity, began his travels through Nubia in the early 19th century. In the centre of the town is a mosque with a Fatimid brick minaret, built in AD 1081. The base is square, with a tapering cylindrical second tier and an octagonal drum.

Of the **Temple of Khnum** only the pronaos (hypostyle hall) survives, the remainder is destroyed or buried beneath the modern city. Esna is generally a rather underrated temple, yet it has many interesting features peculiar to itself. Much of the relief decoration is elegant. The pronaos was decorated under many Roman emperors whose figures and complex cartouches may be found here: Claudius, Titus and Vespasian on the façade; Titus, Domitian and Trajan smite their enemies on the exterior side walls. Most notable is the scene of Septimius Severus, his wife Julia Domna and their sons Caracalla and Geta, the last figure erased after Caracalla had him murdered in AD 211. The latest emperor referred to is Decius, killed in AD 251. The 24 columns of the pronaos are particularly handsome, with splendid capitals:

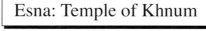

Esna: Temple of Khnum

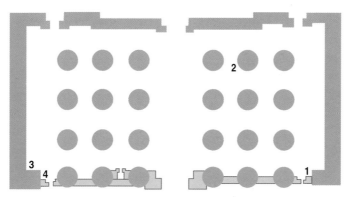

Legend
1   Hymn to Khnum written entirely in crocodile hieroglyphs.
2   Emperor presenting a laurel wreath.
3   Septimius Severus, Julia Domna, Caracalla and (erased) Geta.
4   Hymn to Khnum written entirely in ram hieroglyphs.

© Airphoto International Ltd 2004

note the large insects carved on top of the middle column, central aisle—is it a locust or a scarab? (or a frog?) Most unusual are the two hymns to the temple's presiding deity, Khnum, one carved completely in hieroglyphs of rams, the other in crocodiles. These are to be found on the narrow walls of the entrance façade, above the level of the screen walls. This way of writing was typical of the esoteric priesthood of the late Ptolemaic and Roman periods. The scenes on the columns merit attention. One shows the emperor dancing; another shows him offering a laurel wreath. The rear wall of the pronaos belongs to the inner part of the temple and was decorated by Ptolemy VI.

Between Esna and Edfu on the west bank lies the site of Kom el-Ahmar, the ancient **Nekhen** (Hierakonpolis). One of the most important Pre-Dynastic sites, Nekhen was the capital of the Upper Egyptian kingdom before the unification of the Two Lands by Menes. The main cult here was that of a form of Horus, known as Nekheny, 'He of Nekhen'. Many important artefacts were excavated here in 1896–1898, including the Narmer Palette (Cairo, Egyptian Museum); the superb gold falcon head from a cult image of the god (Cairo); and the large copper statue of Pepi I

(Cairo). New excavations at the site were opened by Michael Hoffmann in 1980, and have continued after his death (1990) under Barbara Adams (d.2002) and Renée Friedman. Their work has considerably advanced knowledge of the Pre-Dynastic town, and also the history of much later phases, notably the 20th Dynasty.

On the opposite side of the river to Nekhen lies its twin city, the modern site of el-Kab. This ancient city, called **Nekheb**, was dedicated to its eponymous vulture goddess, Nekhbet, one of the king's patrons. Spectacular city walls of mud-brick enclose the ancient town site. The whole enclosure is 566 metres by 548 metres, and the walls are over 11 metres thick. The southwest corner has been lost into the river. Although there have been excavations here, there is relatively little to see within the walls. The quay for the temple can still be seen a little further along the bank. No doubt it was by this that the image of the goddess Hathor entered the city to rest overnight on her journey from Dendera to Edfu for the 'Feast of the Beautiful Meeting' (see Edfu, below). The ruins of the adjacent temples of Nekhbet and Thoth stand near the centre of the town. These were rebuilt many times. The surviving temples are predominantly the work of Amenhotep II and Ramesses II, but examination of exposed foundations shows the names of earlier rulers whose monuments have been recycled. There are Late Period additions, and here the cartouche of the 29th-dynasty pharaoh Hakor is prominent: one of relatively few monuments on which it can be found. There are remains of a double circular wall, which may be part of the Early Dynastic town enclosure. The foundations of a number of late dwellings (Ptolemaic–Roman) can be found in the southwest corner of the site.

There are some good, if small, tombs of early 18th-dynasty date in the cliffs. This involves a pleasant walk, crossing the railway tracks and road. The tombs have some important historical texts.

Ahmose Pennekhbet, Overseer of the Seal and Royal Herald, carries an important autobiographical text recording his military career under the early 18th-dynasty pharaohs. Ahmose played a role in the expulsion of the Hyksos in the reign of his like-named sovereign. He accompanied later pharaohs on their campaigns in Nubia and Asia, ending his career in the reign of Hatshepsut.

The **tomb of Paheri**, Mayor of Nekheb, has some good relief sculpture. Paheri was the grandson of Ahmose son of Ebana, whose tomb is further along the cliff.

Ahmose son of Ebana was a soldier in the wars of the pharaoh Ahmose, and was rewarded with land, slaves and gold by the pharaoh. This may have laid the family fortune, as his grandson, Paheri, rose to become mayor of the city and honoured his grandfather with this tomb.

El-Kab: Tomb of Paheri

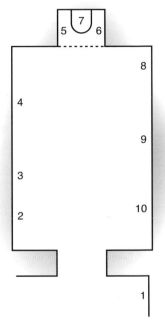

Paheri, Mayor of Nekheb
(Early-to-mid-18th Dynasty)

The tomb has good decoration in painted relief.

1 Paheri and a hymn to Nekhbet.

2 Agricultural scenes, with ploughing, sowing grain, reaping and threshing. One of Paheri's offices was Scribe of the Corn Accounts for the area from Armant-Gebelein to Nekheb. Two boats are full of grain, and two others have Paheri's chariots and horses. Paheri watches the counting of gold.

3 Upper register: Paheri with the child prince Wadjmose, son of Thutmose I, on his knee. Below: Paheri and his wife, with a scene of the vintage, and scenes of fishing and fowling.

4 The funeral of Paheri: the sarcophagus is towed in the top register. Below is an obscure rite, the dragging of the *tekenu*; this is shown as a wrapped bundle on a sledge, with a human head projecting. Earlier Egyptologists understood this as a human sacrifice, but it may represent the parts of the body that were removed during mummification but not placed in the canopic jars, being buried separately. In the bottom register Paheri worships Osiris.

5 Paheri's son makes offerings to his parents. Long text in praise of Paheri.

6 Statue of Paheri with his wife and mother.

7 Paheri makes offerings to two princes and to his parents.

8 Paheri's son and other relatives with list of offerings.

9 Banqueting scene with large figures of Paheri's grandfather, Ahmose son of Ebana, and his wife; Paheri's father and mother; Paheri, with a monkey beneath his chair, and his wife. Musicians in the bottom register.

10 Paheri and his family with offerings and prayers.

Source: Robert Morkot

El-Kab: Tomb of Ahmose son of Ebana

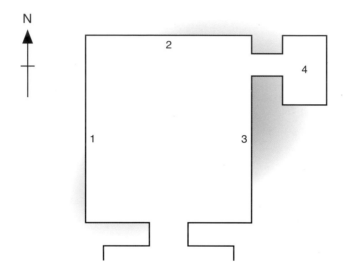

(Early 18th Dynasty)

The tomb was constructed by Ahmose's grandson, Paheri.

1 The descendants of Ahmose: Ahmose seems to have founded the family fortunes in the wars against the Hyksos.
2 Paheri and family members make offerings to his grandfather Ahmose and his wife, and to Ahmose's father Baba and his mother Ebana.
3 Paheri's dedication text, and the autobiographical inscription of Ahmose, narrating his role in the wars against the Hyksos.
4 Burial chamber.

Setau, High Priest of Nekhbet, served in the 20th Dynasty. The tomb has scenes relating to the jubilee festival of Ramesses III. Setau, who may have been a descendant of the like-named Viceroy of Nubia in the reign of Ramesses II, made good marriage connections for his family with the High Priest of Horus at Nekhen and the High Priest of Amun at Thebes.

For those with the time, there are further monuments in the wadi to the south of the tombs. The wadi clearly played an important religious role in relation to the town. At its entrance are two temples, the rock-cut Ptolemaic temple is probably on the site of an earlier shrine. Close by is the stone-built chapel known as **el-Hammam** ('the Bath'). This was built by Setau, Viceroy of Nubia in the reign of Ramesses II. Setau appears to have had a family connection with el-Kab, and his wife, Mutnofret, was a Chantress of Nekhbet. Continuing into the wadi, the centre of it is dominated by the outcrop known as the Vulture Rock because of its shape. This is covered with rock drawings and inscriptions dating from the Pre-Dynastic period onwards. A further 4 kilometres into the wadi brings the visitor to another box-like stone shrine. It is unimposing on the outside, which is plain except for the added scene of the crown prince Khaemwaset before his father, Ramesses II, and texts announcing the jubilee festivals of that pharaoh, and a number of rock drawings. Inside, the chapel is a surprise, with splendid reliefs of Thutmose IV and Amenhotep III, brightly coloured.

EDFU

E dfu is an almost perfectly preserved temple, but it has to be said that when this temple is full of tourist groups it lacks atmosphere. If it is visited when empty (which is almost impossible), particularly very late in the afternoon, it can leave a wonderful impression. Amongst the acres of reliefs are some important, if aesthetically rather dull, mythological cycles. There are also some very fine examples of Ptolemaic relief sculpture.

The building history of this temple is well documented. Founded by Ptolemy III on 23 August 237 BC, its interior structure was completed, excepting the pronaos (first hypostyle), the court and pylons, on 17 August 212 BC. The relief decoration of the walls was finished by 206 BC when the great door of the sanctuary was set in place. A major revolt broke out in Upper Egypt at the death of Ptolemy IV, during which time the temple was occupied by rebel troops. Two Theban-backed rebel pharaohs, Haronnophris (205–199 BC) and his successor Chaonnophris (197–186 BC), controlled the region for 20 years, until the Ptolemaic forces suppressed the rebellion in 186 BC. Only then could the furnishing of the temple be completed, and the dedication took place on 10 September 142 BC in the presence

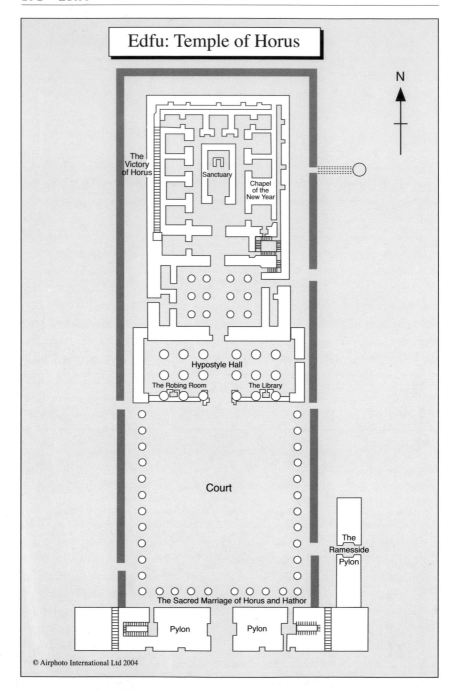

Edfu: Temple of Horus

N

The Victory of Horus

Sanctuary

Chapel of the New Year

Hypostyle Hall

The Robing Room

The Library

Court

The Ramesside Pylon

The Sacred Marriage of Horus and Hathor

Pylon

Pylon

© Airphoto International Ltd 2004

of Ptolemy VIII Euergetes II. The pronaos was begun in 140 BC, finished in 124 BC, and decorated between 122 and 116 BC. The enclosure wall, the forecourt and pylons were begun the same year, and dedicated on 7 February 70 BC. The great cedar doors of the pylon were set in place on 5 December 57 BC, in the reign of Ptolemy XII Auletes.

The modern access brings the visitor to the rear of the temple. To the west of the temple are the extensive ruins of the city mounds, which have been partly excavated. The rear of the enclosure wall is dominated by the large figures of Ptolemy X Alexander I and his wife Berenike III (carved and decorated 101–88 BC) offering to Horus, Hathor and Hor-sema-tawy (Harsomtus). The mass of the temple can be seen rising up inside the enclosure, and, as at Dendera, the pronaos is considerably higher than the sanctuary and its surrounding chapels. Remains of the Ramesside pylon can be found by walking around to the east side of the temple; note the orientation was altered by 90 degrees. Even after the Ptolemaic rebuilding of the temple, the processional way from the river passed through the Ramesside pylon into the court through the side gate. This route was lined with statues of falcons.

The temple is very similar in plan to Dendera, but here the pylon and forecourt have been completed. The *mammisi*, built in the reign of Ptolemy VIII Euergetes II, stands outside the temple, and is very similar in architecture and decoration to the Roman *mammisi* at Dendera, which was modelled on it, and is better preserved. The *mammisi* was used during the 'Feast of the Beautiful Meeting' when Hathor came here to celebrate her marriage with Horus.

Many blocks from earlier structures, excavated in the first courtyard during restoration work in the 1980s, are stored in the area outside the main temple. These include a large group of finely carved blocks with reliefs depicting a Kushite pharaoh, which were recarved in the 26th Dynasty, probably in the reign of Psamtik II. In style these blocks are very similar to monuments of the reigns of Shabaqo and Shebitqo at Karnak and Medinet Habu. There are also blocks with the names of the obscure 17th-dynasty Theban ruler, Sekhem-re Semen-tawy Djehuty.

The pylon is one of the best preserved on a large scale, and is justly famous. The two massive towers carry conventional scenes of Ptolemy XII Auletes smiting Egypt's enemies before the temple's patron deity, Horus. Smaller figures of Hathor are tucked rather awkwardly in the narrow space between the niches for the flagstaffs and the central gateway. On the upper part each tower carries two scenes of the pharaoh before seated deities. The central gateway originally had massive doors of cedar

(preceding page) *At Edfu, a large panel on the screen between the columns of the main hall depicts Ptolemy Soter II in characteristic Egyptian style with an elaborate crown, in idealized form.*

plated with copper, no doubt figured with divine images in coloured metals and perhaps inlaid glass.

The long court splendidly frames the imposing façade of the pronaos. Enclosed by the pylon and the colonnades, this sense of isolation is lost in damaged and unfinished temples such as Esna and Dendera. The colonnades have elaborate floral capitals and the walls are covered in good raised relief. The most important group of scenes is found on the back of the pylons, low down. These show the voyage of the goddess Hathor from Dendera for the 'Feast of the Beautiful Meeting'. The barge of the goddess, carrying her sacred barque, is met and then towed by that of her husband. Breaking her journey from Dendera, Hathor resided at Karnak, with the goddess Mut, and at el-Kab with Nekhbet.

The columns of the pronaos mix date palm and composite floral capitals. The screen walls of the façade carry some well-executed reliefs, depicting Ptolemy VIII Euergetes II. Although he was named Physkon ('Fatty') by the Alexandrians, his waistline here is very trim. The columns carry one register of scenes, with bands of protective *ankh* and *was*-sceptres, serpents, vultures and falcon-headed sphinxes below, and similar groups above. The scenes along the central axis refer to the principal deities, Horus and Hathor and their sanctuaries at Edfu, Dendera and Mesen (in the Delta). The other scenes show the gods of the main sanctuaries of Egypt. There are two small chambers on the interior of the screen walls. One was the robing room in which the king was purified before he could perform the rites. The other chamber contained the temple library. The architraves and ceiling have protective figures of Hathor and scenes of the hours of day and night.

The temple proper begins with the façade at the back of the pronaos. The central door opens onto a hypostyle hall supported by 12 columns with composite floral capitals. Two important inscriptions at the entrance list all of the forms of Horus, and all of the gods of this temple and their shrines. The walls of the hall are decorated with scenes in elegant bas-relief showing processions of the sacred barques.

Surrounding the hypostyle are four chambers. The first on the west is the Chamber of the Nile, used for bringing in the water used in purification. A door here gives access to the ambulatory around the temple, although the well is actually closer to the door in the east wall. The second chamber is the laboratory, used for the preparation of perfumes and unguents: there are recipes carved on the wall. On the east side one doorway leads to the external door for offerings and to the temple treasury.

The Hall of Offerings gives access to the stairways to the roof and to the vestibule, immediately in front of the sanctuary. Called in Egyptian the Chapel of the Ennead, this

vestibule was where the statues and sacred barques of the gods who resided in the temple gathered on festival days. The sanctuary is essentially a massive freestanding stone version of the ancient 'tent shrine' at the heart of the temple. The form is typical, with framing torus moulding and cavetto cornice. The doorway, also framed by a torus and with cavetto cornice with winged sun disc, carries scenes of the daily offering rites. The façade of the sanctuary flanking the doorway has columns of text naming the forms of Horus, the gods of the temple, the emblems of Horus and elements of his body. The reliefs within the sanctuary have suffered mutilation. They depicted scenes of the daily liturgy and the offerings of Ptolemy IV Philopator to his ancestors, Ptolemy II and Arsinoe. The focus of the chamber is the magnificent granite naos (shrine) of Nakhthorheb (Nectanebo II). The naos has a pyramidal roof, and was originally sealed with two cedar-wood doors plated with copper and gold, as the texts tell us. The polish on the stone resembles metal. Within it the god's image resided. As can been imagined, this statue was not huge, but probably made of precious metals; perhaps, like a surviving cult image of Horus, of silver overlaid with gold and inlaid with lapis lazuli. The use of the 30th Dynasty naos linked the new Ptolemaic temple with its predecessors on the site.

The layout of the inner part of the temple is essentially the same as that at Dendera, but with one chapel less on the east and west. Unlike those at Dendera, the crypts here were never decorated. The chapels surrounding the sanctuary are dedicated to forms of Horus and other associated gods. Moving from the sanctuary west–north–east the first chapel is that of Min, in his forms as the fertility god of Koptos and Thebes (Min-Amun) and as the royal god Min-Horus. In the second chapel Horus dominates the decoration, but this room was primarily used for vestments. The Chapel of the Ennead of the temple emphasized the solar aspect of Horus. The next is dedicated to Osiris; with the double chapel at the corner of the temple containing the Tomb of Osiris and the Chamber of the West. In the chapel on the main axis of the temple, called the Chamber of the Victor, there is a close association of Horus with Mesen, his sanctuary in the Delta. This room now contains a replica of the sacred barque. The double chapel at the temple's northeast corner is dedicated to Khonsu and Hathor. Next comes the Chapel of the Throne of Ra, with scenes relating to the king's coronation. In the Chapel of the Spread Wings, the lioness-headed goddess, Menhyt, a form of the burning solar Eye of Ra, was revered. A doorway leads to the Chapel of the New Year with its elevated *wabet* and open court. The ceiling carries an outstretched figure of the goddess Nut with the solar barque in the 12 hours of day and 12 hours of night. The decoration is similar to that at Dendera, but lacks the unusual details specific to that shrine.

Winnowing wheat near Edfu

Returning to the hypostyle hall, access to the ambulatory around the inner part of the temple is gained from either doorway. The ambulatory has some important long texts and reliefs narrating the mythic cycles important at Edfu. These include the 'Origin of the Temple' and the mystery play of Horus (the 'Festival of Victory'). Many of the scenes in the ambulatory have blank cartouches as they were carved at the time of the conflict between Ptolemy IX Soter II and Ptolemy X Alexander I (88 BC). Immediately to the south (right) of the door from the hypostyle and the treasury is a good scene of the coronation of pharaoh by Nekhbet and Wadjet. On the east wall is the access to the temple's supply of water for offerings and purification. Between this and the northeast corner is the text describing the mythical origin of the temple. It tells how an island with a reed emerged from the primeval waters, and how the falcon, flying across the water alighted on it. Spirits emerged from the waters and enclosed the reed ('the perch'), creating the first sanctuary. At the angle of the north wall is a large hieroglyphic text naming the deified Imhotep, the architect of the Step Pyramid in the Third Dynasty. On the west outside wall of the temple and the inner west wall of the ambulatory are the triumph of Horus over the hippopotamus, which was performed as a mystery play. The wall culminates in a scene in which the king and gods close a clap-net on the forces of evil represented as human, bird and fish (there is a similar scene in the pronaos at Esna).

SILSILA

Those travelling by river will pass through the Silsila Gorge, one of the narrowest points on the river. A little to the north of Silsila the limestone, which forms the landscape of much of Egypt, is replaced by sandstone, which continues far into Sudan and creates an entirely different landscape. The river cut easily through the sandstone hills at Silsila, creating the gorge. This became a cult centre of the Nile flood and also a major quarrying area. There are many New Kingdom chapels here, and there are moves to make the site more easily accessible to visitors.

The most important monument is the large speos of Horemheb, but many other smaller chapels can be seen from the river on the west bank. The chapel of Horemheb was probably begun in the reign of Tutankhamun, but was left unfinished. It carries a number of later inscriptions from the 19th and 20th dynasties.

On the east bank are the main workings where some ram-headed sphinxes still remain. The sandstone used to build Amenhotep III's Luxor temple and Akhenaten's Karnak temples was quarried here.

The basin of Kom Ombo is broad and fertile, the site of some of the earliest known settlements. Later it was an important terminus for the caravan route to Sudan, achieving greatest prominence in the Ptolemaic Period when, it is believed, African elephants were trained here for the Ptolemaic army.

KOM OMBO

Kom Ombo has a commanding situation, overlooking the river. The river's eastward movement has destroyed the front parts of the precinct and much of the *mammisi*. The temple is surrounded by the unexcavated mounds of the town. It is an attractive ruin, especially in the late afternoon, with very handsome columns in the pronaos and a very fine style of relief throughout much of the temple.

Kom Ombo is significant as two temples combined in one: all its features are doubled; there are two processional ways and sanctuaries. Two gods, Harwer (Haroeris, Horus-the-Elder) and Sobek, with their respective consorts and children, were worshipped next to each other, although they have no connection. In this respect this temple is different from Abydos where the seven shrines were all part of one temple.

In the forecourt much of the relief is covered in a very thin layer of plaster that carried the paint. Also on the columns, one of the figures of the hawk god, Harwer, originally had an inlaid eye. The columns carry the name of the emperor Tiberius (AD 14–37), in a variety of hieroglyphic spellings. At the centre of the court is a large altar base. The façade of the pronaos is particularly handsome with its double entrance crowned by winged sun discs. The screen walls have some splendid images of the patron deities.

Passing into the temple proper, the hypostyle hall is decorated in bas-relief with scenes of Ptolemy VIII Euergetes II accompanied by his sister (and ex-wife) Kleopatra II and her daughter, his wife, Kleopatra III. This image of apparent harmony was presumably carved before the dynastic feud of 132–124 BC that brought civil war to Upper Egypt. Scenes further in the temple also depict Kleopatra II, but with her first husband, her and Euergetes' brother, Ptolemy VI Philometor. The scale of this part of the temple is much more modest than the comparable halls of Edfu or Dendera. The Hall of Offerings and the two sanctuaries are badly ruined. Beneath the sanctuary rooms is a hidden chamber for the pronouncement of oracles.

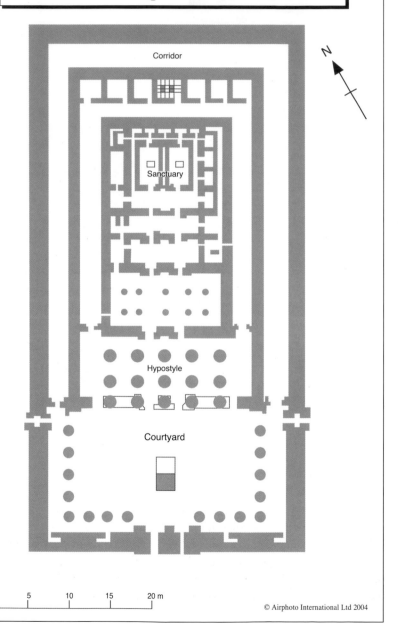

Kom Ombo: Temple of Sobek and Horus

Corridor

Sanctuary

Hypostyle

Courtyard

© Airphoto International Ltd 2004

0   5   10   15   20 m

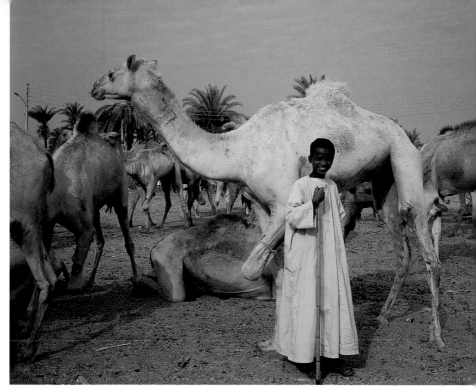

Daraw, near Kom Ombo, was the starting point for one of the long roads through the Eastern Desert to Sudan, and today is the site of a major camel market, with most of the animals coming from Sudan.

Unusually there are two ambulatories running around the temple. The inner ambulatory is entered from doors in the pronaos, and was presumably originally roofed in. The outer ambulatory, as at Edfu, is entered from the courtyard and was open. Along the rear wall of the inner ambulatory is a row of rooms. The central one has a staircase leading to the roof, and in the others are reliefs in varied states of completion: informative as to the technique of carving. The reliefs in the outer ambulatory are worth examining. The most unusual is the group of implements on a table; these are often said to be surgeons' instruments. The reliefs in the middle of the outer wall are of the Antonine emperors, with some crudely added figures at the far end. They are the emperor Macrinus and his small son, Diadumenianus, who reigned briefly after the murder of Caracalla and before the victory of Elagabalus (AD 218). These are amongst the latest depictions of Roman emperors in Pharaonic costume. In the centre of the back wall of the temple is the place where ordinary people could make their prayers and petitions to the gods inside the temple. It takes the form of a niche that originally contained a statue, and is flanked by 'hearing ears' and large images of the gods Sobek and Harwer. There are also some unusual depictions of the four winds, which take the forms of a winged bull, a falcon, a bull and a many-headed snake. There is a number of graffiti of mummified crocodiles on wheeled trolleys.

In the outer parts of the precinct are a deep circular well with staircase and the remains of the *mammisi*. Although little is left of this structure, there is a large relief showing Ptolemy VIII Euergetes II on a papyrus skiff pulling himself through a marsh towards Amun-Ra-Kamutef, with flocks of birds taking wing at the king's approach. The small chapel of Hathor near the entrance into the enclosure is filled with mummified crocodiles. There are also some Roman period statues here.

ASWAN

A swan is still one of the most attractive towns in Egypt, despite enormous expansion in the past decade. Spreading along the river with the islands and surrounding desert, it has been a major resort for over a hundred years. It is a pleasant town in which to relax but it also has many monuments within easy reach. The large market is a good place to buy gifts, notably Nubian products and spices.

Because of the Cataract, this region always marked the natural frontier between Egypt and Nubia, and later it became the gathering place for the army and fleets sent to bring Nubia under Egyptian control. The Cataract, which lay to the south of town, is now largely lost beneath the reservoir between the Old Dam and the High Dam, although some impression may be gained by sailing round the islands near Sehel.

The earliest town site was on the island of Elephantine, but by the Roman Period the mainland town had expanded. Less excavation has been done beneath the modern town, so the history of Aswan itself is less well known than that of Elephantine.

Elephantine is the largest island in the river, and also the northernmost of the Cataract. The name is the Greek version of the ancient Egyptian name, Abu, meaning both an 'elephant' and 'ivory'. It is uncertain why this name was given to the island: the rocks in the river do resemble bathing elephants, but it is more likely to have been because this was an important ivory trading centre. Excavations have been carried out on the island for many years by the German Archaeological Institute and have revealed much of the site's history, including the remains of the early settlement within a circular wall.

The **Temple of Khnum** dominates the ruin-field. The temple itself is badly ruined, the visible remains dating from the Ramesside and Graeco-Roman periods. In the paved floor of the large outer court are the column bases of the earlier Ramesside temple. The great gateway carries the cartouches of Alexander, not 'the Great' but his infant son, Alexander IV of Macedon, whose brief rule was recognized by the satrap Ptolemy, later Ptolemy I Soter. Many blocks of earlier structures may be noted, reused in the foundations or as building material. The area with the sarcophagi of the sacred rams of Khnum is also visible (one of the mummified animals is displayed in the museum). On the main axis is the Roman quay of the temple, a purely symbolic feature standing high above the river. A number of obelisks and monuments have been re-erected on the parapet, and there are inscriptions on the rocks, both at this level and below at water level.

Recently, the monuments excavated and consolidated by the German Institute behind the Khnum temple have become accessible. The New Kingdom **Temple of Satet**, built by Hatshepsut, is surrounded by a colonnade of square piers. It stands on the site of an ancient shrine which lies beneath it. The original chapel was a cleft in the rocks. This was developed into a simple early temple in the Old Kingdom, and enlarged into a more formal shrine in the late Old Kingdom and Middle Kingdom. The whole of this early temple was filled in, and a new floor level created for the 18th Dynasty structure. A direct spiritual connection between the two sanctuaries was maintained by sinking a shaft from the new one to the old one. The Middle Kingdom chapel dedicated to the local official Heqaib is roofed-over. Many fine statues in the museum originated here.

The **Nilometer** is a long steep stairway running down to the water's edge. This is of Roman date, although there were earlier ones here, as this was the most important place to measure the height of the flood. Marble plaques date from the late 19th century AD, when the Nilometer was reused.

At the southern end of the island, a group of small monuments has been re-erected. All of these come from Kalabsha and were found built into the foundations of the Augustan temple. The most complete is the small chapel, its door jambs carrying the cartouches of the Meroitic king, Arqamani. On the side exterior walls there are some good scenes showing Emperor Augustus, but here the cartouche carries the name Rhomy ('the Roman').

The **Tombs of the Nobles**, cut into the hill of Qubbet el-Hawwa, are worth visiting. They can be dangerous, with many tombs' shafts lying open; torches should

be taken. Snakes are also reputed to be a problem here. The tomb of Sirenput II (tomb 31) is beautifully decorated with carved statues and painted scenes. The background is an attractive blue, with excellent large detailed hieroglyphs. Slightly unusual are the elephant hieroglyphs used in the name of Abu. The tomb of Harkhuf contains an important historical text narrating his expeditions into Nubia, although the tomb lacks architectural or artistic interest.

The **tomb of the Aga Khan** is a fine example of modern Islamic architecture and also a good vantage point from which to survey the whole of the town. The monastery of St Simeon lies at the end of the wadi leading up from the Nile. It is possible to take camels from the landing place to St Simeon, then on to the Tombs of the Nobles. The monastery is a well-preserved example of early Christian architecture, with paintings surviving in parts of the church.

Aswan is from the Greek name Syene, after the Egyptian word *swenet*, meaning 'trade', denoting the town's importance as a market and caravan. Little remains of the ancient town which lies beneath the southern end of the modern city. A Ptolemaic Temple of Isis can be found close to the road to Philae. It is usually shut; the interior decoration was never completed, and it is of minor interest. The roof height is about the same as modern street level, showing the rise in the town over the centuries. Many blocks from Roman temples were built into the Byzantine city walls nearby: the cartouches of Domitian can be noted amongst them. More important are the numerous inscriptions on the rocks along the river and in the park next to the Cataract Hotel.

NUBIA MUSEUM

Aswan boasts a magnificent new museum devoted to the history and archaeology of Nubia. It is in a prominent position at the southern end of the city, close to the Old Cataract Hotel. Many fine objects have been brought from Cairo to a more appropriate setting here. The museum is arranged chronologically and contains some splendid examples of art and archaeology reflecting the history of Nubia.

The display begins with objects of the Nubian cultures contemporary with the Egyptian Pre-Dynastic. One of their most notable products was very fine 'eggshell' pottery with burnished interior and patterns, often in red, imitating basketwork. A number of statues and stelae record the Egyptian activities of the Old and Middle Kingdoms. One of the broken statues of Khafre from the valley temple of the Second Pyramid at Giza is carved in diorite from the quarries near Toshka. There

One of the most famous hotels in Egypt, the Cataract Hotel at Aswan commands superb views over the river, Elephantine Island.

are also some reconstruction models of the Second Cataract fortresses. The most aesthetically impressive monuments are in the later part of the display. In a case of smaller statues, note especially the figure of Iriketakana, a Nubian official in Egypt, shown with pendulous breasts and potbelly. It is a remarkable image, as is the purplish red quartzite statue of Haremakhet, High Priest of Amun and eldest son of King Shabaqo. The modelling of the skull and the prince's facial features are particularly fine.

The central gallery is dominated by a colossal statue of Ramesses II, from the Temple of Gerf Hussein. It is similar to those at Abu Simbel, with well-preserved paint. Its slightly clumsy appearance is due to the grainy soft sandstone from which the temple was carved, which forced solidity on the sculptors. Amongst the most important of the many fine pieces in this section are the black granite head from a colossal statue of Taharqo, the crown originally covered in gold foil. Complete and identical statues of this king and his successors were recovered from the temples of Gebel Barkal (now in Khartoum and the Boston Museum of Fine Arts). A colossal red granite head probably represents Taharqo's immediate predecessor, Shebitqo. The statue of the God's Wife of Amun, Amenirdis I, is a superb example of late 25th-dynasty sculpture. In the highly polished black granite favoured at the time, it shows the Kushite princess with typically slender ideal Egyptian proportions, although some relief depictions of her conform to the totally different, and much more ample, Kushite ideal. The black granite kneeling statue of Nehi, Viceroy of Kush, in the reign of Thutmose III was found on Elephantine. At some point the pleats of the kilt have been smoothed away.

The Meroitic period (c.300 BC–AD 400) is represented by statues of *ba*-birds and other objects from tombs in the cemeteries throughout Lower Nubia. During the Second Archaeological Survey of Nubia in the 1930s, two large cemeteries of enormous tumuli were excavated by Bryan Emery and Laurence Kirwan at Ballana and Qustul, south of Abu Simbel. These burials represent the last of the pre-Christian kingdoms of Nubia, the so-called 'X-Group' or Ballana culture. Some of the splendid objects from these rich burials are displayed here, including some of the silver crowns set with carnelians that were found on the skulls of the dead kings and queens. Two horse models are decorated with silver horse trappings from the burials.

The last of the lower galleries are concerned with the Christian and Islamic periods, and the UNESCO salvage operations and the building of the High Dam.

(preceding pages) *Kom Ombo, the Birth House*

Particularly striking are the frescoes from the church at Abdalla Nirqe (10th century AD). Christianity spread throughout Nubia, and three large Christian kingdoms succeeded Meroe. Churches and cathedrals were built at many sites, some using material from earlier temples, others adapting the temples structures themselves. Many of these buildings were decorated with elaborate frescoes, some showing continuity from the preceding cultural periods. The finest group of frescoes was salvaged from the cathedral at Faras, just beyond the Egyptian border, in Sudan (Khartoum and Warsaw). The last section of the display is devoted to the distinctive culture and customs of the Nubian people.

The garden surrounding the museum has a number of monuments including historical inscriptions of the Nubian kings from Gebel Barkal (Sudan). The massive black granite stele of Piye, covered on both faces and the edges with an inscription, records the conquest of Egypt by the Kushites around 730 BC. The other stelae record events in the reigns of Tanwetamani (664–656 BC) and Harsiyotef (c.380 BC).

Quarries and Islands

Aswan was always a major centre of quarrying, principally for granite. Signs of this work can be seen in many places: on islands in the river, some of which have been completely quarried away, and in the two mainland quarries to the south of the town. The most famous remaining example is the **Unfinished Obelisk**. This monolith, about 42 metres long and weighing about 1,197 tons, would have been the largest obelisk ever quarried by the Egyptians. Unfortunately, the stone was flawed and the work had to be abandoned. Now encroached upon by houses and shops, this site has lost any atmosphere that there may once have been. Those with time can visit the southern quarries by continuing past the turning for the island of Philae towards Shellal (approximately 4.5 kilometres). Here an unfinished, 6-metre-long Osiride statue can be seen along with sarcophagi and other fragments.

One of the great pleasures of Aswan is sailing around the Cataract's remaining rocks and islands. One island usually visited is Plantation Island (formerly Kitchener Island), which lies near Elephantine. This large island was presented to Lord Kitchener after the Sudan campaign, and has been turned into a botanical garden with many tropical trees and shrubs. Further south is **Sehel Island**, which once had a sanctuary of Anuket; its main interest today lies in the mountain of granite boulders at the southern end. These are covered with inscriptions, over 250 in number. Graffito is an inappropriate term for a rock-inscription of this type,

Sailing in feluccas at sunset is one of the pleasures of the river at Aswan.

some of which have figures that are life-size. Many of them are carved, with great skill, in almost inaccessible positions on vertical rocks. Traces of paint may also be noted on some of them. These inscriptions record local priests and their families, and the viceroys of Nubia and their subordinates. Climbing to the top of the hill gives a splendid view of the remains of the Cataract and of the Old Aswan Dam. The 'Famine Stele' is located on this high point. The stele claims to be a decree of Djoser of the Third Dynasty, but was actually carved by the Ptolemaic priests of Khnum who were trying to establish their prior claim to land over the priests of Isis of Philae. Around the south and east sides of Sehel, the Middle Kingdom pharaohs cleared a channel through the Cataract.

Many of the rapids and islands of the Cataract were lost beneath the Old Dam and the reservoir between the Old and High dams. Only the highest points of Bigga, el-Heisa and Awad remain. These three large islands marked the southern end of the Cataract, and were, in the last century, noted for their beauty. Of all the islands, Philae, lying low and thickly covered with palms, was considered the 'Pearl of the Nile'.

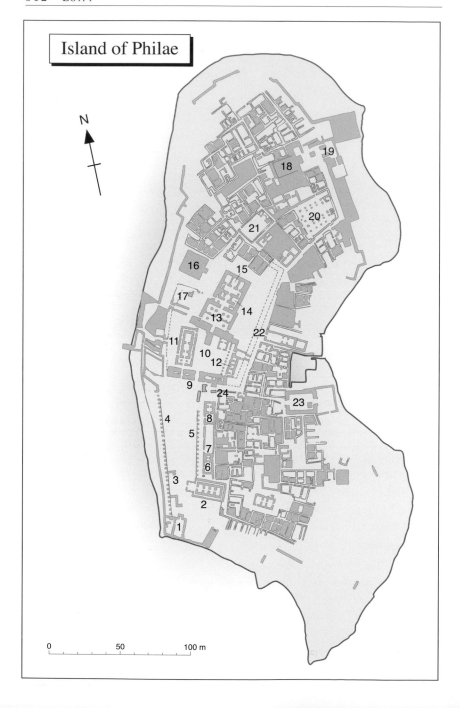

Island of Philae

N

0   50   100 m

Island of Philae: Precinct of Isis

The plan of Philae follows an early 20th-century survey that shows the remains of the Late Antique (Coptic) town that surrounded the temples. The mud-brick walls were lost with the creation of the reservoir, and the remains therefore cannot be seen at the temples' new location on Agilkia Island, opened in 1980.

1 Kiosk of Nakhtnebef (Nectanebo I).
2 Temple of Arensnuphis.
3 Nilometer.
4 Roman colonnade with windows towards (old site of) Bigga and reliefs of the Julio-Claudian emperors; elaborate floral capitals, some combining Egyptian and classical elements (eg acanthus leaves and Ionic volutes).
5 Roman colonnade with unfinished capitals.
6 Chapel of Mandulis.
7 Chapels (most destroyed).
8 Temple of Imhotep with dedicatory inscription in Greek over door.
9 Site of the original enclosure wall with the Gate of Nakhtnebef flanked by the later towers of the Pylon of Ptolemy XII Auletes. The west tower incorporates the earlier gate (Ptolemy VI) leading to the *mammisi*.
10 Court with colonnade of Ptolemy VIII Euergetes II to east. The remains of the hill of granite boulders on which the original small temple stood is visible, with the stele carrying the 'Second Decree of Philae' (Ptolemy VI). The west side of the court is formed by the external colonnade of the *mammisi* added by Euergetes II to harmonize the court.
11 The *mammisi* (birth house) of Ptolemy VI and Ptolemy VIII. On the west external wall inscriptions recording early travellers and the return of the British Sudan Expedition.
12 The Meroitic Chamber, with incised figures and texts of Meroitic envoys.
13 Main temple. Pylon of Euergetes II, decoration completed by Auletes; combined court and pillared hall of Temple of Isis on the site of the small 26th Dynasty temple; later converted into a church.
14 Reliefs of Ptolemy II.
15 Sanctuary of Isis with fine relief decoration.
16 Temple of Harendotes (Horus the Avenger).
17 Gate of Hadrian.
18 Temple of Augustus.
19 Quay and Gateway of Diocletian.
20 Large Church (destroyed).
21 Small Church (destroyed).
22 Temple of Hathor as goddess of music and dancing (Ptolemy VI and Ptolemy Euergetes II).
23 Kiosk of Trajan.
24 Gate of Ptolemy II Philadelphos.

Source: Robert Morkot

PHILAE

T he temples were removed from their original island and re-erected here on Agilkia: the cofferdam put around the temples before their removal is still visible in the reservoir. The dismantling of the temples allowed their foundations and the building history to be reconstructed. Blocks with the names of Ramesses II and kings of the 26th Dynasty were found in the foundations of the temple when it was dismantled. The earliest elements still standing as part of the present temple are the Gate and Kiosk of Nakhtnebef (Nectanebo I). The kiosk, now at the end of the colonnade court, was dismantled and moved, probably twice in ancient times. (This can be seen from the orientation of the figures: the crowns are on the wrong sides.)

The main part of the temple was constructed by Ptolemy II and enlarged by his successors. Photographs taken at the end of the 19th century show the temples surrounded by the brick buildings of the late Roman and Byzantine town. Philae had become a major pilgrimage centre in the Roman Period, and there were doubtless many hostels catering for the pilgrims.

The main **Temple of Isis** is approached through a long courtyard flanked by colonnades. These are Roman and interesting for the variety of vegetal capitals, some combining elements derived from the Ionic and Corinthian orders. Many are unfinished, but they are valuable examples of how Egyptian artisans worked. The pylon, built by Ptolemy XII Auletes, incorporates the original Gate of Nakhtnebef (Nectanebo I) and forms an interesting comparison in scale and decoration with that decorated and dedicated by Auletes at Edfu. Two Roman granite lions flank the steps. There is also the stump of an obelisk. A second obelisk was removed from here in 1819 and now stands in the park of an English country house, Kingston Lacy in Dorset.

Passing through the pylon, the temple proper is seen, elevated on a higher rocky hill. The left side of the court is filled with the *mammisi* of Ptolemy VIII Euergetes II, the right side with a series of chapels behind the colonnade. To the right is a massive boulder, its face smoothed and covered by a long hieroglyphic decree. Steps lead up to the gateway and pylon. The temple is quite small, the court and hypostyle being one room, with open sky at the front and, originally, low screen walls separating off the back part. Many Christian additions can be seen from when it was converted into a church. There is some good low-relief decoration in the small open court; from the

Colossal deeply cut figures of the goddess Isis and her son Horus dominate the façade of the goddesss temple at Philae.

reign of Ptolemy II, it retains affinities with the art of the 30th Dynasty. The decoration of the sanctuary rooms is also elegant, with large figures of deities, including the deified Queen Arsinoe.

Complexes of chapels surround the temple, and the enclosure wall is clearly visible. From the hypostyle hall a door leads to the **Gate of Hadrian**, which faced the Island of Bigga. It was from this point that the statue of the goddess would cross over for the rituals of Osiris. There are two unusual reliefs on the long walls: to the left, the body of Osiris is conveyed across the river on the back of a crocodile; on the right, Isis, cow-headed, waters a grove from which the soul of Osiris (a human-headed bird) emerges, and behind is the rocky mass of Bigga, with the figure of the Nile god Hapi beneath it, encircled by a snake, the waters of the river issuing from two vases.

At the end of the island are the scanty remains of the Temple of Augustus and the **Quay and Gate of Diocletian**. A paved street runs around the other side of the temple, with the small **Temple of Hathor**. The interior is ruined, but the columns of the court have a charming series of figures of baboons and of the dwarf god, Bes, playing musical instruments. Isolated on this side of the island is the **Kiosk of Trajan**, known to early European travellers as 'Pharaoh's Bed'. The kiosk as an architectural form was originally a light and delicate structure in wood. It here achieves its most monumental: unfinished and only partly decorated, there is little to distract from its massiveness.

NUBIA

N ubia is the land between the First and Fourth cataracts of the Nile, although the name is often used today to include the region as far south as Khartoum. Ancient Nubia, Kush, was brought under direct Egyptian control at several periods during the Old Kingdom, the Middle Kingdom and the New Kingdom. It also had periods of independence under powerful indigenous rulers. During one of these periods (in the eighth century BC) the Kushite kings conquered Egypt and ruled there as the 25th Dynasty (c.750–656 BC). The Assyrians eventually forced them out, but the Kushite state continued until the fourth century AD, with its main centres at Napata, near the Fourth Cataract, and at Meroe.

To the Egyptians, Nubia was a source of luxury goods. Ivory and ebony were brought from the region of the central Sudan, with ostrich eggs and feathers, animal skins and incense. From the deserts of Nubia came stones, and, most importantly, gold. Parts of Nubia were also significant as cattle-breeding areas.

During the periods of Egyptian domination many large fortresses and temples were built in Nubia. Sadly, with the building of the Aswan Dam, some of these monuments were lost beneath the waters of Lake Nasser, but others were saved and removed to higher ground. Some were given by the Egyptian Government to countries which had helped in the salvage operations, so today there are Egyptian temples in New York, Madrid and Leiden.

ASWAN DAM

There are two dams, the Old Aswan Dam built by the British in 1898 and the High Dam completed in 1964. The High Dam has created a reservoir (Lake Nubia, or Lake Nasser), drowning Nubia, and extending for 500 kilometres (310 miles), passing beyond the Egyptian border into Sudan. There has been considerable debate about the merits and faults of the dam and the lake ever since the project was begun. There have certainly been many detrimental effects, but, at the same time, it is certain that without it Egypt would have suffered from the famines which have afflicted Sudan and Ethiopia in the past two decades.

LAKE NUBIA

Cruise boats now operate between Aswan and Abu Simbel and can be joined at either point. They visit the temples which were salvaged and rebuilt on the shores of Lake Nasser. The voyage on the lake is itself a pleasant experience.

NEW KALABSHA

Just south of the High Dam, the temples of Kalabsha and Beit el-Wali and the small Kiosk of Kertassi have been re-erected. The **Temple of Kalabsha** originally stood some 50 kilometres south of Aswan. A large temple built in the reign of Augustus, it was dedicated to Merul, better known from the Greek form of his name, Mandulis, a Nubian sun god equated with Horus and Apollo. The temple is a good example of the classic plan. It is still possible to climb the pylon and onto the roof in order to look down on the court: looking in all other directions merely reveals the ugliness of the whole area of the dam. The relief decoration of the interior rooms is undamaged but not exciting; the real interest of this temple is the large number of graffiti on the façade of the pronaos. To the right of the entrance, on the screen between the two columns, is a long decree of Aurelius Besarion, Governor of Ombos c.AD 250, ordering the expulsion of all pigs from the town for religious reasons. On the second column is one of the longest Meroitic texts known, that of King Kharamadoye; unfortunately, it cannot be completely

understood. On the narrow end wall is the inscription of Silko, King of the Noubades, c.AD 450. Silko, wearing a Roman cuirass with his cloak flying behind him, is on horseback spearing an enemy. Above, a rather naive figure of Victory hovers, crowning Silko with a Meroitic crown, similar to those from the tombs of Ballana and Qustul. Below is a long inscription in corrupt Greek, recording the king's campaigns.

Although Kalabsha flourished in the later Ptolemaic and Roman periods, it was an old centre, probably founded in the New Kingdom. When Kalabsha temple was dismantled to bring it to this new site, blocks of earlier shrines were discovered built into its foundations. Of these, a small chapel and parts of gateways can be seen, re-erected at the southern end of Elephantine Island. A large gateway erected by Augustus was given to the German Government in gratitude for help in moving the temples (now in Berlin).

The pretty little **Kiosk of Kertassi** once had a lovely situation 40 kilometres south of Aswan. A collection of other monuments is now stored here: slabs cut from the Nubian hills, with prehistoric rock-drawings; the stele of Sety I from Qasr Ibrim, now sliced into four pieces; and sad remnants of the Temple of Gerf Hussein, destined to be reconstructed.

The small temple from **Beit el-Wali** lies behind Kalabsha, up a winding path, and is easily missed. The earliest of Ramesses II's Nubian temples, it is unpretentious in style and scale but has some nice relief decoration. A gate leads into a long hall, partly rock-cut and originally with a vaulted roof. This was later converted into a church. The scenes show campaigns of Ramesses II against Nubia and Libya. The hall itself, supported by two rather squat proto-Doric columns, has some very good raised relief decoration and two rock-cut triads of the king with deities. Inside the sanctuary, on either side of the door, the king is suckled by goddesses, Anuket and the Nubian Miket.

NEW SEBUA

At New Sebua there are three re-erected temples. **Maharraqa** is undecorated and unexciting. It marked the southern frontier of Roman rule. The **Temple of Dakka** was begun by a Meroitic ruler, and enlarged by various Ptolemies. There is some fine relief decoration. The **Temple of Wadi el-Sebua** is the most elaborate of Ramesses II's Nubian monuments. Its processional way rises up in terraces, flanked by sphinxes, through a stone pylon into the statue-lined court, and then up another terrace into the rock-cut halls and sanctuary. The decoration is, in places, very fine and theologically fascinating (for the specialist).

Temple at Philae Island

AMADA

There are three salvaged monuments at New Amada, the Temple of Amada itself; the Temple of Derr, one of the later temples of Ramesses II; and the rock-cut tomb of Pennut from Aniba.

The **Temple of Amada** was saved by lifting it onto railway tracks and shunting it back to higher ground. The inner rooms of the temple, built by Thutmose III and Amenhotep II, have some fine reliefs with well-preserved colour.

The **Temple of Derr** is similar to Abu Simbel and Wadi el-Sebua, although not so elaborate. The entrance areas of the temple were destroyed long ago, and the first hall of square pillars is not well preserved. There were originally statues of the king attached to the last row of pillars, an unusual position, since in the other temples these line the main axis. The main rock-cut hall is irregular in shape, but rather spacious. The relief decoration, perhaps not as fine as at Sebua or Abu Simbel, is quite elegant. The scenes of the sacred barques in the sanctuary are good.

In the hill a little way beyond the Temple of Derr is the **tomb of Pennut**, removed from Aniba (ancient Miam), the principal seat of the Egyptian administration in Nubia in the New Kingdom. Pennut was the governor of Wawat in the reign of Ramesses VI. The decoration is in carved and painted relief, and typical of any Egyptian tomb of the same period. Although intact when photographed by George Steindorff during his excavations at Aniba, the tomb suffered terribly at the hands of antiquities thieves later in the 20th century. The scenes include the weighing of the heart and introduction of the deceased into the presence of Osiris. A procession of members of Pennut's family shows how important it was in Nubia, and had been one of the leading families for several generations. The most important scene shows Pennut being rewarded by the viceroy in the presence of the pharaoh. The accompanying text tells us that Pennut had dedicated a statue (which is shown in the scene) of the king in the Temple of Aniba, and given some fields from his own land in order to endow it with offerings. The text gives precise details of where the fields were and who owned the adjoining ones. Doubtless this was a way of evading tax, since Pennut could become priest of the statue, and continue to enjoy the 'reversion' of offerings, whilst the land became exempt from tax.

The ancient town of **Aniba** (Miam) had fortress walls built during the 12th Dynasty and renewed in the New Kingdom. There was a temple to the principal god, Horus Lord of Miam, which had dedications by many pharaohs and high officials. Near the town were large cemeteries of the local population (known in archaeology as the 'C-Group') dating from the Middle Kingdom to early New Kingdom, and the Egyptian-style tombs of the later New Kingdom, each with a steep-sided pyramid above it. Aniba and its cemeteries were excavated by George Steindorff, and there are large collections of artefacts from here in the Ägyptisches Museum in Leipzig, and the Nubia Museum in Aswan. A little to the north of the town, at el-Lessiya, was a rock-cut temple of the reign of Thutmose III. This was salvaged during the UNESCO campaign and given to the Italian Government. It is now displayed in the Museo Egizio in Turin. Opposite Aniba lay the hill of Qasr Ibrim. This has a number of chapels cut into the lower part, again salvaged, and being reconstructed at New Sebua. On another outcrop was the stele of Sety I, for a long time at New Kalabsha.

The boat sails past **Qasr Ibrim**, now an island, but once a hilltop fortress on the edge of the valley. A fragile archaeological site, Ibrim has been the focus of excavations by the Egypt Exploration Society since the early 1960s. It can no longer be visited (from 2001 lying in a military zone). The earliest occupation levels belong to the 10th–8th centuries BC. Ibrim became a centre of religious importance in the Meroitic and Christian periods, and continued to be occupied into Ottoman times. The site is dominated by the cathedral, which is surrounded by a mass of streets and houses. Unfortunately considerable parts of the island and its remains have disappeared under the rising waters of the lake in recent years. There was a fortification wall with gates and towers that dated back to the time of the Kushite king Taharqo (690–664 BC), and probably earlier. This wall was renewed and extended during the Meroitic period when a large stone podium, identical in style to a temple quay, was also constructed. There were several temples, some with painted plaster decoration, dating to the time of Taharqo. The site was significant because of the remarkably well-preserved remains of cloth (some cotton), leather and basketry.

ABU SIMBEL

A bu Simbel, despite being removed from its original site, is still one of the most spectacular sites in the Nile Valley. The temples were removed between 1964 and 1968, being re-erected 65 metres above and 210 metres further inland than their original position.

The two temples are carved from the rock. The main temple is dedicated to **Ramesses II** as one of the four state gods of Egypt. The façade takes the form of a pylon surmounted by a row of baboons adoring the rising sun. It is dominated by the

AN INTREPID EXPLORER:
JOHANN LUDWIG BURCKHARDT

Johann Ludwig (John Lewis) Burckhardt was the quintessential 19th-century European adventurer-scholar. Born in Switzerland in 1784, he was educated in Germany. He arrived in England in 1806 with an introduction to the renowned explorer and botanist, Sir Joseph Banks, president of the Royal Society, who, as head of the African Association, was looking for someone to join an Arab trading caravan travelling to Timbuktu.

After some preparatory courses at Cambridge University in Arabic, medicine, surgery and astronomy, he set off for Aleppo in Syria in 1809, where he spent the next three years, in the guise of a learned Muslim by the name of Sheik Ibrahim, perfecting his Arabic and his knowledge of Arabic customs, culture, religion and the Koran. During this time he travelled to Palmyra, Damascus, Lebanon, Baalbek (Heliopolis), Bashan and the remote desert region northeast of Aleppo. In the summer of 1812, he set out for Cairo, disguised as a simple Bedouin, via the relatively uncharted wilds east of the Dead Sea. On this journey, Burckhardt became the first Westerner to rediscover and describe the ruins of the ancient lost city of Petra.

From Egypt, he made two journeys into Nubia and Sudan. On the first, in 1813, he rediscovered the temples of Abu Simbel, sand-covered and unknown to Europeans. The second journey took 'Sheik Ibrahim' across the Eastern Desert to Shendi in northern Sudan and from there to the Red Sea. Crossing to Arabia he spent three months living in the holy cities of Mecca and Medina, returning to Cairo in 1817, finally ready for his mission of tracing the Niger and finding Timbuktu. He was not to make it—he died that October of dysentery in Cairo at the age of 33 before the camel train set off. His tomb still lies in Cairo's northeastern cemetery.

Burckhardt left behind him over 800 volumes of manuscripts, bequeathed to the library at Cambridge University, along with journals, notes and letters to England, all of which played an invaluable role in opening up the Near East to the Western world. His journals, published by the African Association, include: *Travels in Arabia* (1829); *Travels in Nubia* (1819); *Travels in Syria and the Holy Land* (1822); *Notes on the Bedouin and Wahábys* (1830); and *Arabic Proverbs* (1830).

The façade of the main temple at Abu Simbel is dominated by four seated colossi of Ramesses II, here representing the sun god.

Abu Simbel: Temple of Ramesses II and Ra-Harakhty

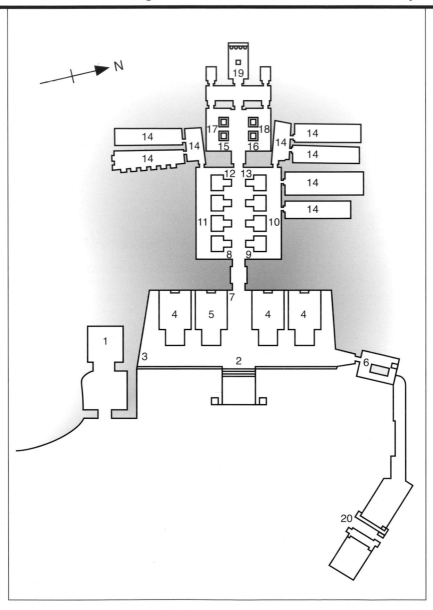

Abu Simbel: Temple of Ramesses II and Ra-Harakhty

1 Chapel of Thoth (*mammisi*): usually closed.

2 Terrace with statues of living and Osiride king and falcon images of Horus.

3 The 'Marriage Stele' with scene showing the Hittite king conducting his daughter to Ramesses.

4 Colossi of Ramesses II accompanied by varying combinations of his wife Nefertari, his mother, Tuya, and his children.

5 Colossus of Ramesses II flanked by his wife Nefertari, his mother, Tuya, and with his eldest son Amun-hir-khepeshef. There are Greek inscriptions on the left leg of the colossus, naming members of the army sent by Psamtik II to attack Napata.

6 Solar chapel with mini pylon.

7 Cryptographic inscription with names and titles of Ramesses II.

8 Ramesses smites Nubians in front of Amun-Ra. Group of the eight eldest princes headed by Amun-hir-khepeshef, Pre-hir-wenemef, Ramesses and Khaemwaset.

9 Ramesses smites captives in front of Ra-Harakhty. Group of nine princesses including Bint-Anath.

10 The Battle of Qadesh. One of the most accessible versions of the scene, with lots of detail of the royal encampment.

11 Upper register: five offering scenes, far right, Amun seated within a Holy Mountain with uraeus (either Abu Simbel itself or Gebel Barkal). Lower register, military scenes: the king and his sons attack a Syrian fort; Ramesses smites a Libyan (repeats a scene at Karnak, note the deeply cut figure of the king); Ramesses in his chariot (note the alteration to the bow and to the crown).

12 Ramesses brings Nubian captives to seated images of Amun-Ra, the deified Ramesses and Mut. The image of the king was added later, and the alterations are quite clearly visible.

13 Ramesses brings Hittite captives to seated images of Ra-Harakhty, the deified Ramesses (added later) and the lioness-headed Ius-aas.

14 Each of the side rooms is generally described as a treasury, although they may have been cult rooms of some sort. The scenes show Ramesses offering to a range of deities including numerous forms of his deified self.

15 Ramesses offers to Amun and Mut.

16 Ramesses offers to Min-Amun and Isis.

17 The sacred barque of Amun-Ra.

18 The sacred barque of the deified Ramesses.

19 Sanctuary with (left to right) statues of Ptah, Amun-Ra, Ramesses and Ra-Harakhty.

20 Mud-brick pylon (restored) with stone gateway leading to Temple of Nefertari.

Source: Robert Morkot

Abu Simbel: Temple of Nefertari and Hathor of Ibshek

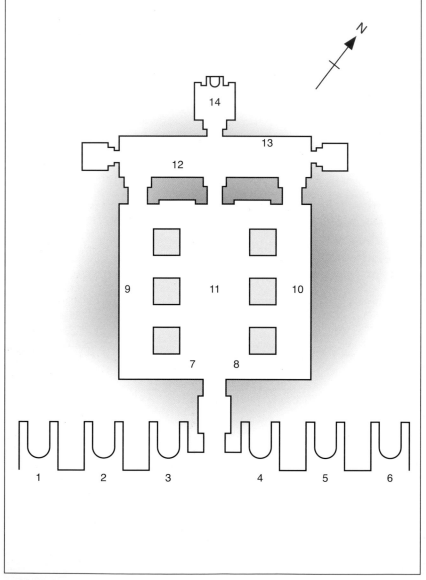

(preceding pages) *Colossal statues of Ramesses II line the hall of the temple at Abu Simbel*

Abu Simbel: Temple of Nefertari and Hathor of Ibshek

1 Ramesses II with sons.

2 Nefertari with daughters.

3 Ramesses II as 'Ruler of the Two Lands, Beloved of Amun', with sons. Doorway: lintel with scenes of Ramesses offering to Amun-Ra and to Horus of Meha; entrance with scenes of Ramesses offering flowers to Hathor of Ibshek and Nefertari playing sistra to Isis, Mother of the Gods.

4 Ramesses II as 'Sun of the Rulers, Beloved of Atum' with sons.

5 Nefertari with daughters.

6 Ramesses II with sons.

7 Ramesses smites a Nubian before Amun-Ra, Nefertari behind.

8 Ramesses smites a Libyan before Horus of Meha, Nefertari behind.

9 Wall: Ramesses receives *menat*-collar from Hathor of Ibshek; Seth and Horus of Meha crown Ramesses; Nefertari offers flowers to Anuket; Ramesses offers Maat to Amun-Ra, Lord of Thrones of the Two Lands. Pillars (read together): Nefertari offers to Maat and Hathor.

10 Wall: Ramesses offers to Ptah; to Herishef; Nefertari plays sistra to Hathor of Iunyt; Ramesses offers to Harakhty the Great God, Lord of Nubia. Pillars (read together): Ramesses offers to Mut and Khonsu.

11 Square pillars with Hathor-headed sistra on central aisle. The images on the east (entrance) face of each pillar face the aisle: Nefertari twice; Ramesses and Thoth; Nefertari and Khnum. On leaving the temple, the pillars show Isis and Weret-Hekau (the Great of Magic); Horus of Baki and Satjet; Horus of Miam and Horus of Buhen. The west wall to the inner chambers has scenes of Nefertari playing sistra and offering flowers to Hathor of Ibshek and to Mut.

12 Nefertari crowned by Hathor of Ibshek and Isis. Opposite: Ramesses offers to Amun, and a scene with the falcon-headed forms of Horus in Nubia, Horus of Buhen, Baki and Miam. On the end wall Nefertari offers to Hathor of Ibshek as a cow in a boat on a papyrus swamp.

13 Ramesses and Nefertari offer flowers to Tawosret ('the Powerful One') a form of Hathor. Opposite: Ramesses offers to Harakhty; and a small scene with the Cataract deities Khnum, Satjet and Anuket. On the end wall Ramesses offers to Hathor of Thebes as a cow in a boat on a papyrus swamp.

14 The Sanctuary: Nefertari offers to Mut and Hathor of Iunyt (Dendera); Ramesses offers to divine forms of himself and Nefertari. The end wall has a carved shrine with a figure of the Hathor cow, crowned with plumes, emerging.

Source: Robert Morkot

four seated colossi of the king, flanked by smaller figures of his wife, Nefertari, and his mother, Queen Mut-Tuya. Various sons and daughters are seen standing by his feet. These colossi are very similar in concept to the Colossi of Memnon at Thebes (although no sons were shown there), and represent the king as the sun god. The temple is set on a low terrace, which itself is lined with large statues, but these are generally ignored because of the scale of the façade behind. The statues show the king living, striding and dead, in the form of Osiris, mummiform with hands crossed on his chest. There are also falcons, representing the forms of Horus. At the north end of the terrace is a solar chapel; the altar with its obelisks, scarab and baboons is now in the Nubia Museum. A number of inscriptions are carved in the recesses at the ends of the façade, the most important being the one at the south end, the 'Marriage Stele'. This inscription records Ramesses II's marriage to Maat-Hor-neferu-Ra, daughter of the king of the Hittites.

The second colossus fell in antiquity, possibly during the reign of Ramesses II himself. The colossus adjacent to the doorway was also damaged and required restoration (easily visible) in the reign of Sety II, whose cartouches are carved here. Over the doorway is a large niche with a striking image of a falcon-headed man: this is the king himself, appearing as the sun god. On either side of this figure, two smaller and damaged figures can be seen. They are the goddess Maat and the dog-headed sceptre (in Egyptian, *user*, meaning 'powerful'); this group in fact makes up the king's throne name, User-Maat-Ra. On either side of the niche are relief figures of the king wearing the blue crown; he is offering a small group comprising the same hieroglyphs: the king offers his name to his own image.

On the (left) jamb of the door is a large inscription that looks like a series of deities: it is, but this is a cryptic text which actually reads as the king's titulary. Such writing is common in the jewellery of Tutankhamun and became typical of the Ptolemaic temples.

The first hall is supported by eight square pillars with statues of the king. Those on the north side have the double crown, those on the south the white crown. This hall can be compared with the open court of temples such as that of Ramesses III at Karnak. The reliefs on the north wall show the Battle of Qadesh. More easily accessible than most reliefs of this campaign, there is much worth examining in the detail of life in the camp. A series of rooms off this hall, probably added later, are often termed treasuries but were most likely for rituals associated with the king's jubilee festivals.

The decoration of the temple was started at the entrance whilst the inner parts were still being hewn. For this reason, the reliefs in this first hall show at what point the king became a god. On either side of the door into the second hall are triads—the king flanked by two deities—but close examination shows that the figure of the king has been added. In the inner parts the divine king is intended from the beginning of the design. Over the doorway itself are two unusual images, a sphinx with a ram's head and one with a falcon's head. These exist in sculpture, but are less often seen in relief. When Belzoni entered the temple in 1817, he found two such falcon-headed sphinxes flanking this very door (now in London, British Museum).

A short ramp leads into the second hall, supported by four square pillars. Here the decoration shows religious scenes. The sanctuary has seated statues of Ramesses flanked by Amun, Ptah and Ra-Harakhty.

The small temple is dedicated to **Nefertari** as a manifestation of the goddess Hathor. Its façade, in the shape of a double pylon, has six colossal figures, two of the queen and four of the king.

The first hall is divided into three aisles by six pillars with sistra carved on their faces. The coarse sandstone means that the sculpture in this temple lacks crispness, but the figures have a slender elegance. The scenes are simple and uncluttered, which, combined with the colour scheme of gold and white, lends a lightness and charm to the whole design. The small hall beyond has a, so far, unique scene showing Nefertari crowned by the goddesses Hathor and Isis. In the sanctuary a cow image emerges from the cliff, between two sistrum-shaped columns, protecting a figure of the king.

All over the cliff surrounding the temples are large inscriptions carved by various viceroys of Nubia, mostly of the reign of Ramesses II.

LOWER EGYPT

T he Delta is one of the most populous and agriculturally rich regions of Egypt, as it was in ancient times. North of Cairo, the Nile now divides into two main branches—in antiquity there were seven—the Rosetta (western) and Damietta (eastern). Broad and flat, crossed by waterways, the landscape is very different from that of the enclosed valley.

Recently, fears have been expressed that with ecological problems increasing, the Delta might suffer extensive flooding. Much of the region is very low-lying and it is estimated that if the sea rose by 2.7 metres (9 feet), much of it would vanish. Even with only a 45-centimetre (18-inch) rise, Alexandria and Port Said would be swamped and the impact on fishing (in the lagoons) and agriculture would be catastrophic.

The Delta contains numerous ancient sites, although these are not frequently on the tourist route. Many are not easy to reach, and, for some, special permission is required. It is also fair to say that many of the Delta sites lack the splendour and immediate appeal of the Upper Egyptian monuments. Although there are many city mounds and ruins, the Delta has received less archaeological attention than other parts of Egypt. In any case, many of its great monuments were pillaged, firstly for the building of Alexandria and later by the Romans. Fortunately, archaeology here is now increasing, with remarkable results. Some of Egypt's most ancient towns and venerable cult centres were situated in the Delta, endowed with monuments by many kings: Buto, probably the capital of Lower Egypt before the unification, always played an important role in the kingship, its patron deity being Wadjet, the cobra goddess who adorns the king's forehead. Sau (usually known by the Greek form, Sais), also important in the earliest phases of Egyptian history, was the cult centre of the goddess Neith, wife of Seth and mother of the crocodile god, Sobek. Strategically placed, controlling routes from Memphis to Sinai and Asia, Per-Bastet (Greek: Bubastis) was another town to achieve early importance. Although there were major towns such as these, much of the Delta seems to have remained papyrus marsh until the New Kingdom, only then being brought under agriculture. So it was in the later periods that the Delta rose to its greatest importance, with many ruling families coming from this region. The process began when Ramesses II founded his new residence city at Per-Ramesses, near modern Faqus. In the Third Intermediate Period, the Libyans, who had been settled in the Delta by the Ramesside kings, gained power, using Djanet

(Tanis) and Per-Bastet (Bubastis) as their principal centres. The 26th Dynasty originated in the city of Sau (Sais), in the western Delta, and the 30th Dynasty at Samannud.

Djanet and Per-Bastet are the two sites usually visited; both are possible in a long day-trip from Cairo. For those wishing to visit Delta towns and sites on the way to Alexandria, Tanta makes a convenient stopping place, with several good hotels. In the heart of the Delta, it is also on the main Cairo–Alexandria road. For those wishing to visit Tanis and Bubastis from Cairo, take the main road to Benha—near Tell Atrib, ancient Athribis—(48 kilometres), then the road to Zagazig (37 kilometres).

ZAGAZIG

Z agazig is a large and important town with Tell Basta, the ruins of ancient Per-Bastet, 'Domain of Bastet' (Greek: Bubastis), lying on its outskirts. An important city from the Old Kingdom onwards, its greatest importance came in the Third Intermediate Period, when it was the residence city of some of the Libyan kings. During the Late Period the festivals of the goddess Bastet made the city a pilgrimage centre. Bastet, daughter of the sun god, was originally shown as a lioness, but by the Late Period she was most commonly associated with the cat. Her imagery caused her to be identified with the other violent goddesses, Sakhmet and Mut. The Greeks equated her with Artemis. According to Herodotos, the festival of Bastet was the most important in Egypt, with, he says, upwards of seven hundred thousand people attending. The pilgrims came to the town in barges, playing music and singing, and more wine was consumed than in all the rest of the year!

Today, the ruins of the **Temple of Bastet** occupy a large area filled with fallen granite columns and weathered granite statues. Herodotos describes the splendours of this temple, saying that while other temples might be larger or more lavish, none was a greater pleasure to look at. The temple was encircled by broad canals (which made it almost an island), their banks shaded with trees, and inside the enclosure, around the temple itself, was a grove of very tall trees. Few trees now shade the flat expanse of coarse grass where the vestiges of this sanctuary lie. The Libyan kings Osorkon I and Osorkon II added columned halls and courts to the ancient temple, and it is the remnants of these that can be seen today. Many granite blocks of the Festival Hall of Osorkon II are now in European museums (Berlin; London, British Museum), but some remain on the site, their relief decoration marred by centuries of contact with the wet ground. There are also many granite statues, some dyads, some triads, mostly from

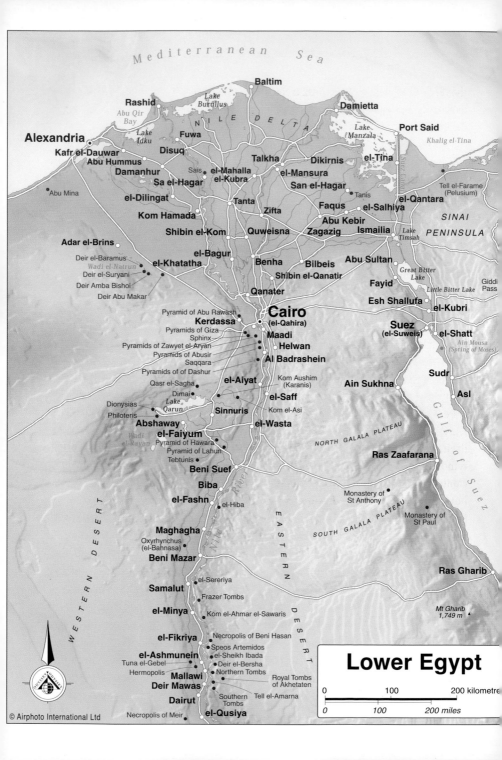

M e d i t e r r a n e a n   S e a

Baltim

Rashid
*Abu Qir
Bay*
*Lake
Burullus*

Damietta

Fuwa

N   I   L   E   D   E   L   T   A

*Lake
Manzala*

Port Said

Khalig el-Tina

Alexandria
Kafr el-Dauwar
*Lake
Idku*
Abu Hummus
Disuq

Damanhur
Sa el-Hagar
Sais
el-Mahalla
el-Kubra
Talkha
Dikirnis
el-Tina

Abu Mina
el-Dilingat

Tanta
Zifta

el-Mansura
San el-Hagar
Tanis

el-Salhiya
el-Qantara

Tell el-Farame
(Pelusium)

SINAI

Kom Hamada

Quweisna
Faqus
Abu Kebir

PENINSULA

Adar el-Brins
Shibin el-Kom
Zagazig
Ismailia
*Lake
Timsah*

Deir el-Baramus
Wadi el-Natrun
el-Khatatha
el-Bagur
Benha
Bilbeis
Abu Sultan

Deir el-Suryani
Deir Amba Bishoi
Shibin el-Qanatir
*Great Bitter
Lake*

Deir Abu Makar
Qanater
Fayid
Little Bitter Lake
Giddi
Pass

Esh Shallufa
el-Kubri

Pyramid of Abu Rawash
Kerdassa
Cairo
(el-Qahira)
Suez
(el-Suweis)
el-Shatt

Pyramids of Giza
Sphinx
Maadi
*Ain Mousa
(Spring of Moses)*

Pyramids of Zawyet el-Aryan
Helwan
Pyramids of Abusir
Saqqara
Al Badrashein
Sudr

Pyramids of of Dashur
Asl

Qasr el-Sagha
el-Aiyat
Kom Aushim
(Karanis)

Dimai
el-Saff
Ain Sukhna

*Lake
Qarun*
Kom el-Asi
Dionysias
Philoteris
Sinnuris

Abshaway
el-Wasta

el-Faiyum
*Wadi
el-Rayan*
Pyramid of Hawara
NORTH GALALA PLATEAU

Pyramid of Lahun
Tebtunis

Beni Suef
Ras Zaafarana

Biba

el-Fashn
el-Hiba

Monastery of
St Anthony

Maghagha
Oxyrhynchus
(el-Bahnasa)
*E
A
S
T
E
R
N*
SOUTH GALALA PLATEAU
Monastery of
St Paul

Beni Mazar

Nile
River

Ras Gharib

Samalut
el-Sereriya

Frazer Tombs
*Mt Gharib
1,749 m*

el-Minya
Kom el-Ahmar el-Sawaris

*D
E
S
E
R
T*

el-Fikriya
Necropolis of Beni Hasan

el-Ashmunein
Speos Artemidos
el-Sheikh Ibada

Tuna el-Gebel
Deir el-Bersha

Hermopolis
Northern Tombs

Mallawi
Royal Tombs
of Akhetaten

Deir Mawas
Southern
Tombs

Dairut
Tell el-Amarna

Necropolis of Meir
el-Qusiya

W E S T E R N   D E S E R T

© Airphoto International Ltd

Lower Egypt

0   100   200 kilometre

0   100   200 miles

the reign of Ramesses II. In 2002 a colossal statue (originally about 11 metres) of a queen was excavated amongst the ruins. It carries inscriptions naming Ramesses II, and the excavators suggest that it may represent Queen Merytamun.

Archaeologists have worked at Tell Basta on and off for over a hundred years. Labib Habachi uncovered monuments of the Old Kingdom and the tombs of some late-Ramesside viceroys of Nubia (sarcophagus in the Egyptian Museum garden). Habachi's excavations lie on the other side of the main road from the temple, but may not be accessible as some areas of the site are frequently shut.

TANIS

Tanis is reached by taking the road to Faqus from Zagazig (37 kilometres), then that via el-Huseiniya to San el-Hagar (another 37 kilometres). The approach is not inspiring, ascending the hill of rich brown mud, but the view down into the remnants of the vast temple area and mounds of the city is quite breathtaking. The temples are almost the only parts of the site actually excavated to date. Much of the stone (a lot of it granite) and most of the statues, obelisks and columns that litter the site were actually brought from the site of Per-Ramesses (probably modern Qantir, near Faqus). Ramesses II had built his new residence city at Per-Ramesses, with Djanet (Tanis) as its port. By the time of the death of Ramesses XI, Djanet had supplanted Per-Ramesses in importance, perhaps because of the drying-up of that branch of the Nile, so the kings of the 21st Dynasty set about removing huge quantities of stone and monuments to build temples in their new capital. Statuary was removed from the site in the early years of the 19th century, but the first controlled excavations were by Mariette between 1859 and 1861 on behalf of the Antiquities Service. Mariette was followed by Flinders Petrie, and more recently French archaeologists have worked here. Pierre Montet excavated between 1927 and 1955, making his most important discoveries, the royal tombs, in 1939–1940. Work continues.

The major monument is the **Temple of Amun** built by Pa-seba-kha-en-niut (Psusennes) and added to by other Libyan kings, notably Sheshonq III. The temple comprised a series of pylons and courts; it is entered through the **Gate of Sheshonq III**, flanked by colossi (of Ramesses II). Beyond this was an avenue leading to the temple proper, with (originally) over 15 obelisks. In this outer area was the burial place of a number of Libyan kings. Their tombs were constructed of massive reused stone blocks and were entered from above. For this reason the tombs look rather

THE FEAST OF DRUNKENNESS

H erodotos describes the festival held in honour of the cat goddess, Bastet, whom he equates with the Greek goddess, Artemis, in her city of Per-Bastet (Bubastis), modern Zagazig in the eastern Delta.

The procedure at Bubastis is this: they come in barges, men and women together, a great number in each boat; on the way, some of the women keep up a continual clatter with castanets and some of the men play flutes, while the rest, both men and women, sing and clap their hands. Whenever they pass a town on the river-bank, they bring the barge close in-shore, some of the women continuing to act as I have said, while others shout abuse at the women of the place, or start dancing, or stand up and hitch up their skirts. When they reach Bubastis they celebrate the festival with elaborate sacrifices, and more wine is consumed than during all the rest of the year. The numbers that meet there, are, according to native report, as many as seven hundred thousand men and women.

This riotous festival had its parallel at Hathor's great shrine at Dendera. It celebrated one of the myths in which the sun god Ra sent his daughter, the 'Eye of Ra', to destroy humankind. In the form of a lioness (as Sakhmet, Tefnut or Bastet) she ravaged the world, until Ra was left with the prospect of no people to rule. In order to pacify her and bring her back, the god Thoth brewed beer coloured with red ochre, and filled a field with it: the goddess, thinking it was blood, drank it and became drunk and so could be taken back to Ra. The myth encapsulates those dualities which are central to Egyptian religion: the violent form which must be pacified, yet it always retains the risk of once again becoming violent. So the lioness becomes a cat, or the wild cow of the marshes a domestic cow.

roughly constructed on the outside, like unfinished mastabas. They would originally have been beneath the pavement of the court, probably with chapels above (as at Medinet Habu). It is sometimes possible to enter the tombs. The **tomb of Osorkon II** (tomb one) has some fine relief decoration. One chamber was converted for the burial of Takeloth II and the sarcophagi are still in place. In tomb three, built for Pa-seba-kha-en-niut (Psusennes), there were several burials. The finds included the king's silver coffin, mask and jewellery and a massive sarcophagus originally made for Merneptah's tomb in the Valley of the Kings. From the other burials in the tomb came the hawk-faced silver coffin of Sheshonq II, and the beautiful, gold face-mask of the general, Wen-djeba-en-djed. All of this may be seen in the Egyptian Museum. Tomb five, isolated, was that of Sheshonq III.

The temple is badly robbed of its architecture, but remains impressive, with many shattered obelisks and statues. Of note, a small queen's figure against the leg of one of the Ramesside colossi has the description 'Daughter of the Great Chief of the Khatti, Maat-Hor-neferu-Ra': this is the Hittite princess whose marriage to Ramesses II (recorded on a stele at Abu Simbel) sealed the peace treaty between Egypt and the Hittites. Climbing the enclosure wall at the end of the temple, you can look into the outer enclosure where there are a number of granite palmiform columns. These date to the Old Kingdom but were reused by Ramesses II and then Osorkon II. To the east of the main Amun temple are the remains of the 30th-dynasty temple. Here one can look out over a flat plain once filled by the waters of Lake Manzala: one of the reasons for the city becoming important as a port. The silting-up of the Delta means that the coast now lies much further away.

A second enclosure contains the remains of the **Temple of Mut**, where the Syrian goddess Astarte was also worshipped. A large dyad of Amun with the lioness-headed goddess sits amid the ruins. Near the French dig house is a collection of sculptures, including an especially attractive, very large foot. Numerous splendid sculptures were removed by Mariette from Tanis to the Egyptian Museum, including the black granite sphinxes of Amenemhat III, first reused by Ramesses II at Per-Ramesses, then brought here.

Between Tanta and Damanhur (near Ityai el-Barud) is the site of the Greek trading settlement of **Naukratis**, founded in the 26th Dynasty. It is extremely difficult to locate and is not an inspiring site: the town area excavated by Flinders Petrie is now filled with a lake and only remnants of the Great Temenos (sanctuaries of Egyptian gods) stand in the village. An important town and described by Herodotos, as a site it has little to offer.

IN THE BELLY OF THE BEAST

'Oh, Heaven help us! What is that dreadful noise? Run, run! Has somebody been killed?'

'Do not distress yourself, kind-hearted sir. It is only the merchants of Alexandria, buying cotton.'

'But they are murdering one another surely.'

'Not so. They merely gesticulate.'

'Does any place exist whence one could view their gestures safely?'

'There is such a place.'

'I shall come to no bodily harm there?'

'None, none.'

'Then conduct me, pray.'

And mounting to an upper chamber we looked down into a stupendous Hall.

It is usual to compare such visions to Dante's Inferno, but this really did resemble it, because it was marked out into the concentric circles of which the Florentine speaks. Divided from each other by ornamental balustrades, they increased in torment as they decreased in size, so that the inmost ring was congested beyond redemption with perspiring souls. They shouted and waved and spat at each other across the central basin which was empty but for a permanent official who sat there, fixed in ice. Now and then he rang a little bell, and now and then another official, who dwelt upon a ladder far away, climbed and wrote upon a board with chalk. The merchants hit their heads and howled. A terrible calm ensued. Something worse was coming. While it gathered we spoke.

'Oh, name this place!'

'It is none other than the Bourse. Cotton is sold at this end, Stocks and Shares at that.'

And I perceived a duplicate fabric at the farther end of the Hall, a subsidiary or rather a superseded Hell, for its circles were deserted, it was lashed by no everlasting wind, and such souls as loitered against its balustrades seemed pensive in their mien. This was the Stock Exchange—such a great name in England, but negligable here where only cotton counts. Cotton shirts and cotton wool and reels of cotton would not come to us if merchants did not suffer in Alexandria. Nay, Alexandria herself could not have re-arisen from the waves, there would be no French gardens, no English church at Bulkeley, possibly not even any drains...

Help! oh, help! help! Oh, horrible, too horrible! For the storm had broken. With the scream of a devil in pain a stout Greek fell sideways over the balustrade, then righted himself, then fell again, and as he fell and rose he chanted, 'Teekoty Peapot, Teekoty Peapot.' He was offering to sell cotton. Towards him, bull-shouldered, moved a lout in a tarboosh. Everyone else screamed too, using odd little rhythms to advertise their individuality. Some shouted unnoticed, others would evoke a kindred soul, and right across the central pool business would be transacted. They seemed to have evolved a new sense. They communicated by means unknown to normal men. A wave of the notebook, and the thing was done. And the imitation marble pillars shook, and the ceiling that was painted to look like sculpture trembled, and Time himself stood still in the person of a sham-renaissance clock. And a British officer who was watching the scene said—never mind what he said.

Hence, hence!

E M Forster, Pharos and Pharillon, Hogarth Press, London, 1923

Forster (1879–1970) was an English author and critic, and a member of the Bloomsbury group. After gaining fame as a novelist, Forster spent his 46 remaining years publishing mainly short stories and non-fiction. Of his five important novels, four appeared before World War I. Between the years 1912 and 1913 Forster travelled in India. From 1914 to 1915 he worked for the National Gallery in London. Following the outbreak of World War I, Forster joined the Red Cross and served in Alexandria, Egypt. There he met the Greek poet C P Cavafy, and a selection of his poems was published in 1923. In 1921 Forster returned to India, working as a private secretary to the Maharajah of Dewas. In 1949 Forster refused a knighthood. He was made a Companion of Honour in 1953 and in 1969 he accepted an Order of Merit.

Alexandria can be reached directly from Cairo by the desert road, which allows a visit to the monasteries of Wadi el-Natrun.

WADI EL-NATRUN

T he pyramids road from Cairo towards Alexandria skirts the desert edges, passing Abu Rawash, site of the northernmost (unfinished) pyramid complex. Chosen by Djedefre, immediate successor of Khufu (Cheops), as his burial place, little remains here, but some fine sculptures can be seen in the Egyptian Museum.

The Wadi el-Natrun is a desert depression, about 25 metres (82 feet) below sea level. It has about 25 lakes which dry up in spring, leaving rich deposits of sodium carbonate. In the early centuries AD, this was one of the major centres of monasticism, but only four monasteries are still occupied. The road to the largest monastery, Deir Makaryus, lies some 89 kilometres (60 miles) north of Giza. Founded by St Makarios the Great (300–390), whose relics are preserved here, it has seen much restoration and new building in recent years, and has a large community of monks. Within the enclosure are several ancient churches containing many relics. The Qasr (fortress), a feature common to all Egyptian monasteries, is an imposing building with chapels inside. Some of the interesting early frescoes have recently been cleaned, and the main church has fine painted decoration in the apse.

The other monasteries are visited by the road from the Rest House further along the main Alexandria road, 103 kilometres (64 miles) from Giza. The two central monasteries are Deir Amba Bishoi (St Pshoi, a disciple of St Makarios), currently the residence of the Coptic Patriarch, Pope Shenouda II, and the Deir el-Suryani (Monastery of the Syrians). Syrian merchants bought the monastery, which was already old, in the eighth century, for the use of Syrian monks. Deir el-Baramus, the Monastery of the Romans, is the most northerly in the wadi still occupied. A new road has made access quite easy. It is named after St Maximum and St Domitius, two brothers who served in the Roman army and later sought guidance from St Makarios. This is probably the oldest monastery in the wadi, and because of its remoteness and small size, it conveys the spirit of desert retreat and prayer. The main church contains the relics of St Moses the Black and St Theodosios. It has fine woodwork, and the column of St Arsanious is a handsome Corinthian piece. Adjacent to the church are the ancient refectory with its stone table and benches, and the old oil and wine presses. The barrenness of the surroundings and the lushness of the cultivation within the walls are best appreciated from the roof.

ALEXANDRIA

Alexandria was founded by the 25-year-old Alexander the Great in 332 BC, on his way to the Oasis of Siwa. The city was built on the spur of land between the sea and Lake Maryut, on the site of a small Egyptian town, Rhakote, probably originally a Ramesside fort. Alexander left Egypt to campaign in the East and never returned, dying at Babylon in 323 BC. The quarrels between his generals saw Egypt seized by Ptolemy, who brought Alexander's body with him. Originally taken to Memphis, it was later brought to Alexandria, where it was buried in great splendour in a glass coffin, to be subsequently joined by the bodies of the Ptolemaic family. Under the Ptolemies, Alexandria became the most important city in the eastern Mediterranean and the focus of the Ptolemaic possessions, extending around the coast of Syria and Southern Anatolia and to the islands of the Aegean. Alexandria retained considerable importance under the Roman Empire, but declined after the Arab conquest of Egypt by Amr ibn al-As, with the building of Fustat and Cairo. Amr wrote to the caliph that, 'I have taken a city of which I can only say that it contains 4,000 palaces, 4,000 baths, 400 theatres, 1,200 greengrocers and 40,000 Jews.'

Sun, sea and sand, Alexandria

The European expansion into Egypt in the late 18th and early 19th centuries saw the rise of Alexandria as a port, its importance increasing when the Suez Canal was opened in 1869. Large and cosmopolitan, the city flourished and became one of the most valuable commercial centres of the Mediterranean. Its position ensured it a key place in the 1939–1945 war, and in subsequent events. Alexandria has also become a semi-fictional city. Unlike, for example, Rome or Athens, there is little remaining of the ancient city; it is not possible to see the tomb of Alexander, or where Kleopatra committed suicide; the Great Lighthouse and the Great Library have vanished. Imagination and memory therefore, take over. Constantine Cavafy (1863–1933) evoked the ancient city and explored it in his own *fin de siècle* world. E M Forster lived in Alexandria during the 1914–1918 war, and wrote a set of essays and the best guidebook to this city. He emphasized also the contrast between the somewhat ordinary merchant port and its vanished past. The literary image was captured most famously in the *Alexandria Quartet* of Lawrence Durrell, but other writers have added to it, notably Robert Liddell (the biographer of Cavafy) and Olivia Manning. In contrast to these external, European views, *Miramar*, by Egypt's own Nobel prize–winning writer, Naguib Mahfouz, gives a view from the inside.

ALEXANDRIA TODAY: A TOUR OF THE CITY

Alexandria, as Durrell has written, is essentially a city that exists through writing; that Alexandria is also a human city. Ptolemaic and Roman Alexandria may have had beautiful and splendid buildings, but the city's significance has been through its people and its thought, both emotional and intellectual. Similarly, the life of mercantile Alexandria was its communities, not its architecture. Fragments of Cavafy's and Durrell's Alexandria still exist; the dusky art-nouveau splendour of Pastroudis café, the Cecil Hotel, the villas built in eclectic and extravagant style—and some attempt is being made to preserve this legacy before it is all replaced by concrete apartment blocks, but, although modern Alexandria has atmosphere and is an exciting city, it is not the ancient, nor the literary, city.

What was the ancient Alexandria like? While many fragments of architecture and statuary may be found in the recently opened Museum of Antiquities of the new Library of Alexandria, and in the various archaeological areas of the city, a real impression can perhaps better be gained from the ruins of such cities as Jerash in Jordan or Lepcis Magna in Libya.

Alexandria was laid out on a grid plan. The main east–west street, the Canopic Way, still exists in part as the Sharia Hurreya (Tariq Abd al-Nasser). At the eastern end it was closed by the Gate of the Sun, at the west end by the Gate of the Moon. The main north–south street, the present Sharia el-Nebi Daniel, ran from the Great Harbour (now the East Harbour) to the Lake Harbour, on Lake Maryut. Much deeper then than now, this lake connected with the Nile, forming a valuable link in the navigation system. Near the junction of the two main streets was the Soma, the burial place of Alexander (near the Mosque of Nebi Daniel); also home of the Mouseion (university) and the Great Library. The only archaeological remains visible in this area are at **Kom el-Dikka**, where a small Roman theatre has been excavated. Thirteen rows of marble seats (accommodating about 800 people), and some of the columns which supported its domed roof, give a good impression of one of Alexandria's less ostentatious public buildings. Nearby, a large bathhouse has been excavated by the Polish expedition.

Some of the most important parts of the city were on the shore. In ancient times **Pharos** was an island at the entrance to the harbour connected to the mainland by a causeway called the Heptastadion. It was on this island, now called Ras el-Tin, that the Great Lighthouse was built, its site today marked by the Fort of Qaitbay. The Heptastadion ('Seven Leagues') has silted up over the centuries and is now densely built up. The Corniche (Sharia 26 July) describes a great arc as it sweeps towards the fort. The Lighthouse, one of the Seven Wonders of the ancient world, was built in the reign of Ptolemy II to a design of Sostratos of Knidos. It stood 120 metres high, inside a colonnaded court. The bottom stage, some 60 metres tall, was square, with a second octagonal tier and finally a cylindrical drum, surmounted by the light and a statue of Poseidon. The Lighthouse was destroyed by earthquakes in AD 1100 and AD 1307. Sultan Qaitbay built the present fort on its remains in AD 1480.

Emergency underwater excavations to the east of Qaitbay Fort, carried out in 1994 and 1995 under the direction of Jean-Yves Empereur, found massive architectural elements and sculptures that may have formed part of the Pharos complex. The crown and base of a colossal statue, originally more than 12 metres high, certainly belong to the statue found here in 1961. This colossus represented a Ptolemaic queen in the guise of Isis. A companion statue of a king and parts of another comparable pair were also located. Amongst the other remains identified on the site are numerous columns; a dozen sphinxes with the names of Ramesses II and Psamtik II; and obelisks of Sety I, Ramesses II and Psamtik II. Some of these monuments have been raised and moved to Kom el-Dikka.

Standing in Midan Sa'ad Zaghlul, outside the Cecil Hotel, near the end of Rue Nebi Daniel, the Pharos lies ahead, with the vast area of the Royal Palace extended on a promontory to the right, some of it now lost beneath the sea. The position now occupied by Ramla Station in Midan Sa'ad Zaghlul is the site of the Caesareum, the Temple of Augustus. Nothing of it remains. Founded by Kleopatra in honour of Mark Antony, it stood near the shore at the centre of the great harbour, a lavish temple, with porticoes, propylaea, parks and libraries. With the adoption of Christianity, it became the Cathedral of Alexandria, and was finally destroyed in AD 912. In front of the temple stood two red granite obelisks. Carved for Thutmose III, they originally stood at Heliopolis and were transferred here in 13 BC, at the completion of the temple. Rather than being placed directly on their plinths, each stood on four massive bronze crabs (two of these have been recovered).

Though one fell in the earthquake of AD 1307, the other remained standing until the 19th century. Only then were these '**Kleopatra's Needles**' removed, the fallen one being sent in 1877 to London where it was set up on the Thames embankment. The other was despatched two years later to the USA, to adorn New York's Central Park.

One of the main foci of the city was the Serapeum, the Temple of Serapis, on the hill of Rhakote. Osiris had been worshipped here, and Serapis, who absorbed many of his characteristics, was also a deity of death and resurrection. Combining Egyptian features with aspects of some Greek gods—Zeus and Helios (solar), Hades (death), Asklepios (healing) and Dionysos (fertility)—Serapis became one of the most important deities of the Hellenistic and Roman worlds. The temple housed a library, not the Great Library, but nevertheless important. The Serapeum and its library were sacked by the Christians in AD 391. A number of temples were included in the complex and it is possible to visit some of the galleries which lay beneath the Temple of Anubis; here mummified jackals were buried. The site is dominated by **Pompey's Pillar**, a single monolith of Aswan granite set up in honour of the emperor Diocletian in AD 297, probably originally with a statue of him (perhaps equestrian) on top. European visitors in the Middle Ages thought that a ball containing the head of Pompey (slain on landing in Egypt in 48 BC) had been displayed here. A large number of sphinxes and statues are gathered here, some of which are New Kingdom and were brought from Delta sites. There are also two large red granite sphinxes, their features typical of the Ptolemaic kings, and some statues of priests of Isis and Serapis of Graeco-Roman date. A large diorite statue of the Apis bull, dating from the reign of

Hadrian, was removed to the Graeco-Roman Museum. In one corner of the site is the seven-metre statue of **Isis-Pharia**, found in 1961 in the sea near the Fort of Qaitbay, where its crown (1.9 metres high) and base, as well as parts of other companion statues, were found in 1994–1995.

The catacombs of **Kom el-Shugafa** are one of the most important surviving sites. Probably dating from the early second century AD, the complex is entered via a spiral staircase round an open well. A vestibule leads into the Rotunda, off which lies the Banqueting Hall for funerary feasts. A staircase leads down to a chamber with three sarcophagi; the architecture here is in the mixed style. This chamber was only ritually used: the bodies were actually placed in the surrounding passage, where niches could accommodate nearly 300 mummies. From the stairwell two other rooms can be reached, the Painted Tomb and the Hall of Caracalla. The former has Egyptian funerary deities and sphinxes delicately painted on stucco. The latter was thus named because when opened, it contained the skeletons of men and horses and was fancifully associated with one of the deeds of that emperor: on a visit to the city in AD 215, Caracalla had ordered a review of the city's youth on the pretext of creating a regiment in honour of Alexander; when they assembled he had them massacred. The hall is, in fact, another catacomb lined with tomb niches in the usual fashion.

The Anfoushy Necropolis, on the promontory of Ras el-Tin, has rock-cut tombs of the third to second centuries BC. The painted decoration includes imitation marble and alabaster panelling, geometrical designs and mythological scenes.

THE GRAECO-ROMAN MUSEUM

The museum contains thousands of objects, not all from the region. Often neglected, this museum well repays a long visit. There are many fascinating exhibits from the Graeco-Roman towns of the Faiyum region, which bring alive the ruins of such sites as Karanis and Dimai. A case of glass vessels is particularly exquisite, due in part to the lustrous quality, some of it produced by decay. Of the official monuments of the city, a room contains sculptures of the Ptolemies and Roman emperors. Of note are the colossal granite head of Ptolemy IV from Abu Qir, with curly hair, *nemes*-headdress and a rather oddly shaped double crown, originally with inlaid eyes; two heads of Ptolemy VI, one in Egyptian style with inlaid eyes and *nemes*-headdress, the other Hellenistic, in marble. Of the Roman emperors, there is a large marble head of Augustus, a statue of Marcus Aurelius from the area of the Zizinia Theatre, and a bronze head of Hadrian with inlaid eyes. There is a splendid collection of terracotta Tanagra figurines. Named after the city in north Greece where they were first excavated, they were probably made by Athenian artisans working in Alexandria. The most typical examples show a standing, draped female figure. They give a better impression of clothes and hairstyles of the period than the more formal statuary.

The museum courtyard has a mass of statues and fragments, including many Pharaonic pieces. Particularly notable are the rather woolly ram and the leg of a granite colossus of a Ptolemy in Pharaonic costume. Note also the colossal green granite head of a king in the guise of Osiris. This was discovered near Nuzha (in the southeast of the city) in the ruins of a temple which is often said to be the Thesmophorion (the Temple of Demeter-Isis), but the identification of this temple with the Thesmophorion remains uncertain, as the ruins form part of Augustus' new town of Nikopolis. Its companion, a queen as Isis, was removed to Belgium. Traditionally identified as Mark Antony and Kleopatra, they originally flanked the entrance to the temple. A small chapel of the crocodile god, Pnepheros, from Theadelphia in the Faiyum, has been reconstructed here: its wooden doors, frescoes and portable shrine are housed inside the museum.

SUEZ CANAL

lthough Suez is not a popular tourist destination, it has been an important city since the opening of the canal linking the Mediterranean with the Red Sea in 1869.

The idea of opening a canal between the Mediterranean and the Red Sea dates back to 2100 BC. The earliest attempt to connect the Red Sea with the Nile, and thereby with the Mediterranean, was undertaken by Nekau II (Necho) during the 26th Dynasty. According to Herodotos, 120,000 men lost their lives in this ambitious project, which was only abandoned when an oracle warned the king that invading foreigners would be the only ones to profit by it. In around 500 BC, Darius I completed the project. His canal ran from the Red Sea to the Great Bitter Lake and proceeded west to Bubastis, the modern-day Zagazig. The Ptolemies maintained the canal, and in AD 98, the Roman emperor Trajan improved it and extended it to Babylon (Old Cairo). Amr ibn al-As, the Arab conqueror of Egypt, restored the canal in order to supply Arabia with corn. It was abandoned 100 years later in order to starve out Medina which had revolted against the caliph. The canal then became unserviceable.

The Venetians frequently contemplated constructing a canal through the isthmus to recover the trade they had lost when the new route around the Cape of Good Hope was discovered. In 1671, Leibniz recommended the construction of such a canal to Louis XIV. The idea obsessed, amongst others, Sultan Mustafa III, Ali Bey, the Mamluk prince, and Napoleon Bonaparte, who, in 1798, undertook preliminary works, but as a result of a serious miscalculation by the chief engineer, Lepère, abandoned the project, thinking it was not feasible. A few decades later, the French Consul Ferdinand de Lesseps became convinced of the feasibility of the operation, but since neither Mohammed Ali nor his son, Abbas, gave permission for the work he had to wait for Ali's other son, Said Pasha, to be crowned. In 1854, the new ruler finally agreed to start the project. Work commenced in 1859 and was finished in November 1869. It was a magnificent inauguration, graced by a host of European princes and the Empress Eugénie herself. Giuseppe Verdi composed *Aïda* for the occasion, which was performed at the Cairo Opera Theatre.

Egypt's ruler, Khedive Ismail, had financed a third of the canal's construction, which contributed largely to his bankruptcy. In 1875, his shares were purchased by the British Government. The canal then became a focal point in the fight for the

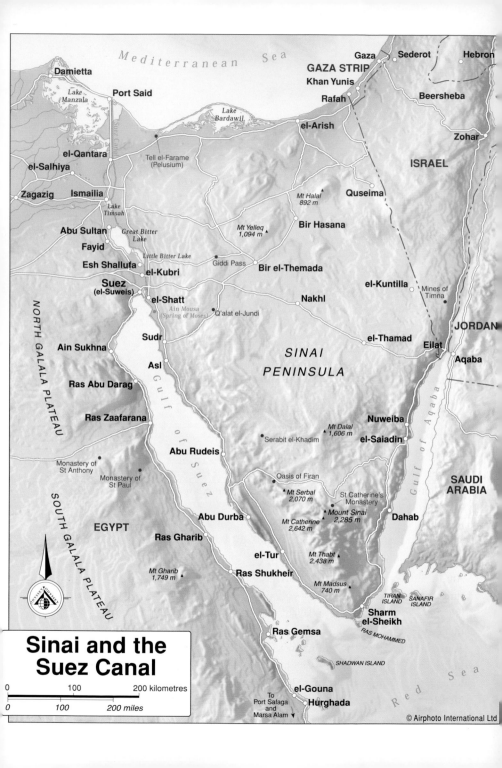

Mediterranean Sea

Damietta

Lake Manzala

Port Said

Lake Bardawil

GAZA STRIP

Gaza

Sederot

Hebron

Khan Yunis

Rafah

Beersheba

el-Arish

el-Qantara

Tell el-Farame (Pelusium)

ISRAEL

el-Salhiya

Zohar

Zagazig

Ismailia

Lake Timsah

Mt Halal 892 m

Quseima

Abu Sultan

Great Bitter Lake

Mt Yelleq 1,094 m

Bir Hasana

Fayid

Little Bitter Lake

Giddi Pass

Esh Shallufa

el-Kubri

Bir el-Themada

Suez (el-Suweis)

el-Shatt

Ain Mousa (Spring of Moses)

Q'alat el-Jundi

Nakhl

el-Kuntilla

Mines of Timna

NORTH GALALA PLATEAU

Ain Sukhna

Sudr

SINAI PENINSULA

el-Thamad

Eilat

JORDAN

Aqaba

Asl

Ras Abu Darag

Gulf of Suez

Ras Zaafarana

Mt Dalal 1,606 m

Nuweiba

Gulf of Aqaba

el-Saiadin

Abu Rudeis

Serabit el-Khadim

SAUDI ARABIA

Monastery of St Anthony

Monastery of St Paul

Oasis of Firan

Mt Serbal 2,070 m

St Catherine's Monastery

SOUTH GALALA PLATEAU

Abu Durba

Mt Catherine 2,642 m

Mount Sinai 2,285 m

Dahab

EGYPT

Ras Gharib

el-Tur

Mt Thabt 2,438 m

Mt Gharib 1,749 m

Ras Shukheir

Mt Madsus 740 m

TIRAN ISLAND

SANAFIR ISLAND

Sharm el-Sheikh

RAS MOHAMMED

Ras Gemsa

SHADWAN ISLAND

Red Sea

Sinai and the Suez Canal

0   100   200 kilometres

0   100   200 miles

el-Gouna

To Port Safaga and Marsa Alam

Hurghada

© Airphoto International Ltd

Suez Canal near Ismailia

independence of Egypt, which started at the onset of the 20th century and ended in 1952 with Nasser's revolution. In July 1956, Nasser nationalized the Suez Canal Company in reaction to the continued control of Egypt by the West and with the intention of using its enormous proceeds to construct the High Dam at Aswan. Israel, France and Britain invaded Egypt three months later, which the world considered an outrage, forcing the invaders to retreat. The Six Day (Arab–Israeli) war in 1967 closed the canal for eight years. In 1975, President Anwar Sadat officially reopened it after a year spent clearing it of some 700,000 mines with the help of 5,000 American, French and British soldiers. Today, an average of 90 ships a day pass through the canal, transporting 14 per cent of the world's trade. Average transit time is 15 hours. The ships cross at Ballah and the Bitter lakes where the canal widens. The increasing amount of traffic requires that continuous improvements be made. The Suez Canal is now 173 kilometres (107.5 miles) long—originally, it was 161 kilometres (100 miles) long—and no less than 200 metres (656 feet) wide at water level. Depth is never less than 20 metres (66 feet). Since the Red Sea and the Mediterranean are at the same level no locks are necessary.

CANAL TOWNS

The Isthmus of Suez may be visited by ship on an interesting 171-kilometre (106-mile) cruise, which departs from Suez and stops at Port Taufiq, Esh Shallufa, Gineifa, Le Deversoir, Serapeum, Ismailia, el-Gisr, el-Fidan, el-Qantara and Port Said. The crossing can also be made by car or train on the western bank. Trains depart from the Midan Ramses Station in Cairo and buses from Midan el-Tahrir.

ISMAILIA

From Cairo the fastest and most convenient way to Ismailia is the 128-kilometre (80-mile) route across the desert. A slow but fascinating route is by road through Bilbeis, along the course of the Ismailia Canal which offers glimpses of Delta life. Ismailia is also accessible from Cairo by rail. Travel time is two hours and 40 minutes and trains depart twice daily. There are also buses to Ismailia at the el-Olali Terminal. An alternative would be the so-called collective taxi, which departs when all seats are taken.

The city derives its name from Khedive Ismail, the sovereign nephew of Mohammed Ali, remembered for his contributions to the achievement of the Suez Canal project. Today, Ismailia is one of the most pleasant of Egyptian cities, evoking a turn-of-the-century charm with its cool, tree-lined boulevards graced by fashionable *fin-de-siècle* resort-inspired houses. Fortunately, the past wars have caused minimal damage, sparing its historic centre which sprawls along the shores of Lake Timsah (also known as the Lake of Crocodiles). During the closure of the canal, Ismailia lost half of its population, which diminished to a mere 200,000. The lake shore is dotted with well-kept public parks and lush gardens, among them the Garden of Stelae, where remarkable finds from various archaeological excavations are to be found. Many of the excavated materials are attributed to Ramesses II. After years of closure to the public on account of war, the museum has been reopened, displaying a wide collection of interesting treasures covering the long span of Egypt's past from prehistory to the Byzantine era. A stone sphinx guards the entrance to the museum.

There is a swimming club along the canal, offering refreshments, a sandy beach and a good view of passing ships. North of the city are numerous resorts and clubs equipped with water sports facilities.

PORT SAID

Established in 1859 as a base for the construction and operation of the canal, Port Said lies 80 kilometres (50 miles) north of Ismailia at the mouth of the canal on the Mediterranean. Named Port Said in honour of Said Pasha, the city occupies a strip of land between the Mediterranean and the vast, brackish Lake Manzala. Although the city is lacking in places of particular artistic or archaeological interest, it offers the best location for viewing the canal.

SUEZ

Some 88 kilometres (55 miles) from Ismailia and 134 kilometres (83 miles) from Cairo, Suez (el-Suweis) is situated on the southern end of the canal. It was heavily damaged during the 1967 and 1973 wars. Suez is now an industrial centre producing petrochemicals, fertilizers and cement. These factories and industrial complexes are concentrated around Port Tanfiq. The small park situated along the canal affords excellent views of the Red Sea and Sinai. The Ataga Hills (Gebel Ataga) to the southwest are also scenic. Suez also offers very good views of the ships passing through the canal.

EASTERN DESERT AND THE RED SEA COAST

AIN SUKHNA

Some 55 kilometres (34 miles) south of Suez is the town of Ain Sukhna, the nearest bathing resort to Cairo, once famous for its silver sand and many types of fish and coral. The landscape is partially disfigured by the immense cistern of a huge oil pipeline that carries raw material from the Red Sea to Alexandria. Apart from the bathing facilities, the hot thermal springs of the sulphuric type are also famous.

RAS ZAAFARANA

A further 70 kilometres (43.5 miles) south on a narrow winding road overlooking the sea is Ras Zaafarana, a small port with a lighthouse and a petrol station, situated at the headland of the same name, on the outlet of the modest Wadi Araba. A secondary road departs from Ras Zaafarana heading west, along which, after about 30 kilometres (19 miles) on the left-hand side, you meet the crossroads of the **Monastery of St Anthony**, or Deir Mar Antonius.

After a further 14 kilometres (8.7 miles) of road, you will come to this most ancient monastery in Egypt. St Anthony (*c*.AD 252–356) was born near Ehnasiya (Herakleopolis) in Middle Egypt. Anthony's contemporary, St Athanasius, the Patriarch of Alexandria, recorded his life in the first classic of Christian biography. Anthony came from a wealthy family, and at the age of twenty he inherited a fortune. After hearing a reading of Matthew XIX: 21 in church, he gave everything to the poor, and took up the ascetic life, eventually finding a cave in the Red Sea hills. Here he was tormented by the flatteries and temptations of the devil. This has formed the subject of many fine paintings, particularly by artists of the northern European schools, and inspired a number of literary works, most notably Gustave Flaubert's *La Tentation de St Antoine*.

Christian monasticism originated in the Egyptian desert before spreading to other countries. At the request of his followers, St Anthony abandoned his solitary life for a period of a few years in order to establish a monastic community, the first in Christendom. He then retuned to his solitary ways. Shortly after, St Pachomius, a disciple of the great spiritual leader St Palomen, founded a number of communities

An irrigation canal, Qena

in Upper Egypt, around Nag Hammadi, itself an important seat of Gnosticism. Pachomius established the rules of the monastic life, forbidding the more extreme self-indulgent exhibitions of 'mortification of the flesh' that had become characteristic amongst ascetics (St Palomen was said to have died from excessive fasting). These regulations set times for eating, prayer, work and sleep, and established the monastic communities as examples of spiritual life without excess.

The Monastery of St Anthony is surrounded by high walls, and has frequently suffered attack in its history. Extensive conservation work here, carried out by the American Research Center in Cairo, was completed in 2001. The first building dates back to the fourth century, but little of this remains except for the southern walls and the church dedicated to St Anthony, built by his disciples on the place where he was buried. The walls are adorned with paintings (12th or 13th century) showing St George, and the fathers of the church. Walls enclose everything necessary to the monastery's life: a spring, a garden, an orchard, a mill and a library. The Bedouins, who occupied the monastery at the end of the 15th century, deliberately destroyed much of the library's contents by using it as fuel for their kitchens, which they placed in the old church of St Anthony. After this invasion, the normal life of the monastery was resumed, but without its previous prosperity. About 30 monks live here today. The cave (*magharah*) of St Anthony can be visited by following a steep footpath climbing the mountain for about 400 metres (1,313 feet) above the monastery. The walk offers some excellent views of the valley.

Returning to the coast road and continuing south from Ras Zaafarana, after about 25 kilometres (15.5 miles), you will meet the crossroad that leads to the **Monastery of St Paul** or Deir Mar Boulos. After following an unasphalted road for about 10 kilometres (6.2 miles) and crossing a steep ridge, you reach a monastery, similar to that of St Anthony, though smaller and less rich. St Paul of Thebes was an older contemporary of St Anthony. Coptic iconography often associates both saints, showing them with the raven, which, according to tradition, brought St Paul his daily bread during his 60-year-long hermitage. (St Paul is believed to have lived from AD 228 to 342.) The monastery has had few alterations through the centuries, thus keeping its homogeneous and ancient aspect, even though the frescoes adorning the church of St Paul were badly restored at the beginning of the 18th century. The church was built over the cave where the saint lived and where his remains are kept.

There are other churches inside the monastery's walls. St Michael's is the biggest, built in the 17th century. The monastery has a spring, mills, ovens, gardens and orchards within its walls. From the hill there is a panoramic view of the Red Sea down to the massive Mountain of Moses in Sinai. The colours are fantastic, especially at sunset.

Another 80 kilometres (50 miles) along the well-surfaced coastal road is the oil zone of Ras Gharib, surrounded by the massive Gebel Gharib, a mountain range 1,749 metres (5,800 feet) high. There are 150 oil wells here. At Ras Gemsa, 330 kilometres (205 miles) from Suez, a headland marks the end of the Gulf of Suez. Opposite the headland, the small Tawila islands face Ras Mohammed, the southernmost part of Sinai. On the eastern slope of the plateau of Abu Sar el-Qibli, 55 kilometres (34 miles) from Ras Mohammed, are the ruins of ancient Myos Hormos, once an important harbour on the Red Sea. Much of it is now buried in sand. From here a rough road leads to Qena through 200 kilometres (124 miles) of stark desert back to the Nile.

HURGHADA

Hurghada (el-Ghardaga) is the major tourist destination on this part of the coast. Until a few years ago, this was a modest fishing village; today it boasts major oil installations, military posts and an airport with daily flights to Cairo. The small town of Hurghada is not particularly attractive, consisting of low houses overlooked by minarets of small mosques and the governor's palace. The **Institute of Hydrobiology** is very interesting. Do not miss the aquarium and museum with their complete collections of flora and fauna of the Red Sea. From here you can hire a boat for a trip to the coral reefs. The Red Sea's warm waters are an ideal habitat for rare species of fish and fascinating coral reefs which may be observed through the bottoms of these boats. The *reis* (captain) manoeuvres the *houri* (boat) expertly over the reefs and shallows. Hurghada offers full scuba-diving facilities as well as three- and four-star resort hotels.

ISLANDS AND AQUASPORTS ACTIVITIES OFF HURGHADA

1   Shadwan Island: Diving, snorkelling, fishing. No swimming.
2   Shaab Abu Shiban: Diving from boat, snorkelling, swimming.
3   Shaab el-Erg: Diving from boat, all kinds of fishing, snorkelling.
4   Umm Gammar Island: Professional diving, snorkelling.
5   Shasb Saghir Umm Gammae: Diving.

6 Careless Reef: Diving.
7 Giftun el-Kabir Island: Beaches, snorkelling, diving, fishing, swimming.
8 Giftun el-Saghir Island: Beaches, snorkelling, diving, fishing, swimming.
9 Abu Ramada Island: Diving.
10 Shaab Abu Ramada: Fishing.
11 Dishet el-Dhaba: Beaches, swimming.
12 Shaab Abu Hashish: Diving, snorkelling, swimming, fishing, beach.
13 Sharm el-Arab: Diving, swimming, fishing.
14 Abu Minqar Island: Beaches, swimming.

From Hurghada you can arrange an excursion to **Mons Porphyrites**, the 'Mountain of Porphyry'. It is a 130-kilometre (81-mile) journey south, and includes a return trip which requires trekking through rough terrain. The Romans mined the nearby 1,661-metre (5,451-foot) Gebel Abu Dukhan (Father of Smoke) for porphyry. This beautiful purple-red stone was used in temples, baths, sarcophagi and statues in the imperial city. The emperor Hadrian erected a temple at the quarries, as well as houses for the workers, most of which are now in total ruin. Much is now known about the work and communities here and at Mons Claudianus from excavation and survey work carried out over the past 20 years.

PORT SAFAGA

Sixty kilometres (37 miles) from Hurghada (460 kilometres or 286 miles from Suez) is Port Safaga, or Bur Safaga. This small port town has 7,000 inhabitants. It has a fine beach, faced by a small island. There is a scuba centre with instructors and a scuba equipment hire service; fishing boats may be hired for trips to the nearby islands and reefs. The most interesting excursion you can make from here, though, is to Mons Claudianus.

Since 2002 a restriction has been operating on travel in the whole of the Eastern Desert: south of Aswan this covered the entire area between the Red Sea and the Nile Valley, in Upper Egypt it affects the road through the Wadi Hammamat, and all regions south. It is advisable to seek local advice before attempting to travel in these areas.

MONS CLAUDIANUS

The 'Mountain of Claudius' can be reached by following a surfaced road up from Port Safaga to the turning on the right for the Roman camp in the Wadi Umm Husein. The round trip from Port Safaga is 95 kilometres (59 miles). Quartz diorite gneiss was

Coptic priest with Bible, Qena

quarried here during the Roman Period. During the reign of Nero and in the time of Hadrian and Trajan, buildings in Imperial Rome were decorated with architectural elements hewn out of the granite. In Rome, one can still see them in the columns of the portico of the Pantheon, in Hadrian's Villa, in public baths built by Diocletian and in the columns and floor of the Temple of Venus, amongst other places. The site on Mons Claudianus has a Roman camp, dwellings, workshops, stables and a *dromos*. A temple erected by Trajan on a further elevated site has collapsed in ruins, but the remains of a staircase leading to it can still be seen. The camp was surrounded by a granite wall with defence towers at the corners. The entire site was well protected from Bedouin attacks. Northeast of the camp was a bath and a temple, and there were walls all around the camp. In the quarries, you can still see blocks of stones among unfinished flooring slabs, architraves and inscribed columns.

The new 175-kilometre (109-mile) road from Port Safaga to **Qena** is well surfaced, running through the valleys in the Eastern Desert, where gold was mined and granite quarried during Pharaonic times. It is a very beautiful drive. From the Red Sea coast, the road to Qena is the best route for visiting the Nile Valley sites between Dendera and Luxor. In antiquity, the Eastern Desert routes between the Nile and the Red Sea were vital for trade with the seaports and the land of Punt (probably in the region of modern-day Ethiopia, Eritrea and Sudan).

QOSEIR

Eighty-five kilometres (53 miles) further on is the small port of Qoseir. Known as the 'White Harbour' during Ptolemaic times, Qoseir was the end of the desert route for caravans crossing the Wadi Hammamat. Later the town was fortified by Sultan Selim. Until the 19th century it was the starting point for pilgrims travelling to Mecca.

Today, its narrow streets are lined with colourful bazaars with a distinct Bedouin flavour, and you can take boat trips from here to the long coral reef opposite the port. Qoseir is also an important port for the export of phosphate. A 220-kilometre (137-mile) road links the port town with Qena.

The road to **Quft**, 190-kilometres (118-miles) long, is generally smooth and crosses the desert through the famous **Wadi Hammamat**, the 'Rehenu Valley' of the Egyptians, who quarried its hard, dark stone for the statues and sarcophagi of the pharaohs, particularly during the Old and Middle Kingdoms. This was the Niger or Thebaicus Lapis of the ancients. Layers of Nubian sandstone embedded with primary crystalline rocks rise to peaks of up to 2,000 metres (6,564 feet). During the Pharaonic period, these hard stones, breccia, black and green basalt were intensively quarried, along with carnelian and rock crystal. Qoseir was a busy port and ships from the Sinai Peninsula brought turquoise and malachite. There was also a great deal of trading activity with the legendary land of Punt. The caravan route across the desert ran from Leukos Limen (Qoseir) on the Red Sea coast to Koptos (Quft) in the Nile Valley. After crossing the Wadi Adi Ambanga, the road continues along the Wadi Beida, and climbs the mountain to el-Itema-Hokheben, passing the Wadi Rosafa which is marked by a large well, and finally through the Wadi Abu Siran. The road now climbs to the top of a rugged pass. On the way down is **Bir Es Sidd**, where the Ababda Bedouins live near a spring. They were originally nomads belonging to the Baga Bedouin tribe, but have now settled here, raising goats, camels and sheep. Beyond Bir Es Sidd are the formidable Hammamat mountains. Near Bir el-Hammamat, in an area settled during the Roman times, are interesting fragments of unfinished sarcophagi, and granite was also quarried here in ancient times. One of the earliest expeditions to Hammamat took place during the reign of King Isesi in the Fifth Dynasty. Later Menthuhotep III followed suit and sent his men to the quarry. Under Ramesses IV, more than 8,000 soldiers and labourers were employed to procure blocks of sandstone and granite for the Temple of Amun in Thebes. In the valleys, one can find rocks with inscriptions left by ancient expeditions describing their great undertakings, their prayers and thanks to the gods. There are representations of the sacred boat of Sokar and stelae depicting the king in prayer. In the pass of Mutraq Es-Selam is a commemorative inscription of Amenhotep IV flanked by graffiti scrawled by travellers, quarrymen, soldiers and Bedouins. Further on, at Qasr el-Banat, are sandstone rocks with inscriptions in Greek, Arabic and Coptic. The Qasr el-Banat is actually a rock eroded to the shape of a tower, whence the name of the place meaning 'Castle of Maidens' is derived. The road passes the ruins of a Roman watering station and arrives at Laqeita, a village of the Ababda Bedouins. The Roman road, Via Publica, which linked Koptos (Quft) and Berenike, once crossed here. There is a fragmentary inscription bearing the name of Tiberius near the principal well. The road continues on to Quft. From here one can reach Qena by following the line of ruined semaphore towers built by Mohammed Ali and used as signalling towers for transmitting messages. Because the road from Qoseir and Marsa Alam is rather bad, make sure your vehicle is in excellent running condition and take along an extra supply of petrol and plenty of drinking water.

DIVING IN THE RED SEA

ALL ABOARD THE LIVEABOARD

On the Red Sea, few miles north of the Sudanese border, our inflatable dinghy whisks us the hundred metres to the drop-off point over Fury Shoal. The sun is barely over the horizon. On a count of three we slide backwards into the inky blue waters.

At 30 metres we level off, having lost sight of the reef. In all directions there is just the blue. Brilliant, mysterious, its intensity dazzles us as and we hang there waiting, watching. After what seems like an eternity our dive guide points below. We descend another few metres. At first we can see nothing other than the blue. Then a shadow and a vague shape emerges, a thin grey brushstroke on a deep blue, almost plum, canvas. Sharks, grey, sleek, dangerous and beautiful, they emerge from the depths, first the white tips and then the hammerheads.

Welcome to the world of liveaboard diving in some of the best waters that the planet has to offer. Liveaboard diving, essentially a scuba-diving cruise boat—you stay on the boat rather than a hotel—has increased dramatically in popularity over the last few years and Marsa Alam is fast becoming the new liveaboard capital of the Red Sea. Situated midway between Hurghada and the Sudanese border, the low-key resort has benefited from the opening of an international airport in 2002. Charter flights arrive from all over Europe and domestic flights from Cairo, the region's major international airport.

The Red Sea is part of the Indo-Pacific Coral Reef region, which includes the world's richest marine life, and it draws divers from all over the world. Some of the Red Sea's best and most pristine dive sites are located in the 'Deep South', as the area south of Marsa Alam is known.

Until the opening of the airport, Marsa Alam was pretty much a dusty isolated one-horse town with just a couple of hotels and a dive safari camp. Now luxury hotels are sprouting up everywhere and there is a brand new port from where the liveaboards depart. Marsa Alam also boasts some of the best shore diving on the Red Sea, and none better than at Red Sea Diving Safari's Ecolodge Shargra Village, a dive safari camp, a few kilometres outside Marsa Alam (redsea-divingsafari.com).

Hossan Helmy, Red Sea's proprietor, has been surveying and diving these waters since 1988, which has enabled him to grab the best fringing reef on the coast. The dive camp has two types of traditional Egyptian accommodation, *madyafah* chalets and *mandarah* bungalows, and well as tents for the budget-conscious guest. The camp organizes daily trips for shore-based diving along the coast and day-boat diving to some of the best reefs in the Red Sea, including the legendary Elphinstone and Dolphin reefs. Divers can opt for unlimited diving on the 'house' reef. Just kit up, walk the five metres to the water, plop in, and voilà... paradise. Hossan is probably the most knowledgeable and environmentally aware person on the whole coast. He is a great host and even if you are not staying at the safari village, drop in and see him.

Relaxing at Marsa Alam, the new centre for 'serious' Red Sea diving, ideal for both liveaboard and shore-based diving.

Marsa Alam is developing as a resort in its own right, attracting visitors from all over Europe, particularly as a winter break destination. The hotels are largely self-contained, providing a variety of activities and entertainment. Most guests never leave the hotel unless it is to go diving. Marsa Alam is a great place to learn to dive; courses and dive packages are usually cheaper if pre-booked with the tour operator. Marsa Alam has the only recompression chamber south of Hurghada. A road is being constructed that leads straight to the Nile Valley, but due to the security situation and logistical problems it is not yet open. But Allah willing it should be by early 2005.

The image of liveaboards has improved dramatically over the past few years. Once the preserve of dive club fanatics, boring everyone with tall tales of wreck diving in freezing, murky Scottish waters, they now increasingly appeal to the humble recreational diver. The Red Sea also boasts some of the most luxurious, state-of-the-art dive boats to be found anywhere, ideal for divers and non-divers alike.

Most of the liveaboards that depart from Marsa Alam are of seven-day duration, although the Ecolodge also offers three-day excursions, ideal for those wishing to combine with a hotel. There are a variety of liveaboard excursions available, including to The Brothers, probably the best-known dive site in the Red Sea. Other itineraries include the Offshore Marine Park Islands and the increasingly popular 'Deep South' trips. Fury Shoal and St John's Reef have some of the most spectacular and pristine hard corals to be found anywhere in the world.

Egypt has the greatest temperature change of any tropical waters in the world. It only warms up for a very brief period of time each year. That is why, unlike much of Asia and the Pacific, where the effects of El Niño have caused widespread coral bleaching, the Red Sea corals, both hard and soft, are in superb condition. The southern diving differs from the traditional 'wall' diving found further north. On St John's Reef there are an abundance of ergs and habilis. These pinnacles rise majestically from the depths in a subaqua lunar landscape. On many of the reefs in the south, yours may be the only boats there, a far cry from the often-overcrowded northern reefs.

The most southerly dive camp in Egypt is operated by our friends at Red Sea Diving Safaris at Marsa Wadi Lahami. This will appeal to those who really want to escape the shackles of mass tourism. If you dream of solitude, sea, sand and desert then look no further. Eat, sleep and dive.

The best way to book dive holidays in Egypt is through specialist dive operators, usually staffed by divers (conventional travel agents rarely have first-hand knowledge of diving products) and from the Internet. Oonas Divers (+44 (0) 1323 648924; oonasdivers.com) in the UK are a long-established dive operator with a long association with Red Sea Diving Safaris. Libra Holidays/Goldenjoy offer both hotel and liveaboard diving holidays at most Red Sea destinations (libraholidays.co.uk).

The best hotel in Marsa Alam is the Iberotel Coraya Beach Resort (accessible through hotels.net).

The cost of diving in Egypt compares favourably with other destinations. Although not quite as cheap as Southeast Asia, in general standards are higher and equipment better.

Other Egyptian Dive Destinations

Hurghada

Hurghada is a sprawling resort spread out over 20 kilometres of coastline. It is not an attractive resort and lacks much character, but has some fabulous hotels (as well as plenty of budget accommodation), excellent reefs and some world-class wreck diving. It is also just a three-hour drive from Luxor and the Nile Valley.

El-Gouna

Just 20 kilometres north of Hurghada, el-Gouna is ideal for those who find Hurghada too large and impersonal. It is far more tasteful and better planned than Hurghada.

Safaga

Located south of Hurghada, Safaga is a pleasant, laid-back resort that, once again, will appeal to those wishing to escape the frenetic pace of Hurghada.

Sharm el-Sheikh

Located near the tip of the Sinai Peninsula, Sharm el-Sheikh is an attractive resort with plenty of non-diving activities available. The best of the Red Sea hotels are here, and it has some truly world-class dive sites such as Ras Mohammed, as well as some superb sites in the Straits of Tiran. The Thistlegorm, one of the world's top wrecks, is within striking distance. Sharm el-Sheikh also boast the best nightlife in the Red Sea and is ideal for those looking for more than just diving.

Dahab

Situated 80 kilometres north of Sharm el-Sheikh, Dahab is the backpacking chill-zone in the Middle East. Incredibly cheap accommodation (as low as $2 a night) and a laid-back atmosphere attracts travellers and hippies like bees to honey. The diving is largely shore based, accessed by four-wheel-drive vehicles, and the legendary Dahab Blue Hole is renowned worldwide. Adrenaline junkies be warned: many divers attempting to dive through an archway at 65 metres that connects the Blue Hole to the open sea tragically lose their lives.

Useful Websites

egypttreasures.gov.eg (This is the official Egyptian Tourism Ministry site)

hotels.net

libraholidays.co.uk

oonasdivers.com

redsea.com

redsea-divingsafari.com

© Christopher Coplans, January 2004

Further along this road is the small fishing port of **Marsa Mubarak**. At the end of the wadi, seven kilometres (4.4 miles) away, are the ancient gold mines of Umm Rus. Further along the coast is Marsa Alam.

The small port of **Marsa Alam** boasts an ideal fishing centre with organized trips for anglers. Sharks, lobsters, turtles and muraena are among the great catches. There is a rest house at the port. From Marsa Alam, 230 kilometres (143 miles) of desert road leads to Edfu. This road goes through Wadi Abu Karalia to Bir Besah. From this area, beautifully encircled by mountains, the road passes the ruins of ancient mines, then proceeds to Wadi Barramiya and finally into the Wadi Miah and the Temple of el-Kanayis.

Discovered in 1816 by Frédéric Cailliaud, the **Temple of el-Kanayis** in Wadi Miah was built by Sety I near an ancient watering station and was dedicated to the god, Amun-Ra. The vestibule is built of sandstone blocks with four papyrus columns adorned with bud-capitals. The central span of the ceiling is decorated with vultures. Reliefs on the walls depict scenes of the king's victories over Nubians and Asiatics. The next chamber was hewn out of rock, with four square pillars and reliefs on the walls recording the sinking of the wells, the building of the temple and the king's offering to the gods. In the rear wall there are three niches. The central niche was dedicated to Amun, the left one to Sety, and the one on the right to Ra-Harakhty. This sanctuary is similar to those in the Ramesside rock temples in Nubia. To the east, on an adjoining rock, are three stelae. The first has an Asiatic goddess on horseback; the second has a dedication of the official in charge of the sinking of the well; and the third shows Yuny, Viceroy of Nubia, kneeling before the king. On a higher rock is an inscription of an earlier viceroy, Merymose, dating from the time of Amenhotep III.

The coastal road from Marsa Alam to the Sudanese border is bad; 145 kilometres (90 miles) from Marsa Alam is Berenike, the last Egyptian town before the border crossing.

BERENIKE

S ituated on the bay of Ras Benas, Berenike was built on coral and founded by Ptolemy II Philadelphos in about 275 BC. He named the town after his mother, establishing it as an important entrepôt for trading with the ports on the eastern shore of the Red Sea and those in the Indian Ocean. Berenike was then as vital as Myos Hormos as a port town. However, the ruins of a temple of Serapis,

Potters at work, Qena

built by Trajan and Tiberius, are all that is left of its ancient glory. A representation on the external wall shows Emperor Tiberius before the god Min, and another depicts offerings to the tutelary deity of the Green Mine. In fact, just north of Berenike, in the desert near Wadi Sakeit, are the remains of ancient emerald mines which were worked until the Middle Ages. Today Berenike is famous for its fishing, and has some of Egypt's best health spas. Berenike is accessible by bus from Luxor, Hurghada, Safaga and Qena. Beyond Berenike, a track leads to Halayib, on the border of Sudan. You can also reach this point by way of a desert road from Kom Ombo.

Sinai Peninsula

T he Sinai Peninsula is a rugged triangle of desert and mountain flanked by the two gulfs of the Red Sea. From the Early Dynastic period onwards, the pharaohs sent expeditions here in search of copper and turquoise. The goddess Hathor, as the 'Lady of Turquoise', became the guardian of the region, and temples were raised in her honour near the turquoise and copper mines. The first written alphabet in history, Protosemitic, was used in inscriptions here.

Sinai is a land of mountains rising to over 2,600 metres (8,530 feet), but it also offers some of the finest unspoilt beaches of the Red Sea and the Mediterranean. The temperatures reach 42°C (107°F) in the summer.

Today, promising oilfields have taken the place of turquoise and copper as a source of wealth. The areas of Abu Rudeis and el-Arish are rich in oil deposits and the near future should see a considerable increase of population as new installations are established. The main places of interest in Sinai are Wadi Maghara, Serabit el-Khadim, and, of course, the Monastery of St Catherine and the Wadi Firan.

Turquoise was mined at Wadi Maghara and at Serabit el-Khadim. Although the inscriptional evidence emphasizes the precious stone, there is evidence that copper was mined and smelted at the same sites. Numerous inscriptions record Egyptian expeditions from the Early Dynastic period to the end of the New Kingdom. Some of these inscriptions were removed to Cairo (Egyptian Museum).

At Serabit el-Khadim there is a temple dedicated to the goddess Hathor, guardian and patroness of the miners. It is unusual in design, having a series of long narrow halls added in front of the sanctuary at different periods. Official stelae and gifts were presented to the temple by the mining expeditions. Amongst the many royal monuments, Thutmose III and Hatshepsut are particularly prominent. A superb head broken from a small statue depicting Queen Tiye, wife of Amenhotep III, was found in excavations here (Cairo, Egyptian Museum). There is also a temple of Sopdu, the god who presided over the eastern borders of Egypt. The celebrated inscriptions in the Protosemitic script were discovered here.

The other focus of Egyptian mining activity in Sinai was at Timna (now in Israel). This site also had a temple dedicated to Hathor, where official expeditions and their workers left numerous inscriptions and votive objects. The evidence from Timna dates its exploitation to the New Kingdom, activity coming to an end in the middle of the 20th Dynasty, in the reign of Ramesses VI or VII.

GULF OF AQABA TOWNS

SHARM EL-SHEIKH

On the southernmost tip of Sinai is one of the most accessible destinations on the peninsula, linked to Cairo by efficient public transport. At Naama Beach, eight kilometres (five miles) away, there are a couple of three-star hotels and a campsite. **Ras Mohammed** provides a commanding view of Asia on the left and Africa on the right. Once an important city, Ras Mohammed was the point of arrival for pilgrims heading for Mecca. Further down the coastal road is Nabq. Here, a sparkling stretch of beach is refreshed by mangroves. Nearby you can see the exotic colours of a Bedouin encampment shimmering in the sun. The **Fort of Nasrani**, within the same area, offers panoramic vistas of the islets of Tiran, scattered at the mouth of the Gulf of Aqaba.

DAHAB

Further on lies Dahab, another 'pearl' of the gulf which has become the focus of tourism development plans. Swaying palms, fine sands and an extraordinary underwater landscape are the major attractions. Snorkelling is a popular sport here. A few kilometres beyond, towards the Israeli border, is the Island of Coral, marked by the ruins of a fort built by the Crusaders. Boat trips can be arranged. The coastal road is relaxing and beautiful, winding through long stretches of beach, coves and deserted rocky promontories. Dahab has a three-star hotel.

NUWEIBA

Ninety-two kilometres (57 miles) north of Sharm el-Sheikh is another good place for underwater fun. You will see both the imposing mountains of the Sinai and green oases along palm-fringed beaches. Nuweiba has a three-star hotel.

Further up the western coast of the Gulf of Aqaba is **Taba**, right next to the Israeli port of Eilat. The resort town boasts the luxurious Sonesta Beach Hotel. These towns dotted along the coast of the Gulf of Aqaba offer some of the world's best scuba diving.

BIBLICAL SINAI

The most famous historical event in Sinai is the 'Exodus' of the Israelites led by Moses. Although there is no direct archaeological evidence to corroborate the biblical narrative, it has generally been dated to the reign of the pharaoh Merneptah (*c.*1213–1203 BC), son of Ramesses II. This date rests solely on

Madonna and Child, St Catherine's Monastery

two pieces of evidence. The biblical record states that the Israelites were set to work on the city of Per-Ramesses in the Delta, which was built in the reigns of Sety I and Ramesses II, and it has therefore been understood that the latter was the 'Pharaoh who knew not Joseph'. The so-called 'Israel Stele' of Merneptah, discovered at Thebes and now in the Egyptian Museum, Cairo, is actually a record of a Libyan war, but names Israel amongst the states of southwestern Asia that greet the pharaoh: Israel was, therefore, no longer in Egypt. There is no archaeological evidence to support this 19th Dynasty date for the events. Indeed, the traditional date for the Exodus calculated from other biblical evidence is much earlier, 1445 BC. This derives from the statement that Solomon completed the temple in Jerusalem 480 years after the Israelites left Egypt: Solomon's temple can be dated to around 965 BC. This would place the Exodus in the reign of Amenhotep II, in the 18th Dynasty. The lack of Egyptian evidence, both archaeological and textual, has long been a mystery, and has been explained in many ways, some writers even suggest that it may not have been a real historical event. Perhaps, as some scholars have argued, there is something in the ancient tradition (preserved in writers such as Josephos) that the Israelites were connected with the Hyksos, and that the Exodus took place at the beginning of the 18th Dynasty when the Hyksos were driven out of Egypt.

Whenever the Exodus happened, a host of miraculous events is described during the arduous journey in search of the 'Promised Land'. Foremost was the parting of the Red Sea, permitting their passage into the forbidding Sinai Peninsula which was bereft of life and vegetation. Heavenly manna, however, rained on them, appeasing their hunger, and to quench their thirst Moses produced water by striking a rock with his staff. The final divine gesture manifested itself when, after having reached the heights of **Gebel Mousa**, also known as the Mountain of Moses or Mount Sinai, Moses received the Ten Commandments.

Sinai was the birthplace of the deep-rooted Judaeo-Christian tradition. Many of the places here are mentioned in biblical stories and are still identifiable today in the stark, mysterious landscape. The miracles and mysteries of Sinai do not end with the story of Moses. The remains of St Catherine, the martyred Christian from Alexandria, are believed to have been transported by angels to Mount Catherine, or Gebel Katerin, from whence it was taken to the celebrated monastery that now carries her name.

Thirty-seven kilometres (23 miles) from Suez is el-Shatt, which faces the industrial zone of Port Taufiq. Eight kilometres (five miles) beyond, a road on the right takes you a kilometre further to the Spring of Moses (Ain Mousa). Twelve springs of water irrigate

(right) *St Catherine's Monastery, Mount Sinai in the background*
(preceding pages) *Mountains above St Catherine's Monastery*

the small but luxuriantly verdant oasis. Tradition claims that the southernmost spring was sweetened when Moses threw a log into it (Exodus 15: 25).

The **Oasis of Firan** (ancient Pharan) lies 208 kilometres (129 miles) from Suez and is the largest and most fertile on the peninsula. The oasis is situated near the foot of Gebel Serbal, 2,078 metres (6,820 feet) high, and extends for over four kilometres (2.5 miles). It has a settled population, and is cultivated with date palms, tamarisk, maize and other cereals. There is evidence for settlement by the Nabataeans here, probably from the second century BC to the time of annexation of their kingdom and principal city, Petra, by the emperor Trajan in AD 106. The population of Firan converted to Christianity in the early fourth century AD and the town became a focus for pilgrims, as it is the supposed site of the battle between the Israelites and the Amalekites. Egeria, a noble lady of Aquitaine, who left an account of her extensive pilgrimage to the Holy Land in the late fourth century, recorded that, at Firan, she was shown the place where Moses sat with his arms raised to heaven, supported by Aaron and Hur, to invoke God's aid while Joshua led the Israelites to victory (Exodus 17: 8–16). This site may be identified with the chapel (probably fourth century) that stands on top of Gebel Takhuna, which dominates Firan. Here also is the place where Moses struck a boulder with his staff to supply water to the thirsty Israelites (Exodus 17: 2–7). By the sixth century, Firan was the seat of a bishop, and there are ruins of a basilica and several churches of that period. One of the churches was dedicated to Saints Cosmas and Damian, who were martyred in the reign of Diocletian. They were doctors, and this church has buildings attached that show it served as a hospital and hostel for pilgrims.

From the Oasis of Firan, the road passes through valleys and gorges before rising in a succession of hairpin bends over an area covered with tamarisk and manna trees, named after the biblical manna. After crossing the rugged pass of el-Buweid, one enters the Wadi Sheikh. Here is the tomb of Nebi Saleh, where Bedouin pilgrims flock annually. Twelve kilometres (7.5 miles) on is the **Chapel of Aaron** (Harun) where the Golden Calf is said to have been fashioned. From Wadi Sheikh, a six-kilometre (3.7-mile) track leads to the Monastery of St Catherine, situated at the foot of Mount Sinai (Gebel Mousa).

MONASTERY OF ST CATHERINE

The Greek Orthodox Monastery of St Catherine stands in a valley surrounded by Gebel Safsaga, Gebel Katerin and Gebel Mousa. In AD 342, the Empress Helen, the mother of Constantine I the Great, ordered a chapel to be built here on the site where God revealed himself to Moses in the form of the Burning Bush. The site became a

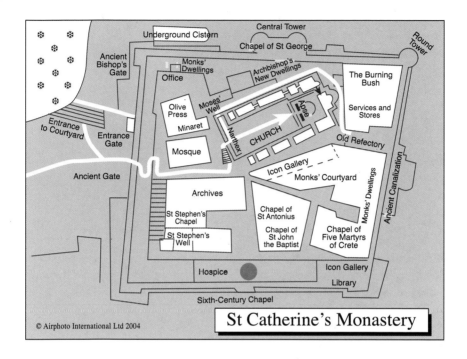

St Catherine's Monastery

© Airphoto International Ltd 2004

focus of pilgrimage and the area was enclosed with a fortified wall in about AD 537 at the order of the emperor Justinian I, who also built the Church of the Virgin and, later, in 562, the Basilica of the Transfiguration.

A veritable fortress with rampart walls, the monastery successfully protected monks throughout history from marauding Bedouins. Hermits and pilgrims met here to retrace the path of the Exodus, safe from attack by soldiers. The monastery has preserved its special character. The thick walls are 12 to 15 metres (40 to 50 feet) high. The door that now serves as the entrance was built at a much later period: initially, there was only a small door nine metres (30 feet) off the ground, from where provisions necessary to the monks' survival were lifted in through a system of pulleys. The monks, in turn, often fed nomads who rested outside the walls. Inside the great walls are buildings from different eras, with small yards, kitchen gardens and stairs crossed by narrow climbing streets. In this centre of Christian faith there is also a mosque, probably built in the 11th century for the servants of the monastery. In the mosque are a wooden throne with Kufic inscriptions (a form of Arabic script) and a *minbar* of the Fatimid Period. Both items date from the reign of the seventh Fatimid Caliph, al-Mustali (AD 1094–1101).

A Fatimid-style 11th-century gate leads to the long arcaded porch of the **Basilica**, and then to a sixth-century Byzantine gateway. Beyond is the narthex. The floor is of white marble and porphyry. Twelve granite columns, representing the 12 months of the year, divide the church interior into three aisles. On the south are the chapels of Saints Cosmas and Damian, St Simeon Stylites, and Saints Joachim and Anna, the parents of the Virgin. On the north are the chapels of St Marisa, St Constantine and St Helena, and of St Antipas. Gifts are laid on both sides of the 13th-century iconostasis. In the apse is a sixth-century mosaic, probably executed by an artist from Constantinople. It depicts the Transfiguration of Christ who is flanked by Moses and Elias, and the Saints John and James. The scene is surrounded by 31 portraits of prophets, apostles and saints. Two scenes in the corners show Moses receiving the Tablets of the Law and Moses and the Burning Bush.

The Church is dedicated to St Catherine of Alexandria who was martyred in AD 306, in the reign of the emperor Maxentius. Although she does not appear in the historical record before AD 800, tradition has it that Catherine came from an aristocratic family in Alexandria, and converted to Christianity after having a vision of the Virgin and Child. She was learned and successfully defended her faith in dispute with a group of leading scholars. Nevertheless, her execution was ordered. The first attempt was to break her on a wheel, but this burst apart when she touched it: the spiked wheel is her symbol. She was therefore beheaded. Her remains were taken to Sinai by angels, where they were found on the top of Mount Catherine in about 800. Her feast day is November 25. The relics of the Saint are preserved in an 18th-century marble tomb, to the right of the altar, beneath a canopy. Two silver reliquaries inlaid with precious stones stand behind the iconostasis. One was donated by Czar Alexander II in 1860, and the other was a gift of the future Czar Peter and the Regent Sophia in 1688.

Immediately behind the chancel is the monastery's most celebrated and holiest place, the **Chapel of the Burning Bush**, traditionally the actual site of the biblical event. This was not incorporated into Justinian's church until the medieval period.

Another pride of the monastery is its rich library, containing some 3,500 manuscripts in Greek, Arabic, Armenian, Hebrew, Slavic and other languages. The extensive collection of manuscripts is said to rank second only to that of the Vatican. Between 1844 and 1859, the German scholar Konstantin von Tischendorf discovered a biblical manuscript, the *Codex Sinaiticus* from the fourth century. This precious document is now preserved in the British Museum in London, having been presented to Czar Alexander II and later sold by the Soviet Government.

Chapel of the Burning Bush, St Catherine's Monastery

Two thousand icons dating from the sixth century to the end of the Byzantine Period in the 15th century are housed in the monastery's library. There are also fascinating paintings in wax (encaustic) from the fifth and sixth centuries. Other treasures include fine sacerdotal ornaments. In the garden is the charnel house or ossuary. The last remains of the monks lie in two crypts.

THE HOLY MOUNTAINS

Mount Moses (Mount Sinai or the Holy Peak) is a three-hour walk from the monastery, entailing a climb up 3,750 steps carved out of hard granite by monks who had made a vow to accomplish this task. This is the mountain where God gave Moses the Ten Commandments. It is probable that the Mountain of the Law, known as Mount Horeb in the Old Testament, was in fact Gebel Serbal. Nonetheless, pre-Christian Nabataean inscriptions refer to Mount Sinai as a sacred mountain. Islam also considers the mountain sacred. Here Mohammed's horse, Boraq, touched the stone steps when he ascended to heaven. The steps pass the Fountain of Moses, a small chapel of the Virgin, and two arches, the Gates of St Stephen and the Gate of the Law. On the summit is the Chapel of the Holy Trinity, built in 1934 on the site of a smaller chapel dating back to the fourth century.

The ascent of **Mount Catherine** (Gebel Katerin) takes five hours, but follows a very interesting route. On the way up, you pass the Chapel of Aaron, the monastery of the garden convent of the Holy Apostles, a pavilion built by King Fuad and the Monastery of the Forty Martyrs. The Chapel of St Catherine, built by the monk Callistes, is at the peak. It is believed that the headless body of the martyred Saint Catherine was transported by angels and laid on the summit of this mountain. Nearby is Gebel Sebir, which takes about 25 minutes to climb from Mount Catherine. On its summit stands an observatory of the Smith Institute of Meteorology of California. Solar radiation was first measured here between 1933 and 1938.

Egyptian Oases

O nce difficult to travel to, the oases of the Western Desert are now relatively easy to visit. With government attempts to encourage settlement in some areas, their population and industries have grown, yet they remain, in many ways, isolated and very traditional societies.

A visit through the oases of the Western Desert is possible on a loop road starting from either Cairo or Asyut. The roads have been considerably improved in recent years, and four-wheel drive vehicles are no longer necessary for the main route, although vital for off-road travel. Many hikers use the bus service, which can be taken from either Cairo or Asyut/Kharga.

The roads between Farafra, Bahariya, Dakhla, Kharga and the Nile Valley are good. The road from Marsa Matruh to Siwa has also been asphalted: there is a rest house and petrol station approximately halfway. The routes between Siwa and Bahariya are still true desert roads. Increasing numbers of people are travelling in the desert, and care should be taken to preserve this fragile environment. It is all too common to find, in what seem to be totally remote places, discarded plastic water bottles and other rubbish.

Faiyum

B ecause the oasis of el-Faiyum is situated so close to Cairo, covers such a vast area and is connected to the Nile Valley, it does not really conform to the traditional perception of an oasis. The pharaohs of the 12th Dynasty developed the Faiyum extensively, placing their pyramids near the entrance from the Nile Valley, at Hawara and Illahun. During the Graeco-Roman Period, the lake was drained and the region settled and intensively farmed. Easily accessible by either the desert road from Giza or the valley road from Beni Suef, it is an attractive region with many ancient sites. The eerie Lake Qarun in the north has shrunk since ancient times when it was a vast lake and reservoir covering much of the cultivable land.

Around the edge of the Faiyum depression are many large ancient sites, some of which require special permission to visit. The most accessible, and one of the most interesting, is **Kom Aushim**, the ancient site of Karanis, at the point where the Giza road enters the oasis. A small museum houses objects excavated here and at other Faiyum sites, notably Medinet Faiyum itself. The site is large, with two temples and many streets. The main excavations were carried out under the auspices of the University of Michigan, beginning in 1924. Many of the buildings are sufficiently well preserved for the visitor to gain a good impression of what a large agricultural village in Ptolemaic–Roman Egypt was like. The population here was, as in most Faiyum villages, predominantly Greek speaking: many of them were descended from veterans of the Ptolemaic army. There may have been significant numbers of Egyptians absorbed into these villages, but the culture was very mixed, and social life focused on institutions that were of Greek origin as well as traditional Egyptian temples.

At Karanis, the temples are of cut stone, but undecorated. The South Temple was dedicated to the local crocodile deities Pnepheros and Petesuchos. The North Temple may also have the crocodile god in one of his manifestations as principal deity, but Isis was probably worshipped alongside him, as at Soknopaiou Nesos. In both temples the large altar is hollow so that oracles could be delivered from inside it. In the walls of the sanctuary is a deep niche in which the mummified crocodile, image of the temple's deity, was kept. A dedicatory inscription in Greek is dated to year 7 of the emperor Nero (AD 60/61). In front of the main façade of the temple was a colonnaded court, with a number of ceremonial buildings. That on the south side of the court has an imposing stone gateway carrying a dedicatory inscription of the emperor Vespasian (AD 69–79). The building was a dining room, and has a large hall that was used for the sacred banquets, perhaps involving remains of the sacrifices offered in the temple. Apollonios, superintendent of the granaries, dedicated the north gateway into the temple precinct in the reign of Commodus (AD 180–192).

The North Temple is small, but has finely executed masonry. In the inner court, the excavators found the upper part of a marble statue of Isis, and a small statue of Soknopaios with a crocodile body and falcon head. A small Roman bathhouse can be found in one of the streets behind the North Temple. There are well-preserved granaries and dovecots among the other buildings.

Near Karanis is **Kom Umm el-Atl**, the ancient Bacchias, currently being excavated by a joint team from the Universities of Bologna and Lecce. There are extensive mud-brick ruins here, but the site is not as imposing as Karanis. The remains of the temple of the crocodile god, who was worshipped here with the name Soknobkonneus, dominate the area. The settlement was in occupation from the early Ptolemaic period into later Roman times, when many of the Faiyum villages and towns suffered from economic decline.

A schoolgirl from the Bahariya Oasis region

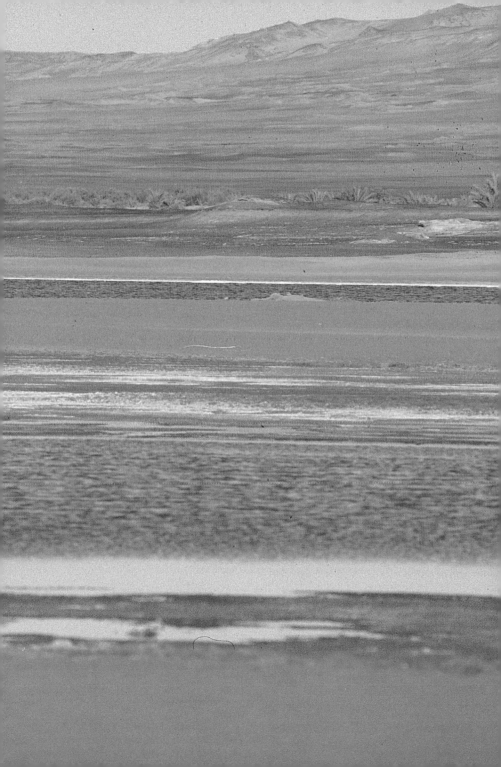

On the north side of the lake (no asphalt road, four-wheel drive necessary), a track begins opposite the Karanis site and leads to the **Temple of Qasr el-Sagha**. Spectacularly situated, this unusual temple dates from the Middle Kingdom, but its external construction is more like that of the Fourth-dynasty granite Temple of Khafre at Giza. Unfortunately the building has been marred by excessive modern graffiti. The interior consists of a broad, narrow hall with seven shrines and small rooms off either end. A second door at the right-hand end of the façade leads into a very narrow passage in the interior of the wall. This ends in a spyhole onto the main entrance, but exactly why is unknown. A little further on is the Graeco-Roman site of **Dimai** (ancient Soknopaiou Nesos), where the massive enclosure walls of the temple still reach to a height of 10 metres. There are extensive ruins of the town, which stood on the edge of the lake, now receded. There are some well-preserved buildings with vaulted subterranean rooms. A paved processional way runs from the temple through the middle of the town towards the lake. The site was excavated in the 1920s, yielding great numbers of papyri from which it was possible to reconstruct the economic history of the town.

More easily accessible is **Qasr Qarun**, ancient Dionysias, with its Ptolemaic temple and scattered remains of the town site. Lying at the far end of the lake on the road which runs around the outside of the oasis, a visit here also allows a full view of the life and landscape of this rich agricultural region. The temple here is a typical monumental stone construction of the Ptolemaic Period. The undecorated exterior is imposing in its massiveness, a late, and remarkably similar, version of the 'tent-shrine' found in the Step Pyramid complex of Djoser some two thousand years earlier. A large Roman fortress was built in the reign of Diocletian as a protection against invasions across the desert. The remains of the walls and some of the buildings (notably the basilica) can be seen. Although excavated, most of the ruins have been covered over by sand.

Medinet el-Faiyum, the major town in the oasis, is the site of the ancient Krokodilopolis (Egyptian: Shedit), the remains of which have all but vanished. On the outskirts of the town (on the main Cairo–Faiyum road), the obelisk from Abgig has been re-erected. This monolith was set up by Senusret I and is decorated, although its surface has been badly weathered. The whole of Faiyum was devoted to the worship of the crocodile god, Sobek, and most of the ancient temples were dedicated to his different forms, the chief one being here in Medinet el-Faiyum. The temple may have been connected to the lake by a canal that was flanked by the two

(preceding pages) *Farmers returning from the fields, Bahariya Oasis*

seated colossi of Amenemhat III at Biahmu. Little remains of these statues but some of the blocks from their bases, which originally stood some 10 metres high. The colossi were probably similar to (even prototypes of) the Colossi of Memnon at Thebes. Each appears to have stood within its own enclosure. Herodotos says that they were on pyramids in the lake, and it seems that at the time of his travels, the waters of the lake had expanded to flood them. The site is in a very pleasant position between the village of Sinuris and Medinet el-Faiyum.

Two important sites, Medinet Madi and Umm el-Breigat, on the southern fringe of the Faiyum are more difficult to reach. They may be closed to visitors if archaeological teams are working.

MEDINET MADI

The enormous archaeological site of Medinet Madi (Narmouthis) has been the subject of archaeological investigation since the early 20th century. The first major excavations were carried out under the auspices of the University of Milan, directed by Professor Achille Vogliano. Since 1966 there have been further excavations, and the present work is conducted by a joint team from the Universities of Pisa and Messina directed by Professors Edda Bresciani and Rosario Pintaudi. They have worked on the Late Antique (Coptic) areas of the site, and have recently uncovered a twin shrine for crocodile gods.

Vogliano's excavations revealed that the town had 12th Dynasty origins. The principal monument is a small temple built by Amenemhat III and dedicated to Sobek, his consort (here) the harvest goddess Renenutet, and their son, a form of Horus (no doubt identified with the pharaoh). In the Ptolemaic and Roman periods Renenutet was assimilated with Isis-Thermouthis, who had a Ptolemaic temple on the site. She is depicted with the rearing head and spread hood of the cobra in place of a human head. The Middle Kingdom temple is reached by a long *dromos* that is lined with sphinxes and lions and passes through a processional kiosk and gateways, all of Ptolemaic date. Preceding the temple is a small court, its gate flanked by two lion statues. A colonnaded pronaos was added to the older temple in Ptolemaic times: it is a miniature version of the type found at Edfu. The Middle Kingdom temple is modest in scale, comprising an outer hall with two columns and a sanctuary with three shrines. The style of these is similar to the inner part of Qasr el-Sagha. The central niche contained a statue of Renenutet flanked by the temple's builders, Amenemhat III and Amenemhat IV. The other niches had statues of Amenemhat III

(following pages) *Eroded landscape, Farafra Oasis*

and Sobek. Behind the Middle Kingdom temple, and joining to its rear wall is a Ptolemaic 'contra-temple', with its own pylon entrance and processional way.

In 1998 the joint Pisa–Messina team uncovered and restored a twin shrine dedicated to crocodile gods. It is built of mud-brick with stone gates and naos, and is of the same type as the temple from Theadelphia reconstructed in the Alexandria Museum. A stone gate with cavetto cornice opens onto a courtyard with the naos at the rear. The naos has two shrines, with the usual type of niche at the back into which the mummified crocodiles could be pushed. The naos has much of its original painted decoration surviving.

UMM EL-BREIGAT

This very large site at Umm el-Breigat (Tebtunis) has been the focus of excavations (the earlier ones not particularly scientific) since 1900. The present work, begun in 1988, is a joint mission by the French Institute in Cairo (IFAO) and the Institute of Papyrology of Milan University, directed by Professor Claudio Gallazzi. The town itself may, like Medinet Madi, have Middle Kingdom origins, and the enclosure of the temple seems to date back to the early Libyan period (22nd Dynasty). The temple of the crocodile god, here called Soknebtunis, is Ptolemaic with Roman additions. In the Late Antique (Byzantine) period the town was renamed Theodosiopolis, and became the capital of a new nome, Theodosiopolites. The town continued to flourish after the Arab conquest, but the desert was encroaching and the water supply was becoming a problem: by the 13th century it had been completely abandoned. The earliest work on the site discovered a vast number of papyri, which are one of the most significant sources of information on life in the Faiyum in Ptolemaic and Roman times. Recent discoveries of papyri have supplemented our knowledge and have revealed that there was a Jewish community here in the second century BC: other villages had a Jewish element in the population (one even had the Jewish name, Magdola), and there was a synagogue in Arsinoe (Medinet el-Faiyum).

In addition to the Temple of Soknebtunis, with its *dromos*, lion statues and Roman kiosk, there was a **chapel of Isis-Thermouthis** (the Egyptian Renenutet), and an Osiris temple (this, at present, is known only from texts). The current excavations have shown that at least parts of the town were laid out on a grid plan. Amongst the important new discoveries is a large public bath complex, dating to the second century BC, one of the finest surviving from Hellenistic Egypt.

BAHARIYA AND FARAFRA

Bahariya is a vast depression, with water in the northern part where the agriculture is concentrated. At one time, camping was the only option for travellers, and there are hot springs near Bawiti, at Bir Ghaba, the usual camping place, but there are now some new hotels in Bawiti and Qasr. The oasis has many fine antiquities—some are currently inaccessible because of the danger of thefts, but the visit and landscape are nevertheless spectacular.

There have been some important new finds in Bahariya in the past few years. One dig by the University of Pennsylvania highlighted an aspect of Egypt that is rarely considered: its dinosaurs. The German palaeontologist Ernst von Stromer had collected fossils in Bahariya Oasis in the early 20th century. They were housed in the museum in Munich, but were lost when it was destroyed in 1944. The Pennsylvania expedition found parts of the skeleton of a large sauropod that they named *Paralatitan stromeri*, in honour of their predecessor. This plant-eater was one of the largest dinosaurs known, weighing some 60–70 tons and measuring up to 30.5 metres (80–100 feet). The dinosaur belongs to the same family as the largest known sauropod, *Argentinosaurus*, and lived about the same time during the Late Cretaceous (146 to 65 million years ago). At that time, the region was an area of shallow water, forest, tidal flats and channels, rather similar, the palaeontologists say, to the Everglades. A variety of other fossils were also discovered, belonging to species of fish, crab, coelacanth and crocodile. The region is also known to have been the home of large carnivorous dinosaurs, similar in size to *Tyrannosaurus*, and called *Carcharodontosaurus*.

Of considerably more recent date, the second important archaeological find is the Valley of the Golden Mummies. This was, as so often, accidental: the subsequent excavation has been under the direction of one of Egypt's most important archaeologists, Dr Zahi Hawass. The extensive catacombs, of Ptolemaic–Roman date, contain hundreds, and probably thousands, of mummies, many with painted and gilded wrappings. Understandably, access to this area is currently very limited.

The other antiquities are concentrated in the area of Bawiti and Qasr. A group of important 26th Dynasty tombs at **Qarat al-Subi**, in Bawiti, was cleared by Ahmed Fakhry in 1938. One group of tombs belonged to Pedi-Astarte, his descendants and cousins: clearly this was the most important family in the oasis. The name Pedi-Astarte is very unusual, Astarte being a Syrian goddess who was introduced into the Egyptian pantheon in the 18th Dynasty. Pedi-Astarte was a High Priest of Khonsu and Priest of Horus sometime in the middle of the 26th Dynasty. The little that survived of the paintings in his tomb was religious in subject. The most impressive of the tombs was that of Djed-Amun-ef-ankh, Governor of Bahariya in the reign of Ahmose II (Amasis), towards the end of the 26th Dynasty. Djed-Amun-ef-ankh succeeded his brother, Sheben-Khonsu, as Governor of the Oasis: they were both descended from a man named Harkheb who was also the ancestor of Pedi-Astarte.

Also in Bawiti, at **Qarat Qasr Salim**, Fakhry excavated a group of tombs of the family of another man named Djed-Amun-ef-ankh, apparently not related to the governor. Djed-Amun-ef-ankh's tomb has four large pillars supporting the ceiling of the roughly square main chamber. The whole tomb was decorated with painted religious scenes. Adjacent is the tomb of Bannentiu: Fakhry used this spelling for consistency, although the name appears in a variety of ways in the tomb, and was perhaps Libyan. The tomb, like most of the others here, is entered by a deep shaft and has a square chamber supported by square pillars, with side chambers. There was an interesting group of painted religious scenes depicting the journeys of the moon god and of the sun god. Unfortunately the paintings began to deteriorate shortly after the tomb was opened.

Contemporary with the tombs was a chapel, possibly part of a larger temple, constructed in the reign of Ahmose II by the Governor Djed-Amun-ef-ankh who was, unusually, depicted following the pharaoh. The relief sculpture was of high quality and depicted the governor and pharaoh with a number of the important deities of the oasis, notably Ha, god of the desert. The chapel was one of four at Ain el-Muftillah that have been re-covered with sand to protect them.

In about 1916 the villagers found a large gallery containing mummified ibises and bronze votive images. They called the area **Qarat al-Farargi**, 'Hill of the Chicken Merchant', thinking that the mummified birds were chickens. Many of the mummies were stripped of their gilt casings, and the bronze statues dispersed through dealers. The galleries were examined and mapped by Ahmed Fakhry, and date, as so many other antiquities in this oasis, to the 26th Dynasty. Also in the main town there was a Roman Triumphal Arch. This was described and illustrated by travellers in the early 19th century, but hardly anything remains. The arch was about 7 metres (25 feet) in length and stood on a large platform, one side of which was level with the village of Qasr, but other dropped some 10 metres (33 feet) to the plain. This is an eccentric placing of an arch and there must have been something on the other side! It perhaps had a stairway, with the arch forming the entrance to a temple complex.

Farmer hoeing, Kharga Oasis

Although the significant excavated remains are of the Late to Roman periods, other sources show that Bahariya was important much earlier. There is a scene in the tomb of Rekhmire at Thebes showing the produce of the oasis, and other texts refer to its vineyards. One significant monument of New Kingdom date was excavated by Ahmed Fakhry at **Qarat al-Hilwa** south of Qasr; the tomb of Amenhotep, the Governor of the Oasis. This tomb suffered severe damage following Fakhry's original work here. The tomb-chapel has a court with two halls, the outer supported by two, the inner by four, pillars. There was apparently a pyramid surmounting the chapel, a feature familiar from contemporary tombs at Thebes and Memphis. Although the precise date of the tomb is uncertain, the style of the incised relief decoration and the costumes points to the late 18th or early 19th dynasties.

To the west of Bawiti–Qasr is one of the other important monuments of Bahariya, **Qasr el-Migysbah**, near el-Tibniya, close to the point where the road to Siwa leaves the oasis. This complex was excavated by Ahmed Fakhry between 1938 and 1942. It is a small temple built in soft sandstone. The inscriptions reveal that it was constructed in the name of Alexander the Great, but there is relatively little to be seen of the relief decoration, which has been badly eroded. Even less survives of the many brick buildings that enclosed the two-roomed sanctuary. A granite altar, also inscribed for Alexander, was removed to Cairo (Egyptian Museum). It is significant as the only monument in the oasis that carries Alexander's name: although the Greek and Roman biographers narrate his journey to Siwa, he is not named in any of the temples there.

Leaving the oasis for Farafra, the depression is covered with the **Black Desert**. Rising out of the Bahariya depression, there are splendid views back, with the great sand dunes spilling over from the high desert. After a fairly short distance across the plateau, the road descends into the Farafra depression. The northern part of this is taken up with the **White Desert**, a complete contrast to the landscape of Bahariya. Here chalk formations dominate, many weathered into fantastic and surreal shapes. Beautiful during the daytime, at night this landscape is ghostly as the formations take on the appearance of icebergs: indeed, in the winter cold it can seem more like the Arctic than the Sahara.

The town of **Farafra** stands on a small hill, surrounded by verdant gardens. A hot spring a short distance outside the town is the usual camping place. Little survey or excavation work has been done in Farafra, although some Roman sites are known: they are difficult to reach and not particularly interesting. The drive from Farafra to Dakhla is quite easy, passing close to the Great Sand Sea.

DAKHLA

D akhla is a very rich and beautiful oasis. One major group of monuments is found immediately on entering the area from Farafra. The medieval town of el-Qasr still preserves its winding streets and alleys, which have the flavour of the *One Thousand Nights and a Night*. Many of the houses have handsome, carved wooden lintels with the dates of their construction. The most notable building, the house of Abu Nafri, has jambs made of blocks taken from a temple, probably nearby Deir el-Hagar. Climb the minaret of the mosque to get a good view over the town.

Very close to el-Qasr are the painted Ptolemaic–Roman **tombs of el-Muzawwaqa**. Many lie open and are undecorated, but the two most worthwhile should be visited. In the tombs of Petubastis and Petosiris, the combination of Egyptian and Hellenistic-Roman motifs, painted in bright colours and rather naive style, is very attractive. They also have some good zodiac ceilings.

The **Temple of Deir el-Hagar** was a picturesque ruin, retaining something of the appearance of temples as drawn by early Western artists such as David Roberts. It is currently being restored.

Next to the road from el-Qasr to Mut lies the vast town site of Amheida. Although there are some fine painted rooms here, they are presently inaccessible and the remainder of the site has little to offer. **Mut**, the major town in the oasis, has a number of hotels. The ruins here are not well preserved and the medieval town is not as appealing as el-Qasr. Between Dakhla and Kharga are the magnificent Old Kingdom mastabas at **Balat** and the town site of **Ain Asil**, both currently under excavation. The sites are reached from the charming village of **Ezbet Bashendi**, which itself has a number of fine Roman tombs. Of these, the most significant is the **tomb of Kitines**, with good relief decoration.

KHARGA

K harga city is a vast, spread-out, rather ugly settlement. It has several hotels. The most important monument is the **Temple of Hibis** to the north. Built on the shores of the lake, its foundations began to collapse in antiquity. The main part of the temple is currently inaccessible but the outer sections can be viewed. It is a handsome structure built by the Persian king, Darius, between 510–490 BC. Darius is shown here as a typical pharaoh. A kiosk, rather like the Kiosk of Trajan at Philae, was added on to the front (30th Dynasty), but, unusually, joined with the temple itself.

On the hill nearby is the small **Fortress of Nadura** with a temple built in the reign of Hadrian, badly ruined but with good views down onto Hibis. Close to Hibis is the **Necropolis of el-Bagawat**. Dating from the fourth to fifth centuries AD, the many tomb-chapels are splendid examples of what can be achieved with mud-brick: cupolas, false windows and engaged columns with Corinthian capitals are all modelled with virtuosity. Inside the chapels are good examples of early Christian painted decoration.

South of Kharga is the spectacular **Fortress of Ghueidah** atop its hill: inside is a mass of buildings with another temple at its heart. The original shrine was a small chapel, now the sanctuary, built in the Persian period. The temple was considerably enlarged in Ptolemaic times. The fort has a commanding position over the Darb el-Arbain, the 'Forty Days Road', and controlled access to the town of Kharga from the south.

A little further on the back road stands the **Temple of Qasr Zaiyan**. The temple itself is a small stone-built shrine of classic Egyptian form. There is an inscription in Greek on one of the lintels, dating to the reign of Antoninus Pius (AD 140). The temple stands within a mud-brick enclosure wall, with a processional way leading to it. The rest of the enclosure is filled with the remains of mud-brick buildings.

Further south along the Forty Days Road is **New Baris**, a village designed by Hassan Fathy. As in the cemetery of Bagawat, mud-brick is the building material but Fathy's splendid design is simple and unornamented. It was begun in 1967 but never completed. Further south, on a side road to the west, lies the great **Fortress of Dush**, guarding the ancient road to Edfu. With commanding aspect, its walls enclose a temple with other buildings and a necropolis surrounding it. Recent excavations by French archaeologists have recovered a gold priestly crown from one of the tombs (Cairo, Egyptian Museum). It is not possible to travel south beyond the checkpoints without permission. Here the Forty Days Road continues parallel to the Nile, eventually reaching Darfur and Kordofan in Sudan. This formed the great slave route, which ran from Sudan to Asyut in former times.

A number of small Late Roman and Byzantine forts lie to the north of Kharga, again mostly inaccessible without good maps, four-wheel drive vehicles and a local driver. The Fortress of el-Qasr controlled the ancient road that crossed the desert plateau to Girga. It was built in the reign of Diocletian, and is typical of the period, with banded brick wall, rounded corner towers, and semicircular towers along the walls. The walls are well preserved but little remains inside. There are numerous graffiti from 20th century army occupation. The fort stood near a supply of good water, and there was a temple and cemetery—and presumably settlement—nearby.

Qasr el-Someira and Qasr el-Gib are almost identical small forts visible from the main road to Asyut. They are within signalling distance of each other, and stand on small hills. Each was roughly square with round corner towers (all now collapsed). Inside they had three floors with a small central court. The interiors are ruined. Watch out for snakes.

SIWA

Siwa lies deep in the desert, close to the Libyan border. Occupied by people of Berber descent, it had its own traditions and culture and was independent until Mohammed Ali brought it under his rule in 1820. Until recently, it remained remote and difficult to control from Cairo. It is now easily accessible from Marsa Matruh, along the metalled road which has brought many changes, not least that Siwa has become a major tourist centre and consequently is losing many of its old traditions. The traditional jewellery is being sold, and soon there will be little left of its unique culture.

Siwa is a beautiful place, with palm groves set between lakes. The main archaeological sites are the **Oracle Temple of Amun** at Aghurmi, the nearby Temple of Umm Ubeida, and the tombs and medieval Qasr in Siwa town itself.

Siwa was one of the most important oracles of the ancient world. It was here that Alexander the Great communed with Amun (Ammon), and was acknowledged as his son. The temple, built in the 26th Dynasty, is surprisingly small and unimpressive but stands in the middle of the imposing medieval fortress. The plain façade had engaged Doric half-columns added to it during the Ptolemaic Period. The interior is also plain except for fragments of relief decoration in the sanctuary. A broad cornice runs around the wall of the sanctuary, to support a low ceiling, perhaps for an oracle chamber above. A narrow passage leads behind the sanctuary, giving access to this chamber and to one below. The hill on which the temple stands has been eroded over the centuries, and there has been work here recently to ensure that the temple does not collapse.

In the palm groves nearby is the **Temple of Umm Ubeida**. Dating from the reign of Nakhthorheb (Nectanebo II, 30th Dynasty) the restored walls are covered with relief, still carrying bright blue paint in places. Here we can see one of the Libyan chiefs who ruled the oasis acting on behalf of the pharaoh. This temple was probably connected by a processional way to the Oracle Temple. Greek and Roman sources describe the carrying of the oracle shrine in procession.

In the town of Siwa is another **fortified medieval town**, its winding streets leading to the top of the hill, where there are splendid views over the oasis. On a small hill just out of the town are the tombs. Some of these have splendid painted decoration, recently cleaned and conserved. Most notable is the tomb of Siamun with fine drawing in mixed Hellenistic and Egyptian style.

VISITING EGYPT

WHEN TO GO

T he best time to visit Egypt is during the winter months, from November to March, when the nights are cool and the days are not oppressively sultry. However, prices tend to be higher at this time and the hotels are often fully booked.

April weather is unpredictable and often very windy. From May to September, when the weather becomes much warmer, Cairo can be very hot and Upper Egypt particularly torrid. However, most hotels are air-conditioned and all first-class establishments have a swimming pool. By October, the worst of the summer heat has dissipated.

Visitors are usually advised to plan trips to archaeological sites during the cooler parts of the day, either in the very early morning or late afternoon. But if travelling in April–May or September–early October, it can actually be worthwhile to disregard this and begin visits to some of the notoriously uncomfortable sites, such as the Valley of the Kings, or Karnak temples, in the earlier afternoon: although fiercely hot, there are usually few other visitors, and the temperatures can only become more bearable as the afternoon advances. Armed with the appropriate array of sunhats, fly-whisks, fans, sunglasses and bottles of water, and not endeavouring to see everything in one visit, this is one way to combat the crowds.

During Ramadan, the holy month of fasting, faithful Muslims abstain from both food and drink from sunrise to sunset, and the pace of life generally slows down as the month proceeds. Opening times for museums and monuments can vary during this period. As with all other Islamic festivals and holidays, Ramadan is determined by the lunar calendar, and is therefore observed 10–12 days earlier each year. Muslim holidays are: Mouled el-Navi, the 'Birth of the Prophet'; Eid el-Adha, the Bairam, celebrating the end of the annual pilgrimage to Mecca; and Eid el-Fitr.

As in all Islamic countries, Friday is Egypt's day of prayer and rest. On this day, opening times can be different, and some major monuments, notably the Giza pyramids, are the place where families will go and enjoy a day out and picnic: they can, consequently, be very busy, but this is balanced by a festive and welcoming atmosphere.

The following dates are official public holidays:

1 January	New Year's Day
22 February	Union Day
1 May	Labour Day
18 June	Anniversary of British Evacuation
23 July	Anniversary of Egyptian Revolution
6 October	Egyptian Military Forces Day
24 October	Anniversary of Suez
23 December	Victory Day

CURRENCY

The unit of currency is the Egyptian pound (LE), which is divided into 100 piastres. Notes come in one, five, ten, 20, 50 and 100 LE. Visitors may bring in an unlimited amount of foreign currency. All money-change receipts issued by banks should be retained throughout the duration of the stay. Upon departure, Egyptian pounds may be reconverted into foreign currency only upon presentation of valid receipts from banks or officially recognized moneychangers. The Egyptian government has successfully curbed the black market, and with a currently very favourable exchange rate, Western visitors have no need to change money this way. However, many tourists take advantage of the black market, but laws exist against this, and, if applied, they are severe. Travellers' cheques may be changed easily at banks or official moneychangers. Credit cards are gaining in popularity in Egypt, and are widely accepted in large hotels, luxury restaurants and shops with a regular tourist clientele.

TIME ZONE

Egyptian Standard Time is two hours ahead of Greenwich Mean Time, seven hours ahead of the east coast of the United States (Eastern Standard Time) and ten hours ahead of the west coast (Pacific Time). Egyptian Summer Time from May till September is three hours ahead (GMT plus three).

Organized Tours

A popular tourist destination, Egypt is included in the programs of most major international travel agencies. Organized tours are generally very helpful for those travellers who wish to visit the principal tourist sights and archaeological zones in comfort, without the painstaking research involved in the planning of an itinerary and means of transportation.

Organized tours can also prove to be time and money saving. Almost always, in fact, the total cost of an individual tour is considerably higher than that of a group. Major travel agencies offer a number of travel plans. The criteria you should keep in mind are: duration of stay, the season, the composition of the trip (how much time will be allotted for sightseeing and how much for free time), the means of transportation and the price. If you want to savour and discover Egypt, avoid hectic tours that visit dozens of sunny Mediterranean destinations and mystical Middle Eastern lands in just 15 days, for they promise the tourist only fleeting contact with places that deserve to be visited at length. A number of companies will arrange specific itineraries for individuals, couples and small groups.

Passport and Visas

V isitors to Egypt are required to have a passport or equivalent documents valid for at least six months from the date of entry. A tourist visa may be obtained at Egyptian embassies or consulates abroad and is valid for 30 days, renewable for up to six months. The requirements for a visa application are a valid passport, a photograph and the payment of the entry tax, which will be demanded upon arrival. The visa may also be obtained upon arrival at a port or frontier, but to avoid unnecessary queuing, it would be advisable to obtain one beforehand and to request a longer duration of stay to allow for some flexibility in your travel plans. Those who join organized tours will usually be included on a collective visa, obtained by their travel agency. Visa extensions of up to six months can be applied for, and are issued at the Passports Office, Mugamma, Palace of the Governor, Room 16, Midan el-Tahrir, Cairo.

Egyptian embassies abroad also issue special student visas valid for one year. Information on business visas or working permits may be obtained from Egyptian embassies and consulates. Once in Egypt, visitors are required to register with the Mugamma or the nearest police station within seven days of arrival. Hotels register their guests; those who stay in pensions or private homes must register personally.

HEALTH

An anti-smallpox vaccination is not now required. However, visitors from endemic zones must present a valid certificate of anti-cholera and anti-yellow fever vaccinations. The anti-cholera vaccination is valid for six months from the sixth day after inoculation. The yellow fever vaccination, on the other hand, is valid for ten years from the tenth day after inoculation.

Health regulations are constantly changing to keep pace with worldwide epidemic trends and medical advances, and Egyptian authorities are very strict on public health. Visitors arriving from infected areas without proper certification must stay in quarantine for a certain period before they are allowed entry. Check beforehand with your local World Health Organization office for information.

SECURITY

Over the past 15 years there have been occasional security incidents involving foreign tourists. These have been rare, and most were random attacks in Middle Egypt, in the region of el-Minya and Mallawi. Tourists have, on a number of occasions, been recommended not to travel through this part of the country. As a result of incidents in and near Luxor, in which some tourists were killed in early 1996, security at main archaeological sites and at airports has been considerably increased. When visiting some sites, such as Abydos and Dendera, coaches now usually travel in convoy accompanied by police. Visitors travelling in small groups who wish to visit sites out of the main tourist centres are advised to seek, and respect, any advice from the local security authorities. Tourist police stations are located in all places of major interest, in ports, air terminals and stations. The Tourist Police, who can be identified by their armbands, will assist visitors in all sorts of situations.

Inevitably, if there is a period of increased political tension in the wider region, there may be increased security in Egypt. Up-to-date advice on travel is issued by governments through their Foreign Offices, and is available through www sources. A few examples include the British Foreign and Commonwealth Office (www.fco.gov.uk/travel), US State Department (www.travel.state.gov/travel_warnings.html) or Australian Department of Foreign Affairs and Trade (www.dfat.gov.au/travel/).

HOTELS

E gypt has a large number of four- and five-star hotels, run by the usual international chains. Many of the more expensive organized tours use these hotels, as do some cheaper package tours. Exclusivity, which might be associated with these names elsewhere, is not therefore to be guaranteed. It has to be said that most of these hotels are international in style, and whilst they offer first-class accommodation, they lack character. This particularly applies to some of the large Cairo hotels, such as the Ramses Hilton, the Semiramis Intercontinental and the Sheraton (both Cairo and Gezira Tower), all of which have their merits. Those visitors wishing to find something more distinctive should look at some of the former palaces.

CAIRO

The **Cairo Marriott** must be the most opulent hotel in the city. Standing next to the Gezira Sporting Club (which occupies what was originally part of its gardens), the hotel was built by the Khedive Ismail as part of his extravagant preparations for the opening of the Suez Canal by the Empress Eugénie. The Hungarian engineer and architect Julius Franz (later Franz Pasha) designed the building around a much smaller palace complex. Franz founded the Museum of Arab Art (now the Museum of Islamic Art) in Cairo in 1881 and was influential in the conservation of Egypt's Islamic heritage. His extensive knowledge resulted in an Orientalist fantasy, combining 'Arabic' styles, not all Egyptian, with Second Empire Baroque, and using lavish quantities of marble, *mushrabiya* work and gilded stucco. It may not be subtle, but it is splendid. Much of the furniture, and the fittings, were made in France, and large quantities of cast iron arches and the stucco decorations were prefabricated in Germany. In 1880, the Khedive's creditors seized the palace along with his other assets. In 1908, the Lebanese Prince Michael Lutfallah bought it for his private residence. The Egyptian Government acquired it in 1960, since when it has been a hotel, being extensively and carefully restored in the 1970s. The new hotel wings flank the palace itself, and have all the expected modern facilities: 1,250 rooms, including over 100 business and executive suites, and seven presidential suites, eight restaurants, five bars and a casino. The hotel stands in one of the most select parts of Cairo, close to many embassies and to restaurants and smart shops.
Cairo Marriott Hotel, Sharia el-Gezira, Zamalek
Tel: (+20)-2-735-8888; fax: (+20)-2-735-6667; www.marriott.com/property/propertyPage/CAIEG

For a long time the Cairo **Nile Hilton** was the main luxury hotel in the centre of the city. It is now rather faded, and its rooms seem quite small compared with many of the newer hotels. For convenience, however, it remains well situated, between the Nile and Tahrir Square. It is right next to the Egyptian Museum, and not as dangerous to get in and out of as the newer, and more luxurious, Ramses Hilton nearby, which is marooned on a traffic island. Of the two, the Cairo Hilton certainly has more character, and it is a lively meeting place, with good restaurants, bars and shops.

Nile Hilton Hotel, Tahrir Square

Tel: (+20)-2-578-0444/0666; fax: (+20)-2-578-0475; www.hilton.com/hotels/CAIHITW/

The **Windsor Hotel** has both character and style, but it is not of the same quality as the Marriott. It is one of the oldest hotels in the city; originally, it is said, a bathhouse (some of the louche associations of which it retained in the 1970s). It was once the annexe to Shepheard's Hotel, and, following the Revolution, was sold to a Coptic family. This three-star hotel has not been lavishly modernized, and is situated in a busy part of central Cairo, so visitors have no doubt as to which country they are in. The Windsor may not have the slick comforts of some of the more modern hotels, but for many of us it belongs to our vivid memories of the first visit to Egypt.

Windsor Hotel, 19 Alfi Bei Street, Cairo

Tel: (+20)-2-591-5810/5277; fax: (+20)-2-592-1621; www.windsorcairo.com/mainpage.htm

Another favoured older hotel is the **Victoria**, situated near the Opera Square in central Cairo. This too has an old-world flavour. The main criticism is that the bathroom units, which have been inserted into the spacious bedrooms, are rather small: a bit like climbing into a cupboard.

Victoria Hotel, 66 Sharia el-Gumhuriyya, Cairo

Tel: (+20)-2-589-2290; fax: (+20)-2-591-3008

The **Four Seasons Hotel Cario at the First Residence** is a new luxury hotel in Giza, with 269 rooms and suites.

Four Seasons Hotel, 35 Giza Street, Giza

Tel: (+20)-2-573-1212; fax: (+20)-2- 569-3088; www.fourseasons.com/cairofr/index.html

The **Mena House Hotel** is situated at the foot of Giza plateau. It was built by the Khedive for his lavish entertainments at the time of the opening of the Suez Canal. The building, with its contents, later became a private home and then a hotel. The original building has been considerably enlarged, but still exists at the heart of the main hotel. Newer wings, with a total of 520 rooms, enclose a large garden and pool area with restaurants.

Mena House Oberoi, Pyramids Road, Giza

Tel: (+20)-2-383-3222/3444; fax: (+20)-2-383-7777; www.oberoimenahouse.com/menahouse.asp; email: obmhosgm@oberoi.com.eg

FAIYUM AND THE OASES

For anyone wishing to explore the sites of the Faiyum, the **Auberge du Lac** is the place to stay. Situated halfway along the south side of Lake Qarun, it is also an ideal place to recuperate, and favoured by Egyptians at the weekend. King Faruq built the hotel as a shooting lodge in an eclectic style, best described as 'golf-club-oriental'. One eccentricity is that most (if not all) rooms have only a double bed, but this is generally large enough for two whose acquaintance is not completely new.

Auberge du Lac, Lake Qarun, Faiyum

Cairo tel: (+20)-2-358-2356, fax: (+20)-2-359-5717; Faiyum tel: (+20)-84-70002/712730, fax: (+20)-84-710730; see www.touregypt.net/magazine/mag09012000/magf2b.htm

The **Oasis Panorama Hotel** is the new place to stay when visiting Bahariya Oasis.

Oasis Panorama Hotel, Bawiti, Bahariya Oasis

Cairo tel: (+20)-2-847-3354/2700/2894, fax: (+20)-2-847-3896; mobile: (+20)-0-12-426-3567; www.oasispanorama.com/; email: info@oasispanorama.com

CAIRO TO LUXOR

There are many hotels between Cairo and Luxor that are more than adequate for the moderately well-travelled, but none that offer luxury. The **Lotus**, in el-Minya, was always a favourite stopping point on the long drive south, and convenient for Beni Hasan and Amarna.

The **Aluminium Hotel** at Nag Hammadi was the major hotel on the southward land journey between el-Minya and Luxor: large, adequate, but with a number of eccentricities. Built to serve as accommodation for the aluminium factory, it had a large number of 'duplexes' with two bedrooms on two floors, plus (former) kitchen and bathroom: these suites are rather large for one person. This, combined with a lack of heating (not needed in summer), and a tendency to have power cuts, made winter visits unappealing: I remember one January, a small group of us sitting down to a candlelit dinner in overcoats (rather too much like being at home), almost the only residents in the vast dining room.

(following pages) *Pyramid of Khufu (Cheops), Giza*

LUXOR

Even into the 1980s Luxor was a relatively small town, with the large, if rather rundown old hotels, the Winter Palace and the Luxor, still operating alongside the newer Etap, and a group of smaller hotels such as the Savoy. Then there was a building boom. The Sheraton, a long walk to the south of the town, and the **Mövenpick Jolie Ville** (www.moevenpick-hotels.com/en/hotels/hotels/HKLXRHH/), still further out, were the first new hotels, followed by the Hilton, an equally inconvenient way north. Since then the road between central Luxor and the Sheraton has been completely built up, and is now dominated by an array of lavish, rather vulgar, hotels and numerous shops.

The **Mercure**, still known to many as the Etap, near the museum, remains a favourite hotel with regular Luxor visitors, and is close to the centre of the town. It has nice gardens and pool, and lacks the unnecessary glitz of many of the new hotels. The **Savoy** is quite an old hotel, not grand, but pleasant. The **Sheraton** has the expected facilities and very attractive grounds, but for location and character the Old Winter Palace is unsurpassed.

The **Winter Palace** was built in 1886, and was the place where archaeologists, and writers such as Thomas Mann, rubbed shoulders with European royalty and nobility, and the rich of all nations. The most famous of its archaeological occupants was, no doubt, Howard Carter. The tower, the New Winter Palace, was added in the 1960s and the older hotel became somewhat rundown, but it has been considerably restored in recent years. The New Winter Palace has also been revamped, and new hotel wings have been built in the very extensive grounds. This returns the whole complex to its former pre-eminence amongst Luxor's hotels. The Old Winter Palace has superb rooms and a very fine formal restaurant. Following the old, if expensive, tradition, some archaeologists have once again chosen to make the Winter Palace their Luxor base.

Old Winter Palace, Corniche el-Nil, Luxor
Tel: (+20)-95-380-422; fax: (+20)-95-384-087

ASWAN

Like Luxor, Aswan has grown considerably in the past 20 years, with a consequent increase in the number of characterless new hotels, most situated on (and marring) the islands in the river.

The rambling **Oberoi** dominates the northern part of Elephantine Island. The hotel has excellent facilities and lovely grounds: it is a pity that the tower (which for

THE ENGLISHMAN ORIENTALIZED

I saw this daily phenomenon of sunset with pleasure, for I was engaged at that hour to dine with our old friend J—, who has established himself here in the most complete Oriental fashion.

You remember J—, and what a dandy he was, the faultlessness of his boots and cravats, the brilliancy of his waistcoats and kid gloves; we have seen his splendour in Regent Street, in the Tuilleries, or on the Toledo. My first object on arriving here was to find out his house, which he has taken far away from the haunts of European civilization, in the Arab quarter. It is situated in a cool, shady, narrow alley...

...J—appeared. Could it be the exquisite of the Europa and the Trois Frères? A man—in a long yellow gown, with a long beard, somewhat tinged with grey, and with his head shaved, and wearing on it first a white wadded cotton night-cap, second, a red tarboosh—made his appearance and welcomed me cordially. It was some time, as the Americans say, before I could 'realise' the semillant J. of old times.

He shuffled off his outer slippers before he curled up on the divan beside me. He clapped his hands, and languidly called 'Mustapha.' Mustapha came with more lights, pipes, and coffee; and then we fell to talking about London, and I gave him the last news of the comrades of that dear city. As we talked, his Oriental coolness and languor gave way to British cordiality; he was the most amusing companion of the —— club once more.

He has adopted himself outwardly, however, to the Oriental life. When he goes abroad he rides a grey horse with red housings, and has two servants to walk beside him. He wears a very handsome grave costume of dark blue, consisting of an embroidered jacket and gaiters, and a pair of trowsers, which would make a set of dresses for an English family. His beard curls nobly over his chest, his Damascus scimitar on his thigh. His red cap gives him a venerable and Bey-like appearance. There is no gewgaw or parade about him, as in some of your dandified young Agas. I should say that he is Major General of Engineers, or a grave officer of State. We and the Turkified European, who found us at dinner, sat smoking in solemn divan.

His dinners were excellent; they were cooked by a regular Egyptian female cook. We had delicate cucumbers stuffed with forced meats; yellow smoking pilaffs, the pride of the Oriental cuisine; kid and fowls à l'Aboukir and à la Pyramide; a number

of little savoury plates of legumes of the vegetable-marrow sort; kibobs with an excellent sauce of plums and piquant herbs. We ended the repast with ruby pomegranates, pulled to pieces, deliciously cool and pleasant. For the meats, we certainly ate them with the Infidel knife and fork; but for the fruit, we put our hands into the dish and flicked them into our mouths in what cannot but be the true Oriental manner. I asked for lamb and pistachio nuts, and cream-tarts au poivre; but J.'s cook did not furnish us with either of those historic dishes. And for drink, we had water freshened in the porous little pots of grey clay, at whose spout every traveller in the East has sucked delighted. Also it must be confessed, we drank certain sherbets, prepared by the two great rivals, Hadji Hodson and Bass Bey—the bitterest and most delicious of draughts! O divine Hodson! A camel's load of thy beer came from Beyrout to Jerusalem while we were there. How shall I ever forget the joy inspired by one of those foaming cool flasks? ...

Cairo is magnificently picturesque: it is fine to have palm-trees in your gardens, and ride about on a camel; but, after all, I was anxious to know what were the particular excitements of Eastern life, which detained J., who is a town-bred man, from his natural pleasures and occupations in London; where his family don't hear from him, where his room is still kept ready at home, and his name is on the list at his Club; and where his neglected sisters tremble to think that their Frederick is going about with a great beard and a crooked sword, dressed up like an odious Turk. In a 'lark' such a costume may be very well; but home, London, a razor, your sister to make tea, a pair of Christian breeches in lieu of those enormous Turkish shulwars, are vastly more convenient in the long run. What was it that kept him away from these decent and accustomed delights?

It couldn't be the black eyes in the balcony—upon his honour she was only the black cook, who has done the pilaff, and stuffed the cucumbers. No, it was an indulgence of laziness such as Europeans, Englishmen at least, don't know how to enjoy. Here he lives like a languid Lotus-eater—a dreamy, hazy, lazy, tobaccofied life. He was away from evening parties, he said; he needn't wear white kid gloves, or starched neckcloths, or read a newspaper. And even this life at Cairo was too civilized for him; Englishmen passed through; old acquaintances would call; the great pleasure of pleasures was life in the desert—under the tents, with still more nothing to do than in Cairo; now smoking, now cantering on Arabs, and no crowd to jostle you; solemn contemplations of the stars at night, as the camels were picketed, and the fires and the pipes were lighted.

William Makepeace Thackeray, Notes of a Journey from Cornhill to Grand Cairo, Smith, Elder and Co, London, 1846

William Makepeace Thackeray was born in Calcutta in 1811, and by the time of his death in 1863 was one of the leading figures in the literary life of Britain, as novelist and, particularly, essayist. His style is noted for its cynicism and sharp wit. In 1844, still making his name as a writer, Thackeray travelled around the eastern Mediterranean courtesy of the Peninsula and Oriental Company. The resulting *Notes of a Journey from Cornhill to Grand Cairo* includes an account of his visit to his 'old friend J.', which combines acute observation of Cairo with mockery of the fashion for pretend-living in the oriental manner (a pretence emphasized by the consumption of beer). 'J' was the artist John Frederick Lewis (1805–1875), who had travelled widely around the Mediterranean region before settling in a grand house in the Ezbekiya district of Cairo in 1841. Returning to England in 1851, his Orientalist paintings received great critical acclaim.

a long time was unused) was allowed to form a blot on the landscape. Although modern in style, it is old enough to have some character, and is wonderfully situated.
Aswan Oberoi, Elephantine Island, P O Box 62, Aswan
Tel: (+20)-97-314-666/667; fax: (+20)-97-303-651

Those seeking old-fashioned style will gravitate to the **Old Cataract**, which has some impressive (and very expensive) suites and a range of other rooms. The Old Cataract was built in 1899 by Thomas Cook, and enlarged shortly afterwards. It is famous for its terrace bar, which has splendid views over Elephantine Island, and to the west bank: a good place to watch the sunset. The internal decoration is splendidly Orientalist, especially in the main dining room. The hotel has featured in films such as *Death on the Nile*, based on the Hercule Poirot mystery by Agatha Christie. Some of the rooms along the wings have rather uninteresting views, but are considerably cheaper than the lavish suites on the Nile front.
Sofitel Old Cataract Aswan, Abtal el-Tahrir Street, Aswan
Tel: (+20)-97-316-000; fax: (+20)-97-316-011; www.sofitel.com/sofitel/fichehotel/gb/sof/resort/1666/fiche_hotel.shtml; email: H1666@accor-hotels.com

ALEXANDRIA

The only hotel worth staying at in the centre of Alexandria is the **Cecil**. This is a relatively small hotel with 83 rooms, recently updated to its former grandeur after a period of being supplanted by newer hotels on the city's edges. The Cecil was built in 1929 and witnessed the final years of Alexandria's importance.
Sofitel Cecil Alexandria, 16 Sa'ad Zaghlul Square, 1726 Alexandria
Tel: (+20)-3-487-7173; fax: (+20)-3-485-5655; www.sofitel.com/sofitel/fichehotel/gb/sof/1726/fiche_hotel.shtml; email: h1726@accor-hotels.com

NILE CRUISES

A Nile cruise is probably the highlight of most visits to Egypt. In the 19th century wealthy travellers hired a *dahabiya* and crew in Cairo. The racy exploits of French novelist Gustave Flaubert and his travelling companion Maxime du Camp (who took some of the earliest photographs of Egypt) provide an alternative to the worthy descriptions of monuments and 'oriental' life that characterize so much travel literature of the same period. Of the more sedate narratives, *A Thousand Miles up the Nile*, by Amelia Edwards, gives a splendid account of the boat she and her companions shared in 1873, fully equipped with piano. In the early 20th century, it was fashionable—for those who were rich enough—to sail one's own yacht; but the majority came on Mr Cook's boats. Although there has been a tendency, from before Amelia Edwards, for the independent traveller to look down on Mr Cook's cruises, they have included such notable figures as the poet Rainer Maria Rilke, who sailed to Aswan on the steamer *Ramses the Great* in 1911. The number of cruise boats grew enormously in the boom years of the late 1980s.

A variety of cruise boats run from Cairo to Aswan and vice versa. Major hotels also have their own boats offering various services and facilities. Smaller than regular cruise vessels, Nile boats can accommodate from 20 to 150 passengers in relatively spacious cabins. Other than the regular service facilities, bigger boats offer swimming pools, solariums, recreation areas, evening entertainment (of varying levels of ghastliness) and laundry and beauty parlour services. It has to be said that the majority of cruise boats lack character, both externally (some look like shoeboxes) and internally. A number of the older boats that still operated into the early 1990s have, sadly, been retired. They may have lacked some of the modern features of other boats, but more than compensated in their character and more intimate scale.

Cruises depart from Cairo, Luxor and Aswan and last from four to 16 days, depending on the route and itinerary. Almost all of the bigger boats are equipped with air conditioning, making these trips very pleasant even at the height of summer. However, it is still advisable to travel in Upper Egypt during the cooler months, since sightseeing ashore can be very hot unless you visit in the very early morning or at the end of the day. Fares during the summer are considerably lower, sometimes only a little more than half the fares in winter, because of the intense heat.

The largest number of cruise boats operate between Luxor and Aswan, with stops at Esna, Edfu and Kom Ombo to see the Ptolemaic temples. This cruise usually takes four days. Unfortunately, the enormous increase in the number of boats has caused problems, notably at the Esna barrage, and they are often moored, four abreast, pumping out diesel fumes. Some cruises add a short northward extension to include Dendera and Abydos, but only a small number go the whole distance between Cairo and Aswan. Those that do make stops at the interesting sites of Tell el-Amarna, Ashmunein, Beni Hasan and Medum, and see the rich agricultural region of Middle Egypt. Due to security problems in Middle Egypt in recent years, few cruises have operated the full length of the river.

Cruise boats also operate on Lake Nubia (Lake Nasser). There was originally one boat, *The Eugénie*, in the mid-1990s, but this has now increased to three (maybe now four). Unfortunately the boats seem to sail at the same time, rather than passing each other, which can lead to large groups at sites.

Many people now enjoy the Nile cruise, once the preserve of the rich.

USEFUL WEBSITES

TOURS

Numerous tour companies offer a wide range of possible ways to see all or parts of Egypt at varying prices: some have lecturers; some use cruise boats. If you have specific requests—or do not want to travel with the herd—a number of companies will organize a tour specifically to your requirements, but obviously at a price.

The Egyptian Tourist Authority sponsors two of the most useful sites:

Tour Egypt: www.touregypt.net

Tour Egypt Monthly is an extremely useful online magazine that covers all aspects of Egypt, ancient and modern: http://www.touregypt.net/magazine/

TOUR OPERATORS

Tour operators offering a wide range of options, and who will accommodate specific requirements, include:

UK-Based Tour Operators:

Ancient World Tours: www.ancient.co.uk

Bales Tours: www.balesworldwide.com

Eastmar Travel: www.eastmar-travel.com

First48: www.first48.com

Martin Randall Travel: www.martinrandall.com

Misr Travel (in German): www.misr-travel.com

Saga Holidays:www.saga.co.uk/travel

Travel Egypt: www.travelegypt.com

US-Based Tour Operators:

Abercrombie & Kent: www.abercrombiekent.com

Atlas Cruises & Tours: www.rivercruisetours.com

Brendan Worldwide Vacations: www.brendantours.com

Cox & Kings USA: www.coxandkingsusa.com

Geographic Expeditions: www.geoex.com

Globus Tours: www.globus-tour.com

Travcoa: www.travcoa.com

World Expeditions: www.worldexpeditions.net

Australia-Based Tour Operators:

Intrepid Travel: www.intrepidtravel.com

MadeEasy Tours: www.madeeasytours.com.au/

Peregrine Adventures: www.peregrine.net.au

World Expeditons: http://www.worldexpeditions.com.au/index.php

SHOPPING

For information on the sorts of souvenirs that you can buy in Egypt see:
http://www.ishoparoundtheworld.com/egypt.php3

VISITING EGYPTIAN TREASURES

MUSEUMS IN EGYPT

Egypt has a large number of museums covering all aspects of its culture and society from ancient to modern times. As well as those devoted to Pharaonic, Graeco-Roman, Coptic and Islamic art and archaeology, there are medical, geological and natural history collections, as well as displays of royal carriages and jewellery in Cairo and Alexandria. Visits to the museums considerably enrich the experience of visiting the sites themselves and usually present the material within a chronological framework that eases comprehension of the vast span of Egyptian civilization. Most major towns in Egypt have museums, but not all of them are open regularly.

A list of museums can be found at: www.egyptvoyager.com/museums_list.htm and at http://www.touregypt.net/museums.htm

CAIRO

Egyptian Museum

The largest and most important collection of antiquities of the Pharaonic period, including the treasures of Tutankhamun and many other famous pieces. See also Cairo and Surroundings chapter, Egyptian Museum section; and Special Topic later in this chapter, Treasures of Tutankhamun.

Tahrir Square, Cairo

http://www.egyptianmuseum.gov.eg

Coptic Museum

Situated within the Roman fortress of Babylon (Old Cairo), the Coptic Museum is another neglected treasure. Founded by Marcus Simaika Pasha in 1908, the building itself has some beautiful old wooden ceilings and *mushrabiya* work. Although the collections include Coptic Christian artefacts of the later Islamic periods, the most interesting exhibits are the early sculptures, stelae and other artefacts of Roman and Late Antique (Byzantine) Egypt. These combine elements of Pharaonic Egyptian, classical and Christian iconography.

Sharia Abu al-Sayfayn, Old Cairo

Museum of Islamic Art

A magnificent—and unfairly neglected—museum, housing an enormous collection of artefacts showing the full range of Islamic production, from many regions. The collections are arranged chronologically and thematically. Of particular note are the enamelled glass mosque lamps of Mamluk date, most from the late 13th to late 14th centuries.

352 Maydan Ahmad Mahir (Bab el-Khalk), entrance in Sharia Bur Said, Cairo

Gayer-Anderson Museum

Also known as Beit el-Kritliyya, this is an annex of the Museum of Islamic Art, adjacent to the Mosque of ibn Tulun on Sharia Tulun. The museum comprises two houses that stand on either side of a small alley, but are connected on the upper floors. These two houses, built in 1540 and 1631, were acquired and restored by Robert Gayer-Anderson between 1934 and 1942, using furniture and artefacts from old Ottoman houses and palaces in Cairo, with a room brought from Damascus. The most impressive feature is the *qa'a* (central covered courtyard), which rises through two floors. With a marble floor, mosaic fountain and *mushrabiya* screens, it is the best-preserved example in Cairo.

Giza Boat Museum

Adjacent to the Great Pyramid, many visitors find the Boat Museum more rewarding. The enormous cedar-wood boat is amazingly elegant and simple in design. The surrounding display includes much of the original rope that held the planks together, as well as details of how the boat was excavated and restored.

LUXOR AND KARNAK

Luxor Museum

On the corniche, a short way north of the Etap-Mercure Hotel, the Luxor Museum has a small but very fine display of statues and artefacts from the Luxor region. Of particular significance are the statues excavated from a cache in the great court of the Luxor temple in 1989. See also Luxor and Karnak chapter, Luxor Museum section.

Sharia Nahr el-Nil, Luxor

Karnak Open Air Museum

Constantly enlarged, the Open Air Museum houses some of the monuments recovered during excavation that had been dismantled in ancient times, many used as fill in the Third Pylon built by Amenhotep III. There are some beautiful small buildings, and many with superb sculptural decoration. Of particular note are the White Chapel of Senusret I, covered with superb low relief sculpture, the Alabaster Barque Shrine of Amenhotep I, with its distinctive portraits of the king, and the Red Chapel of Hatshepsut and Thutmose III. See also Luxor and Karnak chapter, Temples of Karnak section: Open Air Museum.

UPPER EGYPT

Nubia Museum

A beautiful new museum housing material excavated in Nubia and northern Sudan, and a display about the UNESCO campaign and the construction of the High Dam at Aswan. There is also a display about Nubian culture before the creation of the lake. See also Upper Egypt, South of Luxor chapter, Aswan section: Nubia Museum.

el-Fanadek Street, 81111, Aswan

www.numibia.net/nubia/

LOWER EGYPT

Alexandria, Graeco-Roman Museum

Founded in 1892, the museum contains a magnificent collection of statuary and artefacts from Alexandria itself and from sites in the Faiyum. There is a good array of statues of the Ptolemies and the Roman emperors. In the garden there are fragments of colossi in mixed Egyptian–Hellenistic style, more examples of which have been recovered in recent years, and others can be seen in the Open Air Museum around Pompey's Pillar.

Mathaf al-Romani, near Gamal Abdel Nasser Road, Alexandria

www.grm.gov.eg/

Tutankhamun's treasures on display in the Egyptian Museum, Cairo

Aerial view of Muslim cemetery, el-Minya

Egyptian Oases

Kom Aushim, Karanis Museum

At the entrance to the site. A small museum, but containing many interesting 'daily life' objects from the excavations, as well as some Pharaonic material from the region.

Selection of Museums around the World

E very major museum collection in the world has some Egyptian artefacts, and usually one or more mummies. In some countries, such as Britain and Germany, almost every small museum has collections, some of them excellent. The following list focuses on the most significant museums outside Egypt, or museums that have particularly important pieces. When the museums were created, most in the 19th century, attitudes were very different to those of today. Now, there are many who regard those years as a time of pillage: but this argument is countered by those who claim that much would otherwise have been destroyed. Anyone who visits the Egyptian Museum in Cairo will soon become aware of the enormous task of conservation and restoration that faces the Antiquities Service— and the basements of the museum are filled with even more than is on display. Whatever our present view of the morality of museums, they do allow us to care for, see and enjoy some of the finest of the artistic creations of Egypt, and artefacts that give an idea of how its people lived.

AUSTRALIA

Sydney

Nicholson Museum

The Egyptian collection was formed by Sir Charles Nicholson during his visit to Egypt in 1857 and was the first in Australia.

University of Sydney, Camperdown Campus, Sydney NSW 2006
http://www.usyd.edu.au/nicholson/

AUSTRIA

Vienna

Kunsthistorisches Museum

Having its origins in the 18th century, the Vienna collection is large with many impressive pieces. It is housed in a building that is itself impressive, with painted decoration by Gustav Klimt and Egyptian wall paintings by Ernst Weidenbach, who had accompanied Lepsius and the Prussian Expedition (1842–1845). The collection's particular strength is the rich array of statuary and sculpture of all periods. One of the most remarkable pieces is the head of a king in the *nemes*-headcloth acquired in the 18th century. For many years the polished style suggested to scholars that this was a Late Period statue, until the remainder was excavated on Elephantine Island and revealed it to be the head of a king Amenemhat of the 13th Dynasty.

Maria Theresien-Platz, A-1010 Wein
http://www.khm.at/

BELGIUM

Brussels

Les Musées royaux d'Art et d'Histoire

Parc du Cinquantenaire 10, B-1000 Bruxelles
http://www.kmkg-mrah.be/fr/cinquantenaire/kmkg_egypte/documents_fr/verzameling.html

CANADA

Toronto

Royal Ontario Museum

100 Queen's Park, Toronto, Ontario M5S 2C6
http://www.rom.on.ca/

DENMARK

Copenhagen

National Museum of Denmark
Ny Vestergade 10, DK-1220 Copenhagen
http://www.natmus.dk/

Ny Carlsberg Glyptotek
Dantes Plads 7, DK-1556 Copenhagen
http://www.glyptoteket.dk/

FRANCE

Paris

Musée du Louvre

The core of the Egyptian collection was purchased by Jean-François Champollion from the sale of the collection of Henry Salt. This was supplemented by Champollion's own expedition to Egypt in 1828–1829 and numerous other bequests and excavations. Every aspect of ancient Egypt is represented, from large scale monuments to amulets, jewellery and a linen dress. Amongst the most renowned early artefacts are: the Pre-Dynastic Gebel el-Arak knife, a silex (flint) blade with carved ivory handle decorated with scenes showing Mesopotamian influence (authenticity has been doubted); the Bull Palette, a splendid example of Pre-Dynastic sculpture; the stele of King Djet 'Serpent' from his tomb at Abydos; the stele of Nefertiabet, a superb painted Old Kingdom sculpted panel; the quartzite head of Djedefre, surely one of the finest royal sculptures to have survived; and the seated scribe. The Middle and New Kingdoms are represented by a splendid group of royal sculptures, including one of the colossi of Akhenaten from Karnak, some fine relief sculpture from Memphite tombs and a scene from a pillar in the tomb of Sety I. There is a superb display of furniture and basketwork from Deir el-Medina. Especially fine are some Libyan and Kushite period metal statues. The finest is probably the very large bronze image of the God's Wife of Amun, Karomama, acquired by Champollion. Slim and elegant in a tight-fitting pleated dress, she wears a wonderful collar inlaid in gold and silver wires. A superb kneeling bronze figure of the Kushite king Taharqo has been crudely fixed to a much older statue of the god Hemen, an obscure falcon god of Hefat (Moalla, south of Luxor), which is itself wrapped in gold foil. Amongst the equally impressive Late Period works is a group of sphinxes and lions from the avenue leading to the Serapeum complex at Saqqara. The Ptolemaic and Roman periods are represented by

TREASURES OF TUTANKHAMUN:
ON THE MOVE AGAIN

F rom June 2005 the treasures of King Tutankhamun are visiting the United States for the first time in nearly three decades. An exhibition, organized by the Egyptian Supreme Council of Antiquities, National Geographic, Arts and Exhibitions International and AEG Live Exhibitions, are taking the artefacts—discovered in the Valley of the Kings by Egyptologists Lord Carnarvon and Howard Carter in 1922—on a tour of at least three American cities. More than 130 treasures, which rarely leave their permanent home at the Egyptian Museum in Cairo, were originally lent exclusively to the Antikenmuseum Basel und Sammlung Ludwig (Basel Museum of Ancient Art) in 2004 for display in its new department of Egyptian art. However, the volume of interest generated during the brief exhibition—620,000 visitors over three months—led to an extension of the tour, first to the Kunst und Ausstellungshalle (Art and Exhibition Hall) in Bonn and then across the Atlantic.

In the United States the exhibition, entitled *Tutankhamun and the Golden Age of the Pharaohs*, opens on 16 June 2005 at the **Los Angeles County Museum of Art** (LACMA), after which it visits the **Museum of Art, Fort Lauderdale** (December 2005) and the **Field Museum, Chicago** (May 2006). A further tour of European museums is planned for 2007, the itinerary for which, at time of press, has not yet been finalized.

The only previous Tutankhamun exhibition in America, a seven-city tour between 1976 and 1979, contained less material than the present display, but still managed to attract over eight million visitors. The new exhibition, by contrast, will be far more comprehensive, containing many items that have never been seen outside Egypt,

(above) *Funerary mask of Tutankhamun, shown wearing the* nemes-headdress, *with the vulture of Nekhbet and rearing cobra of Wadjet on his forehead; gold, semiprecious stones, quartz and glass paste.*

allowing the visitor to understand the wider context in which Tutankhamun lived. At the heart of the current tour are 50 objects found in Tutankhamun's tomb. These include the golden diadem set with precious stones that was found on the head of his corpse, and which it is thought he wore in life; a canopic bust depicting the head of the pharaoh; the jewelled container holding his mummified organs; and the dagger that was discovered in the wrappings of his mummy. Other notable items are a golden shrine portraying Tutankhamun's wife, Ankhesenamun, statues, collars, fans, mirrors and precious vessels. Visitors can also enter a full-size replica of the inner burial chamber.

More than 70 artefacts from other royal tombs of the 18th Dynasty are accompanying the relics of Tutankhamun around the United States: material from the celebrated funerary chamber of Yuya and Tjuyu, the great-grandparents of Tutankhamun, as well as items from the graves of the pharaohs Amenhotep II and Thutmose IV.

It is hoped that the tour will raise US$40 million to fund a new museum for antiquities in Egypt, as well as paying for the restoration of other monuments, including the pyramids.

Gold sarcophagus of Tutankhamun, decorated with semiprecious stones and glass paste, showing the king with the divine beard of the pharaoh and the royal sceptre and flail held in his crossed hands.

Useful websites

Exhibition website: www.kingtut.org
LACMA: www.lacma.org
Museum of Art, Fort Lauderdale: www.moafl.org
Field Museum, Chicago: www.fieldmuseum.org

Scene from the backrest of Tutankhamun's throne, depicting the king and his wife, Ankhesenamun; gold leaf on wood, silver, glass paste and semiprecious stones.

Photos courtesy of the Egyptian Government, Ministry of Culture.

fine coffins and a group of Ptolemaic royal heads (in the classical sculpture galleries). There is some very fine Coptic material, notably a stylized acanthus capital from the monastery at Bawit, and a collection of sculptures (perhaps from Herakleopolis-Ehnasiya) and textiles showing that extraordinary blend of classical and Christian styles that is characteristic of the period.

Palais du Louvre, 75058 Paris Cedex 01

http://www.louvre.fr/

Place de la Concorde Obelisk

A gift to France from Mohammed Ali (as guides never cease to remind us, he received a clock in exchange, now in the Alabaster Mosque, that stopped working). This is the western obelisk from the outside pylon of Luxor temple, and is slightly shorter than its remaining companion. The obelisk arrived France in 1833 in the reign of Louis Philippe.

GERMANY

Berlin

Ägyptisches Museum und Papyrussammlung

The core of the collection was formed by Giuseppe Passalacqua and purchased by Friedrich Wilhelm IV of Prussia. It was later considerably enlarged by the acquisitions of the Prussian Expedition led by Richard Lepsius and the major German excavations, notably at Abusir and Amarna. The main collection, formerly displayed in the Bodemuseum on Museum Island, is currently closed while the Lepsius Museum is being restored. A large collection of fine pieces is displayed in the Egyptian Museum in Charlottenburg. Amongst the most celebrated are a tiny boxwood head generally believed to depict Queen Tiye, wife of Amenhotep III, and the painted bust of Nefertiti. Of particular fascination is the array of plaster 'masks' from Amarna. These images, which are now recognized as sculptors' models, are slightly disturbing, but they do give a sense of looking at the real faces of some of Akhenaten's most powerful courtiers. It is shame that, apart from the king and queen, we cannot identify most of them. Two, however, are fairly certain: a lady with large earrings is generally recognized as Akhenaten's second wife, Kiya, and one of the most striking faces is probably Ay, who later became king—in this case the profile is very similar to that found in reliefs in Ay's tomb.

Charlottenburg, Schlossstrasse 70, D-14059 Berlin-Charlottenburg.

http://www.smb.spk-berlin.de/amp/e/s.html

Hannover

Kestner-Museum

The original collection was formed by August Kestner (1777–1853) in Rome and given to the city in 1884—it has since been supplemented by many other acquisitions. The museum focuses on the 'minor' or 'applied' arts, rather than monumental pieces. It has a fine group of relief sculpture and some important small sculptures. Most notable are a beautiful head of Amenhotep III and a New Kingdom dyad of a priest named Kinebu and his wife Iset.

Trammplatz, 3, D-30159 Hannover

http://www.hannover.de/deutsch/kultur/museen/mus_mus/mus_all/kestner/kes_engl.htm

Hildesheim

Roemer und Pelizaeus Museum

Am Steine 1-2, D-31134 Hildesheim

http://www.rpmuseum.de/alt_aegypten/alt_aegypten_index.html

Leipzig

Ägyptisches Museum der Universität Leipzig

Egyptology has a long tradition in Leipzig; it is one of the most significant university departments in Germany with some eminent professors in its history. This important collection contains large numbers of artefacts from the University's own excavations at Giza, Qaw and those directed by George Steindorff at Aniba in Lower Nubia.

Burgstrasse 21, D-04109 Leipzig

http://www.uni-leipzig.de/~egypt/Museum.htm

Munich

Staatliches Museum Ägyptischer Kunst

A wide-ranging collection with many fine pieces from all periods. Unusual is a statue in red marble of Antinous wearing the royal headcloth and kilt, although otherwise in the classical style. It was dug up at Hadrian's Villa at Tivoli and restored in the 18th century. The *Venus of Meroe* is a rather intriguing plastered and painted sandstone statue from the Royal Bath (probably a nymphaeum) in the Sudanese city—it is one of a number of pieces executed following classical traditions that were set up in this rather enigmatic structure (first century AD). Also from Meroe is some splendid jewellery removed by an Italian doctor, Giuseppe Ferlini, from the pyramid

tomb of the Nubian queen, Amanishakheto (first century BC) in 1834. There is also some good Coptic material.

Hofgartenstrasse, D-80333 München

http://www.aegyptisches-museum-muenchen.com/de/

GREECE

Athens

National Archaeological Museum

The museum's most significant Egyptian antiquities are bronzes of the Libyan to Saite periods acquired in the late 19th century: a magnificent statue of the Libyan princess Takushit, inlaid with images of deities in gold wire; a kneeling figure of the Kushite pharaoh Shabaqo; and a large kneeling bronze royal figure of the 25th to early 26th dynasties.

Patission 44 St, Athens 10682

http://www.culture.gr/

IRELAND

Dublin

Museum of Archaeology and History

A collection of mostly smaller artefacts dating from the Pre-Dynastic to medieval periods, many acquired through the excavations of Flinders Petrie and others in the late 19th and early 20th centuries.

National Museum of Ireland, Kildare Street, Dublin 2

http://www.museum.ie/archaeology/

ITALY

Bologna

Museo Civico Archeologico di Bologna

Via dell'Archiginnasio 2, I-40124 Bologna

http://www.comune.bologna.it/museoarcheologico/

Florence

Museo Archeologico Nazionale e Museo Egizio di Firenze

Ippolito Rosellini (1800–1843) was born in Pisa, then part of the Grand Duchy of Tuscany. He studied Oriental languages in Bologna and later worked with Champollion in Italy and in Paris. In 1828–1829 he and a group of Italian scholars joined

A Nubian man gazes at the head of Ramesses II, entrance to the Temple of Luxor

Champollion and his team to form the Franco-Tuscan Expedition to Egypt. Besides copying the inscriptions and scenes on the monuments, they did some small excavations and formed large collections of antiquities. Amongst the larger pieces is a beautifully sculpted and painted relief panel, cut from a pillar in the tomb of Sety I in the Valley of the Kings. The chariot, excavated at Thebes, is one of the few complete Egyptian chariots surviving (the rest were found in the tomb of Tutankhamun).

Via della Colonna 38, I-50121 Firenze

http://www.mega.it/archeo.toscana/esamueg.htm

Rome

The ancient Egyptian antiquities in Rome are rather different to those found elsewhere in museum collections that are the result of excavation or collection by travellers. Many of those in Rome were taken to the city in the first and second centuries AD, most to be used in the temples of Isis and Serapis, or at Hadrian's Villa at Tivoli. (See also later in this chapter: Visiting Ancient Egypt in Rome.)

Musei Capitolini (Capitoline Museum)

The courtyard contains grey granite columns with relief scenes of priests—these come from the colonnades of the Iseum, the Temple of Isis on the Campus Martius. There is also a basalt sphinx of Ahmose II (Amasis). The two sphinx-like lions flanking the long ramp (the *cordonata*) rising from the Piazza d'Aracoeli to the Campidoglio (Capitoline Hill) were probably amongst the sculptures brought by Domitian to his renewed Temple of Isis following its destruction by fire in AD 80. By the 15th century the lions had been placed in front of the Lateran Palace. They were transferred to Michelangelo's new Campidoglio and converted into fountains in 1587. They have served as models for numerous lions elsewhere in Europe.

Piazza del Campidoglio 1, I-00186 Rome

http://www.museicapitolini.org/en/index_msie.htm

Museo Nazionale delle Terme (Baths of Diocletian)

The museum, one of the most significant displays of ancient art and artefacts, is partly housed in the Baths of Diocletian. Amongst the many fine works are the important collection of the Ludovisi family, and that from Museo Kircheriano (of Athanasius Kircher), as well as the wonderful paintings from the house of Augustus's wife Livia. Amongst the Roman works, there are many pieces of Egyptian statuary on display here.

Viale delle Terme di Diocleziano and Piazza della Repubblica, Rome

Vatican Museums and Galleries

The **Museo Gregoriano Egiziano** was inaugurated in 1839 by Gregory XVI in response to the flowering of Egyptology as an academic discipline elsewhere in Europe. The collection is particularly rich in antiquities that were taken to Rome by the emperors for dedication in, and decoration of, the temples of Isis and Serapis in the city and the villa of Hadrian at Tivoli. Many of these sculptures were excavated during the papal restorations and building works throughout the city from the Renaissance onwards. Many of them were restored in the 18th century: a feature once criticized is now of interest in our understanding of the 'reception of antiquity' in the West. The black granite lions of Nakhtnebef (Nectanebo I), from the Iseum, are of a rare type, recumbent with head at right angles to the body; the lion is shown resting after the hunt, an image of the king as universal conqueror. The statue of Udjahorresnet (upper part restored) is covered with important historical inscriptions that record events in the Persian conquest of Egypt by Cambyses and Darius. The colossal black granite statue of a queen is one of the most imposing female images from Egypt. The statue depicts Queen Tiye, wife of Amenhotep III, but was later recut for Mut-Tuya (Tuya), mother of Ramesses II. The feet were restored in the 18th century, and the image of princess Henutmire at the side is restored, wearing a mini-skirt! Originally from Heliopolis, the three red granite early Ptolemaic statues were used to ornament an Egyptian style pavilion built for the emperor Caligula in the Gardens of Sallust on the Pincian Hill: they depict Ptolemy II, Arsinoe II and Philotera. Amongst a group of statues from the Canopus of Hadrian's Villa at Tivoli is a marble Antinous in classical style, but wearing Egyptian costume. Another striking statue in classical style depicts Anubis. The canine head emerging without wig from the relaxed posture of the body is far more unnerving than the formal Egyptian image of the god.

The **Braccio Nuovo** is a sculpture gallery that contains a colossal marble statue of the Nile found in 1513, along with a similar statue of the Tiber (now in the Louvre), near the site of the Iseum. Probably a Roman sculpture based on a Hellenistic model, the reclining god, depicted with long hair and beard, rests against a sphinx while holding a cornucopia, symbolizing the wealth of the land, and is surrounded by 16 restored *erotes* (small babies) representing the 16 cubits of a very high Nile. This statue served as a model for a monument in St Paul's Cathedral, London, commemorating George Blagdon Westcott who died in the Battle of Abu Qir. Also in the gallery is another influential sculpture, probably carved in Pergamon in the reign of Hadrian, unearthed in the early 16th century. It depicts a reclining female figure and is generally known as the *Dying Kleopatra*, although the actual subject is unknown.

Renaissance Rome Reinterprets Egypt: The Borgia Apartments in the Vatican

During the early Renaissance a large number of manuscripts and books arrived in Italy from the eastern Mediterranean. Amongst these were the *Hieroglyphics of Horapollo* and the *Hermetic Corpus*. Along with Plutarch's work *On Isis and Osiris*, these books stimulated interest in ancient Egypt and its 'wisdom', much of which was thought to be found in the symbolism of hieroglyphics. There were many translations and interpretations of the writings on Egypt, but links with Christianity were also sought. So, the Osiris legend was regarded as an imperfect prefiguring of the passion and resurrection of Christ. It also became widely believed that the spiritual wisdom of Egypt had been passed to Moses: this is reflected in the decoration of Siena Cathedral of 1488 where Thoth (as Hermes Trismegistus) is called the contemporary and teacher of Moses.

One of the most bizarre manifestations of the Italian Renaissance's renewed interest in Egypt appeared in the works of the Dominican abbot Giovanni Nanni (*c*.1432–1502). A man of his time, Nanni was renowned as a preacher and author; he was also a skilled politician, who acted as confidential secretary to the Borgia pope, Alexander VI (reigned 1492–1503)—until he was murdered by the pope's son, Cesare. Nanni, writing under the Latinized name Annius, attempted to show that Italic culture did not owe its origins to Greece, but that Osiris himself had travelled to Italy and taught the people agriculture and viticulture. He based his claim on a late version of the Osiris legend, preserved in the work of Diodorus of Sicily, in which Osiris was a world conqueror. Clearly, in this version, Osiris has been merged with the other world conquerors of classical texts: Dionysus (Bacchus), the bringer of wine and viticulture; and Sesostris, a composite figure in classical literature. As proof of his claim, Annius produced 12 ancient texts that he had 'rediscovered'. These texts not only supported Annius's own claim, but each other, and had confirmation and illustration in genuine ancient authors. But the whole was a brilliant and erudite fraud and all of the texts were written by Annius himself.

In addition to his main thesis, Annius was able to provide an ancient ancestry for the papal family, in which the Borgia were descended directly from the 'Egyptian

Hercules', son of Osiris. The heraldic emblem of the Borgia, a bull, was now revealed to be no less than the sacred Apis bull of Memphis. It was probably Annius who devised the scheme for the allegorical paintings executed by Pinturicchio (1454–1513) and his workshop between 1492 and 1494 in the Borgia apartments in the Vatican (the Sala dei Santi, now housing the Museum of Modern Catholic Art).

The south wall of the Sala dei Santi, where the papal throne was placed, is dominated by a scene of St Catherine of Alexandria debating with the emperor Maxentius and the scholars of Alexandria. The subject of their dispute was the 'Incarnation and Passion of Christ'. By the time of the painting's composition, the legend of St Catherine had been elaborated. Not just the daughter of a noble Alexandrian family, Catherine was now said to be the niece of the emperor Constantine: Maxentius's persecution of her was therefore a goad to his rival. When Maxentius brought his armies to Rome to confront Constantine, he was defeated at the Battle of the Milvian Bridge. It was immediately prior to this battle that Constantine had his famous vision of the cross that marks a turning point in the rise of Christianity in the Roman Empire. At the centre of the Pinturicchio's painting of the dispute is a triumphal arch, modelled on that which Constantine built (near the Colosseum) to celebrate his victory over Maxentius. The whole scene therefore alludes to the triumph of Christianity. The arch is surmounted by the Apis bull which is, throughout the decorative scheme, used as an allusion to the Borgia pope. The arch and the Apis/Borgia bull would have been directly above the papal throne. The Latin inscription on the arch reads: 'To the cultivator of peace', alluding to Christ, Apis and the Pope.

The vault of the Sala dei Santi, with a rich blue and gold background, carries four scenes of the Osiris legend, which here prefigures the death and resurrection of Christ. The first shows the murder and dismemberment of Osiris. In the second, Isis gathers her husband's remains and places them in the tomb she has built. This tomb is a pyramid, richly patterned and gilded, standing inside an elaborate classical shrine. In the third scene the pyramid appears again, and by its side stands the Apis: this represents Osiris's resurrection as the Apis, but also alludes to Christ's resurrection and Borgia's elevation to the papacy. The last scene is a procession with an elaborate shrine housing the bull (paralleling the tomb of Osiris). The accompanying Latin text tells us: 'They had no sooner begun the sacred rites than the bones rose up as a bull displayed to the people.' In formulating this elaborate iconographic scheme, Annius was fortunate that the Borgia arms (which form the centrepiece of the vaulted ceiling) actually included a bull; his task would have been more difficult with the pawnbroker's balls of the Medici (Leo X).

We might now laugh at such elaborate symbolism and interpretation, but we belong to a different world. Annius was one of a number of writers who were interested in the symbolism of Egyptian hieroglyphic writing, which was detailed in the *Hieroglyphics of Horapollo* and to a lesser extent in other ancient writers such as Apuleius (in his novel *The Golden Ass*). In one of the most significant parts of his work, Annius repeated Diodorus's claim that in his campaigns, Osiris had set up columns with hieroglyphic inscriptions to commemorate his victories. Conveniently, one of these columns was still preserved in the church of San Lorenzo in Annius's home town of Viterbo. Annius claimed to be able to read its inscription, which, he said, stated that it had been set up by Osiris after he had liberated the Italian people and taught them agriculture. This fabricated hieroglyphic text was the first, but by no means the last, of the Renaissance; hieroglyphic studies increased, leading ultimately to some important discoveries by Athanasius Kircher, which would be invaluable in the eventual decipherment.

On a number of occasions during his stay in Rome in 1644, the influential English traveller and diarist John Evelyn (1620–1705/06) met Athanasius Kircher and discussed hieroglyphics with him. Evelyn's diary contains a number of observations on the Egyptian antiquities he saw in the city, particularly the obelisks and their inscriptions. Nor was Annius totally forgotten: in November 1644, on his way to Rome, Evelyn stopped at Viterbo and commented on the inscription there that reputedly recorded Osiris's conquest of Italy. Evelyn's interest in hieroglyphics and Egyptian antiquities was only one aspect of his Italian tour, but it may have been even more significant if politics had not intervened. From Rome, Evelyn travelled to Venice, where he planned, like many before him, to join a ship to the Holy Land and 'Grand Cairo'. He was prevented from undertaking the voyage by events in the eastern Mediterranean, but was given a collection of small Egyptian antiquities brought back by the (English) ship's captain from the 'mummy pits' of Saqqara. Although politically and economically Venice was in decline, the city had for centuries been the main port for trade and pilgrimage with the eastern Mediterranean, and particularly with Alexandria and Cairo.

Also worth looking at in the Vatican is the **Museum of Modern Catholic Art**, not, alas, for its displays, but for the decoration of the rooms where it is housed (in the Sala dei Santi near the Sistine Chapel). The apartments were decorated by Pinturicchio for the notorious Pope Alexander VI Borgia (reigned 1492–1503). The scenes include the dispute of St Catherine of Alexandria with the emperor Maxentius (ruled AD 306–312) and the legend of Osiris and the Apis bull. The Renaissance renewal of interest in Egypt naturally embraced Isis and Osiris, stimulated particularly by study of Plutarch's *On Isis and Osiris*. There were obvious parallels to be drawn between the god's death and resurrection and that of Christ and it was interpreted as an imperfect prefiguring of the passion (for further detail see Special Topic on Renaissance Rome in this chapter).

00120 Vatican City

http://www.christusrex.org/www1/vaticano/EG-Egiziano.html

Turin

Museo Egizio

The most impressive of the Egyptian collections in Italy, and one of the most significant outside Egypt, Turin houses some justly famous works. The collection in Turin goes back to the 17th century when the Duke of Savoy acquired the Mensa Isiaca, a bronze slab elaborately inlaid with Egyptian figures and hieroglyphs in copper, silver and niello. The piece had been found in Rome in 1527 and entered the collection of Cardinal Bembo, becoming one of the most celebrated of Egyptian antiquities during the Renaissance. It is now recognized as of Roman date, but even so, it is one of the most important artefacts in the history of European interest in ancient Egypt. Some statues and small objects entered the ducal collection during the 18th century, but the major acquisition was the collection—some 5,300 artefacts— of Bernardino Drovetti, Napoleon's consul in Egypt (1824). The emphasis was large sculpture, much of Theban origin and dating from the New Kingdom. Later additions to expand and supplement the historical range were through the excavations of Ernesto Schiaparelli and Giulio Farina. More recently the Egyptian government gave Thutmose III's rock-cut chapel from el-Lessiya (Ellessiya), which was rescued during the UNESCO campaign in Nubia.

Highlights of the collection are the statuary, including the spectacular seated Ramesses II wearing the blue crown and long pleated robe; a statue of Sety II from outside his triple barque shrine at Karnak (companion in the Louvre); and a seated Amun with Tutankhamun. There is a rich array of material from Schiaparelli's excavations at Deir el-Medina, including objects from the tomb of Kha, notably loaves of bread, a bed with its mattress and sheets, and a wonderful pair of papyrus sandals; these are human artefacts that really bring us much closer to the inhabitants of that village. Amongst the more peculiar objects is a small wooden figure of Queen Tiye as a hippopotamus.

Via Accademia delle Scienze 6, I-10123 Torino

http://www.museoegizio.org/

NETHERLANDS

Leiden

Rijksmuseum van Oudheden

Rapenburg 28, 2301 EW Leiden

http://www.rmo.nl/new/home.html

RUSSIA

Moscow

Pushkin State Museum of Fine Arts

Oriental Department, Ulitsa Volkhonka 12, 121019 Moscow

http://www.museum.ru/gmii/

St Petersburg

State Hermitage Museum

Dvortsovaya Naberezhnaya (Palace Embankment) 34, 190000, St Petersburg

http://www.hermitagemuseum.org/

SPAIN

Barcelona

Museu Egipci de Barcelona

València 284, E-08007 Barcelona

http://www.fundclos.com/

Madrid

Museo Arqueológico Nacional

Serrano, 13, E-28001 Madrid

http://www.man.es/

SUDAN

Khartoum

Sudan National Museum

The Sudan National Museum contains a superb collection of material from excavations in Nubia and north Sudan. In the garden are several of the temples from the fortresses at the Second Cataract: Buhen, Semna and Kumma. These were built by Thutmose III and Hatshepsut and have fine relief decoration. All that remains of the temple of Aksha, built by Ramesses II, is a wall and part of a gate with images of the deified king. The collection celebrates the rich indigenous cultures of Nubia—neighbours, trading partners and at times rivals of Pharaonic Egypt. Amongst the larger sculptures are statues of the Kushite kings from Gebel Barkal. The wide range of smaller objects complements the Nubia Museum in Aswan. The Upper Gallery contains some of the outstanding frescoes from the cathedral at Faras, depicting saints with the Nubian kings and queens. Remarkably these Christian rulers wear crowns that retain some of the features of Egyptian regalia, notably ram's horns.

El Neel Avenue, Khartoum

SWEDEN

Stockholm

Medelhavsmuseet

Fredsgatan 2, Gustav Adolfs Torg, S-11484 Stockholm
http://www.medelhavsmuseet.se/

SWITZERLAND

Geneva

Musée d'Art et d'Histoire

Rue Charles-Galland 2, CH-1206 Genève
http://mah.ville-ge.ch/

TURKEY

Istanbul

The Topkapi Palace Museum (Topkapi Sarayi)

The great complex of the Topkapi Palace was the heart of the Ottoman Empire. The splendour of the building, and its political intrigues, made it the focus of western European fantasies about 'the Orient'. The museum is filled with works from within the Ottoman Empire and from its trading links along the Silk Road to China and East Asia. The ancient heritage of the lands that later formed the Ottoman Empire is preserved in the Archaeological Museum and the Museum of the Ancient Orient, inside the first courtyard of the Palace. The latter contains an array of Egyptian antiquities on different scales. Amongst the notable items on display are: the upper part of a fine 12th-dynasty statue of a queen, with a remarkably undamaged face; a statue of a type typical of the Late Period, depicting a kneeling official holding a shrine with a statue of Osiris; and a colossal granite sphinx. The last is now missing its head and forepaws, but is interesting as it was excavated in the old city of Istanbul and may have been brought along with the obelisk to adorn the Hippodrome.

Sultan Ahmet, Eminonu, Istanbul

http://www.ee.bilkent.edu.tr/~history/topkapi.html

http://english.istanbul.gov.tr/

Atmeidan Obelisk

This red granite obelisk, nearly 20 metres high in its broken state (originally about 30 metres), was one of a pair dedicated by Thutmose III at Karnak, at the west side of the gateway of the Seventh Pylon. The ramps used for the removal of the obelisk are still in the court. It may have been taken to Alexandria with the Lateran obelisk, in the reign of Constantine (AD 306–337) or Constantius II (AD 351–361), but did not arrive in Constantinople until the time of Theodosius (AD 379–395), who had it set up in the Hippodrome. The massive sculptured pedestal carries scenes showing the obelisk on the barge and in the Hippodrome.

UNITED KINGDOM

Bolton

Bolton Museums, Art Gallery & Aquarium

Much of the collection was formed through donations from the excavations of Flinders Petrie and the Egypt Exploration Society.

Le Mans Crescent, Bolton, Lancs BL1 1SE

http://www.boltonmuseums.org.uk/HTML/archaeology_egyptology_ancient.asp

Cambridge

Fitzwilliam Museum

The display collection is dominated by a red granite sarcophagus lid with an attached statue of Ramesses III as Osiris. The lid was removed by Belzoni from the king's tomb in Thebes. Also of particular note is the beautiful head of Amenemhat III (the Grenfell Head) in shelly greywacke.

Trumpington Street, Cambridge CB2 1RB

http://www.fitzmuseum.cam.ac.uk/

Durham

Oriental Museum

University of Durham, Elvet Hill, Durham DH1 3TH

http://www.dur.ac.uk/oriental.museum/gallery/egypt/

Edinburgh

Royal Museum

The renowned art historian, Cyril Aldred was curator of the Egyptian collection for many years and supplemented it with some astute acquisitions. Most notable of those was the faience plaque depicting the Libyan king Iuput emerging as a child from a lotus flower (a companion piece is in the Brooklyn Museum of Art). There is an unusual large sandstone statue of a deity from John Garstang's excavations at Meroe in northern Sudan.

National Museums of Scotland, Chambers Street, Edinburgh EH1 1JF

http://www.nms.ac.uk/royal/index.htm

Glasgow

The Burrell Collection

This has its origins in the private collection of a Glasgow shipowner who was involved in bringing Kleopatra's Needle to London. There are some fine Egyptian pieces, notably a 12th-dynasty queen's head with a finely modelled Hathorian wig.

Pollock Country Park, 2060 Pollockshaws Road, Glasgow G43 1AT

http://www.glasgowmuseums.com/

Kingston Lacy

Kingston Lacy House

The house was enlarged and filled with his spectacular collections by William Bankes (1786–1855), who travelled in Egypt and the Near East between 1815 and 1819, going as far as Abu Simbel. He employed Linant de Bellefonds to make drawings and watercolours of the monuments of northern Sudan and later sent him to Naqa, Musawarrat es-Sufra and Meroe. Although Linant's drawings were amongst the earliest to record any of the Meroitic monuments of Sudan, they were not published.

A special exhibition in the house includes some Egyptian monuments, with part of a splendid divine statue of the reign of Amenhotep III and some of the paintings commissioned from Linant. In the park facing the house is the obelisk from in front of the pylon of the Temple of Isis at Philae, removed by Belzoni and subject of one of the most colourful incidents in Belzoni's decidedly colourful career. The obelisk is important because of the bilingual inscription, written in Greek and Egyptian hieroglyphics—Bankes was interested in the decipherment of hieroglyphics. There are also some sarcophagi.

Kingston Lacy House, Wimborne Minster, Dorset BH21 4EA
http://www.nationaltrust.org.uk/main/

London

British Museum

The earliest Egyptian antiquities were given to the British Museum in the mid-18th century. A major gift by King George III of the antiquities captured by the British from the French in Egypt included the Rosetta Stone, still one of the museum's most celebrated artefacts (and ongoing subject of ownership disputes). The trustees reluctantly (under)paid Henry Salt for his first collection of antiquities, but rejected the sarcophagus of Sety I. Numerous acquisitions throughout the 19th and 20th centuries, by purchase, gift and excavation, have made this one of the largest collections outside Egypt. Every aspect of ancient Egyptian culture is represented. In recent years the displays have been revitalized. The new Enlightenment Gallery in the King's Library contains Egyptian antiquities and explains how the modern museum has developed and changed.

Great Russell Street, London WC1B 3DG
http://www.thebritishmuseum.ac.uk/

John Soane Museum

The house of the architect Sir John Soane, created from three adjoining terraced houses and filled with his extraordinary collection. There are some small Egyptian artefacts, but Soane's most important acquisition was the alabaster sarcophagus of Sety I, bought from Henry Salt for £2,000 after it had been rejected by the Trustees of the British Museum (who paid Salt £2,000 for the rest of his collection). The sarcophagus had been removed by Belzoni from Sety's tomb in the Valley of the Kings.

13 Lincoln's Inn Fields, London WC2A 3BP
http://www.soane.org/

ISLAMIC ART IN MUSEUMS

Most of the world's major museums house important collections of art from Muslim countries, which include considerable numbers of objects from Egypt. Some were made there and went abroad centuries ago as items of trade and official gifts; others were acquired during the colonial period when Europeans were working in Egypt in a range of capacities. Now there is a growing interest in these collections—over the next few years a number of the most important will be given new galleries and displays: the Victoria and Albert Museum (V&A) in London, the Louvre in Paris, the Metropolitan Museum of Art in New York and the Detroit Institute of Arts. Renewed interest in Islamic art is also coming from wealthy Muslim collectors and a new museum is under construction in the Gulf state of Qatar.

Central to the Islamic holdings of the **V&A** is the collection formed in Egypt in the 19th century by Dr Meymar. This includes the magnificent inlaid wooden *minbar* (pulpit) from the mosque of Sultan Qaitbay. Amongst other notable items is a Fatimid pear-shaped rock crystal ewer, similar to those in St Mark's, Venice. The new Islamic gallery is due to re-open in 2006, but many objects are still on display, including glass and pottery: you just have to search harder. There is also a touring exhibition of a selection of particularly fine pieces, as well as a range of furniture and other objects manufactured in Britain in the 19th century, inspired by the period's interest in Islamic art and design.

One of the most important Egyptian Islamic collections outside Egypt is in the new Museum of Islamic Art of the **Benaki Museum**, Athens. The founder of the museum, cotton trader Antonis Benakis (1873–1954), was born in Alexandria and retired to Greece in 1926. He formed much of his collection in Egypt in the early 20th century, although it contains items from all over the Islamic world, including an important pair of wooden doors from Samarra in Iraq. He amassed some 10,000 objects, including a fine Coptic collection with many important textiles. One of the most imposing features of the new Islamic gallery is the marble-lined interior from a 17th-century Cairo mansion.

V&A: www.vam.ac.uk/collections/asia/islamic_gall/
Benaki Museum: www.benaki.gr/collections/islamic/en/

Kleopatra's Needle

The obelisk is one of a pair of granite obelisks set up by Thutmose III at Heliopolis (the other is now in New York), later moved by Augustus to Alexandria where they stood in front of the temple of the deified Julius Caesar. The obelisks of Rome and Paris have been used to enhance urban spaces, forming the focus of great squares; the New York obelisk adorns a park; how typically English to dump an obelisk, as if it is an embarrassment, on one of the most uninteresting stretches of the Thames Embankment, where it cannot be seen properly and where it does little to enhance the surroundings: a grimy and undignified end.

Leighton House

Not strictly Egyptian, this was the house built by the leading British academic painter of the late 19th century, Frederick, Lord Leighton (1830–1896). Although much of the house is eminently bourgeois, an 'Arab Hall' is attached, richly decorated with tiles collected throughout Syria and the Near East; on the first floor a balcony with *mushrabiya* screens overlooks the hall. The whole is a fine example of the passion for Orientalism—although Leighton as an artist was not Orientalist.

12 Holland Park Road, Kensington, London W14 8LZ
www.rbck.gov.uk/leightonhousemuseum

Petrie Museum of Egyptian Archaeology

The finest teaching collection in the UK, which was formed by Sir Flinders Petrie from excavation and purchase. Particularly important is the sequence of pottery running from the Pre-Dynastic to Islamic periods. There is a large quantity of material from Petrie's excavations at Amarna. Two colossal lions from the excavations at Koptos are displayed in the south cloister of the main College building.

University College London, Malet Place, London WC1E 6BT
http://www.petrie.ucl.ac.uk/

Manchester

Manchester Museum

The Manchester businessman Jesse Haworth was a sponsor of Flinders Petrie's excavations and he built up a large private collection that was given to the museum. Haworth's donation has been considerably enlarged, with a lot of excavated material, notably from the work of the Egypt Exploration Society. There is an impressive collection from Petrie's excavations at Kahun; a fine set of Middle Kingdom coffins and associated material from the intact 'Tomb of the Two Brothers'; and Nubian and

Meroitic objects from the Oxford University Excavations at Faras, Sanam and Kawa in Nubia and Sudan.

University of Manchester, Oxford Road, Manchester M13 9PL
http://museum.man.ac.uk/

Oxford

Ashmolean Museum

The earliest Egyptian antiquities at Oxford were acquired in the 17th century, being supplemented by further gifts of mainly small objects throughout the 18th century, and considerably enlarged by the gift (1865–1892) of the Reverend Greville Chester. From 1884, the majority of material came from the excavations conducted by Flinders Petrie and the University's own digs in Nubia and Sudan, directed by Francis Llewellyn Griffith. This has made the Ashmolean's one of the major teaching collections. It is particularly rich in material from the Pre-Dynastic to Early Dynastic periods, notably the colossal statues of Min from Koptos and the ceremonial mace heads of kings 'Scorpion' and Narmer, the Battlefield Palette, and the statue of Khasekhemwy, all from the cache at Hierakonpolis. Amongst the New Kingdom material is the renowned fragment of a large wall painting excavated by Petrie at Amarna, showing two of the king's youngest daughters. The Ashmolean is particularly rich in sculptures and artefacts excavated by the Oxford Excavations in Nubia in the temples of Kawa and Sanam, and the cemeteries at Sanam, Faras and Firka. The collection spans the whole of Nubian archaeology from the earliest 'A-Group' to Christian periods. Particularly impressive are the sandstone shrines of the 25th-dynasty pharaoh Taharqo and king Aspelta from Kawa; the granite ram of Taharqo from Kawa; and some slabs of relief sculpture from the temple of Tahaqo at Sanam.

Beaumont Street, Oxford OX1 2PH
http://www.ashmol.ox.ac.uk/

Swansea

Egypt Centre and Wellcome Museum

University of Wales Swansea, Singleton Park, Swansea SA2 8PP
http://www.swan.ac.uk/egypt/

UNITED STATES OF AMERICA

Atlanta

Michael C. Carlos Museum of Emory University

571 South Kilgo Circle, Atlanta, GA 30322
http://carlos.emory.edu/COLLECTION/EGYPT/

Baltimore

Walters Art Museum

600 North Charles Street, Baltimore, MA 21201

http://www.thewalters.org/

Boston

Boston Museum of Fine Arts

One of the leading collections in the USA, with a spectacular array of material. One particularly rich holding is from the joint Harvard–Boston excavations, directed by George Reisner. As a result Boston has the largest collections of material from the royal cemeteries in Sudan at el-Kurru, Nuri and Meroe from the first millennium BC to the fifth century AD. There is also large-scale statuary of the 25th-dynasty pharaohs and their Kushite successors from the temples at Gebel Barkal near the Fourth Cataract. Reisner excavated at Kerma, the Kushite capital of a kingdom that rivalled Egypt during the Middle Kingdom and Second Intermediate Period. Resulting from Reisner's excavations at Giza, the museum has one of the finest collections of Old Kingdom royal sculpture outside Egypt. The dyad of Menkaure and his consort is from the same workshop as the triads in the Egyptian Museum, Cairo. The bust of prince Ankh-haf, vizier of Khafre, is extraordinarily lifelike. The wooden coffin of Djehuty-nakht is one of the finest surviving examples of the type, and an excellent example of Middle Kingdom painting.

Avenue of the Arts, 465 Huntington Avenue, Boston, MA 02115-5523

http://www.mfa.org

Chicago

Oriental Institute

The Oriental Institute of Chicago has been one of the leading US institutions working in Egypt. Their principal centre has been Chicago House in Luxor, from where the excavation and recording of many Theban monuments has been pursued with a skill and accuracy rarely achieved by others. The OIC publications are some of the finest, most beautiful—and largest—in Egyptological literature. Amongst their key sites have been the temple of Ramesses III at Medinet with its satellites, the temples of Tutankhamun, Ay and Horemheb; the temple of Khonsu at Karnak; the colonnade hall of the Luxor temple; and important Theban tombs such as that of Kheruef. This work is represented in the museum collection by the colossus of Tutankhamun.

University of Chicago, 1155 East 58th Street, Chicago, IL 60637-1569

http://www-oi.uchicago.edu/

Cincinnati
Cincinnati Art Museum

953 Eden Park Drive, Cincinnati, OH 45202

http://www.cincinnatiartmuseum.org/greatart/tour_egypt.shtml

Cleveland
Museum of Art

11150 East Boulevard, Cleveland, OH 44106-1797

http://www.clemusart.com/

Detroit
Detroit Institute of Arts

5200 Woodward Avenue, Detroit, MI 48202-4008

http://www.dia.org/collections/ancient/egypt/egypt.html

Los Angeles
Los Angeles County Museum of Art

Tutankhamun and the Golden Age of the Pharaohs exhibition opens here in June 2005; see Special Topic earlier in this chapter: Treasures of Tutankhamun.

5905 Wilshire Boulevard, Los Angeles, CA 90036

www.lacma.org

New York
Brooklyn Museum of Art

The Brooklyn Museum has had some leading experts on Egyptian art on its staff. The core is the private collection and library formed by Charles Edwin Wilbour (1833–1896), which came to the museum in 1916, 1935 and 1947, and the Egyptian collection formed by the New York Historical Society. In this remarkably rich collection there are many deservedly famous works. The 12th-dynasty head of a royal woman from a sphinx carved in chlorite was reputedly found at Hadrian's Villa at Tivoli. There are many fine relief blocks of the reign of Akhenaten: originally from Akhetaten, these were reused at Hermopolis by Ramesses II. One particularly important feature of the collection is sculpture of the Late Period. A faience plaque, part of a shrine, carries a superbly modelled image of the obscure Libyan king Iuput; a second panel is in Edinburgh. The Saite Oracle Papyrus is an important document from Thebes dating to the 26th Dynasty, and with a fine painted scene showing the sacred barque of Amun and the leading clergy of the temple.

200 Eastern Parkway, Brooklyn, New York, NY 11238-6052

http://www.brooklynmuseum.org/

Metropolitan Museum of Art

The Met houses one of the foremost displays of Egyptian monuments outside Egypt. The museum has received some major donations, notably that of the collection of Lord Carnarvon, which was given by Edward S Harkness. The museum also financed its own excavations and the copying of Theban tomb paintings. The major excavations were at the 12th-dynasty site of Lisht; at Thebes, important excavations in the temple of Hatshepsut at Deir el-Bahari yielded statuary, and, from the tomb of Meket-re, some of the wonderful tomb models (others in the Egyptian Museum, Cairo). Notable amongst the exhibits are the jewellery of the princess Princess Sit-Hathor-Iunet, daughter of Senusret II from Dashur, and the three foreign wives of Thutmose III, with a superb gold headdress inlaid with rosettes. Amongst the artefacts of the Amarna period are the lower part of a deservedly famous yellow jasper head, probably of Queen Tiye—the most luscious mouth in ancient Egypt; a headless statue of Amenhotep III in a long garment; the head from a canopic jar found in tomb 55 in the Valley of the Kings; and a fine statue of Horemheb, before he became pharaoh, depicted as a scribe. From the 19th Dynasty there is a superb royal head in quartzite, reliefs from the temple of Ramesses I at Abydos and a magnificent double statue of a high official named Yuny, with his wife Renutet. There are many smaller artefacts, furniture and faience, including two renowned ivory pieces, a whip handle in the form of a galloping horse and a gazelle. An extension of the museum houses the Temple of Dendur, where you can get married.

1000 Fifth Avenue, New York, NY 10028-0198

http://www.metmuseum.org

New York Obelisk, Central Park

The pair to that in London, from Alexandria, but originally set up by Thutmose III at Heliopolis.

Philadelphia

University of Pennsylvania Museum of Archaeology and Anthropology

3260 South Street, Philadelphia, PA 19104

http://www.museum.upenn.edu/

San Jose

Rosicrucian Egyptian Museum

1342 Naglee Ave, San Jose, CA 95191

http://www.egyptianmuseum.org/

Visiting Ancient Egypt in Rome: The Nile Flows into the Tiber

The cults of Isis and her associated deities were well established in Italy by the first century BC, but however popular they were, official regulations banned temples to the Egyptian cults within the sacred limits of Rome that had been established early in its history. Kleopatra's extended stay in the city may have stimulated further interest from the Roman elite, but when some private chapels were erected, they were destroyed by the authorities (53 and 50 BC). A temple to Isis built on the Capitol at the city's heart (in 48 BC) was likewise removed. Following the defeat of Kleopatra and conquest of Egypt, Egyptian influence grew in many ways but official policy suppressed the Egyptian cults within the city (21 BC). Nevertheless, the temple of Apollo adjacent to the emperor Augustus's own house had plaques with the image of Isis flanked by two sphinxes, and the house of Augustus's wife, Livia, on the Palatine was decorated with Egyptian motifs.

The Temple of Isis was once again destroyed in the reign of Tiberius (AD 14–37), but Caius Caligula (AD 37–41) had a new temple built on the Campus Martius—hence outside the sacred area of the city. This marks the beginning of official recognition of the cult of Isis, which soon received considerable imperial patronage. The emperor Nero (AD 54–68) and his circle were closely connected with Isiac rites: his wife Poppaea Sabina had a cousin in Pompeii who had a household shrine dedicated to Isis, Osiris, Harpokrates and Anubis, while Poppaea's first husband, the later emperor Otho, who ruled for only a matter of months, himself took part in Isiac rituals.

In AD 69 Vespasian was proclaimed emperor in Alexandria and received an oracle and blessing from Serapis. On his return to Rome the following year, the new emperor and his son Titus spent the night in the Temple of Isis on the Campus Martius before entering Rome in triumph. Fate overtook the temple again in AD 80, when it was destroyed by fire, but it was lavishly rebuilt by Vespasian's younger son, Domitian (r.AD 81–96).

The great Temple of Isis and Serapis on the Campus Martius, known as the Iseum, occupied the area lying to the east and south of the Pantheon. The plan of the temple is known from a marble map of Rome made in the late second century, and by some early, non-scientific, excavations in the area. Two arches formed the entrance to a large courtyard some 70 metres by 140 metres, which stretched northwards as far as today's Via del Seminario. The court probably had lines of obelisks or trees, and shrines for Isis and Serapis. The temple itself was situated in

Rome: Temple of Isis

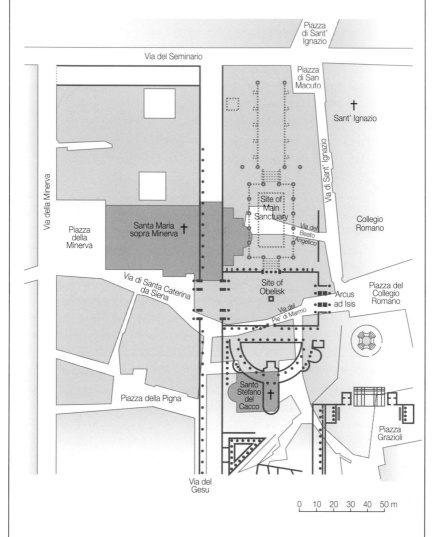

The plan of the Temple of Isis is known from a marble map of Rome that was carved on wall of the Temple of Peace during the reign of Septimius Severus (AD 193–211). Here it is shown over a modern street plan.

Source: Robert Morkot

the area where the rear door of the church of Santa Maria sopra Minerva opens into Via del Beato Angelico. In its courtyard there were several obelisks and it was once thought that the obelisk now in the Piazza Navona, whose inscription honours Domitian, proclaiming him 'Beloved of Isis and Ptah', was one of them. However, more recently a location in a temple dedicated to the Flavian emperors has been proposed as the original site of this obelisk. To the south two large gates, like triumphal arches, entered the precinct. That on the west stood on a line with the south transept of Santa Mari sopra Minerva, at the angle with the Via di Santa Caterina da Siena. On the east, the Arcus ad Isis occupied a position near the junction of the Via del Pie' di Marmo with Via di Sant' Ignazio.

A semicircular sanctuary on the axis of the main enclosure occupied an area as far as Santo Stefano del Cacco. This sanctuary had a semicircular apse with a colossal statue of Isis flanked by Serapis and Anubis. A large water basin had statues of the Nile (Vatican, Braccio Nuovo), the Tiber (Paris, the Louvre) and Oceanus. There were sphinxes and statues from Egypt, and probably several of the obelisks later re-erected in Rome's squares. Early excavations in the area brought many of these statues to light. They entered the papal and Roman princely collections and many can now be seen in the Museo Gregoriano in the Vatican. One particularly significant piece, the Mensa Isiaca, found in 1527, passed from Cardinal Bembo to the Gonzaga family and thence to the Duke of Savoy, becoming one of the first Egyptian pieces in what is now the Museo Egizio in Turin. The Mensa Isiaca was long thought to be a Pharaonic Egyptian piece, and as such was studied, along with the Roman obelisks, by the scholar Athanasius Kircher in his attempts to decipher hieroglyphics. We now recognize the Mensa as a product of Roman Egypt, but none the less interesting for that.

In addition to the Iseum, there were 13 other Egyptian cult centres in Rome—one of the districts was even named after a sanctuary of Isis and Serapis. The cults had enormous popularity with all sectors of Roman society, attested to by the Isiac graffiti found in private houses on the Aventine.

Of the many monuments brought from Egypt to adorn the Iseum, the largest and most impressive were the obelisks that now stand in the Piazza della Rotunda, the Villa Celimontana, the Viale delle Terme and, in Florence, the Boboli Gardens.

OBELISKS OF ROME

Rome has more large obelisks than remain in Egypt. These were mostly removed from Egypt's temples by the Roman emperors, although some, such as the Vatican and Navona obelisks, were commissioned specifically for Rome.

Piazza San Giovanni in Laterano

This granite monolith, some 32 metres in height, was commissioned by Thutmose III and erected 35 years later by Thutmose IV as a single obelisk in the solar court of the eastern temple at Karnak. Scenes carved on the pyramidion show the king before Amun-Ra and Amun-Atum, the morning and evening sun. Augustus intended to move it, but it was not until the reign of Constantine that operations began (in AD 330). The obelisk arrived in Alexandria en route to Constantinople, but the emperor died and Constantius II ordered it to be sent to Rome. In AD 357 it was erected in the Circus Maximus, witnessed by Ammianus Marcellinus, who narrates the story in his history. The obelisk later fell and broke into three pieces. It was re-erected in 1588, in the reign of pope Sixtus V, with a new pedestal telling its history.

Piazza del Popolo

A 23-metre obelisk with inscriptions of Sety I and Ramesses II, who set it up in the temple of Iunu (Heliopolis). This was the first obelisk to be taken from Egypt to Rome where Augustus raised it in 10 BC in the Circus Maximus to symbolize his conquest of Egypt. It was joined in the Circus much later by the obelisk that now stands in front of San Giovanni in Laterano (St John Lateran). In the pontificate of Sixtus V, the obelisk fragments were taken from the Circus Maximus to the Piazza del Popolo, the main entrance to the city from the north (the Porta Flaminia) and where the three main streets of Rome diverge. The obelisk was re-erected in 1589.

Piazza della Rotunda and Villa Celimontana

These form a pair of obelisks set up by Ramesses II in the temple of Ra-Harakhty at Heliopolis, which were later taken to Rome and placed in the Temple of Isis on the Campus Martius. In the pontificate of Clement XI (1700–1721) one obelisk was set up in front of the Pantheon. The second obelisk had been removed long before to the Capitoline Hill (Campidoglio) from where, in 1582, it was presented to Ciriaco Mattei who had it placed in the garden of his Villa Celimontana. Both obelisks are missing their lower portion.

Viale delle Terme

Another pair of obelisks originally set up by Ramesses II in the temple of Ra-Harakhty at Heliopolis and later removed to the Iseum. One of these was excavated near Santa Maria sopra Minerva in 1883 and now stands in the garden near the Baths of Diocletian as a memorial to Italian soldiers killed in Ethiopia in 1885. Its companion, dug up much earlier, adorned the Villa Medici, but was taken to Florence in 1790 where it was set up in the Boboli Gardens.

Montecitorio

A 26th-dynasty obelisk, dedicated by Psamtik II at Heliopolis. It was removed by Augustus in 10 BC and set as the pointer into the vast marble sundial on the Campus Martius (occupying an area centring on the modern Piazza del Parlamento). The obelisk is a little over 21 metres high as it survives, but when complete and serving as the pointer, with its base, pedestal, and crowned with a spiked bronze globe, it stood at 100 Roman feet (30 metres). It appears to have remained standing until the 10th or 11th century AD, but was then buried. Pope Sixtus V ordered its re-erection in 1587, but the damaged state made this impossible. The obelisk was buried again until Pope Benedict XIV (1740–1758) had it re-excavated and restored. It was set in its present position in 1792 by Pius VI.

Piazza della Minerva

A smallish, 26th-dynasty granite obelisk, dedicated by Wahibre (Apries) at Sais. It was one of the obelisks in the Iseum and was rediscovered in 1665 when a wall was being built in the garden of Santa Maria sopra Minerva. The excavation was supervised by Athanasius Kircher, who believed the late Roman tradition that hieroglyphics were a symbolic rather than a purely alphabetic form of writing. The obelisk was raised on the back of an elephant statue designed by Bernini and the Latin inscription on the base reads: 'Let any beholder of the carved images of the wisdom of Egypt on the obelisk carried by the elephant, the strongest of beasts, realize that it takes a robust mind to carry solid wisdom.' The design is taken directly from a Renaissance book, the *Hypnerotomachia Poliphili*, that did much to promote the ideas about hieroglyphic writing that had been derived from works such as the *Hieroglyphics of Horapollo*, a manuscript brought to Italy in the mid-15th century and which explained the philosophical meaning of each sign (this was probably Roman in date). The obelisk was originally one of a pair, two fragments of which were incorporated into the obelisk now at Urbino.

Trinita dei Monti

The 14-metre obelisk at the top of the Spanish Steps carries a late Roman copy of the inscription on the obelisk in the Piazza del Popolo naming Sety I and Ramesses II, which may date to the reign of Hadrian (AD 117–138). Ammianus Marcellinus states that the obelisk was brought to Rome by Augustus and erected in the Gardens of Sallust, where its foundations still remain. Pope Pius VI had it placed in its present position.

Piazza Navona

This granite obelisk, 16.4 metres high, was commissioned by Domitian (AD 81–96) and quarried at Aswan. Earlier scholarship thought that the obelisk was erected in the courtyard of the Iseum, but it is now proposed that it was raised in the temple of the Flavian family that Domitian built on the Quirinal Hill. Maxentius (AD 306–312) transferred the obelisk to the Circus he built on the Appian Way (Via Appia). Innocent X (Pamphili) had the obelisk removed to adorn another circus site, the Piazza Navona, where his family residence stood. The obelisk was raised on Bernini's *Fountain of the Four Rivers* (1651) and surmounted by a dove, the emblem of the Pamphili family, rather than the more usual cross. The inscriptions were the subject of one of Athanasius Kircher's most important studies of hieroglyphics.

Monte Pincio

This nine-metre obelisk has been the subject of much speculation. It was carved at the command of Hadrian to commemorate his lover, Antinous, who drowned in the Nile near Hermopolis in AD 130. Hadrian founded a new city in honour of the deified youth, naming it Antinoöpolis, and a temple was built in his honour in Rome. Scholars thought that hieroglyphic inscription would lead to the tomb of Antinous. The original location of the obelisk is uncertain: some have suggested Hadrian's villa at Tivoli, although the Roman temple seems more likely. It was later moved to the *spina* of the Circus Varianus in the villa of the emperor Elagabalus (parts of which still exists adjacent to Santa Croce in Gerusalemme), eventually being put in its present location by Pius VII (1800–1823).

Vatican Obelisk

The huge uninscribed obelisk, 25 metres tall, now forming the centrepiece of Bernini's spectacular Piazza di San Pietro, was originally set up by Augustus in Alexandria, but was transferred to Rome in AD 37, in the reign of Caligula, when it was placed in the Vatican Circus. It remained standing, regarded as a witness to the martyrdom of St Peter in the Circus, until it was moved to its present location by order of Sixtus V. The difficult task was placed under the direction of Domenico Fontana. The events of the removal and re-erection, between May and September 1586, are recorded by frescoes in the Vatican Library.

Piazza dell' Esquilino and Piazza del Quirinale

Two uninscribed granite obelisks almost 15 metres high that were found near the Mausoleum of Augustus. Ammianus Marcellinus records that they were standing there in the fourth century. Sixtus V had one of the obelisks repaired and raised on the Esquiline Hill in 1587. The second was excavated in 1781; in 1786, following restorations, it was placed by Pius VI at the entrance to the papal summer residence, the Quirinal Palace.

Also worth taking a look at is the obelisk that stands in the grounds of the now ruined **Villa Torlonia** on Via Nomentana. This was raised in 1842, in the presence of the Pope, King Ludwig I of Bavaria and the nobility of Rome. The hieroglyphic inscription was devised by Luigi Ungarelli, who had encouraged the creation of the Museo Gregoriano Egizio in the Vatican. It honours, by placing his names with cartouches, the immensely rich papal banker Alessandro Torlonia, whose family had successfully entered into the ranks of the Roman nobility from poor French origins. Amongst their other acquisitions, the Torlonia family bought the Villa Albani on the Via Salaria which, in the 18th century, had been the home of Cardinal Alessandro Albani and his collections. Albani had employed the art historian Johann Joachim Winckelmann (1717–1768) as librarian and curator. His collections were amongst the most important in Rome, gathered from around the city. In 1733 Albani's uncle, Pope Clement XII bought much of it to establish the Capitoline Museum. Some of it, however, remained, including many of the Egyptian antiquities which had been found around Rome and Tivoli. These included many fine pieces, and were central to the development of western European understanding of Egyptian art in the 18th century.

One of the most striking examples of Roman 'Egyptomania' is the **Pyramid of Caius Cestius** at the Ostia gate. It was built in 330 days, according to the dedicatory inscription, sometime between 18 and 12 BC. The owner was a Roman official, but little is known about him. The pyramid is not like those of the Old or Middle Kingdoms, but resembles the New Kingdom private pyramids and those raised for the royalty of the Sudanese kingdom of Meroe. The pyramid is 30 metres (100 Roman feet) square at the base, and 36.4 metres high (125 Roman feet). It's nice to know that it is built of concrete, faced with marble. It was not unique in Rome: another similar pyramid stood somewhere between the Vatican and the Mausoleum of Hadrian until it was demolished in the 15th or 16th century.

It is worth noting here in passing a more recent example of Egyptomania: the garden buildings in the **Villa Borghese** (and some of the villa's decoration).

Tivoli

Hadrian's Villa (Villa Adriana) is a site of great importance in the history of the rediscovery of the ancient world, especially Rome and Egypt. Huge quantities of sculpture were dug up here in the 18th century and were passed into the great Roman collections, such as that of Cardinal Albani and the papacy: some of the most significant are now in the Vatican museums. Hadrian's vast palace complex probably

EGYPT, VENICE AND THE SILK ROAD: TRADERS AND PILGRIMS

When, in AD 452, the forces of Attila the Hun destroyed Aquileia and the other Roman towns of the region, their populations fled, and, according to tradition, founded Venice in the safety of the islands of the lagoon. From this collection of small island villages, inhabited by fishermen and refugees, Venice rose to become the most important city trading with the eastern Mediterranean, surpassing her early rivals Pisa and Genoa. In 810, Charlemagne, emperor of Western Europe, signed a treaty with the Byzantine emperor formally acknowledging Venice as a vassal of Constantinople, and so it remained until the middle of the 11th century. Byzantine influence in the city was strong, reflected in the marriages of two of its early doges to Byzantine noblewomen, the education of elite Venetian sons at Constantinople, and in the architecture of its great new cathedral, which was built to house the relics of the city's—and the republic's—patron saint, Mark.

St Mark the Evangelist had been adopted as the patron saint because he was believed to have travelled to the north Adriatic in the mid-first century AD, preaching in Aquileia. After his time in Italy St Mark travelled to Egypt, arriving in Alexandria sometime between AD 41 and 43. St Mark may have been drawn to the city because of its large Jewish population, and his first conversion there was reputedly that of a Jewish shoemaker. St Mark is thus regarded as the founder of Christianity in Egypt, and the patriarchs of the Coptic Church are his direct successors, just as the popes are the direct successors of St Peter in the Roman Church.

The Venetian fleet rapidly became important to the Byzantines, both as a defence of the Adriatic and in trade. About AD 828–829 the corpse of St Mark was stolen from Alexandria by the Venetian merchants Buono di Malamocco and Rustico di Torcello, aided by two Greek monks, Stauriacus and Theodore. According to tradition, the body was wrapped in a shroud and carried to the Venetian ship waiting in the port. A 13th-century chronicler commented that: 'If all the spices of the world had been gathered in Alexandria they could not have so perfumed the city.' The authorities pursued the thieves, but they covered the body with pig carcasses and the devout Muslims fled.

The church built in Venice to house the relics was founded in AD 829, but was later destroyed by fire. The present Basilica di San Marco (St Mark's Basilica) was begun in 1063 and dedicated in 1094, although the decoration continued to be added for centuries. The Basilica looks east, to the Byzantine world, for its architecture (it is modelled on the Church of the Holy Apostles in Constantinople) and decoration. Indeed, all merchants were obliged to bring something to decorate the Republic's chief shrine, and, as a result the outer walls are encrusted with sculptures from the east, including the splendid statue in Egyptian 'imperial' porphyry generally called *The Four Tetrarchs*. The statue was brought from Constantinople, and is typical of works of the Tetrarchic Period (many of which were executed in porphyry from the Eastern Desert of Upper Egypt). This group may show the two Augusti, Diocletian and Maximian, with their two Caesars, Galerius and Constantius. The columns of the Basilica's façade were brought from Alexandria.

The interior of the Basilica was lavishly decorated with eastern treasures. The floor is made of different types of marble, with green and purple porphyry from Egypt (much of it sawn from ancient columns). The walls and domes are covered with mosaics, amongst which are scenes showing the voyage of St Mark's remains and the biblical story of Joseph. The latter cycle depicts Joseph's seduction by Potiphar's wife; his time in prison; the pharaoh's dream; and Joseph as vizier. One notable scene shows five pyramids which, following popular medieval tradition, are shown as the granaries where the grain from the seven abundant years was stored. The Treasury of St Mark's houses many splendid objects brought from the east and from the sack of Constantinople. Amongst them is one of the largest and finest surviving rock crystal ewers. The pear-shaped ewer, decorated with text in Kufic script and two seated lions flanking a tree, was made in Egypt in the reign of the Caliph al-Aziz (ruled 975–996). A large rock crystal vase in the Treasury of similar date has elaborate jewelled and metal mountings, as does a second pear-shaped ewer. The carving of rock crystal (probably brought from east Africa) was a speciality of the Fatimid craftsmen, but was short-lived. Rock-crystal vessels of all shapes were highly prized in Europe as reliquaries, and many of those surviving are to be found in cathedral treasuries.

Venice became one of the leading points of departure for pilgrimages to Egypt, Sinai and the Holy Land, and pilgrims from all over Europe made their way to the city to join ships directly to the Levantine cities or to Alexandria. Those who arrived in Alexandria made their way to Cairo, where they might visit the pyramids at Giza— 'Joseph's Granaries'—and the mummy pits of Saqqara (*mummia* became an important Egyptian export because of its supposed medicinal properties). At this time, few travellers went further south of the Cairo region. A few miles north of Cairo, and on the route towards Sinai, lay Matariyya, now part of Heliopolis. Here the pilgrims could visit the site where the Holy Family were traditionally said to have rested on their flight into Egypt, subject of so many paintings. The large hollow sycamore fig (*ficus sycamorus*), known as the Virgin's Tree, was famous as the exact spot of the event: its descendant was drawn by many later travellers. It became the centre of a large Mamluk pleasure garden. In 1553 the Venetian consul was permitted to build a chapel here. From Matariyya, the pilgrims continued on the arduous route across to Sinai in the footsteps of Moses and the Israelites, visiting the site of the Burning Bush, and making their way ultimately to Mount Sinai, where Moses received the Tablets of the Law. They were also able to see the monastery where the relics of St Catherine of Alexandria were kept, before continuing their journey to Jerusalem.

Far more lucrative than pilgrims was the trade that Venice established with the eastern Mediterranean. In its early history, Venice's imports into the Byzantine Empire were arms, slaves, wood and coarse cloth, but Constantinople tried to forbid direct trade with the Islamic rulers of the eastern Mediterranean. However, the problems that beset the Byzantine Empire saw grants of increasing privileges to the trading cities of Italy. When the Crusades cut off Constantinople, Venice was able to enjoy the benefits of direct trade with the Islamic states. The conflict between the Christian states of western Europe and the Byzantines culminated in the Venetian attack on Constantinople in 1204, which allowed the Fourth Crusade to capture and loot the city. With the acquisition of various Greek islands, Venice came to dominate the trade in the eastern Mediterranean, becoming a leading power in Europe and ousting its main rival, Genoa. The two-and-a half centuries of Mamluk rule in Egypt (AD 1250–1517) were the heyday of Venetian–Egyptian trade.

From Egypt the Venetian merchants acquired the exotic and expensive products of long-distance trade via the Gulf and the Silk Road: spices, eastern silks, gold silk cloth, Chinese porcelain and jewels—especially pearls. There were also more locally produced goods, such as potash, which was exported for use in glass manufacture on the Venetian island of Murano, sugar (rose and violet sugars were manufactured in Alexandria), raisins, lemons, dates and capers. The most lucrative trade was no doubt that in spices, which were extensively used in medieval cookery. The spice trade was dominated by a group of merchants based in Egypt and Yemen, known as the Karimi. From 1181 their networks spread by sea through Yemen and the Gulf to Hormuz, and along the Silk Road through Samarkand to China. Egypt was also a leader in the ivory trade: east Africa being the major source of raw ivory and provider of the best quality.

The goods exported by the Venetian merchants were no longer purely of locally Italian origin, but came from all over Europe: Flemish and English wool, with saffron, brocade, satin, velvet and furs—notably sable—from Russia, and glass from the factories on Murano. Although there were expert glass factories in Egypt, those in Damascus seem to have come to end when Timur and the Golden Horde captured the city in 1400: soon after, the workshops of Murano were sending enamelled glass mosque lamps to Syria. Alexandria remained the main centre for the trade, and by 1480 there were 80 Venetian merchants resident in the city. Seven Venetian galleys were usually to be found in the Alexandrian harbour and four more at Beirut (also under Mamluk control).

In the 15th century, the Byzantine Empire was in decline, eventually falling to the Ottoman Turks in 1453. But Mamluk Egypt too was suffering economic crisis, and Qaitbay (died AD 1496) had left an empty treasury which was soon followed by the greatest threat to Mamluk Egypt's control of the spice trade with the east: in 1497 the Portuguese fleet sailed around the Cape of Good Hope and opened the sea route to India. This threatened to give Portugal the monopoly on many exotic goods. The Mamluk sultan, Qansuh al-Ghawri, attempted to regain control of the trade through his territories of Egypt and Syria, placing garrisons on the Arabian coast and sending fleets to patrol the Indian Ocean and prevent the Portuguese from using the routes. In 1506 he sent a large embassy to Venice to try to secure the spice trade. After ten months of negotiation, some agreement was reached and the embassy returned to Egypt, accompanied by a Venetian embassy led by Domenico Trevisan (died 1535) and attended by its own trumpeters. The Venetians were received with ceremony and housed in splendour in Cairo. Conducted to an audience in the citadel, they presented Sultan al-Ghawri with lavish gifts of robes of cloth of gold, of velvet, satin and damask, and with large quantities of sable skins and ermine. Over a period of months, and after many meetings in different splendid palaces, the sultan was assured that the Venetians would continue to trade with Egypt. The Venetians were fully aware of the sultan's economic problems and were able to negotiate favourable terms. However, in Istanbul, the accession of Selim I the Grim (ruled AD 1512–1520) saw a swift change in Ottoman policy, and a move to gain control of Syria and Egypt. In 1516 Selim defeated al-Ghawri and his Mamluk forces in battle near Aleppo and marched on to Egypt, capturing Cairo the following year. Egypt was now under Ottoman rule, and for the next three centuries was reduced to the status of a *pashalik* (a territory ruled by a pasha). As a result the Egyptian trade dwindled, and in 1577 the decline of Alexandria as a significant centre forced the Venetian consul to move to Cairo. After that, although Egypt remained important for some commodities, the bulk of the luxury trade from the Silk Road passed through Istanbul and the Venetians had to vie for influence there with the other European states and private companies (such as the English Levant Company).

included a burial place for his lover Antinous. The Canopus, a long lake with colonnades around it, formed the focus of an elaborate dining hall (probably with ritual overtones). The area was filled with Egyptianized images of Antinous and with ancient Egyptian sculptures: the magnificent head of a 12th-dynasty queen, originally part of a sphinx, is believed to have come from the villa. Although relatively little Egyptian sculpture or architecture remains at the site, anyone pursuing Egypt in Rome should visit the villa: but as one of the most glorious archaeological sites anywhere, excuses are hardly needed.

EGYPTOLOGY WEBSITES

mongst the best and most reliable of the websites that provide information on Egyptology and related matters are:

Abzu (study of the Ancient Near East), Oriental Institute, University of Chicago: http://www.etana.org/abzu/

American Research Center in Egypt: http://www.arce.org

Ancient Near East.net: http://www.ancientneareast.net

Digital Egypt for Universities: http://www.digitalegypt.ucl.ac.uk

Egypt Exploration Society: http://www.ees.ac.uk

Egyptian Museum: http://www.egyptianmuseum.gov.eg

German Institute of Archaeology Cairo: http://www.dainst.org/abteilung.php?id=265

Griffith Institute: http://www.ashmol.ox.ac.uk/Griffith.html

Institut français d'archéologie orientale du Caire (in French): http://www.ifao.egnet.net

Isaac Newton Institute for Mathematical Sciences, Egyptology Resources: http://www.newton.cam.ac.uk/egypt/

Theban Mapping Project: http://www.thebanmappingproject.com

RECOMMENDED READING, MUSIC AND FILM

BOOKS

Books about ancient Egypt tend to be either detailed and academic, or rather broad in scope. There are huge areas of the subject that have no accessible 'popular' account (eg the Middle Kingdom and the New Kingdom).This selection of Egypt-related reading is divided into the following categories:

General Introductions and Historical Background
Specific Historical Periods
Egypt in Context
Art, Architecture and Garden Design
Religion
Pyramids
Akhenaten
Islamic Cairo
Egypt in the West
Collectors, Archaeologists and Travellers
Literature
Holiday Reading
Guidebooks

GENERAL INTRODUCTIONS AND HISTORICAL BACKGROUND

Brewer, Donald and Emily Teeter, *Egypt and the Egyptians*, Cambridge: Cambridge University Press, 1999.

A good general introduction to Egypt and its culture.

Morkot, Robert G, *The Egyptians: An Introduction*, London: Routledge, 2005.

Kemp, Barry, *Ancient Egypt: Anatomy of a Civilization*, London: Routledge, 1989.

One of the best books on ancient Egypt. Kemp really tries to understand and explain how ancient Egypt functioned.

Shaw, Ian (ed), *Oxford History of Ancient Egypt*, Oxford: Oxford University Press, 2000.

This is the most up-to-date general history of Egypt, written by a number of specialists in different periods.

Spencer, A Jeffrey and Stephen Quirke (eds), *The British Museum Book of Ancient Egypt*, London: British Museum Press, 1992.

SPECIFIC HISTORICAL PERIODS

Pre-Dynastic to End of the Old Kingdom

Wilkinson, Toby, *Genesis of the Pharaohs*, London: Thames and Hudson, 2003.
New research and ideas about the origins of Egyptian civilization written in an engaging style.

Andreu, Guillemette, *Egypt in the Age of the Pyramids*, Ithaca, NY: Cornell University Press, 1997.

Malek, Jaromir, *In the Shadow of the Pyramids: Egypt during the Old Kingdom*, Cairo: The American University in Cairo Press, 1986.

New Kingdom

Tyldesley, Joyce, *Hatchepsut: The Female Monarch*, London: Viking, 1996.
Readable, up-to-date account of the historical problems surrounding one of Egypt's most interesting rulers.

Kitchen, Kenneth A, *Pharaoh Triumphant: The Life and Times of Ramesses II, King of Egypt*, Cairo: The American University in Cairo Press, 1982.
An engaging account of one of Egypt's most renowned rulers, by the leading authority on the period.

Late Ptolemaic Periods

Morkot, Robert G, *The Black Pharaohs: Egypt's Nubian Rulers*, London: Rubicon Press, 2000.
Covers Egypt's relations with Nubia, and the rise of the Nubian kingdom that conquered Libyan Egypt, ruling as the 25th Dynasty.

Mysliwiec, Karol, *The Twilight of Ancient Egypt: First Millennium B.C.E.*, Ithaca, NY: Cornell University Press, 2000.
An overview of the, unfairly neglected, thousand years following the end of the New Kingdom.

Hölbl, Günther, *A History of the Ptolemaic Empire*, London: Routledge, 2001.
A detailed account of this important period.

Bowman, Alan K, *Egypt after the Pharaohs*, Oxford: Oxford University Press, 1986. The thousand years of Egyptian history from its conquest by Alexander the Great in 332 BC to that by the Arabs in AD 642 has generally been of little popular appeal. This book surveys and explains the enormous range of archaeological material from this time of great change.

Late Antique Egypt

Bagnall, Roger, *Egypt in Late Antiquity*, Princeton, NJ: Princeton University Press, 1993.

Kamil, Jill, *Coptic Egypt: History and Guide*, Cairo: The American University in Cairo Press, 1993.

Islamic Egypt to 1800

Hillenbrand, Carole, *The Crusades: Islamic Perspectives*, Edinburgh: Edinburgh University Press, 1999.

Inalcik, Halil, *The Ottoman Empire: The Classical Age 1300–1600*, London: Phoenix, 1997.

Irwin, R, *The Middle East in the Middle Ages: The Early Mamluk Sultanate 1250–1382*, London: Croom Helm, 1986.

Petry, Carl F (ed), *Cambridge History of Egypt Volume One: Islamic Egypt 640–1517*, Cambridge: Cambridge University Press, 1998.
A weighty tome, academic, but up to date (library reading).

Runciman, Steven, *A History of the Crusades*, 3 volumes, Penguin, 1978.
A classic history. Currently being reissued.

Walker, Paul E, *Exploring an Islamic Empire: Fatimid History and its Sources*, London: I.B.Tauris, 2002.

Modern Egypt

Daly, M W (ed), *Cambridge History of Egypt Volume Two: Modern Egypt 1517–1990*, Cambridge: Cambridge University Press, 1998.
Another weighty tome, academic, but up to date (library reading).

Perry, Glenn E, *The History of Egypt*, Westport CT: Greenwood Press, 2004.

Vatikiotis, P J, *The History of Modern Egypt: From Muhammad Ali to Mubarak*, 4th edition, London: Weidenfeld and Nicolson, 1991.
The standard work.

Egypt in Context

Kuhrt, Amélie, *The Ancient Near East*, 2 vols, London: Routledge, 1995.

> With chapters on Egypt, this is the most recent survey of the whole region: academic, but readable.

Van De Mieroop, Marc, *History of the Ancient Near East: c.3000–323 BC*, Oxford: Blackwell, 2003.

> An accessible account of the region, but not specifically including Egypt.

Historical Atlases

Baines, John and Jaromir Malek, *The Cultural Atlas of Ancient Egypt*, Facts on File, 1980.

> This is the only large reference atlas for ancient Egyptian archaeology. It has good maps of the Nile Valley with descriptions and plans of the most important archaeological sites.

Manley, Bill, *The Penguin Historical Atlas of Ancient Egypt*, London: Penguin, 1996.

> This is very useful as a supplement to the *Oxford History of Ancient Egypt*. There are good sections giving a historical overview, and maps explaining specific military, administrative and economic aspects of Egyptian history. The format and aims are totally different to the Baines and Malek atlas.

Nicolle, David, *Historical Atlas of the Islamic World*, Facts on File, 2004.

Art, Architecture and Garden Design

Ancient Egyptian Art and Architecture

Aldred, Cyril, *Egyptian Art*, London: Thames and Hudson, World of Art series, 1980.

———, *Jewels of the Pharaohs*, London: Thames and Hudson, 1971.

Arnold, Dieter (translated by Sabine Gardiner and Helen Strudwick), *The Encyclopedia of Ancient Egyptian Architecture*, London: I.B. Tauris, 2003.

Malek, Jaromir, *Egyptian Art*, Oxford: Phaidon, 1999.

Robins, Gay, *The Art of Ancient Egypt*, London: British Museum Press, 1997.

Stevenson Smith, William (revised by William Kelly Simpson), *The Art and Architecture of Ancient Egypt*, London: The Pelican History of Art, 1981.

Wilkinson, Richard H, *Symbol and Magic in Egyptian Art*, London: Thames and Hudson, 1994.

———, *Reading Egyptian Art*, London: Thames and Hudson, 1992.

Late Antique (Coptic) Art

Du Bourguet, Pierre, *Coptic Art*, London: Methuen, Art of the World series, 1971.

> The art of Late Antique, or Coptic, Egypt remains unfairly neglected. This study, although rather old, is one of few general introductions, written by a leading specialist in the field.

Gabra, Gawdat Abdel Sayed et al, *Cairo: the Coptic Museum and Old Churches*, Cairo: Egyptian International Publishing Company, Longman, 1993.

> A good guide to the Coptic Museum by its curator, the leading authority on the subject.

Islamic Art and Architecture

(See also Islamic Cairo section, below.)

Creswell, Keppel A C, *The Muslim Architecture of Egypt*, Oxford: Oxford University Press, 1952–1960.

Ettinghausen, Richard and Oleg Grabar, *The Art and Architecture of Islam: 650–1250*, Pelican History of Art and Yale University Press, 2003.

> Some sections deal specifically with Egypt.

Graber, Oleg and Cynthia Robinson (eds), *Islamic Art and Literature*, Princeton, NJ: Markus Wiener Publishers, 2001.

Hillenbrand, Robert, *Islamic Art and Architecture*, London: Thames and Hudson, World of Art series, 1998.

> Chronologically arranged and covering the entire Islamic world.

Mack, Rosamond E, *Bazaar to Piazza: Islamic Trade and Italian Art, 1300–1600*, Berkeley, CA: University of California Press, 2001.

Howard, Deborah, *Venice and the East: The Impact of the Islamic World on Venetian Architecture 1100–1500*, New Haven and London: Yale University Press, 2000.

Gardens

Brookes, John, *Gardens of Paradise: The History and Design of the Great Islamic Gardens*, London: Weidenfeld and Nicolson, 1987.

> Not specifically Egypt, but analyses the underlying philosophy of the Islamic garden.

Wilkinson, Alix, *The Garden in Ancient Egypt*, London: Rubicon Press, 1998.

> The only book that deals with gardens rather than just plants.

THE PLEASURES OF THE PIPE

T he pipe and the cup of coffee are enjoyed by almost all persons who can afford such luxuries, very early in the morning, and oftentimes during the day. There are many men who are scarcely ever seen without a pipe either in their hand or carried behind them by a servant. The smoker keeps his tobacco for daily use in a purse or bag made of shawl-stuff, or silk, or velvet, which is often accompanied with a small pouch containing a flint and steel, and some agaric tinder, and is usually crammed into his bosom.

The pipe (which is called by many names, such as "shibuk", "ood", &c.,) is generally between four and five feet long: some pipes are shorter, and some are of greater length. The most common kind used in Egypt is made of a kind of wood called "garmashak". The greater part of the stick (from the mouthpiece to about three-quarters of its length) is covered with silk, which is confined at each extremity by gold thread, often intertwined with coloured silks, or by a tube of gilt silver; and at the lower extremity of the convering is a tassel of silk. The covering was originally designed to be moistened with water, in order to cool the pipe, and, consequently, the smoke, by evaporation: but this is only done when the pipe is old, or not handsome. Cherry-stick pipes, which are never covered, are also used by many persons, particularly in the winter. In summer, the smoke is not so cool from the cherry-stick pipe as from the kind before mentioned. The bowl is of baked earth, coloured red or brown. The mouthpiece is composed of two or more pieces of opaque, light-coloured amber, interjoined by ornaments of enamelled gold, agate, jasper, carnelion, or some other precious substance. It is the most costly part of the pipe: some mouthpieces are adorned with diamonds: the price of one of the kind most generally used by persons of the middle orders is from about one to three pounds sterling. A wooden tube passes through it. This is often changed, as it soon becomes foul from the oil of the tobacco. The pipe also requires to be cleaned very often, which is done with tow, by means of a long wire. Many poor men in Cairo gain their livelihood by going about to clean pipes.

The tobacoo smoked by persons of the higher orders, and some others, in Egypt, is of a very mild and delicious flavour. It is mostly from the neighbourhood of El-Ládikeeyeh, in Syria. The best kind is the "mountian tobacco", grown on the hills *about that town. A stronger kind, which takes its name from the town of Soor, sometimes mixed with the former, is used by most persons of the middle orders. In smoking, the people of Egypt and of other countries of the East draw in their breath freely; so that much of the smoke descends into the lungs; and the terms which they use to express "smoking tobacco" signify "drinking smoke", or "drinking tobacco": for the same word signifies both "smoke" and "tobacco". Few of them spit while smoking: I have very seldom seen any do so.*

Some of the Egyptians use the Persian pipe, in which the smoke passes through water. The pipe of this kind most commonly used by persons of the higher classes is called "nárgeeleh", because the vessel that contains the water is a cocoa-nut, of which "nárgeeleh" is an Arabic name. Another kind, which has a glass vase, is called "sheesheh". Each has a very long, flexible tube. A particular kind of tobacco, called "tumbák", from Persia, is used in the water-pipe: it is first washed several times, and put into the pipe-bowl while damp; and two or three pieces of live charcoal are placed on the top. Its flavour is mild, and very agreeable; but the strong inhalation necessary in this mode of smoking is injurious to persons of delicate lungs. In using the Persian pipe, the person as freely draws the smoke into his lungs as he would inhale pure air. The great prevalence of liver-complaints in Arabia is attributed to the general use of the nárgeeleh, and many persons in Egypt suffer severely from the same cause. A kind of pipe commonly called "gózeh", which is similar to the nárgeeleh, except that it has a short cane tube, instead of the snake (or flexible one), and no stand, is used by men of the lowest class, for smoking both the tumbák and the intoxicating "hasheesh" or hemp.

Edward William Lane, An Account of the Manners and Customs of the Modern Egyptians, *Charles Knight, London, 1836*

Lane, 1801–1876, English Arabic scholar, studied the art of engraving briefly before travelling to Egypt in 1825, where he spent three years, twice ascended the Nile, proceeding as far as the Second Cataract, and composed a complete description of Egypt, with a portfolio of 101 drawings. Lane again visited Egypt in 1833–1835, residing mainly in Cairo, but retiring to Luxor during the plague of 1835. Lane took up his residence in the Muslim quarter, and under the name of Mansur Effendi lived the life of an Egyptian scholar. Returning to England in 1849, Lane devoted the remaining 27 years of his life to preparing a thesaurus of the lexicographical knowledge of the Arabs.

Religion

Ancient Egyptian Religion

Hart, George, *A Dictionary of Egyptian Gods and Goddesses*, London: Routledge, 1986 (new edition in press).

A useful guide to *nearly* every deity the visitor will encounter—certainly all the ones that matter.

Quirke, Stephen, *Ancient Egyptian Religion*, London: British Museum Press, 1992.

A very fine, penetrating and readable introduction to the complexities of the subject.

———, *The Cult of Ra, Sun-Worship in Ancient Egypt*, London: Thames and Hudson, 2001.

An excellent analysis of this central element of Egyptian religion.

Roberts, Alison, *Hathor Rising: The Serpent Power of Ancient Egypt*, Totnes: Northgate Publishers, 1995.

———, *My Heart My Mother: Death and Rebirth in Ancient Egypt*, Rottingdean: Northgate Publishers, 2000.

Both books by Roberts are inspiring and innovative studies of the role of the feminine in Egyptian religion.

Taylor, John H, *Death and the Afterlife in Ancient Egypt*, London: British Museum Press, 2001.

If you really need a book on mummification and the rest, this is it.

Late Antique to Christian

Frankfurter, David, *Religion in Roman Egypt: Assimilation and Resistance*, Princeton, NJ: Princeton University Press, 1998.

Islam

Dawood, N J, *The Koran: With Parallel Arabic Texts*, Penguin Classics, 2000.

Waines, David, *An Introduction to Islam*, Cambridge: Cambridge University Press, 2003.

Pyramids

Lehner, Mark, *The Complete Pyramids*, London: Thames and Hudson, 1997.

Verner, Miroslav, *The Pyramids: Their Archaeology and History*, Atlantic Books, 1997.
    These books tell you all that you need to know—and all that there is to know.

Akhenaten

Fascination with the 'heretic' pharaoh never seems to abate. There are numerous books about him and his family. For those who care:

Montserrat, Dominic, *Akhenaten: History, Fantasy and Ancient Egypt*, London: Routledge, 2000.
    Explains the ways in which Egyptologists and others have created an image of Akhenaten, and the ways in which that image has been used, abused and exploited by different interest groups.

Reeves, Nicholas, *Akhenaten: Egypt's False Prophet*, London: Thames and Hudson, 2001.
    The most up-to-date book in terms of archaeology and historical interpretation. This deals fairly with the remarkably insubstantial ancient material on which the image of Akhenaten has been built.

Islamic Cairo

Behrens-Abouseif, Doris, *Islamic Architecture in Cairo: An Introduction*, Cairo: The American University in Cairo Press, 1998.
    Selected monuments from all periods with good plans and information.

——, *The Minarets of Cairo*, Cairo: The American University in Cairo Press, 1985.
    Well illustrated with line drawings and archival photographs, this extremely handy guide focuses attention on one of the joys of the Cairo skyline.

Rabbatt, Nasser O, *The Citadel of Cairo: A New Interpretation of Royal Mamluk Architecture*, Leiden: Brill, 1995.

Rafaat, Samir W, *Cairo, the Glory Years: Who Built What, When, Why and For Whom*, Cairo: The American University in Cairo Press, 2004.
    This examines the sometimes crazy architecture of the city from the late 19th century onwards, and those who were responsible for the extraordinary gothic, oriental, art nouveau and baroque styles that make Cairo what it is.

Rodenbeck, Max, *Cairo: The City Victorious*, Cairo: The American University in Cairo Press, 2000.
    An acclaimed biography of the city.

Williams, Caroline, *Islamic Monuments in Cairo: The Practical Guide*, 5th edition, Cairo: The American University in Cairo Press, 2002.

> This is the best general guidebook to the Islamic monuments written by a specialist in the field.

Egypt in the West

Egyptian Style and 'Egyptomania'

Curl, James Stevens, *The Egyptian Revival*, George Allen and Unwin, 1982.

> A fine study of the influence of the Egyptian style on European art, architecture and decoration. Not to be confused with Egypt's cultural legacy. (A new, expanded edition is in press.)

Humbert, Jean-Marcel and Clifford Price (eds), *Imhotep Today: Egyptianizing Architecture*, London: UCL Press, 2003.

Wisdom of Ancient Egypt

Hornung, Eric (translated by David Lorton), *The Secret Lore of Egypt: Its Impact on the West*, Ithaca, NY: Cornell University Press, 2001.

> A leading Egyptologist considers traditions about Egypt and their influence: the Hermetic corpus, Freemasonry, Rosicrucianism etc.

Ucko, Peter and Timothy Champion (eds), *The Wisdom of Egypt: Changing Visions through the Ages*, London: UCL Press, 2003.

Changing Interpretations of Ancient Egypt

Jeffreys, David (ed), *Views of Ancient Egypt since Napoleon Bonaparte: Imperialism, Colonialism and Modern Appropriations*, London: UCL Press, 2003.

O'Connor, David and Andrew Reid (eds), *Ancient Egypt in Africa*, London: UCL Press, 2003.

Reid, Donald, *Whose Pharaohs? Archaeology, Museums and Egyptian National Identity from Napoleon to World War I*, California: University of California Press, 2002.

Collectors, Archaeologists and Travellers

Arabic Tradition

El Daly, Okasha, *Egyptology: The Missing Millennium, Ancient Egypt in Medieval Arabic Writings*, London: UCL Press, 2005.

Early Travellers (to AD 1800)

Wolff, Anne, *How Many Miles to Babylon? Travels and Adventures to Egypt and Beyond, from 1300 to 1640*, Liverpool: Liverpool University Press, 2003.

   A fascinating collection of episodes showing the range of contacts in a period that is usually neglected.

MacLean, Gerald, *The Rise of Oriental Travel: English Visitors to the Ottoman Empire, 1580–1720*, Basingstoke: Palgrave Macmillan, 2004.

   Although only one of the four travellers spends any time in Egypt, this enjoyable study explores the complexity of the attitudes of English visitors to the Ottoman world.

Early Collectors and Archaeologists

Adkins, Lesley and Roy, *The Keys of Egypt: The Race to Read the Hieroglyphs*, London: HarperCollins, 2001.

   A readable, popular account of the life of Champollion and the decipherment of hieroglyphics.

Drower, Margaret S, *Flinders Petrie: A Life in Archaeology*, Madison: University of Wisconsin Press, 1995.

Manley, Deborah and Peta Ree, *Henry Salt: Artist, Traveller, Diplomat, Egyptologist*, London: Libri, 2001.

Reeves, Nicholas, *Ancient Egypt: The Great Discoveries*, London: Thames and Hudson, 2000.

   A year-by-year chronicle from the Rosetta Stone to the Valley of the Golden Mummies.

Ridley, Ronald, *Napoleon's Proconsul in Egypt: The Life and Times of Bernardino Drovetti*, London: Rubicon Press, 1998.

Usick, Patricia, *Adventures in Egypt and Nubia: The Travels of William John Bankes (1786–1855)*, London: British Museum Press, 2002.

Travel Writing

De Nerval, Gérard (selected, translated from the French and with an Introduction by Norman Glass), *Journey to the Orient*, London: Michael Haag, 1984.

Edwards, Amelia B, *A Thousand Miles Up the Nile*, 1877 (various modern editions available).

> One of the best narratives of a Nile cruise. The 'redoubtable' Miss Edwards came back and pestered the great and the good into creating the Egypt Exploration Fund (now Society) to preserve the monuments and excavate sites.

Flaubert, Gustave (translated and edited by Francis Steegmuller), *Flaubert in Egypt*, London: Michael Haag, 1983.

> More interested in belly dancers than ruins, Flaubert captures the Orientalist appeal of Egypt to the 19th-century Western male.

Manley, Deborah and Sahar Abd el-Hakim (eds), *Traveling through Egypt from 450 BC to the Twentieth Century*, Cairo: The American University in Cairo Press, 2004.

> A collection of excerpts of writing about Egypt from Herodotos onwards, including Pierre Loti and Florence Nightingale, amongst many others.

Thackeray, William M, *From Cornhill to Grand Cairo By Way of Lisbon, Athens, Constantinople, and Jerusalem: Performed in the Steamers of the Peninsula and Oriental Company*, London: Smith, Elder and Co, 1846.

Interpreting Travellers

El Kholy, Nadia and Paul Starkey (eds), *Egypt through the Eyes of Travellers*, ASTENE, 2002.

> A collection of papers on travellers including Lord Valentia, Henry William Beechey, Florence Nightingale, Amelia Edwards, Giovanni Belzoni and Reverend Browne, the Gayer-Anderson Museum, Lord Morton and Maxime du Camp.

Starkey, Paul J (ed), *Interpreting the Orient: Travellers in Egypt and the Near East*, Ithaca, 2001.

——— (ed), *Unfolding the Orient: Travellers in Egypt and the Near East*, Ithaca, 2001.

LITERATURE

European Literature with Egyptian Setting or Themes

Excepting the life of Kleopatra, Ancient Egypt does not seem to have inspired much 'great' literature.

Cavafy, Constantine, *Poems* (various editions available).

> Life and love, much of it set in Alexandria, both ancient and more modern.

Durrell, Lawrence, *The Alexandria Quartet: Justine; Mountolive; Balthazar; Clea*, Faber and Faber, 1968; Penguin USA, 1991.

A remarkable group of novels set mainly in Alexandria in the mixed Egyptian and European community. Includes some splendid purple prose.

Flaubert, Gustave (translated with an Introduction and notes by Kitty Mrosovsky), *The Temptation of St Anthony*, Penguin Books, 1980.

Mann, Thomas, *Joseph in Egypt*, Knopf, 1938.

——, *Joseph the Provider*, Random House, 1944.

Ancient Egyptian Literature

Foster, John L, *Ancient Egyptian Literature: An Anthology*, Austin: University of Texas Press, 2001.

——, *Love Songs of the New Kingdom*, Austin: University of Texas Press, 1992.

Lichtheim, Miriam, *Ancient Egyptian Literature*, Berkeley: University of California Press, 1975–1980.

A comprehensive collection of all genres, in three volumes.

Arabic Literature

The Koran

Easily available in annotated editions from major publishers (eg Penguin, Oxford Classics).

One Thousand Nights and a Night

This huge collection of tales is familiar to most of us through the sanitized versions prepared for children. The complete texts of Sir Richard Burton's rather difficult translation and the more accessible one of J C Mardrus and E Powys Mathers are now available in paperback. A collection of the better-known tales was edited and translated into more modern English by N J Dawood: *Tales from the Thousand and One Nights*, Penguin Classics (first published 1971).

Kritzeck, James (ed), *Anthology of Islamic Literature*, NY: Penguin, 1964.

Contains sections of the Koran and the *One Thousand Nights and a Night* amongst a wide range of poetry and prose from most of the Islamic countries of western Asia and North Africa to Spain.

Modern Egyptian Literature

The most celebrated of modern Egyptian writers is Naguib Mahfouz, who was awarded the Nobel Prize for Literature in 1988. All of Mahfouz's works are now published in translation by the American University in Cairo Press. Although many are set in Cairo, *Miramar* offers an Egyptian view of Alexandria to contrast with the novels by European writers about the city. Notable amongst Mahfouz's other works are: *Children of the Alley*; *Autumn Quail*; *Palace Walk*; *Palace of Desire*; and *Midaq Alley*. The AUC Press publishes many other modern writers, but not all of their books are available outside Egypt (check on www.aucpress.com).

Abdulah, Yaha Taher (translated by Denys Johnson-Davies), *The Mountain of Green Tea*, London: Heinemann, 1984; Cairo: The American University in Cairo Press, 1999.

Hussein, Taha (translated by E H Paxton), *An Egyptian Childhood*, London: Heinemann, 1981.

Ibrahim, Sonallah (translated by Denys Johnson-Davies), *The Smell of It and Other Stories*, London: Heinemann, 1978.

Idris, Yusuf (translated by Wadida Wassef), *The Cheapest Nights and Other Stories*, London: Heinemann, 1978.

—— (translated by Catherine Cobham), *Rings of Burnished Brass*, London: Heinemann, 1984.

Johnson-Davies, Denys (ed), *Egyptian Short Stories*, London: Heinemann, 1978.

Holiday Reading

Numerous novels, of varying degrees of awfulness, have been set in Egypt, both ancient and modern. Earlier Egyptologists, such as George Ebers and Arthur Weigall, themselves penned a goodly number and their modern successors are continuing the tradition. Many recent books set in ancient Egypt or the world of excavation are in the murder-mystery genre, although science fiction and romance are also popular: they are extremely varied in quality. An enormous list of books in all categories, from historical to erotic, has been compiled by Noreen Doyle: 'Ancient Egypt in Fiction'. The list is currently at http://members.aol.com/wenamun/Egyptfiction.html, but will be moving to Egyptomania.org.

Agatha Christie's *Death on the Nile* was made even more famous through the glamorous film version. This Hercule Poirot mystery is set on a luxurious cruise boat.

Christie's *Death Comes as the End* (first published 1944) is, unusually for her, a historical murder, set in New Kingdom Thebes. It exploits the drama of the cliff path between Deir el-Medina and the Valley of the Kings.

Joan Grant wrote four acclaimed novels set in ancient Egypt: *Winged Pharaoh*; *Eyes of Horus*; *Lord of the Horizon*; and *So Moses Was Born*.

Mika Waltari's best-selling novel, *Sinuhe, the Egyptian* was based on the ancient Egyptian story of Sinuhe, but Waltari moved the action from the early 12th Dynasty to the ever-popular reign of Akhenaten.

Although there have been dozens of novels about Akhenaten and his time, that by archaeologist Jacquetta Hawkes, *King of the Two Lands* (1966), is arguably the best. Although the image of Akhenaten projected is the idealistic, and idealized, monotheist, this well-informed novel does have some convincing recreations of the atmosphere of ancient Egypt. Other novels set in this period range from the plain awful to the ludicrous, and occasionally titillating.

The Amelia Peabody mysteries, written by a lapsed Egyptologist, Barbara Mertz (as Elizabeth Peters) are stories of murder and mayhem on excavations (pretty much like the real thing, then). Peters loosely based the characters of Amelia Peabody and Radcliffe Emerson on Amelia Edwards and Flinders Petrie. Beginning with *Crocodile on a Sandbank*, the novels span the period from the late 19th century to the 1920s. The early ones in the series are the best.

Another archaeologist, Paul Sussman, has set his excavation thriller, *The Lost Army of Cambyses* (Bantam, 2001), in the contemporary world, where religious fundamentalism collides with Egyptology.

Other writers in this genre include: Lauren Haney, who has set her series in the 18th Dynasty, in Thebes and Nubia; Paul Doherty; and Lynda S Robinson (the Lord Meren mysteries).

For those who like to be amused, but with only a loose connection to things Egyptian, P G Wodehouse's *Something Fresh* (1915) is a diverting farce that begins when Lord Emsworth inadvertently filches a scarab.

GUIDEBOOKS

General Guidebooks

Humphreys, Andrew et al, *Lonely Planet Egypt*, Lonely Planet Publications, 2004 (ISBN: 1740594630).

Richardson, Dan, *The Rough Guide to Egypt*, Rough Guides Limited, 2003 (ISBN: 1843530503).

This, and the Lonely Planet guide above, has plenty of information for travellers: on hotels of all standards; cafés; restaurants; shopping; and other practical issues.

Specific Regions and Subjects

Fakhry, Ahmed, *Bahriya and Farafra*, Cairo: The American University in Cairo Press, 2003.

A reprint of the classic volume (1974) on these oases by a leading Egyptologist of the region.

———, *Siwa*, Cairo: The American University in Cairo Press, 2003.

A reprint of the 1973 classic on this remote oasis. Fakhry knew better than any other outsider the extraordinary culture that had developed in isolated Siwa and was already vanishing in the mid-20th century.

Gohary, Jocelyn, *Guide to the Nubian Monuments on Lake Nasser*, Cairo: The American University in Cairo Press, 1998.

Kamil, Jill, *Coptic Egypt: History and Guide, Cairo*: The American University in Cairo Press, 1993.

Vivian, Cassandra, *The Western Desert of Egypt: An Explorer's Handbook*, Cairo: The American University in Cairo Press, 2000 (ISBN 977424527X).

Essential for anyone venturing into the Western Desert, this guide has detailed practical information about finding all of the ancient sites, as well as information on the history, archaeology, animals and people.

MUSIC

Although there are many ancient musical instruments surviving, and numerous scenes of the performance of music, we have little evidence for what that music sounded like. The only written music comes from the Ptolemaic and Roman periods, and seems to reflect those traditions, rather than the Egyptian.

The only popular book in English on the subject is: Manniche, Lise, *Music and Musicians in Ancient Egypt*, London: British Museum Press, 1991.

It is likely that some idea of ancient Egyptian religious chant can be gained from in the music of the Coptic Church: *Liturgy of the Coptic Orthodox Church* performed by the choir of St Mark's Cathedral, Cairo, Heidelberg: Christophorus CHR 77200.

ARABIC CLASSICAL MUSIC

With the increase in programs dedicated to World Music on the radio, the sounds of Arabic music are more familiar to Western ears. Although there are similarities in the different regions, the term 'Arabic music' is probably a misnomer, embracing a wide range of local traditions, originating in more ancient styles. Some of the most important musical treatises were written in Egypt and these did synthesize the traditions and establish conventions for performance. Arabic music is generally modal, and relies extensively on improvisation. There are many instruments, one of the most important being the *oud*, a plucked string instrument, ancestor of the European lute.

A wide range of recordings of classical Arab music and modern interpretations can be found through www.maqam.com

Two recent recordings are strictly Ottoman, rather than specifically Egyptian, but gently introduce the ear to the sound world of 'oriental' music.

Dream of the Orient by the combined forces of Concerto Köln and the Turco-German ensemble, Sarband (Deutsche Grammophon: Archiv 474 992-2) is a mixture of traditional Turkish music and European pieces of the 18th century. Mozart's overture to *Die Entführung aus dem Serail*—with full Turkish percussion—is probably the most familiar, and reflects the fascination with, and fear of, the Ottoman Empire. Most of the other European works, by Gluck, Kraus and Sussmayr, belong to a similar 'exotic' and pastiche oriental genre. The 'Concerto Turco', published in Venice in 1787, is a rather enchanting piece of Orientalism based upon real Turkish sources. Most of the traditional Turkish music here was notated by Dmitrie Cantemir (1673–1723), a Moldavian prince who spent several decades in Istanbul.

Invitation to the Seraglio by the London Academy of Ottoman Court Music director Emre Aracı (Warner Classics 2564 61472-2) is rather different: a group of 19th-century pieces, mostly by European composers working for the Sublime Porte (a term referring to the Ottoman ruler), and reflecting the contemporary lament quoted in the notes that 'the ancient Turkish music is in its death throes ... Sultan Mahmud loves Italian music...' There are several pieces by Turkish composers, such as Sultan Abdulaziz (*Invitation to the Waltz*, c.1861) and Ida, the Hungarian-born pianist and wife of Omer Pasha. The remainder have a loosely oriental feel and some incorporate surprisingly familiar tunes. Altogether this collection shows the Westernizing of the later Ottoman Empire and would be good listening amongst the similarly eclectic architecture of Cairo, or in the opulent public rooms of the Marriott Hotel, Mena House, the Old Winter Palace or the ballroom of the Cataract Hotel.

CONTEMPORARY EGYPTIAN MUSIC

The most notable singers of modern Egypt have combined a traditional style with considerable Western influence. Much of it falls into a style that is similar to the Greek *rebetika* (perhaps most closely paralleled in the West by cabaret singers such as Dietrich and Piaf), and has been described as 'melodramatic' when compared with classical Arabic music and that of other countries of the region. The instrumental accompaniment usually combines Arabic instruments such as the *oud*, with a range of Western ones, against a background of lush strings playing in a 'Mantovani-goes-Oriental' style. The performers who are most highly regarded were mostly making their careers from the 1930s to 1970s and recorded their works. In a very short career, Sayyid Darwish (1896–1923) had enormous influence on the development of Egyptian popular music, and on composers and performers such as Mohammed al-Qasabgi (1892–1966), Zakariyya Ahmad (1896–1961), Riyad al-Sunbati (1906–1981) and Mohammed Abdul Wahab (1897–1990), who is widely considered to be the finest. The works of this group were also performed by Egypt's most famous singer, Umm Kulthum (born sometime between 1904 and 1908), who rose to become a national icon in the 1950s and 1960s. It has been estimated that some four million people filled the streets at her Cairo funeral in 1975. A striking figure, tall, with black hair, Umm Kulthum's weekly concerts were broadcast on national radio and brought Egypt to a standstill. Her dramatic songs are easily available in recordings of the live performances, still selling some 300,000 per year in Egypt alone.

Farid al-Atrash (died 1974 aged 'about 60') and his sister, who adopted the stage name Asmahan, were born in the Druze mountains of Syria, but the political situation forced their elite family to flee first to Beirut and then Egypt. Both were highly regarded, and Farid has been styled 'king of the *oud*'. He was noted for melancholy love songs; amongst his most famous compositions are: 'Al Rabia' (Spring) and 'Awel Hamsa' (First Whisper). Another fine performer of this style was Abdel Halem Hafiz, whose recordings are widely available. More recent performers are rather more 'pop' in flavour and lack the smoky cabaret style of the earlier generation.

WESTERN CLASSICAL MUSIC

Ancient Egypt has inspired relatively little Western classical music that is regularly in the repertoire. The main inspirations have been either the biblical episodes or the story of Kleopatra derived from classical sources.

Berlioz, Hector, *La mort de Cléopâtra*, 1829.

Glass, Philip, *Akhnaten*, 1984.

Opera based on the older interpretation of Akhenaten as a mystic, written in Glass's minimalist style: you like it or you don't.

Handel, George Frideric, *Giulio Cesare in Egitto*, 1724.

An opera set in Alexandria, following the love of Caesar for Kleopatra, and the rebellion of her brother, Ptolemy.

———, *Israel in Egypt*, 1738.

Oratorio from biblical sources.

Massenet, Jules, *Thaïs*, 1894.

Opera, based on the novel of 1890 by Anatole France, about the love for, and the conversion to Christianity of, the courtesan Thaïs, by the hermit, Serapion.

Mozart, *The Magic Flute*, 1791.

Sarastro leads Tamino in the search for higher wisdom in the temple of Isis and Osiris. This encapsulates the 18th-century and Masonic vision of Egypt.

Respighi, Ottorino, *Church Windows 1: The Flight into Egypt*, 1925.

One of four pieces based on Gregorian chant; this one inspired by the episode that also attracted so many painters. Originally for piano, but later lushly orchestrated.

Rossini, Gioachino, *Mosè in Egitto* (*Moses in Egypt*), 1818; revised 1827 as *Moïse et Pharaon, ou Le Passage de la Mer Rouge* (*Moses and Pharaoh*).

Saint-Säens, Camille, *Piano Concerto No. 5, 'The Egyptian'*, 1896.

The middle, slow movement is based on the song of a Nubian boatman that Saint-Säens jotted down on his shirt cuff.

Strauss, Richard, *Die Ägyptische Helena* (*The Egyptian Helen*), 1927.

Opera with libretto by Hugo von Hofmannsthal based on ancient sources. Set in Egypt following the Trojan War, the opera narrates the reconciliation of Menelaos and Helen (so not a lot of Egyptian content).

Verdi, Giuseppe, *Aïda*, 1871.

With a plot line written by the Egyptologist August Mariette, the opera is the story of the love of the Egyptian general Radamès for the slave girl Aïda (actually the daughter of Amonasro, the King of 'Ethiopia' [Nubia]), and the vain love of the Egyptian princess Amneris for Radamès.

EGYPT IN FILM

E gypt, in its broadest sense, has inspired a huge number of films, some of them laughable, many of them dreadful. For those interested, the first place to look is Hans van den Berg's website (www.wepwawet.nl/films), which lists over 260 films and gives an outline and cast—with some enjoyably pithy comments. The films fall into the inevitable Egyptian genres, mummy films being by far the most common, with a large number of Kleopatras (not all with literary-historical aspirations), some biblical and a few loosely 'adventure'.

In the vast range of Egyptologist-enters-tomb-and-somehow-revives-mummy-that-seeks-revenge genre, the most highly regarded, by those who like them, is Boris Karloff's *The Mummy* (1932). The mayhem is instigated by a British Museum field expedition (so based on fact, then). The revived mummy, now called Kharis, enjoyed a long career in Hollywood, re-appearing in the Tom Tyler/Lon Chaney Junior, series of films, *The Mummy's Hand/Tomb/Curse* and *Ghost* (of 1940/1942/1944/1944). He then took to comedy in *Abbott and Costello Meet the Mummy* (1955), before encountering Peter Cushing and Christopher Lee in 1959 (*The Mummy*), which experience presumably sent him back to the tomb (or worse, to a job at the British Museum). In many of these films an Egyptologist is found dead, his colleague/assistant is accused, but the mummy did it (yeah, sure!) Occasionally the writer has had the wit to include a real Egyptologist's name, as in *I Was a Teenage Mummy* (1962) in which Professor Flinders Petrie appears with his assistant Peaches LaVerne! Moving away slightly from the straightforward horror (in every sense) of these films, *The Awakening* (1980) with Charlton Heston, Susannah York and Jill Townsend, was based on Bram Stoker's *The Jewel of Seven Stars*: but it's still Egyptologists, tombs and reincarnation. The mummy genre continues, although it doesn't seem to get any better.

A new style was set in 1981 with Harrison Ford's first appearance as Indiana Jones in *Raiders of the Lost Ark*. Sadly, nearly a quarter of a century later some (ageing) Egyptologists still see themselves as this 'hero' and wear the hat in an attempt to convince us. In *Stargate* (1994) James Spader played a different breed of Egyptologist: the cute, floppy-haired, bespectacled genius that nobody believes (it was based on me). Although he was not attacked by mummies, he did go to the other side of the galaxy, never to return: sadly he did not take any of his colleagues with him, only a handful of the US military led by Kurt Russell. But he did meet the evil, if rather beautiful, sun god Ra (Jaye Davidson). Amongst many loose ends, the most striking have to be: why did the Egyptian Antiquities Organization ever allow the Stargate to leave Egypt rather than putting it in one of the dustier side-galleries of the Cairo Museum? How did the US military manage to keep it secret for so long when it had been re-erected on the Giza plateau? And who was the woman with the heavy central European accent? Piffle.

With a good number of murders, but no Egyptologists, *Death on the Nile* (1978) is based on Agatha Christie's novel, with a splendid cast including the poisonous Bette Davis, frosty Maggie Smith, dishy Simon MacCorkindale and gloriously over-the-top Angela Lansbury. Peter Ustinov presides as Hercule Poirot, with David Niven in attendance. Pedants get distressed by the merging of bits of different temples into one (Kom Ombo suddenly becomes Karnak) and some other geographical leaps; suspend your critical faculties and enjoy it for what it is!

Also starring (a younger) Peter Ustinov, with Victor Mature, Michael Wilding and Jean Simmons, amongst others, the 1954 film *The Egyptian* was based on Mika Waltari's best-selling novel set in the reign of Akhenaten.

Kleopatra has been played in film by many of the leading screen icons (and in some films by ladies whose acting skills were not their chief asset). The sultry Theda Bara took the lead in the earliest of the serious Kleopatras (1917), now, alas, preserved only in some still shots. An anagram of 'Arab Death', Theda Bara was born, it was claimed, in the shadow of the pyramids. Cecil B de Mille's version of the story (1934), starring Claudette Colbert, has some spectacular moments, notably the barge scene (with some surging music), but has otherwise been considered vulgar and stolid. In 1945 Claude Rains and Vivien Leigh headed an impressive cast in *Caesar and Cleopatra*, based on a play by George Bernard Shaw. For what was then Britain's most expensive film to date, sand was taken to Egypt in order to get it the right colour. It was not money well spent (especially during a war), as the critic Richard Winnington wrote: 'It cost over a million and a quarter pounds, took two and a half years to make, and well and truly bored one spectator for two and quarter hours.' It should be no surprise then, that the 1963 *Cleopatra*, starring, amongst many thousands, Elizabeth Taylor, Richard Burton and Rex Harrison, took even longer to make and cost far more money (for a long time it was the most expensive film ever made). It is also considered to rank high in the vulgarity and boredom categories: 'It lacks not only the intelligent spectacle of *Lawrence of Arabia* but the spectacular unintelligence of a Cecil B de Mille product...' (John Simon). None of these criticisms could be made of *Carry on Cleo* (1964), part of a series that was famously made on the cheap and at high speed (with plenty of script recycling). Amanda Barrie as the queen and Kenneth ('infamy, infamy, they've all got it in for me') Williams as Caesar were probably as convincing as their predecessors in the same roles, and had more jokes. Amongst many other versions, some only tenuously connected with the historical characters and events, are the French *Astérix et Cléopatre* (1968) and a Mexican musical version. A television series covering Kleopatras I to VII and their Ptolemies was so awful that it has passed into the kitsch classics (rumour has it that the advisor was from the British Museum, could it have been Peaches LaVerne?).

The biblical genre has fared hardly better than the Kleopatras. Mr de Mille had two runs at *The Ten Commandments*, in 1923 and 1956. In the later version, a host of Hollywood stars played major and minor roles, some unlikely. Charlton Heston led as an all-American Moses, with pharaohs Sir Cedric Hardwicke—a suitably patrician Sety I—and Yul Brynner—a passable, if diminutive, Ramesses II. Edward G Robinson and Vincent Price make less likely appearances, and Yvonne de Carlo was preparing for a long run in *The Munsters*. Some of the scenes allude to some well-known Orientalist/biblical paintings, such as Sir Edward Poynter's *Israel in Egypt* (1867; London: Guildhall Art Gallery) and Sir Lawrence Alma-Tadema's *Death of Pharaoh's First-Born Son* (1872; Amsterdam: Rijksmuseum). The critics' verdict? 'A very long haul across a monotonous route, with the director at his pedestrian worse.' Nice chariots though.

Amongst other nonsense was the appalling pseudo-biblical *Land of the Pharaohs* (1955) with Jack Hawkins, James Robertson Justice (performing in his usual, if inappropriately bluff, style) and Joan Collins—as an evil princess (*plus ça change*). The critics seem to rate this slightly higher than this writer, apparently due to the impressive way Miss Collins was entombed alive.

More recently *The English Patient* which has, in part, an Egyptian World War II setting, has been highly praised by some.

So ancient Egypt and Egyptology can hardly be said to have inspired great cinema. Is there anything worth watching? Probably the best film about Egypt, things anciently Egyptian and Egyptological, is *The Night of Counting the Years* (1970). The director was Shadi Abdel-Salam who was encouraged by Roberto Rosellini. He had worked on *Cleopatra* and made a film that is its antithesis. It tells the story of the discovery of the cache of royal mummies at Deir el-Bahari in the late 19th century, looted for years before by the Abd er-Rassoul family and eventually tracked down by Gaston Maspero of the Antiquities Organization. It is much more than a docudrama as it explores the internal relationships and the attitudes to the past of the characters. It won a prize at the Venice Film Festival and is widely acclaimed as a landmark in Egyptian filmmaking.

GLOSSARY

afnet-headaddress: a loose bag-like wig cover.

ankh: symbol of life, like a cross with a looped top.

atef crown: elaborate crown, shaped rather like the white crown, with attached wavy ram horns, ostrich feathers and solar discs, sometimes with pendant uraeuses.

ba-bird: human-headed bird representing the *ba*, one of the souls of a person.

behdet: winged sun disc, a form taken by the god Horus in his conflict with Seth.

ben-ben stone: the sacred stone upon which the solar god alighted at the moment of creation; the origin of the obelisk form.

bennu-bird: the Egyptian 'phoenix', actually a blue heron.

dahabiya: a Nile vessel favoured by 19th-century tourists.

djed; *djed*-pillar: symbol of stability, perhaps the backbone of Osiris.

dom-palm nuts: large, orange-brown fruit with an outer sweet layer of flesh that can be processed and eaten, and a hard inner nut that can be used as vegetable ivory.

dromos: processional way, often lined by sphinxes.

Fields of Yaru: the 'Fields of the Blessed', an idealized Egypt where the deceased is shown working in the fields, ploughing, reaping, pulling flax—not the sort of thing the elite normally did.

heb-sed court: part of a temple complex used for rites associated with the 'jubilee' (*heb-sed*) of a pharaoh.

ished-tree: the persea tree; the gods (usually Amun-Ra or Ra-Harakhty) wrote the name of the king on the leaves of the tree at his coronation.

ka: the 'double' created at the same time as a person at the time of their birth, and with which they are reunited at death.

ka-arms: the *ka* is written in hieroglyphics with a sign of a pair of upraised arms joined, and bent at the elbows.

kalathos: grain measure, worn by some deities (notably Serapis) in the Ptolemiac–Roman periods.

khekher frieze: a series of stylized knots, deriving from the tied fronds of reed architecture, the *khekher* crowns the tops of scenes along with the chequered border.

madrasa: literally 'a place of study'; a school, especially a theological school attached to a mosque.

magharah: a cave.

mammisi: the 'birth house'. In temples of the Ptolemaic–Roman periods, the *mammisi* was a separate building that was used in rites celebrating the birth of the child of the temple's patron deity.

maristan: a hospital.

mastaba: from Arabic meaning 'bench', the mastaba is a flat-topped superstructure above tombs. Sometimes with plain, inclining walls, sometimes with elaborated recessed and painted walls ('palace-façade').

menat-collar: one of the emblems of the goddess Hathor, comprising strings of beads with a heavy counterpoise. It could be used as a musical instrument.

mihrab: niche indicating the direction of Mecca.

minbar: pulpit from which the address at Friday prayer is given.

mushrabiya: wooden lattice-work screens.

muwu-dancers: of ancient origin, the dancers wear tall headdresses and perform in funerary rites, usually shown with highly stylized movements.

naos: the shrine in which the image of a god was kept.

nemes-headdress: a royal wig cover, usually shown striped in gold and blue, with a bag-like back, ending in a pigtail, and pleated lappets at the front.

nemset-vessels: small teapot-shaped vessels used in ritual.

nome: administrative division, 22 in Upper Egypt and 20 in Lower Egypt.

nomarch: ruler of a nome.

Opet Festival or Feast: a festival celebrated at Thebes in which the local god Amun went to celebrate his marriage to his consort Amunet (later Mut) in the Temple of Luxor, which was called the 'Southern Opet'. Opet means 'inner apartments' of a residence.

pronaos: room in front of the main sanctuary of a temple.

qa'a: central covered courtyard, large hall or reception room.

saff tombs: from the Arabic word for a 'row', *saff* tombs are found in the Theban necropolis, cut into the low hills, usually with a colonnade and a row of entrances behind.

sekhem-sceptre: a broad-bladed sceptre on a long handle, used to dedicate offerings.

sed-festival: conventionally celebrated after 30 years of reign (then every three), the *sed*-festival was a time of royal rebirth and confirmation of the ruler's power.

senet: a game in which pieces are moved around a chequered board.

serdab: a feature of mastaba tombs of the Old Kingdom, consisting of a sealed chamber containing a statue of the deceased. The wall into the chapel has a hole so that the *ka* can gain access to the offerings presented outside.

shabti: a 'servant' figure. Forms vary, but often a small mummified figure with a hoe and grain bag on its shoulders, inscribed with a prayer to activate it. Purpose: to save the deceased doing any hard work in the afterlife.

shen: a loop of rope, the symbol of eternity; it can be elongated as the 'cartouche' to contain a royal name.

speos: from Greek, meaning a 'cave' or 'grotto'; speos is a term used for rock-cut temples both small and large (eg Speos Artemidos, Abu Simbel).

spina: the central part of the Roman Hippodrome around which the chariots raced.

talatat: relatively small blocks of stone that can be carried by one man: a feature of the buildings of Akhenaten.

tekenu: appearing in funerary rites with the *muwu*-dancers, the *tekenu* were once thought to be human sacrifices. Depicted as bundles with a human head, they may be the parts of the body not kept in the canopic jars.

temenos: the entire precinct of a temple, with an enclosing wall: temple, *mammisi*, storage rooms, houses, hospital, sacred lake.

udjat eye: the eye of the god Horus, a symbol of health and completeness.

uraeus: the rearing cobra that spits fire at the king's enemies.

wabet: the 'pure hall'; in temples of Ptolemaic–Roman date usually a small open court with an elevated chapel approached by a flight of steps (eg Dendera, Edfu).

wadjyt: a columned hall, originally with papyrus-shaped columns.

was: a symbol of dominion and divine power. A long straight thin sceptre with a forked end, and sometimes with the head of the animal of Seth. It may derive from the shepherd's staff used to catch snakes.

INDEX

Please note: many place names change over time; these are, in most cases, cross-referenced in the index. Also, museums and related institutions specifically referred to in the text are listed under the current name of the city or town in which they are located.

Bedouin girl, Mount Sinai

Water vendor, Old Cairo

Street scene, Aswan